LOGICS OF DISLOCATION

MAPPINGS: Society/Theory/Space
A Guilford Series

Editors

Michael Dear
*University of
Southern California*

Derek Gregory
*University of
British Columbia*

Nigel Thrift
*University of
Bristol*

APPROACHING HUMAN GEOGRAPHY:
An Introduction to Contemporary Theoretical Debates
Paul Cloke, Chris Philo, and *David Sadler*

THE POWER OF MAPS
Denis Wood (with *John Fels*)

POSTMODERN CONTENTIONS: Epochs, Politics, Space
John Paul Jones III, Wolfgang Natter,
and *Theodore R. Schatzki,* Editors

WRITING WOMEN AND SPACE:
Colonial and Postcolonial Geographies
AlisonBlunt and *Gillian Rose,* Editors

LAW, SPACE, AND THE GEOGRAPHIES OF POWER
Nicholas K. Blomley

GROUND TRUTH:
The Social Implications of Geographic Information Systems
John Pickles, Editor

INDIFFERENT BOUNDARIES:
Spatial Concepts of Human Subjectivity
Kathleen M. Kirby

LOGICS OF DISLOCATION:
Models, Metaphors, and Meanings of Economic Space
Trevor J. Barnes

forthcoming

SPACE, TEXT, AND GENDER:
An Anthropological Study of the Marakwet of Kenya
Henrietta L. Moore

EMANCIPATING SPACE:
Geography, Architecture, and Urban Design
Ross King

Logics of Dislocation

Models, Metaphors, and Meanings of Economic Space

Trevor J. Barnes

THE GUILFORD PRESS
New York   London

Marketed and distributed outside North America by Longman
Group Limited.

Printed in the United States of America

This book is printed on acid-free paper.

Last digit is print number: 9 8 7 6 5 4 3 2 1

Library of Congress Cataloging-in-Publication Data

Barnes, Trevor J.
   Logics of dislocation : models, metaphors, and meanings of
economic space / Trevor J. Barnes.
      p.   cm. — (Mappings)
   Includes bibliographical references and index.
   ISBN 1-57230-033-7 (cloth). — ISBN 1-57230-039-6 (pbk.)
   1. Economic geography. I. Title. II. Series.
HF1025.B333 1996
330—dc20   95-42463
                                                        CIP

Lines from Philip Larkin's poem "Intolerance" are reprinted by
permission of Faber & Faber Ltd. and Farrar, Straus & Giroux.

PREFACE

The only valid tribute to thought . . . is precisely to use it,
to deform it, to make it groan and protest.
                    —Michel Foucault, *Power/Knowledge*

When I drew up for the publishers a prospectus for this book in late 1989, my original intention was to write a monograph that offered a reconceived economic geography, one that was created from the union of various "post"-prefixed theories of the past two decades. My introductory chapter was to be a series of postage-stamp-sized reviews of various "post"-isms. With those slots in place, the remainder of the book would be concerned simply with filling them in with appropriate examples drawn from the economic geographical literature.

In retrospect I now realize that my project was hopelessly ambitious, outrageously presumptuous, and certainly ill conceived. Just as there is no single economic geography to be reconstructed all of a piece, so there is no single body of "post"-prefixed theories. More important, as I wrote it became clear that my original approach was a fundamentally rationalist response to set of writings that shunned such rationality, an attempt to impose order on a body of work that eschewed both closure and regimented structure. But even with that recognition, I've found escaping from an ordered rationality all but impossible. Oscar Wilde said that temptation was the only thing he couldn't resist, and my temptation remains rationalism. Certainly its presence haunts the subsequent chapters in spite of my best efforts. It seems I cannot escape my past, mired as it is in undergraduate studies in economics and geography and postgraduate work in analytical geographical theory.

That past also affects the book in another way, in the selection of the economic geographical debates that I've chosen to review. Apart from the first chapter, which more than most still bears the hallmarks of the book's original conception, I've ignored many of the recent discussions within economic geography of the past fifteen years, preferring instead to use examples taken from spatial science of the 1960s and 1970s. This is so for three reasons.

First, it is a consequence of my own training to which I've already alluded. I often lacked the time, skill, and sometimes inclination to read seriously in areas of economic geography to which I had not already been exposed. Later in the book I speak about the importance of learning a "craft" and "habit," and my habit was spatial science. There is another related reason here as well. The various "post"-prefixed theories that I've chosen to examine I found difficult to grasp, the going painfully slow. For example, Chapter Four, which is about postpositivist philosophies of science, took more than two years to write. It became clear to me that the only way I could do justice to these "post"-prefixed ideas was by putting them to work, that is, to make them groan and protest, as Foucault put it, and not simply to review them as a detached body of ideas—which is often how they are treated in human geography. Moreover, I found I could do that only by bringing such ideas into conjunction with areas of economic geography that I knew very well, which in my case was primarily spatial science.

Another related caveat is that I recognize that there are also gaping holes in my coverage of "post"-prefixed theories. Apart from the first chapter, for example, I say virtually nothing about feminist or postcolonial approaches. This is certainly neither because I think that they are unimportant nor that they wouldn't affect the substance of my argument. Far from it. A feminist history of recent economic geography would provide a very different reading than mine (in that light, see the comments by Massey, 1992, on a feminist interpretation of regional development theory and Rose, 1993, ch. 6, on Marxist uneven development theory). That said, I hope that the account of recent economic geography I've provided here is at least not antithetical to either a feminist or postcolonial narrative of the discipline. Insofar as I acknowledge the partialness and absences within my own stories, I have tried to provide the spaces for, say, a feminist and postcolonial analysis, even though I've not filled them in myself.

The second reason for my concentration on spatial science has to with my own psychological relationship to that movement, which I think can best be described as Oedipal. I continue to be deeply smitten by the logic and orderliness of spatial science and its various manifestations, but at the same time I have an equally strong desire to undermine that very logic and orderliness. This is a consequence again of my past, I think. Geography was in a particularly peculiar state when I studied it as an undergraduate in the mid- to late 1970s. Spatial science was still official orthodoxy, and as a result I duly learned the mantra of laws, theories, and models associated with that movement. But where the real action lay at that time was in Marxism and, in particular, the irregular arrival at the departmental library at University College London (where I was a student), of the latest copy of *Antipode*. Along with others, I eagerly awaited news from subversives across the Atlantic. The result was a Jekyll-and-Hyde existence that involved espousing the tenets of spatial science in my exams, projects, and tutorial essays, while my out-of-class conversations were all about social justice, class oppression, and the irrelevance of r^2.

Finally, there is an intellectual justification. I've never thought that the postspatial science approaches and debates that emerged during the late 1970s and 1980s escaped the rationalism that the 1960s quantitative and theoretical revolution represented. Rather, it always seemed to me that methodologically it was more of the same. It is precisely this issue that forms the entry point for the book. In Chapter One I make the argument that the legacy of the scientific revolution in geography is still very evident in four of the most significant debates that occurred within economic geography since the mid-1970s: in Marxism, critical realism, locality studies, and flexible production. In the remainder of the book I then attempt to illustrate in piecemeal fashion what an alternative nonrationalist, "post"-prefixed economic geography might look like. I use the words "illustrate" and "piecemeal" in very specific senses. I certainly don't want to construct yet another essentialist and foundational approach to economic geography that legislates how economic geographers should undertake to study the material of their discipline. So rather than constructing an overall method, as seductive as that task might be for me, I've tried to illustrate through examples the kind of economic geography that unfolds, for instance, when one thinks of models as metaphors or spatial statistics as just another kind of language or economic value as a social construct. Such an approach also goes to the second idea of the book's piecemeal nature. To counter the idea (one that I myself held and maybe secretly still do) that there can be a monolithic reconstruction of economic geography, I've concentrated on working though comparatively limited "post"-prefixed concepts and theories, refraining from trying to make the grand synthesis.

I recognize, of course, that I've not always been successful. Precisely because of who I am and have been, the inclination to rationalize, essentialize, and satisfy my architectonic inclinations is always close to hand. That I've sometimes been able to resist such inclinations is in part a result of the wonderfully talented group of people I've been fortunate to work with and learn so much from over the many years that I've been writing this book. They include Keith Bassett, Mark Bouman, Noel Castree, Dan Clayton, Michael Curry, Jim Duncan, Steve Gudeman, Les

Hepple, Debby Leslie, David Ley, Fred Lukermann, Cole Harris, Roger Hayter, Dan Hiebert, Ross Nelson, Amanda Ocran, Mischa Penn, Gerry Pratt, Matt Sparke, Nigel Thrift, and Jock Wills. I thank them all.

In addition, I owe two special debts. The first is to Eric Sheppard, who has been wonderfully supportive of my work ever since I was a graduate student. In particular, he provided detailed comments upon many of the chapters in the book and in doing so weeded out a number of errors, misinterpretations, and inconsistencies. And the second is to Derek Gregory, who not only helped me with the book's title[1] but who has been extremely generous both with his books (albeit often unknowingly) and especially with his time and good conversation.

Finally, I also thank my family, particularly my children, Claire and Michael. That they've allowed me to write this preface during the first morning of our summer holiday without insisting that I play chess or Cluedo or have my fortune told is testament to their great magnanimity in the face of a negligent father. It is also a result of my promising that I would dedicate the book to them, which I am most happy to do.

Roberts Creek, Sunshine Coast
August 1994

NOTE

1. The title of the book is a geographical take on Peter Dews's 1987 book *Logics of Disintegration*. I've tried to strive for the same clarity and rigor as Dews in writing this book, although my substantive conclusions are quite different from his. I take up further the significance of my title in the final chapter.

ACKNOWLEDGMENTS

Several of the chapters in this book derive in whole or in part from previously published works. I've resisted the temptation to rewrite the original papers (admittedly not always great), and I have only pruned them in places to avoid too much repetition. In those cases, even, I have repeated the odd example and quote in order to make each chapter self-contained.

I am very grateful to the publishers and editors of the following journals for giving me permission to reprint or adapt these articles: The first half of Chapter Two was published under the same title in *Transactions, Institute of British Geographers*, 14, 299–316 (1989). Chapter Three is a slightly modified version of "Rationality and Relativism: An Interpretive Review of the Homo-economicus Assumption," which first appeared in *Progress in Human Geography*, 12, 473–496 (1988). It is reproduced by permission of Edward Arnold (Publishers) Ltd. Chapter Five is reprinted, with the same title, from *Geografiska Annaler*, 73, 11–20 (1991). Chapter Six is also reprinted, with the same title, from *Environment and Planning A*, 26, 1021–1040 (1994). It is reproduced by permission of Pion Ltd. Chapter Eight is a significantly expanded, combined version of an editorial and a short essay that first appeared in the *Canadian Geographer*, 37, as, respectively, "A Geographical Appreciation of Harold A. Innis," 352–353, and "Knowing Where You Stand: Harold Innis, Staple Theory and Local Models," 357–359 (1993).

The following chapters were originally presented at conferences: A severely truncated version of Chapter Four, at the annual meeting of the Association of American Geographers in San Francisco in March 1994; Chapter Seven, based upon a plenary paper, at the 1989 European Regional Science Conference at St. John's College, Cambridge University, September 1989; and Chapter Nine, based upon a paper I read at the "Fredfest," in honor of the retirement of Fred Lukermann, at the University of Minnesota, Minneapolis, May 1992.

CONTENTS

PART I

SOMEWHERE BETWEEN EXPLANATION AND THE CONDITION OF POSTMODERNITY

ONE

TOWARD A "POST"-PREFIXED ECONOMIC GEOGRAPHY?

Toto, I have a feeling we're not in Kansas anymore.
—Dorothy, from *The Wizard of Oz*

The geographer Fred Lukermann of Minnesota, writing in the mid-1960s about location theory, contrasted two different views of economic geography, ones that I will call, following David Bloor (1983, ch. 8), the Enlightenment and the conservative approaches (see also Chapters Four and Nine of this book). The Enlightenment approach—a belief in rational progress, the individual subject, a monolithic order, and universal truth—was clearly embodied in the location models of spatial science that were in ascendancy at the time Lukermann wrote, and which represented the application of principles of scientific analysis to the problems of geography. At bottom such models assumed that "the world was given and man's success was the result of an objective appraisal or ferreting out of nature's secrets. The world had order, man had only to find it" (Lukermann, 1964a, p. 50). In contrast, the conservative view was much more pessimistic about finding anything, especially order. Characterized by a belief in historical contingency, the central role of social institutions in shaping identity, the irreducible complexity of social life, and the importance of local knowledge, geographical location was not a "problem to be solved, a secret to be discovered, but a continuing sequence of events and experiences to be worked out. The world . . . [does] not [have] a given order but an evolving order, a system which is made by not one of us, but by all of us" (Lukermann, 1964a, p. 50).

Although he recognized these two distinct traditions, Lukermann saw the economic geography of his own time entrenched only in the first. In fact, citing the contemporary enchantment with gravity and potential models—models based upon Newton's original formulations and applied to terrestrial spatial flows (see Chapter Four)—he predicted the retreat of economic geography to the seventeenth century, the historical hearth of the Enlightenment (Lukermann and Porter, 1960). In spite of his efforts to forge an alternative, conservative economic geography (see Chapter Nine for details), Lukermann was clearly writing against the grain, and by the late 1960s he withdrew from economic geography altogether, turning instead to historical studies.

Although much has changed in economic geography since Luker-mann wrote, my argument in this chapter, and indeed this book, will be that the seventeenth century continues to exert a powerful grip on the discipline. While the substance of spatial science was extirpated from economic geography during the late 1970s and early 1980s, its legacy in the form of an adherence to the broader Enlightenment doctrine remained strong. There is, as Aris and Penn (1980) recognize, a "workmanship of habit," and for those who apprenticed in economic geography under the system of spatial science—or even those who apprenticed under appren-tices of spatial science—old times died hard. The consequence was that while much of the post-spatial-science debates during the 1980s around, for example, Marxism, critical realism, locality studies, and flexible production, were an attempt to create something different from the past—to establish new times—many of the participants of those discus-sions continued to sit wholly or in part in the old times. Sloughed off was the vocabulary of spatial science, but its broader logic rooted in the Enlightenment remained. In making this argument, I recognize that some people were more successful in shedding their pasts than others and that no one was advocating a return to spatial science as such. Even advocates of quantitative methods, such as Wrigley and Bennett (1981) and, even more extreme, Oppenshaw (1989), saw themselves as doing something different. But escaping the past was a struggle, the temptation to resurrect some form of times lost often irresistible.

As the debates of the 1980s unfolded, it became clear to some that the broader problem—the common difficulty with many of the attempts to construct a post-spatial-science economic geography—was the contin-ued presence of some form of the Enlightenment view within each. Although there were ongoing substantive disputes about, say, just how widespread flexibility was as a form of industrial organization or the correct geographical boundaries of a locality, wider arguments were made that questioned the very ground rules within which those disputes were conducted. This was the embryonic beginning of what I will call a "post"-prefixed economic geography that, in one form or another, drew inspiration from a number of different "post"-prefixed isms that were then entering human geography and that contested the central tenets of the Enlightenment. The emerging "post"-prefixed economic geography took on many of the characteristics that Lukermann had identified in the alternative, conservative economic geography he had mapped out in the 1950s and 1960s. The result was that economic geography, perhaps the most resilient exemplar of human geography within the Enlightenment project, began to shift position, albeit at a sometimes glacial pace. Given the internal sociology of the discipline, that change has tended to occur most readily on three of the discipline's margins: in studies of its method, in development geography, and in studies about gender. For this reason, Lukermann may in the end be proven wrong. Economic geography might make it to the twentieth century on time after all, although it will still be a close call.

This chapter is divided into three sections. First, I discuss the tradition of the Enlightenment and the various "post"-prefixed positions that came to be counterposed with it. Second, I review four of the most significant debates in economic geography during the 1980s: those around Marxism, critical realism, locality studies, and flexible production. There are of course strong overlaps among these different topics both in terms of intellectual content and the personalities associated with each. For my purposes, though, the most interesting feature is the tension in each debate between, on the one hand, an Enlightenment view that seeks certainties and foundations and, on the other, an often only partially articulated alternative that emphasizes skepticism and historical and geographical contingency. In the final section I examine three areas in which that previously muffled interest in skepticism and contingency emerges more clearly as an embryonic "post"-prefixed economic geography: in the application of poststructural ideas to the discipline's method, in postcolonial approaches to development geography, and in feminist theories about female labor markets.

In this chapter I attempt to cover a vast intellectual terrain. In order to at least introduce my arguments in a chapter as long as this one, I had to cut corners, make leaps of logic, and simplify complex ideas. My justification is that it is important in this first chapter to present, however schematically, a review of the events within economic geography since the 1970s to serve as a context for the book's subsequent, more narrowly defined studies. In many of the later chapters I flesh out the various methodological themes I offer in skeletal form here, but this is the only chapter in which I discuss recent debates within the discipline. That I prefer in the remainder of the book to focus on such topics as the quantitative revolution, spatial interaction models, and the philosophy of science is not, I hope, a result of an inclination to intellectual Luddism but because, as I will argue throughout the book, only by understanding those earlier issues can we both comprehend the shape of contemporary discussions in economic geography and, more important, define a real alternative to the Enlightenment view that hitherto has dominated the discipline.

THE ENLIGHTENMENT
AND "POST"-PREFIXED THEORY

The caveat about cutting corners is particularly germane as I elaborate on the two terms that form this section's title. For behind both lies a series of complex and far-reaching debates to which I cannot do justice here. Furthermore, the very use of these two terms imposes an order and homogeneity that is frequently not there. In later chapters, however, I try to recognize some of the internal differences under each of these two rubrics, and in this sense this section is a promissory note.

The Enlightenment project emerged in the seventeenth and eighteenth centuries in Western Europe and is linked to the rise of a number of other broad intellectual and historical movements such as rationalism (discussed in Chapter Four), experimental science, and modernity itself (Bernstein, 1991). Although the question "What is the Enlightenment?" has vexed philosophers since Kant (Foucault, 1984), I will define it here in terms of four main beliefs.

First and perhaps most important is the assertion of *progress*, which is to be both gauged and achieved through the application of rationality and reason. Gregory (1989a, p. 68) writes: " 'The Enlightenment project' . . . was, above all, a celebration of the power of reason and the progress of rationality, of the ways in which their twin engines propelled modernity into the cobwebbed corners of the traditional world." To think in terms of progress requires some benchmark or norm by which to judge whether change is good (progress) or bad (regress). Under the Enlightenment view that norm is reason and rationality. The twentieth century has progressed since the seventeenth century because, for example, Newton's theory of gravity is only a special case of Einstein's more general theory of relativity or because Leibniz's differential calculus is derivable from Weierstrass's more comprehensive set of mathematical axioms. More generally, the twentieth century is an improvement over the seventeenth century because the same things are done more "efficiently," "simply," and with greater "logical rigor"—that is, more rationally—than in the past.

But rationality and reason are not simply the yardsticks, they are the instruments by which progress occurs. In particular, rationality became the basis of various "foolproof methods" (Curry, 1985a) for attaining progress in fields such as physics, medicine, engineering, and even economic geography (see Chapter Four). Such foolproof methods were not confined to the Western academy, though. As Gregory suggests, there was a wider charter that involved disseminating rationality to the rest of the world. Certainly that occurred through the spread of Western science and technology but also through colonial war and conquest. Here, too, economic geography was no innocent bystander. Its early institutional history was inextricably bound to colonial conquest, administration, and intellectual legitimation (see Hudson, 1977; Livingstone, 1992; Watts, 1993).

Second, the Enlightenment was characterized by a belief in the *inviolability of the human subject*. Individuals were taken to be autonomous, sovereign, and self-consciously directed. More generally, it was assumed that there was "an irreducible, stable, unalienated essence at the core of . . . every human individual" (Bondi, 1993, p. 86). Such a claim, in turn, was clearly linked to a broader humanist position that placed human awareness, agency, consciousness, and creativity at the center of all inquiries (Soper, 1986). The Enlightenment project required this link to humanism because, according to Gregory, it rejected other sources of justification for making moral, epistemological, and aesthetic claims. As Gregory (1994, p. 357) writes, "Constitutionally unable to appeal to myth, tradition or religion as a source of authority, modernity established its own ground of legitimation in a self-contained subjectivity." With that grounding in place, general claims about the Other were legitimated. If every individual subject was *essentially* the same, judgments about the good, the true, and the beautiful became generalizable (Driver, 1992, p. 32).

A third central tenet of the Enlightenment was the belief that the world had order and humans could find it. The key again was rationality: the world was not haphazardly arranged but rationally ordered. So the best way to disclose that order was through rational methods, which reached their pinnacle in logic and mathematics. The consequence of these methods, though, was theoretical *totalization*. Behind all our seemingly ephemeral and evanescent experiences—William James's "blooming, buzzing confusion"—was a hidden order, revealed simply by imposing the iron grid of rationality over the various facets of our lives. Moreover, not to locate that order through the imposition of rationality meant a failure to explain or understand the world in which we lived. While we may experience the world as a set of disconnected shards, the underlying reality was one of coherence and totality, held together by the superordinate power of rationality.

Finally, there was the belief in a *universal truth*, that is, a truth that holds for all times and places. To acquire that truth, it was necessary to make reference to some foundation or essence; something that lay outside the changing external context and therefore could provide the permanence necessary to judge claims to knowledge. What was chosen as that Archimedean point varied with the particular theory of knowledge or epistemology in question. In each case the essence or foundation selected provided a universal touchstone by which to assess claims to truth. For Cartesianism, the *cogito, ergo sum* guaranteed the mind as the backstop of knowledge—no one could doubt the mind because the very act of doubting proved its existence; under logical positivism pieces of the world were mirrored in language because it would be impossible to make this statement about language if they were not; and under Marxism class position, and in particular the position of the workers, was essential to establishing the historical truth of the demise of capitalism because if bourgeois classes knew such a truth, they would never let it happen. Although different in substance, each of these epistemologies adopted the same strategy: find an unimpeachable assumption, and use it as the basis for rationally constructing a system of infallible knowledge.

Almost from the Enlightenment's inception, however, there was an oppositional movement running historically parallel to it and continually contesting its various claims. It is seen in Vico's work, in that of the nineteenth-century German romantics, in Nietzsche, in the American pragmatists, in Mannheim's work on the sociology of knowledge, in the later works of Wittgenstein and Heidegger, and most recently in a variety of "post"-prefixed theorists including poststructuralists such as Foucault and Derrida, post-Marxists such as Laclau and Mouffe, postcolonial theorists such as Said and Spivak, feminists such as Haraway and Fraser, and philosophers such as Rorty and Bernstein. There are significant dissimilarities and disagreements among these authors, but they have been united in their desire to interrupt the Enlightenment project in various ways and to strive toward an alternative. For the most part, I focus in this book on this last and most recent group of anti-Enlightenment thinkers, and for that reason I use the admittedly clumsy term " 'post'-prefixed theory" as a collective moniker. As before, I will characterize it in terms of four main beliefs:

1. There is a rejection of both the epic of progress and the power of rationality and reason (Bernstein, 1991, ch. 2). The idea of progress is often bound up with teleological thinking in which the world is directed in linear terms to move from its current state to some improved one: from the Dark Ages to the Enlightenment, from capitalism to communism, from modernism to postmodernism. For "post"-prefixed theorists, however, to think in these terms is only to be captivated by the seductive metaphor of traditional narrative, which is always moving us toward some redemptive

end point. But if we think history is taking us somewhere, it is only because we have already constructed our myths, images, and stories of the past in such a way that this seems plausible. Instead, it is better to see history as composed of ruptures, disjunctures, and gaping non sequiturs. The same goes for reason and rationality. We find them compelling not because of any inherent qualities but because we've been socialized into their tradition. As Wittgenstein once said about mathematics, its truths are accepted because "we lay it down as a rule, and put it in the archives" (quoted in Bloor, 1983, p. 92).

2. Especially since Foucault's work, "post"-prefixed theorists have constructed a very different version of the subject. Rather than autonomous and self-directed, marked by certain core characteristics, "post"-prefixed subjects are created rather than preexisting, shaped from the outside rather than from the inside, defined by what they are not rather than by what they are. The Enlightenment subject, then, for "post"-prefixed theorists is dead; he—and the gendering is deliberate—has been decentered and displaced, and along with him the whole humanist tradition that equates humanness with the ability to act autonomously. Instead, it is argued that the subject is continually in a state of construction, fabricated from the competing and often contradictory discourses in which all social practices are embedded. One point to note here is that those discourses from which subjectivity is made are always situated within particular social constellations of power and are thus always subject to contestation and change. A second is that there is nothing outside of those discourses—no extradiscursive reality—that provides some deeper foundation.

3. A characteristic of "post"-prefixed theories is the rejection of the Enlightenment notion of a monolithic order. Derrida leads the attack against what he calls the belief in logocentrism. For him, the dream at the heart of Enlightenment philosophy was to locate some foundation or "metaphysics of presence" such as God or Rationality or Truth beyond which we need not go so as to establish how all the bits of the world fit together in a totalized way (see also Chapter Six). In so doing, such philosophers were trying to devise a "vocabulary which is intrinsically and self-evidently final" (Rorty, 1991a, p. 89). Beginning with Saussure's work on language, Derrida consistently shows through his detailed readings of various texts that the Enlightenment dream of a final vocabulary is just that, a dream. Through a process of deconstruction, Derrida shows over and over again that there is no final presence. Rather, meaning is constructed not by what is present but by what is absent. There is no single overriding order but only the disorder of an infinite chain of colliding differences.

4. The most recent sustained attack on essentialist and universalist

epistemologies has come from the American "post"-philosopher Richard Rorty. Rorty maintains that the problem with Western philosophy is that it has been captivated by various ocular metaphors, the most important of which is that the mind "mirrors" nature. Furthermore, once

> the notion of knowledge as accurate representation [is accepted, it] lends itself naturally to the notion that certain sorts of representations, certain expressions, certain processes are "basic," "privileged," and "foundational." In this ocular view, the essence of humans is to discover essences; it is to discover rules, procedures and entities that once grasped allow the world to be seen as it "really" is. From such a viewpoint the world that emerges is a . . . universe . . . made up of very simple, clearly and distinctly knowable things, knowledge of whose essences provide the master-vocabulary. (1979, p. 357)

Rorty goes on to argue, however, that none of those essences is ever able to provide a sufficiently secure foundation on which to construct an ironclad epistemology (for more details see Chapters Two and Five). Instead, we must view those epistemologies not as universal constructs but simply as a set of local social practices of a given time and place. Rather than an architectonic enterprise—constructing complete epistemologies to explain everything—philosophy should be a kind of intellectual anthropology trying to understand how "vocabularies acquire their privileges from the men who use them rather than from their transparency to the real" (Rorty, 1979, p. 368).

In summary, I have laid out in very crude terms two different intellectual traditions. The Enlightenment view represents orthodoxy, and as a number of recent reviews of the development of geography have indicated (Stoddart, 1986; Livingstone, 1992; Gregory, 1994), it is the tradition that has historically defined geography. This is especially true of economic geography, which, through its intellectual links to the "science" of economics and its substantive links to imperialism, was early on integrated within the aims of the Enlightenment project. Of course, along the way there were dissenters, including Fred Lukermann, who beginning in the late 1950s provided a series of penetrating critiques of the latest incarnation of the Enlightenment project in economic geography, spatial science. Lukermann's alternative drew upon the same traditions that later "post"-prefixed theory also incorporated. Supplanting spatial science immediately following its demise sometime during the 1970s, however, was not Lukermann's alternative but a mélange of approaches that uneasily bestrided both the Enlightenment and "post"-prefixed approaches. It is to that mélange that I now turn.

FOUR DEBATES

As I discuss in some detail in Chapter Four, spatial science was attacked during the 1970s by humanistic geographers (Ley, 1978; Wallace, 1978) and especially Marxists, who objected to its method, substance, and politics (Harvey, 1973; Massey, 1973). From the mid-1970s on, an explicit attempt was made to reconstruct a relevant economic geography along political–economic lines (as opposed to the neoclassical approach that was dominant under spatial science; Sheppard and Barnes, 1990, ch. 1). Initially the basis of reconstruction was from a Marxist perspective, albeit with an occasional nod to neo-Ricardianism (Scott, 1976). But over the 1980s that reconstruction broadened with the recognition of various difficulties within the Marxist position itself. Two main alternatives, locality and flexible production approaches, emerged, although both remained within a broadly political–economic tradition. In addition, not so much an approach but a whole way of thinking, critical realism, arose during the same period; it cut across Marxism, locality studies, and flexible production approaches and for a period became the unofficial method of economic geography (at least in the UK). My task in this section is to review these various alternatives to spatial science. My argument will be that each of them displays an ambivalent relationship to both the Enlightenment and "post"-prefixed theory. In each case there was an attempt to move beyond the Enlightenment but never quite the vocabulary or the means to do so. The result was a series of tensions within each of the four debates as participants were torn between the opposing poles of the Enlightenment and "post"-prefixed theory.

Marxism

In order to make the discussion of Marxism manageable, I will focus exclusively on the work of David Harvey, who, since *Social Justice and the City* (1973), remains the most prominent Marxist writer in contemporary economic and human geography. This is not to deny the importance of other Marxists such as Richard Peet, Neil Smith, or Richard Walker but only to admit the special place Harvey occupies.

Throughout Harvey's writings there is often a tension between his tendency toward closure, totality, and fixity and his counterinclination toward openness, partialness, and flux. On the one hand, he speaks of the need for "experience and imagination to get behind the fetishism[s]" (1985a, p. 200) and invokes the aid of novelists as varied as Dickens and Pynchon (Harvey, 1985a, pp. xv–xvi). On the other hand, he says that "ambiguity . . . is no basis for science," and it is as a scientist that he wants to be remembered (Harvey, 1984, p. 8). Or again, Harvey brilliantly draws upon a series of oxymoronic concepts—Pareto's batlike terms that combine two different entities in one—such as "concrete abstraction," "creative destruction," and "symbolic capital" to inform his analysis but lets them then sit cheek by jowl beside a static and pedantic lexicon rooted in the most undialectical parts of Marxist theory (best seen in his *Limits to Capital*, 1982). More generally, Harvey is, in his own words, a "restless analyst" (1985a, p. xv). It is a fitting self-description in all kinds of ways: in terms of the history and geography of his own academic appointments, in terms of the varied subject matter of his inquiries, and, most germane to my argument in this section, in terms of his intellectual position, fitfully moving between the poles of the Enlightenment and anti-Enlightenment traditions.

The fitfulness goes deep, and Harvey applies it in a highly creative way, perhaps best exemplified in his most significant contribution to economic geographical theory, his writings on the geography of accumulation, in which he counterposes the fixity of place with the flux of space to define a capitalist economic landscape beset by creative destruction (see Chapter Two for more details). In many ways that theory is the perfect metonym for Harvey's broader intellectual position as he, too, is pulled between the twin desires of fixity and flux, certainty and ambiguity, and totality and partialness. All this said, Harvey more often than not in his explicit methodological statements capitulates to the first of these terms and as a result presents some version of the Enlightenment view. In contrast, the second of the terms tends to emerge only in his prefaces, footnotes, and asides. Certainly, Harvey provides a series of political and ethical reasons for prosecuting the Enlightenment view and being suspicious of "post"-prefixed theory (seen in the multiauthored debate in the journal *Society and Space* [Harvey, 1987], and in his reply to Deutsche, Massey, and Rose in *Antipode* [Harvey, 1992]). But such a commitment to the Enlightenment, however tempered, creates various problems.

Although Harvey is sometimes outwardly suspicious of the notion of progress and rationality, those ideas frequently lie behind his project. In its most extreme form the belief in progress emerges in his view that only by constructing the right kind of theory will socialism be attained. As he writes in his "Historical Materialist Manifesto," "A theoretical project dedicated to the unification of geographical sensitivities . . . [and] formulated in the tradition of historical materialism . . . is fundamental to our thinking in the prospects for the transition to socialism" (Harvey, 1984, p. 9). He is measuring progress according to the final goal of a socialist state. Theory that helps us on our way to socialism is progressive, while that which impedes us is regressive—"counter-revolutionary" theory, as Harvey (1973, ch. 4) once put it. There are other examples, such as his writings on Paris (Harvey, 1985a, 1985b), but the broad point, as Gregory

(1994, p. 218) suggests, is that Harvey promotes "an essentially *progressive* conception of history in which the past is able to illuminate the present precisely because each is conceived as a moment in the unfolding of a single master-narrative."

There is a similar ambiguity with respect to Harvey's view of rationality. In spite of his statements about the importance of the dialectic, much of his theorizing is rationalist in design in that it attempts to define a common matrix against which various competing claims about the world can be compared. Again, this is perhaps most explicit in his 1984 "Manifesto":

> Geographers cannot remain neutral. But they can strive towards scientific rigor, integrity and honesty. The difference between the two commitments must be understood. There are many windows from which to see the world, but scientific integrity demands we faithfully record and analyze what we can see from any one of those. . . . The intellectual task of geography, therefore, is the construction of a common language, of common frames of reference and theoretical understandings, within which conflicting rights and claims can be properly represented. (Harvey, 1984, p. 8)

On the one hand, then, Harvey offers a seemingly relativist view with his metaphor of many windows on the world; on the other hand, he takes that away by supposing that all those different views are ultimately comparable through a rational common language and frames of language.

Harvey's tendency toward the Enlightenment view contributes to a second problem: Harvey does not have an explicit theory of the subject. Indeed, frequently there are no subjects at all because Harvey's economic landscape is typically a peopleless one. As Castree (1995) argues, however, by drawing together a series of scattered remarks, one can provide at least an interpretation of Harvey's view of the subject. In Castree's reading, Harvey presents subjects within capitalism as ostensibly free, autonomous, and individual. In fact, individuals must have these qualities in order for the free market within capitalism to function. Such qualities, however, are only surface appearances; they are manufactured fetishisms created by capital to mask the inequalities and determinations that really characterize economic life. In the sense that capitalism requires these subject positions in order to exist, such positions are fabricated within the broader system. But Harvey immediately takes back this recognition, supposing that those constructed subjectivities are mere obfuscations of some real individual who lies behind and is autonomous and self-directed. So there is a pregiven (Enlightenment) subject after all; it has only been temporarily hidden by the fetishisms created by capitalism.

Third, Harvey is not even ambivalent about totalization. He writes, "To dissect the totality into isolated fragments is to lose contact with the complex interrelations that intertwine to produce the simple narrative of historico-geographical change that must surely be our goal" (1985a, p. 68). Or again, in the *The Condition of Postmodernity*, he discusses the importance of developing a metatheory "that has the potential to put all such partial views together not simply as a composite vision but as a map that shows how each view can itself be explained by and integrated into some grander conception" (1989, p. 2). It is perhaps this celebration of totality that has drawn fire from Harvey's fiercest critics (Deutsche, 1991; Massey, 1991a; Morris, 1992). In particular, Deutsche argues that Harvey's desire to totalize is a result of his captivation by the Enlightenment celebration of visual metaphors, especially that of the all-encompassing gaze. According to Deutsche, Harvey's model is that of the voyeur who gazes upon the world but on whom the world never gazes back. Harvey thus takes on the role of Foucault's universal intellectual, who stands outside, and not inside, the world that he represents. But in so doing, Harvey creates for himself a particular kind of subject position—one that is autonomous, privileged, and sovereign. Then, too, for Deutsche as well as for Massey, Harvey's commitment to totalization through the gaze entails above all a masculinist stance that attempts to master the world through a single vision. But that vision, of course, precisely because it is blinkered by its masculinist form, is only ever partial, and for evidence of that one need only examine *The Condition of Postmodernity* (1989), which claims to be a general theory of contemporary culture yet "ignores one of the most significant cultural developments of the past twenty years—the emergence of practices in art, film, literature, and criticism that are informed by specific kinds of feminism" (Deutsche, 1991, p. 6; see also Rose, 1993, pp. 5–11).

Finally, there is Harvey's position on the truth. Although he wants to recognize that truths are socially constructed at a given moment in time and space, he also wants to claim that his theory is a valid and accurate representation of the capitalist world. For example, he writes with Allen Scott, "The project of holistic theory construction [can allow us] to move forward to the point where we might hope to reflect the totalizing dynamics of capitalism, as in a mirror" (Harvey and Scott, 1989, p. 226). As discussed above, the very idea of truth as mirror representation has been thoroughly criticized by philosophers such as Rorty (1979). In addition, as Morris (1992) argues, Harvey's mirror talk also serves a rhetorical function in allowing him to separate his work, which he can claim is rooted in the real, from that of postmodernists, whose work floats untethered. Specifically, Morris argues that Harvey sets up two mirrors: the good mirror of historical materialism that ensures mimesis and the bad mirror of postmodernism that distorts. As she writes, for Harvey the first mirror "commands the universal, the [second] is mired in the local; one grasps or penetrates, the other masks or veils; one wants to know reality, the other worships the fetish; one quests for truth, the other lives in illusion" (Morris, 1992, pp. 269–270). Given the way in which the two mirrors are rhetorically constructed, Harvey leaves himself—and us— with no choice about which mirror to accept. Because he defines truth as an undistorted reflection of the world, his mirror of historical materialism wins out every time. Of course, once we move away from ocular metaphors and the whole talk of mirrors, which in part is the intention of "post"-prefixed theory, then Harvey's rhetoric is less persuasive.

In sum, Harvey is rightly regarded as a seminal theorist, if not *the* seminal theorist, within contemporary human geography. His theory, though, is born from contradictory impulses that are ultimately rooted in two very different philosophical traditions, the Enlightenment and "post"- prefixed theory. By remaining partially within the Enlightenment tradition, Harvey remains open to attack by various "post"-prefixed critics such as Deutsche and Morris. Some might respond, though, that Harvey's Marxism depends for its inspiration upon the kind of tension that I've outlined (this seems to be the argument in Berman, 1982, with respect to Marx himself). Against this view, recent work by Laclau and Mouffe (1985) and Resnick and Wolff (1987), both of which I review in Chapter Two, suggest that it is possible to construct a "post"-prefixed Marxism without the taint of the Enlightenment. So while such a tension may be a necessary component of Harvey's own ability to theorize, it is not a necessary component of a reconceived, post-Enlightenment Marxist theory.

Critical Realism

In the same way that I concentrated only on Harvey's work in illustrating the Marxist approach, I will similarly focus exclusively on Andrew Sayer's writings in reviewing critical realism (for reviews of realism by other geographers, see Williams, 1981; Sarre, 1987; Cloke, Philo, and Sadler, 1991, ch. 5; Gregory, 1993). Sayer's work is perhaps the most analytically philosophical of any contemporary human geographer. Lucid, lean, and logical, his studies are forensic in their attention to conceptual distinctions. Sayer presents a complete philosophical system that draws upon the writings of the critical realist philosophers Roy Bhasker and Rom Harré. Sayer's exposition, however, is not simply a regurgitation of other people's ideas; he is also concerned to apply that philosophy to a specific range of empirical phenomena, those that constitute economic geography. In this sense, Sayer's writings share a common purpose with those of 1960s positivists who also attempted to work out the details of a wider philosophy within the disciplinary confines of economic geography.

This is not the only link between Sayer's realism and positivism, however. Although Sayer sets realism in opposition to positivism, I will argue that there remain a number of shared methodological characteristics that partially undermine his claim to critique. In turn, this equivocal relationship forms the basis of yet a second one, that between realism and the Enlightenment tradition. While Sayer's radical philosophy of science seems to put him at odds with the Enlightenment, I will argue that his commitment to the complete packaging of method aligns him with various elements of that project. Like Harvey, Sayer does not go the whole way but remains in a hesitant and complex relationship with positivism, the Enlightenment, and "post"-prefixed theory.

Critical realism was initially conceived as an alternative philosophy of science, established directly in contrast to positivism and, in particular, to the "standard" or hypothetico-deductive model of scientific explanation (see Chapter Four for more details). Specifically, realism challenged positivism's formulation of causation, facticity, and verification.

Proponents of critical realism reject the Humean idea of cause as a constant conjunction—if event a, then event b—found in the standard model and instead speak about necessary causal powers and liabilities contained within objects that are only realized under specific contingent conditions. To use Sayer's (1984, ch. 3) favorite example, a barrel of gunpowder embodies the necessarily causal power to explode, but whether it does or not depends upon the contingent event of someone's throwing in a lighted match. So while recording constant conjunctions of events may produce generalizations and even predictions, they cannot reveal causes. As Sayer (1985b, p. 162) says, "What causes something to happen has nothing to do with . . . the number of times it has happened or been observed to happen." To avoid the categorical mistake of confusing causes with generalizations, Sayer emphasizes the distinction between intensive and extensive research. Intensive research is concerned to identify real *explanatory* causes through a process of "rational abstraction" (defined below), whereas extensive research is concerned only with *recording* the frequency of occurrence of empirical events, that is, in making generalizations. The mistake of positivism was to conflate these two very different activities.

In contrast to the standard view that portrays facts as neutral sensory observations of the world, critical realism suggests that facts are socially constructed and are not independent of theories. For this reason, fact gathering is a hermeneutical process in which we continually negotiate between our inside social world and the outside real world. Moreover, sometimes facts are the beliefs of other people, in which case there is a need for a double hermeneutic, an understanding of others' understanding. Note, however, that in neither case can we make facts anything we like, which is the mistake of idealism. As Sayer (1984, p. 186) says, facts are "theory-laden but not necessarily theory determined." More generally, positivism is wrong in assuming that what is real about the world are surficial empirical observations—facts. For realists, such observations are only the exterior manifestation of ontologically deeper structures that possess causal powers and liabilities. It is these nonapprehendable causal structures that form the real in realism.

Finally, and related to both previous points, realists criticize the standard procedure of verification found within the standard model, one based upon comparing deductively derived predictions of a theory with empirical observations. The problems here are, as already noted, that there is no neutral set of observations against which to compare predictions and that because prediction is expressed only in terms of surficial empirical events, it will not reveal anything about the deeper causal structures that produce the events. More generally, for realists there are sharp distinctions among prediction, verification, and causal structure: good predictions do not verify causal structures, and likewise bad ones to not falsify them. Rather, verification of causal structures can only occur through an intensive form of case-study research employing a large array of confirmatory tests, although none is foolproof (see Sayer, 1984, ch. 7).

It was to counter the errors of positivism and its associated mathematical and statistical apparatus of theory construction and verification that Sayer introduced realism into economic geography in the late 1970s and early 1980s (Sayer, 1979a, 1979b, 1982a, 1982b). Focusing on these three issues, Sayer in a series of critical articles took to task various positivist economic geographers. In a well-known debate, Sayer (1982a) argued that Keeble's (1980, 1982) finding of a statistically significant linear regression between the two variables "percentage loss of metropolitan manufacturing employment" and "number of development grants awarded" said nothing about the causal mechanisms responsible for such a relation. This is because the kind of extensive research Keeble practiced can never address questions of cause that only intensive research methods answer. Then in an attack on urban economic modelers, Sayer (1979b) said that the main problem with models such as the Lowry model and entropy-maximizing techniques was that they took both "things" and people's actions as if they were immutable facts rather than social constructs. Finally, Sayer finds in both Keeble's work and that of the urban economic modelers inappropriate claims of verification. For example, successful predictions of an urban commuting pattern do not verify, say, the entropy model as an explanation because no such causal explanation is ever offered (Sayer, 1976).

If these are the differences between realism and positivism, there are also commonalites that make the break between critical realism and positivism seem less convincing than Sayer suggests. Realism, like the standard model, provides a complete set of methodological strictures for empirical inquiry that are as applicable to physical science as they are to the humanities and social sciences. In this sense, like the standard model, realism offers a form of naturalism—the belief that there is a single logic of inquiry that transcends subject matter. Now, realists do recognize the differences between people and things through, for example, their distinction between the single and the double hermeneutic. But a constant in both cases is the basic critical realist method of explanation: through rational abstraction the researcher locates significant structural relationships, identifies causal powers and liabilities, and through intensive research finally denotes the specific contingent conditions under which such causes are realized. It is as simple or, as Sayer (1987) might say, as hard as that. Admittedly, just because realism shares the naturalism of the standard model, the two are not necessarily identical. But it does suggest a common intellectual origin that upholds the importance of possessing a set of indispensable methodological procedures for explanation that lie outside the particular investigative context.

In spite of Sayer's critique of the traditional notion of objectivity and neutrality of research, he also implicitly shares with proponents of the standard model the belief in a value-free method, untainted by politics. This is best illustrated by the distinction he makes between Marxist social theory and realist method. Sayer (1985b, p. 161) writes that the "association of realism and radical geography is not a necessary one: some radical work has been done using a nomothetic deductive method and acceptance of realist philosophy does not entail acceptance of a radical theory of society" The key word here is "necessary," for if the association between realism and Marxism is not necessary, then following Sayer's own strictures it must be contingent. This implies that if realists are Marxists, then they must justify their politics "by other means" (Sayer, 1985b, p. 161), and likewise if Marxists are to employ realism, they must justify it not on political grounds but on methodological ones. Here, then, is the separation between politics and method. While there might be pragmatic reasons for making this distinction (implied in Sayer, 1982b), the effect is to uphold one of the canons of the standard model that Sayer seeks to undermine.

For all the qualifications, realism, like the standard model, ultimately attempts to explain the world by using a rational set of procedures to connect abstract theories with a set of empirical statements (see Sayer, 1985b, p. 172, for his gloss on this). Archer (1987, p. 390) also recognizes these similarities and polemically likens Sayer's *Method in Social Science* to David Harvey's (1969) manual of the standard model, *Explanation in*

Geography, written fifteen years earlier. He writes, "Both books . . . concentrate on the specific procedures of scientific explanation. . . . [Both] posit an extra-theoretical reality and, then, a gulf between our theories and the real, which can be bridged only by an approximately [*sic*] way no matter how comprehensive those theories may be. The trick . . . [is] to achieve successfully better approximations to the real by continually refining our methodological procedures" (Archer, 1987, p. 390). Thus, in the standard model rationality is central to the process of deduction, while under realism it is manifest in the process of abstraction. In the standard model there are so-called correspondence rules that link observations with abstract theory, while under realism there are specific procedures associated with intensive research that allow investigators to connect empirical phenomena with abstract causal structures (Sayer, 1985b, p. 163). In the standard model theories are tested against the real world observations using predictive success as a criterion, while under realism causal structures are tested against the real-world on the basis of what Sayer (1984, p. 66) calls practical adequacy, that is, on the basis of generating "expectations about the world . . . which are actually realized." Finally, in the standard model the project is to come up with ever better theories as measured by their predictive success, while under realism the task is to delineate ever better accounts of causal structures as gauged by their practical adequacy (Sayer, 1993, p. 330).

In sum, realism and positivism articulate with one another in an intricate way. They are not mutually exclusive but enjoy significant overlap. This complex articulation in turn forms the basis of a similarly involved relationship between realism and the Enlightenment, one that again can be unpacked using the fourfold scheme already employed.

With respect to the first issue of rationality and progress, Sayer is seemingly unwavering. He writes that we should not "doubt the possibility of scientific progress or abandon the Enlightenment project" (1993, p. 321). Or again, "Yet presumably there is . . . scientific progress, otherwise we would be using quill pens and stagecoaches rather than word processors and fax machines" (1993, p. 324). Such a Panglossian position is in turn born from two rationalist conceptions:

As already noted, the initial step in any realist inquiry is identifying rational abstractions, where "a 'rational abstraction' is one which isolates a significant element of the world which has some unity and autonomous force. On the other hand, a poor abstraction or 'chaotic conception' combines the unrelated or divides the indivisible" (1982b, p. 71). Rationality here serves, as in the Enlightenment, as the means of progress. Rational abstractions give us the fax and word processors; chaotic ones do not.

Rationality is also important in that it allows comparability among different theories. That is, rationality provides for commensurability among alternative explanatory accounts and thus provides a basis for comparing one to the other. This point requires a little elaboration. In many of his writings, Sayer (1984, p. 68) attacks Kuhn's idea of incommensurability, arguing that "an illusion of incommensurability is produced by reducing the description of competing systems of thought to those terms which are unique to them, ignoring the wealth of usually more mundane concepts which they share and to which appeal can be made in trying to resolve disputes." Even on its own terms, Sayer's argument is shaky. When we compare a new theory with an old one, our purpose is typically to show all the novel things that the new formulation allows us to accomplish. For example, if we compare Perroux's (1950) growth pole theory with Massey's (1984a) theory of the spatial division of labor we are unlikely to emphasize their common bearing upon regional economies. Instead, we would be much more inclined to stress their *differences*, a consequence of the different metaphors that each employs, one based upon magnetism and the other on geology. The two theories are incommensurable precisely because the two metaphors are incommensurable, and no amount of adjustment in common "mundane concepts" will change this. That Sayer does not recognize this point seems to be a consequence of his belief that there is some common (rational) basis to argument that allows us to know which theory is better than another and hence to achieve progress. For example, he writes, "If we don't follow the protocols of reason and practical adequacy, how should anyone understand us, and why should they believe us?" (Sayer, 1993, p. 340). But ever since Wittgenstein, such a view of language and practice hardly seems tenable. Provided that we are socialized within the rules of a language game, we will achieve understanding, but it might well be an understanding that shuns reason and practical adequacy. The broader problem is that Sayer thinks that within all language games there is a bedrock set of rules based upon reason and practical adequacy that ensure comparability. Wittgenstein in contrast argues that there are a multitude of such rules with no necessary overarching connections among them (Bloor, 1983).

Sayer is more circumspect about subjectivity. He argues that every individual consists of a bundle of causal powers and liabilities that, like those of inanimate objects, are activated by contingent factors (Sayer, 1985a, p. 57). In the case of humans, those causal powers and liabilities are the very beliefs of the individuals themselves, albeit beliefs that are intersubjective and socially constructed. As Sayer writes (1989b, p. 209), "Individual subjectivity is structured through inter-subjective relations and expressed in socially available concepts and language." Given this position, Sayer makes three further claims: (1) that unlike inanimate objects, individual agents have the ability to learn and thus the power to change their causal powers and liabilities over time; (2) that while such change is possible, the intersubjective beliefs that constitute subjectivity are relatively stable and are reproduced through a recursive relationship between the individual agent and the broader social structure; and (3) that in order to understand the subjectivity of individuals and hence the causes of their action, it is necessary for the researcher to engage in some form of interpretive understanding, or *Verstehen*.

How does this view relate to both the Enlightenment and the "post"-prefixed understandings of the subject? On the one hand, Sayer's portrayal seems to shy away from the autonomously self-directed individual of the Enlightenment and instead to follow the poststructural line that subjects are created from wider social beliefs. On the other hand, though, Sayer shares with the Enlightenment both the idea that there is an essential core to humanness—in his case a bundle of causal powers and liabilities—and the view that the beliefs that constitute an individual's subjectivity are not just discourses but are representative of real-world features; that is, discourses stand for something real. How these two different perspectives on individual subjectivity—one social constructionist and the other essentialist—are compatible is unclear.

There is further ambiguity around Sayer's view of totality and order. In one sense, the internal logic of Sayer's scheme makes it one of the most ordered systems of inquiry ever presented in economic geography. His exact and measured language, his finely honed distinctions and relations, and his meticulously worked out steps of inquiry all make for a highly structured method in which everything is in its place. Specifically, the orderliness of realism as a mode of inquiry is predicated upon a limited number of relatively inflexible but intuitively appealing principles often expressed as dualisms, for example, necessity and contingency, causation and generalization, abstraction and concreteness. Such dualisms, once learned, form a basic tool kit, just as hypothesis testing, laws, and regression analysis did for an earlier generation. In both cases, whatever the context, there is always a tool that is appropriate for the problem.

Where realism and positivism diverge is in how much of the messiness of the world they believe can be explained at any given time by their respective tool kits. Positivism attempts to eradicate that messiness altogether by finding the one underlying order that binds everything, while realism attempts only to cordon off the messiness and keep it under control. By that I mean that realism, on the one hand tries to discern ordered structural relations through a process of rational abstraction—the recognition of necessary relations—but, on the other hand, also tries to recognize that not all of the world can be so structured—the recognition of contingent relations. In this sense, the world is always divided into two parts: the ordered part that we can explain by positing causal powers and liabilities, and the disordered part that we cannot because of its contingency. As Sayer (1993, p. 333) writes, "Realism prioritizes the search for necessity rather than for order and it conceptualizes necessity as plural rather than singular, as residing in the causal powers and liabilities of objects, which may in many cases be contingently related to one another. While its ontology includes structures there need be no single or central structure." Although it is true that realism seeks no one structure, the structures that it does discern it apprehends through a single and central method. Its totalization is thus in terms of the method realism uses—one method for all things—rather than the totalization of the things themselves.

Finally, there is the realist stance toward the truth and essentialism. Sayer avers (1) that realism adopts a fallibilist position that recognizes that one can only prove something is false but not true and (2) that realism is nonessentialist and antifoundationalist.

With regard to the first of these, Sayer argues that we can never know absolute truth because the world is socially mediated. All we ever know are falsehoods, not truths. Adopting this fallibilist position, we must, however, "beware of two common non-sequiturs . . . : first, from the fact that knowledge and the material world are different kinds of thing it does *not* follow that there can be no relationship between them; and second, the admission that all knowledge is fallible does not mean all knowledge is equally fallible" (Sayer, 1984, p. 65). In both cases Sayer believes these non sequiturs are made because practical adequacy is not taken into account. There must be some relationship of words to the world, otherwise we would never get anything done. For the same reason, although one can never know the absolute truth, some "nontruths" are for practical purposes more useful than others. By appealing to practical adequacy, Sayer attempts to steer between the Charybdis of absolutism and the Scylla of relativism.

The difficulty with Sayer's position, however, is that if practical adequacy is to accomplish the task he sets it, then it, too, must fall back on either the relativist or absolutist position that he seeks to reject. Recall that the definition of practical adequacy is that knowledge must generate expectations about the world that are realized. This kind of argument is a form of instrumentalism in which knowledge is accepted only on the basis of its results. The trouble with instrumentalism is that different theories can meet the same criterion of practical adequacy. For example, both William Alonso's (1964) and David Harvey's (1973) theory of urban land rent are practically adequate because each accords with our expectations about the urban pattern of land rents. The problem, however, is how to choose between these two very different, practically adequate theories. Sayer is left either to claim that one can't choose between them (a relativist position) or to assert that only one is correct (an absolutist position). Employing practical adequacy as a criterion of theory choice, then, merely postpones the choice between relativism and absolutism but does not dispense with it.

If we turn to the second issue, we find that Sayer argues that realism is not committed to essentialism, and in fact is antifoundationalist (1984, pp. 146–148) The form of this argument is similar to the previous one about never knowing absolute truth. Because we never know reality as it really is, it is impossible to claim that any one of its characteristics is essential. The problem here, though, is that realism is making a very strong claim about the world, that is, the presence of what Sayer terms natural necessity (as opposed to logical necessity that exists only between statements). Natural necessity is the claim that the world is made up of nonapprehendable necessary causal relations. This claim is itself a form of essentialism: it asserts that necessity is a necessary feature of the world if it is to be understood.

In conclusion, following both the demise of spatial science and the increasing doubts raised about Harvey's brand of Marxism, Sayer's critical realism offered many attractive features to economic geographers. It retained a number of methodological precepts into which economic geographers had already been socialized: it upheld scientific rigor and logic, offered a series of clear methodological strictures and steps of inquiry, and insisted on the close link between the theoretical and the empirical. At the same time, however, it avoided many of the criticized features of both positivism and structural Marxism—it eschewed mind-numbing statistical generalization, avoided overarching structural determinations, and disavowed claims to universality and absolute truth, preferring instead an emphasis on local contingency. *Method in Social Science*, then, was the right book for the right time and place. But my argument is that as with Harvey, Sayer totters between Enlightenment and anti-Enlightenment views. This is seen by the very tensions that exist within his argument, as I have tried to make clear. For this reason, Sayer is perhaps another restless analyst.

Localities

Elements of both Marxism and realism were central ingredients of the third debate, around localities. That debate was peculiar in all kinds of ways, not least of which was the vituperative and acidic tone of much of the discussion and the wildly divergent assessments of the idea of locality itself. For example, while Cooke (1989c, p. 272) found locality "a fascinating, complex concept of considerable value," Duncan and Savage thought it at best a "conceptual gap filler" and at worse a "dangerous" idea (1989, pp. 203, 192). There were also other oddities.

Although it was initially conceived as an empirical project, very little attention was ever paid to its substantive results (summarized in Dickens, 1988; Cooke, 1989b; Bagguley et al., 1990). Instead, the focus was theoretical and methodological. Or, again, while the politics of the project was left-wing and its method ostensibly realist (Cochrane, 1987; Massey, 1991b), the two most prominent Marxists in the discipline, Harvey (1987) and Smith (1987), remained sharply critical of it, while the most articulate exponent of realism, Sayer (1991), provided a definitive critique of the use of that method by locality researchers. Finally, the debate was primarily a British affair, often conducted among vying factions of the same project and publishing in what became for a period the disputants' own house journal, *Antipode*. (A notable exception are Cox and Mair, 1988, 1989, and 1991—works that attempted a North American counterpart, although they, too, published their initial methodological proposal in *Antipode*.)

To understand these various oddities, it is helpful to begin with the historical and intellectual origins of the project. The former lie in the deindustrialization of Britain and the accompanying Thatcherite social and political "revolution" of the late 1970s and early 1980s. Because the effects of such change were highly spatially differentiated, the UK Economic and Social Research Council undertook to fund three separate locality projects to investigate various facets of the resulting uneven geography. The stance that each of the projects took toward the locality concept, however, differed markedly from the others. The first, the Social Change and Economic Life program, treated locality as a geographical residual, while the second, the Sussex program, considered locality confused and unusable. It was only the third, the Changing Urban and Regional Systems (CURS) program, headed by Philip Cooke, that made full use of the locality concept and perhaps for that reason garnered the greatest attention (Duncan and Savage, 1991, pp. 155–156). I, too, will focus primarily on Cooke's CURS program.

The intellectual origins of the locality project are more difficult to depict, bound up as they are in a series of debates both within geography and outside it (Savage et al., 1987, p. 28). Three main influences can be detected, however. First, there was the work of the British sociologist Anthony Giddens (1976, 1977) and his idea of "locale." Geographers from the late 1970s became interested in Giddens's notion of structuration—the notion that agency and structure are recursively linked—and tethered that concept to emerging work in time-geography. The argument Giddens made was that in reproducing social structures, individual agents through their everyday actions drew upon various institutional powers and resources embedded in space and time. Social reproduction, then, was not an abstract process occurring in some empyrean realm but took place in particular concrete locales. Furthermore, in prosecuting a structuration perspective, Giddens strove to distance himself from any structural, functionalist, or evolutionary sociology. The locality project took up both these types of concerns. On the one hand, there was the attempt to represent empirically the particularity of everyday life in specific places; on the other, there was the desire to shrug off the functionalism and structural determinacy associated with at least Harvey's brand of Marxism.

A second influence on the CURS program was that of Doreen Massey's writings, and particularly her books *Anatomy of Job Loss* (1982), written with Richard Meegan, and her now classic *Spatial Divisions of Labour* (1984b). From the late 1970s onward, Massey (1978) had argued for the importance of place in understanding regional industrial restructuring. In the *Anatomy of Job Loss*, she suggested that the same process of industrial restructuring could occur through one of three different means: rationalization, technical change, and increased intensity. Her important point was that any of the three strategies a firm chooses will produce a very different outcome not only on employment levels but also on regional economies.

Refining and elaborating this argument in *Spatial Divisions of Labour*, Massey contended that different parts of a firm's operation were carried out at different geographical sites, and over time those sites would be stamped economically, but also socially and culturally, by the division of labor that was created. Geography matters here because places that were initially defined by a particular division of labor influence the kind of investment that is deposited in the next round of accumulation. The idea that places are the result of past layers of investment that in turn determine the nature of yet future layers was subsequently dubbed a geological metaphor by Alan Warde (1985).

Finally, there was the impact of realism. Ever since Gregory's (1978) call for a critical regional geography in the last chapter of his influential *Ideology, Science and Human Geography*, economic geographers were interested in theorizing the specificity and uniqueness of place. The problem was that there seemed no readily available method. With the advent of realism, that changed. As Massey (1984a, p. xv, cited in Massey, 1991b, p. 271) wrote in an initial proposal for the localities project, "But if there are reasons, both in policy and in analysis, why such a set of local studies is important now, it is also the case that this is a propitious moment because both theory and method have been and are still being developed in ways which make such analyses more possible." The theory was her own idea on spatial divisions of labor, and the method, although she never names it, was realism. At least as used by its proponents, realism provided the charter for distinguishing between necessary general economic causal structures that were space-independent and place-specific contingent factors that could trigger those general causal powers. In this way it was possible both to discuss comprehensive theories of economic change and also to deal with the particularities of individual places without reducing one to the other (Cochrane, 1987). As Sayer (1991) subsequently argued, things were unfortunately not this simple. But such a judgment was in some sense moot; it was the belief that they were so simple that launched localities studies as a project.

Given this large amount of antecedent intellectual baggage, it was not surprising that the localities debate began well before many of the empirical studies were ever published. Furthermore, to make matters more complicated, Cooke (1989a, 1990) harnessed his CURS localities project to yet another controversial body of work, postmodernism. Because of these dispersed and often contentious origins, the discussion on localities quickly splintered into several debates, each one effectively autonomous from the others and, apart from the enduring presence of Cooke, involving a different set of participants. Those debates can best be reviewed under three main headings: methodological disputes, definitional controversies, and postmodern anxieties. In each case they exemplified to varying degrees the uneasy relationship between the localities project on the one side and Enlightenment and "post"-prefixed theory on the other.

Methodological Disputes

With respect to method, there were two main bones of contention, both of which were laid bare in Smith's (1987) and Cochrane's (1987) early critiques. First, Smith (1987, p. 62) argued that by documenting "the minutiae of local change," locality researchers were "unable to emerge from [a] morass of statistical information" and as a consequence were also unable "to draw out theoretical or historical conclusions." Locality research had thus fallen into the "daunting abyss of empiricism" (Smith, 1987, p. 60). Second, the very focus on the local made it difficult to provide comparisons and "sustainable generalization" (Smith, 1987, p. 67). In particular, as Cochrane (1987, p. 361) argued, such parochialness mitigated against the formulation of either a "coherent theory of restructuring" or the development of practical policies to combat its effects.

To both claims counterarguments were made. Cooke (1987) suggested that there was no necessity for locality research to be restricted to an empiricist method, and even if this had become the de facto practice, it was not empiricism of the old kind but one that recognized the role of theory in shaping inquiry. Cooke referred here to the importance of

"diagnostic theory" and "clinical inference," although the precise meaning of these terms remained unclear. As for the second charge, Cooke
(1987) argued that Smith and Cochrane were wrong in claiming that the
study of localities produced only small-scale concrete research with no
hope of abstract theorization. For there is no necessary relationship
between geographical scale and level of theoretical abstraction (see also
Massey, 1991b; Sayer, 1991): abstract generalities are derivable from a
study of the local, just as concrete specificity is found at the level of the
global.

Definitional Controversies

Another debate was around the coherence of the definition of a locality—
Urry (1987), for example, recognized ten different definitions, and Gregson (1987a, 1987b) eight. There were two parts to this criticism, both of
which were primarily made by members of a rival locality project, based
at Sussex (Duncan, 1989; Duncan and Savage, 1989). The first was that
in Cooke's account locality was defined in such a way that it possessed
causal efficacy. For the Sussex group, though, such an attribution was
merely a disguised form of spatial determinism or fetishism. According to
the realist line of thought, spatial units, such as localities, can never cause
anything; only objects within space possess causality (Sayer, 1985a).

The second and related argument made by the Sussex group was that
Cooke inappropriately defined "locality" as "a pregiven sociospatial
object" (Duncan and Savage, 1991, p. 157). For the Sussex group,
however, the appropriate scale of analysis depended upon the particular
research question at hand; it cannot be defined *ex ante*, and for that reason
it is necessary to employ a panoply of spatial terms—"area," "region,"
place and so on—and not a single predefined one, locality.

Again, Cooke and others provided counterarguments. With respect
to the first charge, of spatial determinism, Urry (1987) and Massey
(1991b) argued that they never assumed that localities were autonomous
causal entities. Localities are always interacting with a set of broader
structures, and causation follows from their interaction, not from their
mere existence. Cooke (1989a, 1989b, 1990) elaborated this argument by
suggesting that such interaction triggers what he calls proactive powers
embodied within individuals living within a locality, and it is the exercise
of those powers that does the causing and not space as such (Cooke,
1989a, pp. 20–22). Specifically, Cooke's (1989b, p. 296) argument is that
by virtue of certain rights of citizenship, individuals possess the capacity
for local proactive change.

As for the second charge, that localities are pregiven entities, Cooke
(1990) argues that because of broad social and economic processes of

transformation, Western Europe and North America have since the mid-1970s moved from a modernist epoch to the beginnings of a post-modernist one. For Cooke, at least, the appropriate geographical scale of analysis for this emerging postmodernist era is the locality, because as modernism falters, "the burden of responsibility for resolving problems is falling increasingly upon" the proactive individuals who operate at that spatial level (Cooke, 1990, p. 130). There is thus something about the very era in which we live that makes locality the central spatial concept; it is a product of the emerging postmodern times.

Postmodern Anxieties

The final debate was about the relevance of this last idea of postmodernity to the localities project. This is a particularly important issue for this chapter because if such a connection is legitimate, localities research might claim to be the first "post"-prefixed economic geography, thereby under-mining the earlier assertion that it is stuck between the two worlds of the Enlightenment and "post"-prefixed theory. Specifically, Cooke's (1989a, 1990) claims that the universal certainties and monolithic institutions of modernism are now crumpling under the weight of the postmodern recognition of the importance of the local. This is seen in the abstract in various philosophical discussions about the importance of local knowl-edge but also on the ground in the revival of interest in local community and the attendant splintering of the monolithic political, social, and economic institutions that hitherto dominated people's lives.

While this seems a plausible argument, there are two reasons for being suspicious of it: First, there is the elision in Cooke's argument between the abstract local communities that concern postmodern philosophers, liter-ary critics, and the like and "real" geographical communities on the ground. Cooke seems to suggest that because, for example, Rorty in his work on epistemology and McIntyre in his work on morality emphasize the community-defined nature of, respectively, knowledge and morality, this then provides the charter for examining communities (localities) as they are embedded in space and place. But the view, say, that knowledge is relative to the local intellectual community in which it is produced implies neither the existence of local communities on the ground nor their superiority as a form of social organization. Logic chopping by philoso-phers and literary critics can never prove the existence of the type of geographical communities and localities on which Cooke wants economic geographers to focus. The two are of a different order.

Second, if we examine the substance of locality studies, including Cooke's own empirical works, we see little sense of the plurality and difference characteristically associated with postmodernism. Locality research remains, as a number of critics have suggested, highly economistic (Bowlby, Foord, and McDowell, 1986; Rose, 1989; Jackson, 1991; Pratt, 1991). Furthermore, as Rose (1989) argues, even within that economistic reading only particular kinds of predominantly masculine and formal economic activities are investigated. The obverse is the undertheorization and empirical neglect within the locality project of noneconomic factors. Bowlby, Foord, and McDowell (1986, p. 329) write, for example, that "other social relations such as those based on gender, race or religion . . . remain untheorized." Jackson (1991, pp. 215–218) likewise describes the representation of culture and cultural studies by locality studies as "faltering" and "impoverished," and Pratt (1991) argues that it provides no analysis of discursive formations, a mainstay of much of postmodernist analysis. For these reasons, it is easy to accept Massey's (1991b, p. 272) conclusion that while "there are . . . many apparent points of contact [between locality studies and postmodernism] . . . many of these are more the result of the accidents of language than real connections, and none of them amount to real equivalences."

If these three issues represent the substance of the localities debates, in what ways do they illustrate the ambiguous relationship to the Enlightenment and "post"-prefixed theories that I've claimed for them? With respect to the issue of rationality and progress, Cooke is ambiguous on both counts. Although Cooke (1990, ch. 1) presents progress as the epitome of the modernist project, he presents localities and the proactive capacities that they embody as inherently progressive. As he writes, "Localities may yet be a key agent in dissolving [modernism's] blockages and distortions, thus propelling modernity onto a higher plane" (Cooke, 1990, p. 181). The role of localities here is the same that rationality performs in pushing aside premodern obstacles on the path toward the Enlightenment. Similarly, while Cooke decries the rationalism of the Enlightenment, seeing it as yet more universal rules, there is the strong sense throughout both the case studies and accompanying theoretical work (such as Massey's spatial divisions of labor argument) that capitalists represent the very pinnacle of rationality, geographically deploying their investments in an optimal, profit-maximizing fashion. So what locality studies provide is not so much a different theory of capitalist rationality as a better theory, one that offers a more refined account of how geography enters into capitalists' rational calculations of profit and loss.

Second, there is not so much an ambivalence as an absence in the way the locality project deals with the subject. There is sometimes an implicit acknowledgment of structuration, but even that is rare. Perhaps a theory of the subject is most explicit in Cooke's idea of proactivity. After first recognizing that individuals living within localities are vested with particular kinds of rights and powers of citizenship, Cooke (1989b, p. 12) writes, "Locality is thus a base from which subjects can exercise their capacity for pro-activity by making effective individual and collective interventions within and beyond that base." The idea here seems to be that preexisting individuals are provided with certain rights and powers that, depending upon the set of contextual conditions they face, can be exercised in a proactive manner. This conception seems very close to the Enlightenment ideal. Individuals exist autonomously and exercise their agency on the basis of the rights and powers vested in them. There is no sense in Cooke's account that subjectivity is made; in fact if it was, it would likely undermine the very idea of proactivity that he espouses.

Third, locality's stand toward totalization is more ambivalent. On the one hand, the locality project celebrates variety, difference, and context as have few other theories in economic geography (Cooke, 1990; Warf, 1993). Of course, this was in part the basis of Smith's and Cochrane's skepticism about the ability of the locality project to grasp capitalism as a whole. On the other hand, if other critics are right, there is an implicit totalization in locality that is effected through its economism. Pratt (1991, p. 257) writes, for example, "Quite simply, much of what has been written under the guise of 'locality studies' can be labelled economism; that is, the reduction of ideology and culture to the position of a subject in relation to the means of production." Certainly, the empirical studies are informed by the strong sense that the economy undergirds everything else.

Finally, there is the relation between the locality project and issues of truth and essentialism. Whereas Cooke (1989a) aligns himself with the "post"-philosophers in claiming that there is no such thing as absolute truth or universal essences, there remains some vacillation. First, everything about the narrative Cooke (1989b) tells with respect to "the changing face of urban Britain" leads one to think that he believes it to be true. In discussing, say, the decentralization of industrial activity from large urban centers, he never indicates any postmodern agonizing over the claims he makes—no attempts at disrupting the text, experiments in reflexivity, or even scrutiny of his metaphors (see Barnes and Curry, 1992). He offers his representations as the facts. Second, in Cooke's account localities often come across as natural entities, defined by certain essential attributes (Jackson, 1991, p. 226), rather than as socially constructed concepts. Again this goes back to the criticisms made by the Sussex group. Cooke's mistake is in thinking that locality is embodied in a definite real-world entity that possesses distinct geographical boundaries rather than accepting it simply as a potentially useful piece of fiction that as much as anything reflects the time and place in which it was coined as it does the time and place to which it was applied.

In conclusion, to understand the sometimes extreme attention devoted to locality studies, especially given "its limited role in terms of research effort" (Sayer, 1991, p. 283), one again needs to take into account the intellectual context within economic geography when it was introduced. It was a time, as already suggested, in which spatial science and its unrestrained empiricism had been rejected, while the theoretical excesses of Marxism, along with its structural functionalism and teleology, were also under criticism (Duncan and Ley, 1982). Moreover, there was a more general call in the discipline for a reemphasis on particularity and place. Locality studies, tied to the rising star of realism, seemed to offer the illusive third way. It was the best of all possible worlds, combining cautious amounts of theory and empirical work, with an emphasis on the particularity of place. As Rose (1989, p. 317) put it, "For a brief moment . . . [locality studies] glittered as the jewel in the discipline's crown, seeming to integrate geography fully with social theory and at last making it possible to claim with confidence that 'geography matters!' " However, Rose (1989, p. 317) continues, "those heady days are now over. As criticisms . . . mount . . . [locality studies] are looking less and less like diamonds and more and more like paste." While her last conclusion may be too extreme—after all, by the usual academic criteria the localities project was very successful, generating both a large amount of published literature and a vigorous debate—there is nonetheless a lingering sense that it never fulfilled its intellectual promise. This is in part because as a debate its center never held. The various issues of discussion seemed distant from one another and, apart from the constant of Cooke, often involved quite different sets of protagonists. This sense of disjointedness was exacerbated by both the changing and conflicting definitions of "locality" and methodological positions that were skittishly advanced. Did locality mean a local labor market, a set of social relations, or spatially bounded proactive capacities? Should the method be clinical inference, realism, or some derivative of postmodernism? More generally, this lack of focus arose in large part because of the attempt to draw together two incompatible traditions: the Enlightenment and "post"-prefixed theory.

Flexible Production

While the locality debate has fallen onto the margins of economic geographical discourse since the beginning of the 1990s, the discussion around flexible production has become increasingly central. This is odd because the localities debate grappled with many of the same issues as flexible production. In both cases there was an attempt to document the decline of old industrial regions and the rise of new ones; an intent to rethink and retheorize the specificity of place, represented in the locality project by Massey's (1984b) geological metaphor and in flexible production by Storper and Scott's (1988) idea of a territorial complex; and a desire to work out a political economic perspective that did not invoke structural functionalism, seen in the locality project's use of realism and in flexible production by the deployment of the regulationist a posteriori functionalism. Yet despite these congruences of purpose, the locality project now lags, while flexible production excels. The reasons for the discrepancy are partly intellectual and partly sociological; I will examine both in this section.

The rise within economic geography of flexible production, and its various synonyms—post-Fordism, neo-Fordism, flexible specialization, lean production and just-in-time capitalism—has been meteoric[1]; it would seem we are all post-Fordists now. The result is that rarely have so many different people in economic geography been united under such an ostensibly single banner. Harvey (1989) accepts a version of the term; Sayer, who has had an on–off relationship with flexible production at least now in his book with Walker (Sayer and Walker, 1992, chs. 4 and 5) concurs with certain of its characteristics; Cooke (1988) was a believer even during the heyday of his locality pronouncements; and Scott and Storper remain the high priests, bringing back the word from such sacred sites as Orange County, Silicon Valley, Route 128, and the Emilia–Romagna region. This does not mean that there is complete agreement. There are major disputes that cleave along interesting geographical lines (see Chapter Four), but even here critics frequently accept some version of "flexible production," just not the version propounded by the group that they criticize. In this sense, flexible production is an overdetermined term, meaning different things to different people. As a result, much of the acrimony within the debate derives from the clash among competing definitions of "flexible production."[2]

Given the massive burgeoning of discussion since the mid-1980s, seeping in and out of economic geography and other disciplines, it is impossible to provide a complete and detailed review here (for that, see Gertler, 1988, 1992; Dunford, 1990; Tickell and Peck, 1992). In any case, much of the debate is about substantive, empirical issues and not the methodological issues that are the concern of this chapter.

The beginnings of the flexible specialization debate in economic geography are in Allen Scott's work in the late 1970s and early 1980s that he later refined (often in collaboration with Michael Storper), and subsequently dubbed neo-Weberian location theory. Having presented a spatial land use, input–output model based upon Piero Sraffa's (1960) work (Scott, 1976), Scott later took the same basic notion of production interlinkages but elaborated them at the level of the firm using as his theoretical template Oliver Williamson's (1975) institutionally based transactional analysis (Scott, 1983). That analysis provided a means to assess the optimal conditions under which parts of the production process should be carried out either inside or outside the firm. Scott effectively collapses those conditions into two archetypes. First, there is the vertically disintegrated firm that externalizes many of its production linkages and as an entity tends to be small and labor intensive, engages in batch production, makes use of external economies of scale and scope, and because of the need to minimize transportation costs and maximize accessibility to clients, is part of a wider production agglomeration or complex with tight-net interlinkages with similar kinds of firms. Second, there is the vertically integrated firm that internalizes most of its production linkages, and as an entity tends to be large and capital intensive, engages in mass production, makes use of internal economies of scale and scope, and takes on arm's-length relationships with subcontracting firms that are often spatially distant.

In setting out these two archetypes, Scott also sought to embed them within an urban labor market that he made increasingly sophisticated by adding political institutions, housing markets, commuting costs, and social characteristics (for a summary, see Scott, 1988b, 1988c). More generally, this attempt to fuse the firm, the labor market, and distinct urban neighborhoods led Scott to rediscover Alfred Marshall's idea of the industrial district, a concept that subsequently became increasingly pivotal in at least some of the flexible production literature (Pyke, Becattini, and Sengenberger, 1990).

Storper's initial contribution to Scott's firm-level analysis was primarily in recognizing the centrality of new technologies and their importance in creating both different kinds of divisions of labor and locational patterns. In particular, by drawing upon a neo-Schumpeterian analysis of technical change buttressed by both long-wave theory and Perroux's concept of the growth pole, Storper (1985b) presented a model of the creation of new industrial spaces. His important point was that once technologically innovative, propulsive industries are established in a place, they create their own conditions of success (Storper and Walker, 1989, ch. 7). Because many of the high-technology firms are vertically disintegrated and depend upon a sophisticated urban labor market, Storper's idea of new industrial spaces chimed perfectly with Scott's speculations about the firm.

As this was occurring inside economic geography, two related bodies of work were emerging outside of it that later provided Scott and Storper with a wider theoretical platform. They were the writings of the regulationist school on Fordism and post-Fordism and the works of Piore and Sabel on flexible specialization.

The regulationist school is now dominated by its Parisian wing, represented primarily by Alain Lipietz and Robert Boyer (for the historical origins and later factionalization, see Dunford, 1990). Using a bastardized version of Marx's base–superstructure model, the school attempts to address the age-old question of why capitalism survives despite its seeming instability. That question is answered by recognizing two components to any mode of production: the regime of accumulation, which is the relationship between the capital goods and consumption goods sectors, and the mode of social regulation, consisting of the various institutions, norms, habits, and so on that bear upon that regime. The argument, following Marx's discussion of expanded reproduction, is that for capitalism to enjoy uninterrupted economic growth, it is necessary that an appropriate relationship be maintained between department 1 (the capital goods sector) and department 2 (the consumption goods sector) (Desai, 1979). If that relationship is out of line, crisis will follow. The function of the mode of social regulation (MSR) is to maintain that appropriate relationship, that is, to regulate departments 1 and 2 in such a way that they remain balanced. To put it in these terms, however, is not to sink to any crude functionalism. The correct mode of social regulation is discovered, as Lipietz (1986) is at pains to emphasize, by trial and error; it is an a posteriori functionalism, as Hirst and Zeitlin (1991) label it, in which knowledge of the mode's successfulness is established only after the fact.

In turn the regulationists brought this abstract analysis to bear on the recent histories of North American and Western and Northern European capitalism. In the crudest of terms, the thirty years following the end of World War II were dominated by a Fordist regime of accumulation that successfully combined mass production with mass consumption and was able to remain in balance because of the existence of an appropriate MSR, a Keynesian welfare state that ensured both full employment and a guaranteed level of consumption. Note that given the trial-and-error discovery of the MSR, there remained significant national variations in the mode's form reflecting the broader cultural, political, and institutional histories in which that search for balance was conducted.

In the late 1960s and early 1970s, the prevailing Fordist regime of accumulation and its associated mode of social regulation became increasingly unhinged, creating a sustained period of economic crisis. Because this crisis was precipitated by impediments to productivity improvements within Fordism itself, a result of its various rigidities (Walker, 1988), capitalists made themselves more flexible by switching to new technologies, work practices, products, and markets that collectively crystallized in a new regime of accumulation: post-Fordism. While the contours of that new regime have become well defined in the literature, the corresponding mode of social regulation remains as yet only faintly drawn. Some initially linked the new regime to the rise of the political neoconservatism of Margaret Thatcher and Ronald Reagan (Scott, 1988a), but that seems less clear now (Tickell and Peck, 1992; Peck and Tickell, 1992).

However that new MSR is defined, though, regulationists agree that post-Fordism bodes no good for the bulk of the working class; it represents yet one more attempt by capitalists to exploit and oppress the proletariat.

The origins of the MIT school of flexible specialization are in Piore and Sabel's (1984) book *The Second Industrial Divide*. Rather than born from an overarching theoretical question, flexible specialization was the result of a pressing empirical problem: What is causing the changing structure of the contemporary North American and Western European economies? Their answer, again in very crude terms, is that capitalism is experiencing a major industrial transition—the second industrial divide. Industry is moving away from traditional Taylorist work principles of mass production found in the large oligopolies that dominated postwar capitalism and toward limited production runs by small firms using computer-based technology and associated with new work practices including work teams, multiskilled tasking, and a reemphasis on craft labor. Although found at a number of sites, the second industrial divide is burgeoning in the older craft centers such as the "Third Italy" and Germany's Baden–Württemberg region. More generally, the name of the game in this brave new world of the computer chip is flexibility, which itself is a result of the capitalists' need to respond to new consumer demands for niche products. Gone are the days when consumers are willing to accept any color of car providing it is black. Flexibility, therefore, is not driven, as the regulationists argue, by obstacles within the production system but by fundamental changes in consumer demand for much more specialized goods. In addition, and again contrary to what the regulationists believe, this latest turn in capitalism is not necessarily all bad. Industrial flexibility possesses a liberatory potential for workers, as seen in the restoration of worker autonomy that has accompanied the reemergence of traditional and artisanal production and in the recent flowering of industrial democracy (Piore and Sabel, 1984).

Scott's and Storper's studies both complement and benefit from the work of regulationists and the MIT school. The regulationists provide them with a wider macrotheory in which to situate their mesoconcepts (Scott and Storper, 1986). For example, Scott's distinction between vertically disintegrated and integrated firms easily fits under the regulationist distinction between post-Fordist and Fordist regimes of accumulation. Furthermore, that regulationist macrotheory also eschews the discredited functionalism of classical Marxism, allows for local (national) variability, and situates itself within a political–economic tradition, all characteristics Scott and Storper uphold. Scott's and Storper's works benefit the regulationists by concretizing their ideas, seen in Scott's (1988a) delineation of the postwar geography of Fordism and flexible production, while also theoretically extending their basic scheme by applying the notion of a regime of accumulation and a mode of regulation to geographically specific sites, manifest in their idea of a territorial complex and a politics of place (Storper and Scott, 1988; Scott and Storper, 1992). With respect to the MIT school, the overlap is primarily in terms of method and the geographical scale of analysis. Scott and Storper, as well as Piore and Sabel, are committed to detailed empirical accounts of specific geographical regions and the mechanisms required to reproduce them. While Scott rediscovers industrial districts, Sabel rediscovers the regional economy (Sabel, 1989); while Scott and Storper focus on Los Angeles, Piore and Sabel concentrate the Baden–Württemberg and the Emilia–Romagna districts; and while Scott and Storper embed local reproduction within urban labor markets and the politics of place, Piore and Sabel discuss networks of trust and local government.

By linking themselves to *both* the regulationist and flexible specialization theories, however, Scott and Storper create certain tensions in their own work that a number of critics have in turn exploited. Lovering (1990), for example, among other charges levels at them the criticism of eclecticism. Amin and Robbins (1990) attempt to pin Scott and Storper to only one of their theoretical sources—the flexible specialization thesis of Piore and Sabel—and then condemn them through guilt by association. These kinds of tensions in Scott and Storper's work, I would argue, are part of a wider set of ambivalences around the relationship of flexible production to the Enlightenment and "post"-prefixed theory and to which I will now turn.

First, the progressive conception of capitalism put forward in the theory of flexible production has been widely criticized. The argument is that while regulationists depart from Marx in recognizing submodes of capitalism—the various subtypes of Fordism and post-Fordism (Tickell and Peck, 1992)—they nonetheless keep Marx's sense of historical progression, where that progression is measured by the enhanced productivity of capitalism. This version of Marxism is also seen in Piore and Sabel's idea of the second industrial divide, which is more productive than the previous divide because of flexible production techniques. The result in both cases is that history is portrayed as a series of progressive ruptures— Gertler (1992, p. 265) calls it a periodization of "before 'then,' 'then,' and 'now' "—where what progresses is the productivity of production technology. Nineteenth-century machinofacture was less productive than the assembly-line techniques of Fordism, which were less productive than computer assisted designs and computer assisted machines (CAD–CAM) technology of today. Moreover, this same progressivism, it is argued, is embodied in Scott's and Storper's works. Amin and Robbins (1990, p. 15), for example, talk about their "historical teleologism," which is made even more acute because they tie their work to neo-Schumpeterianism and long-wave theory (Amin and Robbins, 1990, p. 9). More generally, the

problem with Scott's and Storper's work for such critics is their presentation of events as both cumulatively progressive and sequentially ordered.
Both characteristics are disputed. For example, forms of flexible production are found in earlier historical epochs (Gertler, 1988), and there is no
neat progression of types of capitalism. As Hudson (1989, p. 20) notes,
following his investigation of British old industrial regions, "There is no
general, simple and unidirectional historical sequence of modes of capital
accumulation." Elements of post-Fordism sit cheek by jowl with elements
of a continuing pre-Fordism. Moreover, even the very progressiveness of,
say, the new technology in flexible production is questionable. Gertler
(1988) argues that it is not necessarily more productive than that which
went before, and may even be less so. For this reason, conceiving history
as a series of progressive ruptures is unwarranted.

Against this must be set the many statements by regulationists (for
example, Lipietz, 1986) and by Scott and Storper (Storper, 1987) that
disavow the progressivism and teleologism of which they are accused. Part
of the problem here, as both Gertler (1992) and Tickell and Peck (1992)
recognize, is the murky relationship the regulationists posit between the
mode and regime, a relationship Scott and Storper (1992) have recently
repackaged in terms of the division between the production complex and
the politics of place. It is not clear whether the regime drives everything
forward (this is the view of Marsden, 1992), which if so would bear out
charges of progressivism, or whether the mode curbs and channels the
regime in unpredictable ways, which would thus mitigate those charges
of inevitability. Until this ambivalent relationship is clarified, the relationship of the regulationists of whatever stripe to "post"-prefixed theory will
also be ambivalent.

Like proponents of the other three approaches (Marxism, realism,
the locality studies), the regulationists make little reference to specific
individual subjects. There are hints in Scott's and Storper's early works
(1986), especially with respect to their notion of mesoconcepts, that
subjects are neither the dupes of structures nor freewheeling agents
(Barnes, 1987b). But those hints have never been elaborated. Graham's
(1991, 1992b) interpretation is that regulationism and flexible specialization "construct a unified historical subject" (1991, p. 40). She argues that
both schools "attempt to create an overarching story of the post-war
period, a master narrative to which all our little narratives can be
subsumed. . . . Th[at] narrative tells the story of the social formation from
a 'universal' point of view" (Graham, 1991, p. 53). The problem is that
the universal subject turns out to be none other than the traditional
Fordist, white, male worker, thus occluding other subject positions such
as women, visible minorities, secondary labor market service workers, and
so on. While this is certainly an important point, it, too, suggests some

ambiguity. There is recognition of the Other—if not at home, then at least abroad—through Lipietz's idea of the "bloody Taylorism" that occurs in the newly industrializing economies (NIEs), and work is gradually being done, particularly on the service sector of conditions of employment and the nature of labor markets for female workers (see Christopherson, 1989a, and also her work with Storper, Christopherson and Storper, 1989).

Perhaps the most significant charge leveled at both regulationism and flexible specialization, and perhaps even more vehemently at Scott and Storper, is that of totalization. This criticism is implicit in Graham's critique but is found more specifically is found in the accusation that flexible production generalizes a few local characteristics to overall economic theory. In this sense, totalization is prosecuted by synecdoche— parts are taken as the whole. For example, Aksoy and Robbins (1992) suggest that Storper generalizes the characteristics of a very particular sector, the movie industry, to the economy at large; Amin and Robbins (1990) argue that the same type of move is made with respect to particular kinds of places: the Third Italy, Silicon Valley, Route 128, and so on are made to stand for the world as a whole (also see Gertler, 1992, p. 267). Even on their own terms, such sectors and regions do not live up to their flexible production billing (Amin, 1989; Aksoy and Robbins, 1992), and many areas, for example, older industrial regions (Hudson, 1989) and even whole countries such as Japan (Sayer, 1989c, p. 666), are completely missed out because they do not fit the template. In sum, Storper and Scott (1988, p. 1) are wrong in asserting the existence of a " 'new' hegemonic model of industrialization, urbanization and regional development"— flexible production. That they believe in this "hegemony" is the result of a "totalizing vision in which they see flexible specialization and locational agglomerations, and only this, wherever they look" (Amin and Robbins, 1990, p. 14).

Again, while there is substance to these various criticisms, some caveats need to be made. Despite the charge of totalization, the flexible production literature tends to acknowledge variety and diversity. For example, Storper (1987, p. 418) says that "capitalist history is n[ot] the product of a totalizing structure" and that the "study of the locality and the particular are keys to understanding how the general structure of capital works" (p. 420). Graham (1991, p. 52) also senses an ambivalence and writes about how regulationists in particular "challenge modernism" through their "explosion of the modernist monolith of capitalism and [its] replace[ment] with capitalisms." Likewise, Scott and Storper (1992) and Salais and Storper (1992) attempt to recognize the local and particular outcomes of unique combinations of the regime and mode in specific places—captured in their alliterative triad of periods, places, and pathways (Scott and Storper, 1992, pp. 20–22). As before, there is ambivalence rather than certainty.

Finally, there is the issue of essentialism and the truth. This is a difficult issue to discuss because different regulationists bring to it different philosophical baggage. Sayer clearly represents a realist line, but so, it seems, do Amin, Robbins, and Peck. There is the historical materialist pitch of Harvey (1989), to some extent shared by Scott (Harvey and Scott, 1989). Finally, there is Storper's (1987) anti-Enlightenment view, which is intriguing but often begs more questions than it answers. Whatever the nature of these philosophical statements, if we examine the substantive work of each of these authors, we see in every case the attempt to match theory with empirical referents; that is, representation itself is rarely problematized. Now, critics such as Amin and Robbins certainly dispute specific representations of Scott and Storper, but only because they overgeneralize or are not sensitive enough to historical context; they do not call into question the epistemological practices of flexible production. More generally, all participants of the debate seem to believe that the world can be more or less represented by our theories (Harvey and Scott, 1989, p. 223, are perhaps the most extreme here).

In sum, flexible production sparked an enormous amount of literature and debate within the discipline that shows no sign of abating. In Kuhn's terms, it is an extremely successful paradigm, one that has become "normal science" and is thus driving out competing paradigms. This takes us back to the question posed at the beginning of this section. From the discussion of both the localities debates and flexible production, we can recognize at least three factors that explain the robustness of the latter over the former.

First, flexible production writers in economic geography quickly coupled themselves to wider debates and movements outside the discipline and also showed that they had something to offer in return (Gertler, 1992, p. 259). For example, Lipietz was an early contributor to Scott and Storper's (1986) influential collection, while Storper in particular increasingly moves in economic rather than geographical circles. By forming these external connections and networks, such economic geographers made themselves indispensable (for more general justification of this point, see Latour, 1987; for an application in economic geography, see Curry, 1992b).

Second, the very flexibility of the flexibility idea itself (although something that Sayer, 1989c, bemoans) lent itself to a more general usage than locality. Locality was always associated with the British context, partly because of its foundation in Massey's geological metaphor. But thought it was appropriate to British regional economies, it seemed less appropriate in North America. Indeed, the most sustained criticism of Scott's and Storper's work comes from British economic geographers.

Finally, flexible production was always more able to link itself to the long-standing preeminence of industrial geography within economic geography. Issues of the firm, its interlinkages, and production technology were already well-defined rubrics in industrial geography, under which especially Scott's work could define itself. In contrast, there was less of a tradition within industrial geography of the type of integrated, multisectoral, place-bound studies that were attempted in the locality project.

For these three reasons, then, flexible production has become the dominant paradigm within the discipline, the wider context against which "normal" research is defined. This is not to imply that flexible production has solved the problems of economic geography. As I tried to make clear here, it is still racked by the recurring ambivalences toward the Enlightenment and "post"-prefixed theory and in this sense is not much different from the other approaches over which it won out during the 1980s.

TOWARD A "POST"-PREFIXED
ECONOMIC GEOGRAPHY

While much has changed in economic geography since the 1970s, there remain, as I've suggested, some strong methodological continuities that bind the discipline to the Enlightenment. In particular, there is the continuing sense that progress is possible. This means that not only do the various approaches examined above make progress an assumption, but also those who believe in them assume that the discipline itself has progressed. Regulationist theory is better than classical Marxism, which is better than spatial science. Again, where it is discussed at all, the conceptualization of the subject typically bears the hallmarks of "Enlightenment man." Many of the recent theories in economic geography, including Harvey's scheme of accumulation, Massey's geological metaphor, and Scott's conception of the firm, all implicitly assume a *Homo economicus* intent on maximizing profits, where *Homo economicus* bears all the typical characteristics of the Enlightenment subject—self-directed, autonomous, and rational (see also Chapters Two and Three). Bound up with these works are other less traditional views of the subject—for example, those that feature the power of local culture to shape consciousness—but they are rarely worked out (Jackson, 1991). Yet again, within contemporary economic geography there remains a tendency toward totalization. This is perhaps clearest in the work of Harvey and of Scott and Storper, but it also emerges in more subtle forms in the locality approach and Sayer's realism. These theories give the impression that there is always only one story to tell, and that it is often economic, masculinist, and white. There is little attempt to fragment the story or to cross boundaries or to blur genres. Finally, there is the overwhelming sense that our theories are mirror representations, however cracked or distorted, of some real set of economic events. In this sense, economic geography remains committed to some form of mimesis.

Despite this inclination toward the Enlightenment, there is, as I have also argued, a countertendency to an anti-Enlightenment stance even within the same approaches. This countertendency has emerged more explicitly over the early 1990s in a body of a work that I have called "post"-prefixed. For the most part, it is found outside of industrial geography, such as in the discipline's methodological discussions, in the geography of economic development, and in the study of female labor markets. To conclude the chapter, I will briefly review each of these topics and discuss the various ways in which these emerging bodies of literature point to a different kind of economic geography, a "post"-prefixed kind.

Method and the Poststructural Turn

While there are now a number of proposals for bringing together post-structural methods and economic geography, I will focus on only one: Julie Graham's advocacy of overdetermination as a basis for a post-Marxist economic geography.

After initially working from within a classical Marxist perspective (Graham et al., 1988), Graham from the late 1980s was influenced by the economists Resnick and Wolff (1987) and their use of the Althusserian concept of overdetermination (for a detailed review of Resnick and Wolff's work, see Chapter Two). In their hands, as well as Graham's, overdetermination was deployed as a critical foil against essentialism, which was the Achilles' heel of classical Marxism. Because under overdetermination every event or structure is multiply caused, where those causes themselves are in turn multiply determined, there is never a final or essential cause of anything. As Graham (1992a, p. 142) writes, "Every aspect of reality participates in constituting the world and, more specifically, in constituting every other aspect." For Graham (1988), at least, the resulting anti-essentialist methodological position has strong resonances with post-modernism, which also eschews final causes. In particular, the task of a postmodernist or post-Marxist economic geography is to trace the over-determined set of causes of economic geographical phenomena, the most important of which, says Graham, are those regarding class.

In an article with Kathy Gibson, Graham has recently fleshed out the empirical entailments of her position (Gibson and Graham, 1992). She is concerned with identifying the overdetermined set of processes that bear upon an individual's class interests. Those class interests themselves, however, are not stable and homogeneous but shift over time and with circumstances. Furthermore, class identity is only one of the many conditions of existence that constitute a subject position. For this reason, class is not an essence but just one of an infinite number of starting points.

More generally, and in contrast to the complete packaging of method found in the approaches reviewed above, economic geographers who practiced overdetermination would (1) recognize their own partiality because of the impossibility of representing every cause; (2) accept the presence of contradictions in all explanation because "since every process exists as the effect of all other processes, each is quite literally a bundle of contradictions" (Wolff and Resnick, 1987, p. 138); (3) by recognizing the concatenation of multiple causes, emphasize "the ceaseless change that characterizes every process in society" (Wolff and Resnick, 1987, p. 138); and finally and perhaps most important (4) by shunning single causes, mark "the ineluctability of difference rather than the search for sameness in a structured world" (Graham, 1988, p. 61). In each of these different ways, then, Graham attempts to map a different kind of economic geography, one that admits from the outset that its stories are fragmented, partial, and contradictory and in which there is no single binding entity such as capitalist reproduction, local proactive forces, or a monolithic flexible production. In that light, Peet's (1992) criticism that Graham's theory is flawed because it "cannot be validated on the basis of its correspondence with the real world" misses her point. Graham's task involves reconceiving the very nature of theory, a prime purpose of which is to shun any talk of correspondence with the real world (see also Resnick and Wolff's [1992] and Graham's [1992a] replies to Peet's criticisms).

Development Geography and Postcolonial Theory

The second area in which "post"-prefixed theory is in evidence is in development geography, which has experienced a renaissance of sorts since the early 1980s. Characterized by an empirical–analytical methodology during the 1960s and early 1970s ("the geography of modernization"), development geography took on a very different complexion following the incorporation of Marxist-inspired development theory in the late 1970s and early 1980s (for a review of that literature, see Corbridge, 1986). Following Booth's (1985) critique of the Marxian tradition in sociology, however, and also a growing dissatisfaction with a similar kind of Marxism found in human geography, Corbridge (1986, 1989) brought the same kind of anti-Marxist arguments to development geography in the late 1980s, albeit not without controversy. The debate was lively and often constructive (see especially Watts, 1988, and Corbridge, 1988), but even before it ended many of its participants began moving on to a related literature that served to emphasize even further the "post" part of post-Marxism, that is, writings about postcolonialism.

To give a crude outline: emerging primarily in literary criticism and anthropology, postcolonial studies sought to emphasize the pivotal role played by Western imperialism in shaping discourses, relations of power, vocabularies, and subject positions of the non-Western Other (Gregory, 1994, pp. 165-205). Moreover, this was not a simple, one-way flow because the very positing of a non-Western Other helped define Western identity itself (Slater, 1993). More generally, the postcolonial literature, along with an already well-established feminist argument, tried to show that the supposed Western universals of rationality and progress were not universals but were designed to serve a particular set of interests, primarily those of European white males living in "developed" regions. Within this Occidental discourse, the West was established as the pinnacle of modernization and civilization (Slater, 1993, p. 426), while the non-West was represented as its antithesis, the homogenized Oriental Other (Said, 1978). This Western view, furthermore, cut across traditional political lines such that conservative and Marxist theorists alike could aspire to Western definitions of development and produce schemes that relied on universal subject positions, epistemological bedrocks, and simplified dualisms (Said, 1978, p. 22).

To flesh out the implications of a postcolonial sensitivity for development geography, let me provide three brief examples. First, it implies that development geographers, and more broadly economic geographers, should reflect critically on the origins of their own discipline and the very relations of power that inhere in their subject of inquiry (Driver, 1992). Foucault is the typical source of inspiration here. Watts, in a superb review of the recent literature from this perspective, argues that it is imperative for economic geographers to provide an archeology of development that "seek[s] to discover the institutions, social processes and economic relations on which the discursive formation of development is articulated" (Watts, 1993, p. 265). With its origins in a biological metaphor aligned to teleological conceptions of history, science, and Western progress, the term "development," argues Watts, was mobilized to serve the interests of the West. By dominating the non-Western Other through various technologies of power and surveillance embodied, for example, in the military, and the colonial police and administration, Western nations imposed a disciplinary power over the non-Western Other. Since 1945 those technologies of power, although less blatant, are even more pervasive and insidious. In particular, it is through various global organizations and their institutional emanations that a new kind of Western discourse field has arisen around development. In this field knowledge and power are inextricably linked. Watts (1993, p. 260) writes, "In the same way that planning in nineteenth-century Europe opened up a realm of state intervention to manage poverty, so the institutions and practices of development attempt to create, and regulate, a realm of the social on a global scale. Development disciplines, as much as the infrastructure and institutions of international governance, attempt to produce governable subjects." The result, as Slater (1993, p. 422) notes, was a "modality of power which is exercised over those who are known as the other, the non-West. Furthermore, when that knowledge is deployed in practice, those who are so known will be subject, or more exactly, subjected to it." Insofar as development geographers were part of that infrastructure, they, too, produced subjected subjects.

Second, doing a "post"-prefixed development geography provides the potential to "learn from other regions," as Slater (1992a) puts it. In examining both traditional development theory (Slater, 1992b) and wider intellectual movements such as Marxism, critical theory, and even postmodernism, Slater concludes that within each there is a strong streak of universalism that entails either ignoring the non-West or, worse, equating the West with the best. Such ethnocentricism, argues Slater, can be partially avoided by learning from other regions, one source of which is the pursuit of development geography. Sources of such learning include non-Western intellectuals such as Said, who emphasizes the processes of "Othering"; the construction of imperial "counter-geographies" that tell the story from the "other side"; and the counterposing of our own experiences with that which is "marginal" and "peripheral." For only in its "outskirts [does] the system . . . reveal its true face" (Slater, 1992a, p. 314).

Finally, a "post"-prefixed development geography would emphasize the centrality of political practice, especially in ethnography and fieldwork. Here the writings of Homi Bhabha and especially Gayatri Spivak are central (see Young, 1990). Both argue that imperialism is not just about appropriating land and resources but also about appropriating a subject. In particular, for Spivak (1988) colonial discourse creates a "subaltern" position defined in terms of nationality or ethnicity. Her project is to retrieve the subaltern, to think through the conditions that allow her or him to speak. In a recent paper Cindi Katz (1992) argues that these issues about the subject are also vital for development geographers to pursue when engaged in ethnographic fieldwork. Drawing upon her research in the Sudan, she examines the ways in which Western intellectuals stage the objects of their inquiry to reinforce the hegemonic (subaltern) subject positions already created by imperialism. Instead, her aim is to redefine the very techniques of representation "in ways that recognize the power embedded in them, thereby enabling the development of new modes of practice and engagement" (Katz, 1992, p. 496). In particular, by prosecuting a "non-innocent ethnography" that attempts to tack between the "macrological structures of power—that is, the global process of capitalism, imperialism, and patriarchy—and the micrological textures of power played out in the material practices of everyday life" (Katz, 1992, p. 500), Katz tries to fulfill the political project of allowing the subaltern to speak. Ethnography, therefore, should not be just thick description but also thick with politics.

Female Labor Markets and Feminist Theory

The final area in which there has been use of "post"-prefixed theory is in discussions of female work and labor practices. In particular, Pratt (1993, pp. 194–195) talks about the recent move in this literature toward "postcolonial feminist geographies" (also see Pratt and Hanson, 1994).

The history of feminist analysis of female work and labor markets mirrors the general history of the use of feminist theory in human geography (usefully discussed by Bowlby et al., 1989). The first phase predominant during the 1970s, was effectively politically liberal and typically used empirical methods to document differences between men and women within the labor market. Two related points were made. First, because of their conventional gender roles as homemakers and caregivers, women do not have the time to search out opportunities in the primary labor market segment and hence end up in secondary segments. Second, precisely because of those gender roles, women need to stay close to home and are therefore spatially trapped (for a review of the literature on women's commuting distances, see Hanson and Pratt, 1995; a different interpretation is given by England, 1993).

While the empirical conclusions of this work remain useful, the wider theoretical framework in which it was placed was increasingly criticized during the early 1980s. Apart from the fact that spatial constraint was equated with only physical distance, such work never provided an account of why women took on the roles they did within the family, presenting them only as passive victims.

The socialist and radical feminist analyses of the early to mid-1980s offered an alternative. MacKenzie and Rose (1983), following the domestic labor debate in Marxism, argued that the traditional domestic responsibilities of women were necessary for the maintenance and reproduction of capitalism as a whole. Specifically, they argued that at least since the nineteenth century women have provided both material support for the reproduction of (male) labor, and ideological support by making the home a safe haven. Their conclusion is that "since home life plays such an important part in the reproduction process, it clearly should not be separate in analytical terms from industrial life, from the 'sphere of reproduction' " (MacKenzie and Rose, 1983, p. 157; see also Rose, 1993, ch. 6). In making this claim, MacKenzie and Rose were in effect exploring the relationship between class and patriarchy (further examined in more abstract terms by Foord and Gregson, 1986, and McDowell, 1986). The more general point was that to understand women's position with respect to the labor market, it was necessary to refer to their structural role within the wider system of capitalism. This in turn led to two kinds of theoretical work.

The first, best exemplified by Nelson (1986), picked up the earlier insight of the spatial entrapment thesis but linked it both to socialist–feminist theoretical concerns and to an emerging empirical trend in the restructuring of service employment, the establishment of back offices in several major North American cities. Precisely because of their domestic responsibilities, suburban women, often white, middle class, and highly educated, were trapped close to home and became a target labor force for decentralizing office employers who found them reliable, pliant, conscientious, and willing to work for wages that were below those offered to comparable employees downtown.

The second type of research that emerged was associated with the localities project, and it made a similar point about the importance of gender. The pioneering contribution was Massey's (1984b, ch. 5) research on south Wales that showed that to understand emerging spatial divisions of labor, it was necessary to study the geography of patriarchy. In this case it was because of years of strong patriarchal relations within the mining communities of south Wales that women there were viewed favorably as an appropriate work force by multinational electronic companies who began investing in the region from the late 1970s. In generalizing this argument, McDowell and Massey (1984, p. 128) concluded, "The contrasting forms of economic development in different parts of the country present distinct conditions for the maintenance of male dominance. *Extremely* schematically, capitalism present[s] patriarchy with different challenges in different parts of the country."

As important as this work was, during the late 1980s and early 1990s this Marxist-inspired feminist theory was criticized for a number of different reasons: First, it fails to problematize the differences among women workers, typically presenting them as a homogeneous group; second, it continues to focus on economic relations, particularly those of capital and class (Bowlby et al., 1989, p. 167); and finally, it presents very general and abstract explanations often undergirded by some form of rationalism rather than attempting more situated and contextually based forms of explanation (Hanson and Pratt, 1995).

The result is that since the late 1980s some feminists have turned toward a form of "postcolonial feminism." For Pratt (1993, p. 195), at least, this movement is characterized by three features: (1) it is no longer focused only on male–female dualism but is more generally concerned with how identity and difference are constructed along a variety of axes, including race, class, sexual orientation, and so on; (2) it deploys a range of social theory that examines the way in which identity and difference are constructed from various social discourses and the power relations embedded within them; (3) there is a movement away from objectivist epistemologies and forms of representation toward ones that strive for some kind of reflexive "situated knowledges" (Harraway, 1991).

In terms of research on women's work and labor markets, elements of a postcolonial feminism have been taken up by nongeographers such as Pringle (1989) and Parr (1990) and within economic geography by Dyck (1989), Hanson and Pratt (1992), Pratt and Hanson (1993, 1994), and McDowell and Court (1994a, 1994b). To exemplify the three features of a postcolonial feminist analysis that Pratt notes, I will conclude by drawing upon her own work with Susan Hanson (Pratt and Hanson, 1994) that examines the segmentation of female labor markets in Worcester, Massachusetts.

Pratt and Hanson are very concerned to examine the construction of a variety of differences in the Worcester labor market; these then become the bases of multiple spatial and social segmentations. In particular, among Worcester female workers they find sharp differences in ethnicity and class. The finding of these multiple cleavages, in turn, casts doubt on the appropriateness of using the effectively essentialist notion of "woman." This is not just a theoretical point but an immensely important practical issue as well. For once created in place, differences among women become the basis of particular kinds of job opportunities, which in turn help to reproduce those very differences (Pratt and Hanson, 1994, p. 11). And it is those differences that are then subsequently exploited by employers who typically are male.

By drawing upon the literature of cultural studies in particular, they attempt to show how difference is constructed and maintained. Unlike most of that literature, however, they are keen to emphasize that geography enters into the construction of identity not only metaphorically through such notions as marginality but in material ways as well (Hanson and Pratt, 1995). In particular, they argue that "identities get hardened and rigidified in part because social life takes place in and through space" (Pratt and Hanson, 1994, p. 6). That is, the competing discourses and institutions of power from which identities are forged take on certain geographies that then shape the spatial patterns of difference. Those patterns for Pratt and Hanson are very fine-grained and localized, and this clearly emerges in their empirical work. In this sense, Pratt and Hanson follow Massey's (1993) observation that in spite of the process of internationalization of material products and images, most people's lives, especially women's, are lived and shaped locally.

Finally, Pratt and Hanson attempt to move away from any objectivist rendering of Worcester's female labor markets by reflexively recognizing their own situated knowledges as white, middle-class professional women (Pratt and Hanson, 1994, p. 14) and by recognizing, as did Katz, the political imperatives within their project, which admits difference among women yet remains committed to the common purpose of feminist social change.

In sum, by offering up a postcolonial feminism, Pratt and Hanson are not rejecting other kinds of feminism that have preceded theirs. Rather than an exclusive project, they see theirs as an additive one. Certainly, their work employs insights from both the spatial entrapment theory and the socialist feminist literature. By staying open to a range of perspectives, they also show by example yet one more of the virtues of "post"-prefixed theory.

CONCLUSION

During the 1970s and 1980s, economic geography moved away from spatial science. The new economic landscape that was theoretically constructed bore little resemblance to the old one; as Dorothy said to Toto, this wasn't Kansas anymore. Gone were the assumptions of isotropic plains, uniform population densities, and distance minimizers. Instead, the new landscape was much more troubled, restless, and unsettled. Punctuated by creative destruction, rocked by the explosive forces of new technologies whose origins lay in tightly clustered urban complexes, and reshaped by the slow but geologically powerful forces of changing spatial divisions of labor, the new landscape was exemplified not by agricultural heartlands such as the American Midwest or the Canadian prairies but by reconfigured industrial spaces such as the Rust Belt, Silicon Valley, and the M-4 corridor.

Such a change in theoretical view was very impressive, requiring much ingenuity, creativity, and effort to achieve. Nor was it without personal cost. Just as the leaders of the quantitative revolution suffered from the dogmatism, closed-mindedness, and entrenched interests of an earlier generation (see the accounts by Warntz, 1984; Berry, 1993; and Chorley, 1995), so, too, did many of the new and often radical geographers who contested what had become the new orthodoxy some fifteen years later—William Bunge was fired, Dick Walker was granted tenure only after a protracted appeal and major petition, while others were never able to secure jobs at all. But as with the quantitative revolution, within only a few years former subversives became part of the "project" (Christopherson, 1989b)—Doreen Massey was offered the chair at the Open University, David Harvey was made the Halford Mackinder Professor of Geography at Oxford, and Allen Scott was given the directorship of the Lewis Center at UCLA.

I don't want to belittle this process of socialization, which was inevitable and in which I myself of course am part. But it does illustrate a theme implicit throughout this chapter, namely, the close links among knowledge, power, and sociological processes within the academy (taken up in more detail in Chapter Four). More important for my purposes here, that process of post-spatial-science economic geographers' becoming part of the project was eased intellectually by the continuation within their work of certain elements that characterized the Enlightenment and its earlier manifestation in spatial science. This was not some simple continuity, as I've stressed, but fraught with ambivalence, complexity, and uncertainty. That said, the fingerprints of the Enlightenment remain all over the four most significant approaches that were advanced in economic geography during the 1980s: Harvey's Marxism, Sayer's critical realism, Cooke's locality approach, and Scott and Storper's flexible production. The result is that each of the four can be criticized from the perspective of the various "post"-prefixed frameworks that, particularly since the 1960s, have contested that Enlightenment position.

That "post"-prefixed perspective is now gradually seeping into various recent works within economic geography. The kind of new economic geography that is emerging abandons any notion of progress, accepts that subjects are made and not given, avoids a homogenizing and totalizing portrayal of the world, and discards any essentialist notions of knowledge. In the remaining chapters of this book I take up and develop these four themes both critically and constructively in order to exemplify the possibilities of a "post"-prefixed economic geography.

NOTES

1. I am being very loose in saying that these terms are synonyms. Each term is associated with a specific spin on "flexibility" that is often contested, as I will explore in the rest of this section. I use "flexible production" as the generic noun because it is the one employed by Scott and Storper, the two economic geographers on whom I most focus in this section.

2. For samples of some of the more vigorous attempts to command that definition, see Gertler (1988, 1989); Schoenberger (1989); Amin and Robbins (1990); Storper (1990, 1993); Scott (1988a, 1991a, 1991b); Lovering (1990, 1991); and Aksoy and Robbins (1992).

PART II

ESSENTIALISM AND RATIONALISM IN ECONOMIC GEOGRAPHY

TWO

PLACE, SPACE, AND THEORIES OF ECONOMIC VALUE
Context and Essentialism in Economic Geography

If Oscar Wilde didn't say that an economist is a person who knows
the price of everything and the value of nothing, he should have.
—Philip Mirowski, "Learning the Meaning of a Dollar"

Out of the recent analysis of urban and regional economic restructuring
has come the call by some economic geographers for a restructuring of
their own discipline. Shunned is the traditional lexicon of spatial laws,
rigid determinism, and formal abstractions (Storper, 1985a; Massey,
1986). Instead, the demand is for a new vocabulary composed of terms
of difference, contingency, and the particularity of place and period
(Massey, 1984b, p. 120; Clark, Gertler, and Whiteman, 1986, p. x; Scott
and Storper, 1986, p. 310; Warf, 1988). My purpose in this chapter is to
discuss these old and new vocabularies of economic geography by situating them within a broader philosophical debate: that between contextual
and essentialist explanations. Specifically, I argue that one way to interpret
the recent emphasis on place in economic geography is in terms of a move
toward contextualism which is at least an important component of many
of the "post"-prefixed theories discussed in the previous chapter. Contextualism, by recognizing and celebrating difference, provides economic

geographers with a charter for treating places as places; it insists that the texture and specificity of place be maintained and not reduced to something less than it is (Barnes and Curry, 1983; Thrift, 1983). In contrast, I argue that the critique of the old vocabulary is interpretable partly as an attack on essentialism. For essentialism contends that to know the world one must make reference to unchanging and universal entities—essences. As such, the logic of essentialism leads to an emaciated view of place in which place is only the surface appearance of a more fundamental essence lying beneath.

To ground this discussion, I will use the vehicle of theories of economic value. In strict terms, a theory of value is simply a theory of price determination. But as Myrdal (1969, p. 15) argues, it has come to take on a broader significance, and is often treated as "the starting point for all economic analysis which really tries to probe beneath the surface." Historically, there have been two main value theories: the Marxian labor theory of value, which argues that prices of commodities are determined by the socially necessary labor time embodied in their production, and the neoclassical utility theory, which argues that exchange values are derivable from the primitives of individual subjective states and natural resource scarcity. I will argue that both these theories of economic value are found in economic geography and, furthermore, represent essentialist approaches. By examining the use of these two value theories in economic geography, I attempt to substantiate my claim that essentialist theories reduce geography to something less than it is. In contrast, to show that a contextual approach allows places to be treated as places, I discuss the possibility of developing a contextual and nonessentialist theory of economic value by drawing upon some recent work that has been completed primarily in economics. I should note that this discussion is programmatic, and it is not until later in the book that I try to work through the details of a contextual value theory (see Chapter Seven). In both this chapter and the later one, I endeavor to demonstrate that a contextual approach is capable of realizing the new vocabulary of uniqueness, specificity, and contingency that some economic geographers are calling for.

Before turning to the examination of contextualism and essentialism in the next section, I need to offer some qualifiers. In making my argument, I am not suggesting that all work in economic geography follows either utility theory or the labor theory of value. Rather, I take the work carried out within these two traditions simply as an exemplar of the broader position of essentialism. Furthermore, not all proponents working within a Marxist or neoclassical framework adopt labor values or utility. In these cases the specific critique provided here does not apply, although the more general criticism of essentialism may still hold.[1] Similarly, I do not argue that work in economic geography should necessarily derive from the application of one of the contextual value theories that I later discuss. I provide these theories only by way of illustration of the possibilities that exist. In any case, to assert the necessity of just a single approach is to undercut the very tenets of contextualism that the theories I discuss represent.

CONTEXTUALISM AND ESSENTIALISM

In recent years perhaps the best-known critic of essentialism in philosophy has been Richard Rorty (1979, 1982), although he freely acknowledges his debt to other twentieth-century philosophers such as Dewey, Heidegger, Wittgenstein, and Gadamer. Rorty, advocating pragmatism, argues that essentialism is a product of a particular metaphor that has captivated Western philosophy, namely, that it is possible for the mind to mirror the world (see also Chapter Five). Rorty (1979, pp. 318–319) further contends that once "the notion of knowledge as accurate representation [is accepted, it] lends itself naturally to the notion that certain sorts of representations, certain expressions, certain processes are 'basic,' 'privileged,' and 'foundational.' " This is because once "such-and-such a line of inquiry has had a stunning success, [then it is sensible to] . . . reshape all inquiry, and all of culture on its model" (1979, p. 367). That model might be Carnap's logic, Collingwood's rational ideas, or Lévi-Strauss's internal coding mechanisms. In each case the model is foundational in that it legislates between genuine and spurious knowledge. Genuine knowledge is able to meet the criteria proposed by the model and thereby guarantees that such knowledge mirrors the world, while spurious knowledge does not. In this view the world that emerges is a "universe . . . made up of very simple, clearly and distinctly knowable things, knowledge of whose essences provide the master-vocabulary" (Rorty, 1979, p. 357). Two related features of the essences that Rorty discusses should be noted. First, by definition essences are unaffected by the thing they explain. The value of beginning with essences stems precisely from their being brought in from outside those circumstances to provide order and explanation; they represent the Archimedean point from which all "real" explanations originate. Second, essences are invariant across time and place. This must be the case, otherwise they could not be a bedrock on which to rest explanation. For the seductiveness of essentialism is in always giving us the same starting point.

Rorty argues that the metaphor of the mind's mirroring the world, and thereby the essentialist method it underpins, is flawed. It is flawed because those who advocate essentialism are caught up in a logical contradiction. Although they want to provide a "foolproof" method by which to establish knowledge, they are unable to provide a justification for that method other than in terms of the method itself—by definition the guarantor of "true" knowledge. The consequence of such a circular argument is that under scrutiny essentialist concepts, such as the labor theory of value and utility (as I will argue below), become logically incoherent (this general point is elaborated further in Chapter Three).

In contrast, Rorty suggests that our language, theories, and laws are ways of "coping" with the world and are not mirror reflections of what is actually there. When we examine the world, we are presented with "brute facts"—the brute fact of the pressure of light waves on our retinas when we look at the celestial system, for example. It is then up to us to interpret them. And when we interpret them, that is, when we cope with the world, we do so from the perspective of the prevailing social practices of a given place and time. For example, the celestial system for Ptolemy represented a geocentric solar system, whereas for Kepler it was a heliocentric one. In each case the astronomer was faced with the same brute facts, but their interpretations are radically different. For Rorty, to make sense of such differences we must know something about the different contexts in which each of the astronomers lived. That is, we must examine in what way the social practices of ancient Greece and the social practices of medieval Germany coped with the world (Koestler, 1964). In making these arguments, Rorty is in effect abandoning the whole project of epistemology. For epistemologists, in establishing ironclad rules of knowledge, are viewing "social practices of justification as more than just such practices" (Rorty, 1979, p. 390), whereas the implications of Rorty's view is that philosophy becomes a kind of intellectual anthropology. Rather than an architectonic enterprise—constructing complete theories to explain everything—the task is to understand how "vocabularies acquire their privileges from the men who use them rather than from their transparency to the real" (Rorty, 1979, p. 368). More generally, by denying philosophical bedrocks, privileged vocabularies, and essential essences, Rorty seeks to keep the "conversation" going. For as soon as we accept essences, we have a closed system, a system impervious to the dynamics, diversity, and difference of the changing contexts in which social practices are embedded.[2]

In the next two sections of this chapter, I provide examples of the use of an essentialist logic in economic geography, namely, the theoretical employment of Marxist labor values and neoclassical utility. First, I argue that by denying context, these two essentialist accounts squash flat the play of difference as embodied in place. As such, the landscapes created are closed; they are sealed against change and diversity. In short, they kill the conversation. Second, I argue that there are fundamental problems with the very nature of labor values and utility because of the essentialist claims that each makes.

PLACE AS MARXIAN LABOR VALUES

The importance of the labor theory of value for carrying out a Marxist economic geography has not always been adequately recognized. It is not that Marxist labor values are merely a useful way to examine economic geography, but rather for many they are the foundation on which that inquiry is based. As Elson (1979, p. i) writes,

> Marx's theory of value . . . is not some small or dispensable part of Marx's investigation of capital; it constitutes the basis on which that investigation takes place. If we decide to reject that theory, we are at the same time rejecting precisely those tools of analysis which are Marx's distinctive contribution to socialist thought.

Elson's point is that the centrality of labor values derives from their definition outside the economic sphere. Maurice Dobb (1940, p. 13) writes, "As used by . . . Marx the concept of labour was an objective one; labour being conceived as the expenditure of a given quantum of human energy." The anchor for labor values, therefore, is a "physiological fact, . . . the expenditure of human brain, nerves, muscles, and sense organs" (Marx, 1976, p. 164). In this sense, labor values satisfy the first of the requirements of an explanatory essence discussed above, namely, lying outside of the thing they explain. By its very definition, "a quantum of human energy" is unaffected by socioeconomic variables. It is simply a physical quantity.

An argument for labor values satisfying the second requirement, invariance across space and time, is put forward by Lippi (1979). Lippi argues that the view of labor values as a "physiological fact" comes about because of a strain of naturalism running through Marx's thought. At the basis of Lippi's (1979, p. xv) claim is a "well-known and frequently quoted passage from a letter to Kugelmann, [where] Marx characterized the concept of value as a 'law of nature' and defined the task of science as the investigation of the *forms* in which the law operates." Specifically, the law is that in all societies humans are able to transform a recalcitrant nature to their purposes only through the act of labor (the expenditure of physiological energy). In this sense, labor time is the ultimate cost of production and thus "the 'immanent' measure of the product, whatever the historical mode of production" (Lippi, 1979, pp. xv–xvi).

Although labor time is the "fundamental universal measure of commodities" (Farjoun and Machover, 1983, p. 84), the value *form* in which labor time is expressed varies historically (Webber, 1987, p. 1303). According to Meek (1976), in a feudal society prices are proportional to labor time and surplus is directly appropriated from the serf by the landowner, while in capitalism prices are generally not proportional to labor values and exploitation of workers by capitalists is hidden under the surface of market appearances (but see Morishima and Cataphores, 1978). Although the form of value differs between the feudal and capitalist mode of production, labor time itself stubbornly remains the essential factor on which both systems are made to depend. As Marx (1976, p. 325) writes, "What distinguishes the economic variations of society—the distinction between for example a society based on slave-labour and a society based on wage-labour—is the form in which . . . surplus labour is in each case extracted from the immediate producer, the worker." In this sense, the centrality of labor values cuts across place and period.

To examine the kind of geography created by starting with labor values, we will look at only one topic in radical economic geography: regional or uneven development. Even this topic is immense, spanning both production and exchange approaches (examples of the former include Walker, 1978; Carney, 1980; Webber, 1982; Browett, 1984; and examples of the latter include Liossatos, 1980; Foot and Webber, 1983; Forbes and Rimmer, 1984; Hadjimichalis, 1987). We will examine here only the production approach that explains uneven development in terms of the conditions of accumulation. Furthermore, we will focus only on the work of two writers: David Harvey (1982, 1985a, 1985b, 1986) and Neil Smith (1982, 1984, 1986). Apart from reasons of brevity, my justification for such a narrow review is that these two accounts are well known, influential, richly developed, and often original and incisive.

Harvey and Smith put forward two types of relationships between labor values and geographical form: a general historical one and a second concerned with the detailed dynamics of capitalist uneven development. The first begins with the proposition that "the historical development of capitalism entails the progressive universalization of value as the form of abstract labour" (Smith, 1984, p. 82). In a world of geographically separated producers, however, this universalization is accomplished only if there is an accompanying "spatial integration," that is, producers in different locations are linked by exchange relations (Smith, 1984, p. 82; Harvey, 1982, p. 375). Such linkage "involves not just the production of geographical space through the development of transportation networks, but the progressive integration and transformation of absolute spaces into relative space" (Smith, 1984, p. 82). By claiming that "spatial integration can be understood as an expression of the universality of value" (Smith, 1984, p. 83), Harvey and Smith are making labor values the master key for understanding geographical complexity. General patterns of spatial integration are simply precipitates of the "universalization of value."

The second argument details the dynamics of spatial integration. Although there are periods of equilibrium, the specific pattern of spatial integration (the relationship between relative and absolute space, in Smith's vocabulary) is continually subject to change, sometimes of a major kind (called the "see-saw of capital" by Smith, 1984, ch. 5, and a "reswitching crisis" by Harvey, 1986). At bottom the motivation of change, including alterations in the geographical landscape, is the ceaseless quest by capitalists for surplus value (in turn defined by labor values; Harvey, 1985b, p. 44; Smith, 1984, p. 49). As Harvey (1985b, p. 37) writes,

> Under capitalism . . . it is *socially necessary labor time* that forms the substance of value, *surplus labor time* that lies at the origin of profit, and the ratio of surplus labor time to *socially necessary turnover time* that defines the rate of profit. . . . Under capitalism, therefore, the meaning of space and the impulse to create new spatial configurations of human affairs can be understood only in relation to such temporal requirements.

Harvey and Smith discuss the geographical manifestations of such temporal requirements in terms of Marx's notion of the "annihilation of space by time." Under the impulse of increasing surplus value, capitalists are intent on reducing capital's turnover time by rejigging the pattern of spatial integration. According to Harvey (1985a, p. 28), "processes as diverse as suburbanization, deindustrialization and restructuring, gentrification and urban renewal . . . are part and parcel of a general process of continuous reshaping of geographical landscapes to match the quest to accelerate turnover time. . . . Familiar places and secure places . . . [are] being annihilated in the 'whirligig of time.' "

Because of various tensions within the landscape, the annihilation of space by time is only ever partial. First, the geographical flux and dispersion implied by that annihilation is partially blocked by forces of spatial inertia and concentration (Harvey, 1982, p. 418). Second, it is diverted by a process that Smith (1984, pp. 99–113) calls "the tendency toward differentiation." If capitalists were completely to annihilate space by time, Smith argues that the world would be composed wholly of relative space—"equalization" in his terms. But equalization is never completely realized because of the countertendency of "differentiation" and the production of absolute space. For to annihilate space by time paradoxically requires that "a portion of the total capital and labour power . . . be immobilized in space" (Harvey, 1986, p. 149). This is because to alter the pattern of spatial integration, new transportation networks and termini, along with an accompanying infrastructure, need to be built. But by the very act of constructing these immobile points of fixed capital (dead labor) to reduce turnover time, absolute space is created, thereby undermining relative space, equalization, and the annihilation of space by time itself. Finally, the annihilation of space by time is frustrated by crisis and devaluation brought about by the very process of annihilation. The argument is that the "produced geographical landscape constituted by fixed and immobile capital [becomes] . . . a prison that inhibits the further progress of accumulation precisely because it creates spatial barriers where there were none before" (Harvey, 1985b, p. 43). As a result, "it is now the created spaces of capitalism, the spaces of its own social reproduction, that have to be annihilated" (Harvey, 1985a, p. 28). But because of the immobilities of labor and capital found in such space, there is devaluation (unemployment and scrapping of capital equipment). The result is crisis, thereby retarding the annihilation of space by time that was supposed to mitigate that crisis in the first place.

For Harvey and Smith, the outcome of these tensions is "the restless formation and re-formation of geographical landscapes"—uneven development (Harvey, 1986, p. 150). But even with this complexity, the shifting geographical transformations are ultimately reducible to a single cause: "contradictions within the value form" (Harvey, 1982, p. 417). Thus, despite the innovative and sophisticated accounts that Harvey and Smith present, space and place are understood ultimately in terms of the ebb and flow of the single essence of labor value. Behind the shifting surface appearances of different places lies the same essential process expressed in labor time. Urban places are deposits of dead labor time awaiting de*valuation*, the spatial integration among places is defined by the universalization of value, and the "geographical landscape [is] beset by a pervasive . . . struggle to reduce turnover time and so gain surplus value" (Harvey, 1985b, p. 42). In short, differences within places, and differences among places, are comprehended by reducing them to "a particular form of the same 'jelly'—general abstract labor" (Georgescu-Roegen, 1968b, p. 264).

One response to these arguments is to say that it does not matter that space and place are reduced to labor values because labor values *are* pivotal to understanding the world. In sifting through the literature, we find at least six justifications of the labor theory of value. I review each of them here, but for reasons already suggested, the essentialist nature of labor value makes it impossible to provide a consistent justification.

First, it is argued that labor values can account for the "riddle of profits" (Wright, 1981, p. 139). If all commodities, including labor, exchange for their value, how can surplus arise, which is in turn converted into profits? Everything, after all, seems to be exchanged for what it is worth. Marx's brilliant insight is to recognize a distinction between the value of labor and the value of labor power. On the one hand, capitalists do not hire labor; what they buy is labor power, that is, the ability to produce. On the other hand, the value of labor is the cost of reproducing it, that is, a culturally defined subsistence wage. Marx argues that at the workplace the value that workers produce with their labor power is greater than the value of their labor. The difference between the two is converted into profit. Although this account is logically impeccable, it is also clear that other logically impeccable accounts can explain the existence of profit without resort to labor values, for example, Sraffa's approach (Steedman, 1977), which is cast in terms of surplus product rather than surplus value.

A second justification is that only if goods exchange in proportion to their values will there exist a behavioral motive to produce anything at all. This argument has its roots in Adam Smith's story about the beaver and the deer. Unless the quarry exchange is in proportion to the labor time invested in the hunt, rational exchange cannot continue in the future. Although this scenario may be the basis for an economist's parable, it is certainly unconvincing as an analytical argument. As soon as we think of a society where bartering no longer holds sway, it is difficult to imagine that labor values are the behavioral motive for production.

The third argument is given the imprimatur of Marx himself. In the first chapter of volume 1 of *Capital*, Marx (1976, pp. 127–128) writes:

> Let us now take two commodities, for example, corn and iron. Whatever their exchange relation may be, it can always be represented by an equation in which a given quantity of corn is equated to some quantity of iron, for instance 1 quarter corn = x cwt of iron. What does this equation signify? . . . [The] two different things . . . are . . . equal to a third thing, which in itself is neither the one nor the other. . . . This common element cannot be . . . [use-values because] . . . the exchange relation of commodities is characterized precisely by its abstraction from . . . use-values. . . . If then we disregard the use-value of commodities, only one common property remains, that of being products of labour.

Here Marx justifies labor as the source of value because it is the only common denominator of all commodities. There are two problems with this view. For one, why does there have to be a common "something" to all commodities before exchange takes place? As Cutler et al. (1977, p. 14) argue, "Exchange may be conceived as being equivalent, in the judicial sense, that is, that both parties to it agree to the equity of the terms of exchange." And even if we accept Marx's argument, why does the common substance have to be labor? Energy expended or even weight could be chosen as the common denominator (an example of an energy theory of value is given by Georgescu-Roegen, 1971). A recent variant on this third justification is Farjoun and Machover's (1983, p. 89) claim that "labour, as a resource, is necessary for the existence of any economic system whatsoever." The validity of this claim, however, rests on demonstrating that there are no other necessary resources in all economies and that one cannot imagine in the future an economy without the resource of labor. With respect to the first issue, land, along with its attributes of relative and absolute location, might well vie with labor as a necessary resource, and with respect to the second issue, one can imagine, at least, an epoch of only the machine.

The fourth justification occurs in Marx's writing (Cutler et al., 1977), but it has been popularized in particular by Rubin (1972). It concerns the functional distribution of labor necessary for the continued reproduction of the economy. The argument is that only if goods exchange on the basis of their labor content is labor distributed among the various lines of production in the correct way to ensure continued reproduction. There are two objections to this view. First, the distribution of labor between sectors that is compatible with equilibrium reproduction will in general not ensure that prices are proportional to labor values. Second, there is no justification for singling out labor values as the basis for continued reproduction of the economy. As Hodgson (1981) points out, any commodity has the potential to be a limiting factor in that it sets the boundary between a reproducible and nonreproducible economic system.

The fifth and sixth arguments are both found in Farjoun and Machover's (1983) work, and in economic geography they are discussed by Webber (1987). The fifth justification is that labor "is, *par excellence*, the essential substance of an economy" because "what economics is all about . . . *is the social productive activity of human beings, social labour*" (Farjoun and Machover, 1983, p. 85). The claim, then, is that the essentialism of labor values is based upon the objective of the academic discipline "economics." But economics over the centuries has had numerous different objectives, and even today there is no agreed-upon definition (see the survey in Caldwell, 1982). Farjoun and Machover, of course, are free to define "economics" as they choose, but to claim that their definition represents the one "real" economics only pushes back doubts about the essentialism of the labor theory of value to doubts about an essentialist economics.

The sixth justification is that unlike valuing commodities in price terms, measurement in labor values "is always quite meaningful and informative, whether the commodities in question are located . . . in the England of 1867, the Germany of 1960, or the India of 1981" (Farjoun and Machover, 1983, p. 96). In making this claim, Farjoun and Machover present an argument based upon practical expediency. One might question, though, how adequate such an argument is in these circumstances.

The convenience of labor values for statisticians does not justify their necessity as a theoretical category. Further, the claim that workers' hours are homogeneous across time and space is disputable. The meaning, the setting, and the valuableness of laboring varies historically and geographically (Polanyi, 1968; Sahlins, 1972).[3]

PLACE AS NEOCLASSICAL UTILITY

Although neoclassical economics is no monolithic entity, in order to understand its various strains, one must begin by examining utility (Dobb, 1940, ch. 5; 1973, ch. 7). Utility, like labor values, is of course only one element of the neoclassical scheme, but it is a critical one; it is the element that "constitutes an implicit definition of the general shape and character of the terrain which it has decided to call 'economic' " (Dobb, 1940, p. 19).

Just as labor values are set within naturalism, many argue that utility is set within the perspective of the natural sciences and in particular physics (Lowe, 1951; Samuelson, 1972; Thoben, 1982). Mirowski (1984a, 1984b, 1986b) has fleshed out the historical details of this general claim. He argues that the metaphor used by neoclassical economics derives not from Newtonian mechanics but from the mid-nineteenth-century physics of energetics. For brevity's sake, I do not explore here the nature and influence of energetics on neoclassical economics. It is sufficient to note two points: First, in applying the framework of energetics "energy became transmuted into 'utility' " by the early neoclassical economists (Mirowski, 1986a, p. 5). Thus, just as energy was "unique, and yet ontologically undefined . . . [and thereby] could only be discussed cogently through the intermediary of its mathematical eidolon," so, too, was utility (Mirowski, 1984a, p. 366). Although utility is symbolically representable within a preference function and takes on unique values, it is very difficult, if not impossible, to define the term (Robinson, 1964, p. 48). The second point is that the neoclassical economists also appropriated the mathematical techniques of energetics, central among which was constrained maximization. The consequence was that neoclassical economists by the very techniques they employed necessarily couched the economic problem in terms of maximization (Barnes, 1987a, and Chapter Three). In particular, just as the early physicists used the technique of constrained maximization to reveal the path of least action of any particle's movement, so neoclassical economists used the same mathematical technique to discover the most efficient (rational) actions required by consumers and producers to maximize utility and profits, respectively (Mirowski, 1984a, 1986a).

Despite the slipperiness of the definition of "utility" (reflected in the plethora of synonyms: "desire," "satisfaction," "want," "pleasure," "welfare," "*ophelimité*"), it nonetheless possesses an essentialist quality. For it is ultimately grounded in an individual's subjective state of consciousness. This does not imply a hedonistic interpretation of utility, only that what is taken as exogenous is some psychological state. The more important point is that, like labor values, such states lie outside of the economic and thereby are the bedrock of explanation. As Dobb (1940, p. 6) writes, "The significance of [the] 'constant' [utility] is . . . that it is some quality which in any particular case can be known *independently* of any of the other variables in the system . . . and [thereby] in an important sense it is on this outside factor that the total situation is made to depend."

Turning now to spatial theory, we will examine the use of utility in two areas: theoretical urban land use models (the "new urban economics") and spatial choice models. It was Alonso's work that codified the neoclassical approach to urban land use theory. At bottom Alonso's (1964, p. 18) question is, "Given . . . tastes, [how will] a simplified family spend whatever money it has available in maximizing its satisfaction?" What makes this a geographical problem is that Alonso poses his question within the context of one-dimensional Euclidean space, space that Alonso calls a city. In order to take space into account, Alonso incorporates distance directly into the householder's utility function. The utility function, then, has three arguments: the quantity of a composite good available for consumption, the amount of land rented, and the distance a householder travels into the central business district to work. Unlike the first two arguments, distance is "unusual" in that "the individual would prefer distance to be smaller rather than larger, so that distance may be thought of as a good with negative utility (that is, satisfaction)" (Alonso, 1964, p. 26). With distance incorporated into the utility function, a preference surface can be drawn in one-dimensional space. The optimal location for a householder with a given income is then derived using the technique of constrained maximization.

The effect of this exercise is to reduce differences within the city for the householder to a single variable, utility. The specific characteristics of neighborhoods—are they lively, sedate, rustic, brash?—that seem important in residential location decisions get lost. They are lost because, as Georgescu-Roegen (1954, p. 515) writes, "*Utility* represents the common essence of all wants, the want into which all wants can be merged." That is, although liveliness, sedateness, and so on may be included within a utility function, such qualities are accounted for only insofar as they are reducible "to a particular form of a general abstract want—utility" (Georgescu-Roegen, 1968b, p. 264). The difference that difference makes in residential neighborhood choice is not valued in and of itself but only as a reflection of some deeper, more fundamental feature of economic life.

Let us now turn to spatial interaction models. It is argued that the problem with aggregate spatial interaction models is their lack of any plausible theoretical underpinnings (Sheppard, 1978, 1979). The early social physics explanations put forward by Carrothers and others are discredited, and what is notable about Wilson's maximizing-entropy derivation is precisely "the *paucity* of theory involved" (Sheppard, 1978, p. 388). In order to provide an adequate explanation of aggregate interaction, spatial theorists have recently turned to examining individual behavior. The leading approach "has stemmed from the utility theoretic formulations of economics, incorporating the presumption of uniformly rational behavior" (Sheppard, 1978, p. 388). (In this light, we should also note the recent burgeoning of research on the random utility approach of discrete choice modeling; see Fischer and Nijkamp, 1985, for a comprehensive review.)

Utility is important in spatial interaction modeling as a metric to evaluate destination choices when traveling. The landscape is composed of a series of islands of different utility levels, each representing a different spatial opportunity. How the actual destination is decided depends upon the model used. In one type "spatial opportunities are determined solely by the non-spatial properties of those opportunities and . . . distance . . . influences travel decisions only by delimiting the range of feasible travel patterns" (Smith, 1975, p. 31). In another type distance directly enters into the utility function. In this case it is not only the attributes of a place that determine utility but also the disutility of travel.

One recent analytical development in spatial interaction modeling is using potential theory to develop place utility fields (Baker, 1982). Here a continuous spatial field of utility is defined with the result that "the decision maker will then have an action space composed of a variable surface of utility for different alternatives in space" (Baker, 1982, p. 11). In this case the contours of place are the "contour lines . . . of equal utility" (Baker, 1982, p. 11).

The outcome of the place utility field model is the absence of any humanly recognizable places. The quirks, nuances, and character of place are steamrollered as geography is expressed in the "colorless blanket of utility" (Georgescu-Roegen, 1968b, p. 264).

It might be argued by some that, as with the case of labor values, reducing the geographical world to utility is not a problem because utility *is* the most fundamental entity in explaining human behavior. The economic literature offers four analytical justifications for using utility theory. I review each of these now, but as with the case of labor values, I find none convincing because of their essentialist claims.

Perhaps the most common justification for utility is that it represents the common denominator of all goods. It allows us to "compare pushpin with poetry, bingo with Beethoven, guns with butter and sex with wisdom" (Hollis, 1983, p. 249). The argument that exchange only takes place if there is a common standard on which to base relative prices is exactly the same one that Marx employed when justifying labor values in the first chapter of *Capital*, volume 1, cited in the previous section. For the same reasons given then, however, such an argument is not sustainable. There is no reason why commodities must share an intrinsic common property for exchange to occur. In fact there is a long intellectual tradition beginning with Veblen and extending through Malinowski, Polanyi, and more recently to Sahlins and Douglas that argues that the meaning of commodities and the very nature of the exchange process are cultural constructions (Gudeman, 1986). As such, the unidimensional variable utility cannot capture all the diverse circumstances in which exchange occurs. Even if it is granted that there is a common denominator to exchange, there is no justification for why utility is the only measure of value. For example, why not exchange based on labor values?

The second justification for utility, which also has a counterpart in Marxism, is that it is the behavioral motive behind economic acts. As Stigler (1973, p. 306) writes, "It can hardly be disputed that the principle of utility is an all-embracing theory of purposive conduct." As such, utility maximization embodied in the rationality postulate becomes "a united framework for understanding behavior that has long been sought by and eluded Bentham, Comte, Marx, and others" (Becker, 1976, p. 14). Despite such claims, the utility-maximizing postulate of neoclassical economics is one of the most battered ideas in the social sciences. Traditionally, it is attacked on its ancillary assumptions: perfect information, the ability and desire to maximize, the pursuit of a single goal, egoistical behavior, and the autonomy of individual preferences (for further details, see Chapter Three). Boland (1981) has argued, however, that the utility maximization postulate is inherently untestable, and as such the ancillary assumptions are never disproved.

I have suggested that a more fruitful line of criticism instead starts with the origins of the *Homo economicus* postulate, which, as we have seen, are in physics (Barnes, 1987a). The central question then becomes, Is the physical metaphor an appropriate one for understanding the social world? I concluded that it is inappropriate for four reasons: First, it mistakes desires as causes, thereby confusing necessary with contingent relations. Second, it denies any deliberation on the part of the individual. As Georgescu-Roegen (1971, p. 343) writes, in the neoclassical scheme "man is not an economic agent simply because there is no economic process. There is only a jigsaw puzzle of fitting given means to given ends, which requires a computer not an agent." Third, using the technique of constrained maximization to express "purposive behavior" the theory is left with no independent specification of the explanatory variable, utility maximization. The problem is that any extremal theory by definition is "committed *to explain everything within their domains*" (Rosenberg, 1979, p. 523). Therefore all aspects of human behavior are maximized. As a result, we cannot refer to any feature of human behavior to explain maximization. For as soon as we do, we are left with the circular statement that utility maximization accounts for maximizing behavior, and human behavior, because it is subject to maximization, accounts for people's maximizing utility. Finally, the physical metaphor recasts the project of social science in teleological terms. As Mirowski (1984b, p. 473) writes, utility maximization

> endows the human drama with a scope and a purpose which it has not had since the intelligentsia broke away from the theological institutions which earlier had performed that function.
>
> Unfortunately, as with all other teleological conceptions of the world, it is only a case of the theorist reasoning in a circle. The theorist . . . *imposes* a constrained maximization algorithm, *correlates* the deduced result with empirical data, and then feels assured that social life has purpose and direction. . . . The rabbit, fresh from being thrust into the hat, reappears, dazed but compliant.

The third justification for utility is that utility is a self-evident fact drawn from experience. Robbins (1935) and Knight (1956) are particularly associated with this view, which has become known as a priorism (Blaug, 1980). The argument is that neither controlled experiments nor historical evidence is sufficient grounds on which to base the fundamental postulates of economics; rather, such grounding is given only by carefully inspecting one's own behavior and experience. There are two criticisms of a priorism as a justification. First, on what basis does the a priori method itself rest? It cannot be a self-evident fact drawn from experience, otherwise we would be led to an infinite regress where acknowledging the usefulness of our experience comes from past experience, and the usefulness of past experience comes from a yet a previous experience, and so on. But if we cannot justify a priorism this way, how can we justify it, because by definition it is only everyday experience that is the basis for true knowledge? Second, in inspecting our experience, we may only rationalize what we find, not distill from it the fundamental axioms of economic life. As Myrdal (1969, p. 94) writes, "If we pay any attention to our [experiences], . . . we do, no doubt, rationalize them in some way. [But] rationalization is not an explanation but becomes itself a phenomenon which has to be explained. Only marginal utility theorists go on accepting it as genuine psychological insight."

The final justification for utility is that it enables economics to be a mathematical science. This rationale is one of the oldest and is found explicitly in Jevons's *Theory of Political Economy*: "It is clear that economics, if it is to be a science at all, must be a mathematical science . . . simply because it deals with quantities" (1970, p. 70). The central quantity for Jevons was utility, measurable on a cardinal scale. We might cite at least three criticisms of this view. Economics can be a science under Jevons's definition without making any reference to utility. For example, the recent rise of analytical political economy shows that neoclassical economics does not have proprietary rights over mathematics (Sheppard and Barnes, 1990, ch. 1; see also my debate with Myers and Papageorgiou, 1991: Barnes, 1991). Second, using the language of mathematics itself, Georgescu-Roegen (1968a) demonstrates that utility is measurable on neither a cardinal nor an ordinal scale. Utility as an entrée to mathematics fails on its own terms. The final criticism is that utility also fails at a fundamental metaphysical level. Specifically, the problem is one of identity. To measure utilities of goods, we must have for each type of commodity a generic exemplar; that is, certain psychologically identifiable attributes must distinguish one type of commodity from another, otherwise there would be no basis for the measurement of utility. The well-known work of Lancaster (1966), however, appears to undermine the notion of generic commodities. Lancaster argues that commodities are not desired for their phenomenological identity but for the qualities they possess. Taking this argument further, Mirowski (1986b, p. 205) suggests that the broader implication is that it gives

> voice to a hesitation that had occurred to many, [namely, that] . . . there is no such thing as a generic commodity. [For example,] to every individual *qua* individual, each apple is different: some bigger, some stunted, some mottled, some worm-ridden, some coated with stuff that will kill me slowly, some McIntosh, some engineered to taste and look like tomatoes. . . . [In short,] reconsideration of these issues raise[s] the possibility that the self-identity of the commodity . . . is not at all psychologically present.

But if we are unable to identity the generic commodity, then there is no basis for quantification and mathematics.

SPACE, PLACE, AND NONESSENTIALIST THEORIES OF THEORY

Having criticized the Marxist and neoclassical value theories for their essentialist stance, let me turn to a number of recent approaches found mainly in economics that attempt to present a nonessentialist value theory.

The origins of this work are in the writings of a small but vocal group of economists who during the mid-1980s made use of postpositivist philosophies of science and to a lesser extent poststructuralist theory. Klamer's (1984) *Conversations with Economists* and McCloskey's (1985) more general *Rhetoric of Economics* were the first, and the motivation of both authors was to remedy what they saw as the yawning gap between the practices of economists and their official methodology, which was rooted in some form of positivism (Caldwell, 1982). Specifically, both argued that in spite of what they say, economists are not concerned with establishing the truth using given, rule-bound methodologies but only in persuading other economists of the force of their position by using a variety of rhetorical ploys and tropes. More generally, there is a disjuncture between economists' public claims to have achieved the highest standards of scientific purity and their private practices, which are sodden with rhetorical excesses. In prosecuting this position, Klamer and McCloskey were in effect raising the same kind of antifoundationalist questions posed by Rorty, emphasizing social practice over essentialist claims to truth.

Whether Klamer and McCloskey meant to situate their work under the poststructural rubric is unclear, but by drawing upon writers such as Wayne Booth, Kenneth Burke, Stanley Fish, Clifford Geertz, and Richard Rorty, that was the consequence (see the comments in Milberg, 1991, p. 93). Certainly, the writings that followed took that direction, emphasizing the inconsistencies of economic essentialism and the need for a poststructural reconstruction (Amariglio, 1988, 1990; Klamer, 1988; Milberg, 1991; Mirowski, 1991; Ruccio, 1991; and various essays in Henderson, Dudley-Evans, and Backhouse, 1993). Ruccio (1991, p. 502) writes, for example, that "the absolute truth claims of economics (and the correct method for making such claims) . . . [should be] given up in favour of an approach that makes central a [postmodernist] analysis of the multiple languages, metaphors, and strategies of persuasion used by contemporary economists." Although many issues have now been critically discussed within this "post"-prefixed turn, I will review here only those works that bear upon the theory of economic value. Specifically, I will examine three attempts to present a nonessentialist value theory: Resnick and Wolff's revamping of the labor theory of value, Mirowski's attempt at providing a social value theory, and Laclau and Mouffe's post-Marxist reconstitution of the economy. Although each of the three cases suffers from the absence of a geography, I will argue that this gap can be bridged precisely because each theory is nonessentialist.

Resnick and Wolff
and an Overdetermined Value Theory

Of the three, Resnick and Wolff's (1987; and Wolff and Resnick, 1987) ideas are probably the best known in economic geography because of their popularization by Julie Graham (1988, 1990, 1991). From the outset Resnick and Wolff claim that their particular brand of Marxism is "strictly antiessentialist and strictly non-reductionist," which in turn implies on their part a "refus[al] to look for the essential cause of any event because . . . [we] do not presume that it exists" (Resnick and Wolff, 1987, pp. 2 and 3). Instead, following Althusser's notion of overdetermination, they argue there is never a single essential cause of anything. As they put it, "no one process in society, nor any subset, can be understood as *the* cause of one or more other social processes. In other words, no process can be the essence of another." Rather, wherever we look, there are multiple causations that are themselves multiply caused. As Schell (1991, p. 9, quoted in Graham, 1991, p. 142) says, under this interpretation of overdetermination, "nothing less than everything is a sufficient explanation for anything."

While it is not a central task of their work, Resnick and Wolff along the way attempt to provide an overdetermined theory of economic value, one that is nonessentialist by its very definition. Their starting point is Marx's notion of socially necessary labor time. This concept usually is defined as the amount of labor time required to produce a good or service using the average or dominant technology in a given economic sector (Sheppard and Barnes, 1990, ch. 3). Such a concept was necessary for Marx because it allowed him to avoid the paradox of lazy workers' producing goods with higher labor values than those produced by energetic workers. By using socially necessary labor time as a benchmark measure of the time average workers take to produce a commodity he avoided this problem.

With socially necessary labor time so defined, Resnick and Wolff apply to it the notion of overdetermination. For them, the main result is that the normal, narrow technical meaning of the concept is extended to include various cultural and social norms, providing a more sensitive contextual account of labor values. As they write (Wolff and Resnick, 1987, p. 162),

> The amount of labor that is socially necessary to produce chairs or any other capitalist commodity is overdetermined by all the processes existing in society. Economic processes of exchange, competition, and lending, for example, will influence how much labor will be required to produce chairs. So too will political and cultural processes ranging from legal factory regulations to technological inventions. In their unique ways each will participate in overdetermining how much labor will be socially necessary to produce chairs.

In this account, then, it is not just average technical efficiency that is important in determining socially necessary labor time but also all those extra-economic factors that directly and indirectly bear upon that efficiency.

The upshot is that labor values are not the essence of value because in arriving at any calculation, it is necessary to take into account through socially necessary labor time their overdetermined causes—causes that are contextually specific. Moreover, this is not a one-way flow, as the overdetermined labor values also overdetermine all other aspects of social, cultural, and political life. For this reason, and to paraphrase Althusser, the moment of the final hour of labor value never arrives.

Mirowski and a Postmodernist Value Theory

The second nonessentialist value theory is Mirowski's social theory of value. Writing since the early 1980s, Mirowski presents a trenchant critique of neoclassical and classical/Marxist economic value theory. Incisive, sarcastic, pungent, and full of memorable prose and acerbic asides, *More Heat Than Light* (1989) is a brilliant combination of biographical and historical evidence plus mathematical and analytical arguments by which Mirowski deconstructs the physical metaphors on which both utility theory and the labor theory of value are predicated.

Mirowski's (1989, p. 4) principal sources of inspiration are various postpositivist philosophers of science, in particular David Bloor from the Edinburgh school (see Chapter Four). Concurring with Bloor that scientific theories and models are based upon metaphors, Mirowski both documents the physicalist metaphorical origins of neoclassical and classical/Marxist economics and demonstrates their respective inadequacies in representing the social world (Mirowski, 1984a). Instead, that social world, says Mirowski, is best examined using institutionalist and pragmatist methods, following Thorstein Veblen and Charles Sanders Peirce (Mirowski, 1988). Those later methods shun any single logic of inquiry, eschew ahistorical entities, embrace interpretation and hermeneutics, and accept that "the community of inquiry is the basic epistemological unit" (Mirowski, 1988, p. 121).

In following such methodological tenets, Mirowski sees as his main substantive task to reconceive traditional value theory. The argument is complex, but the gist is that the history of economics is the history of successive "conservation principles," defined as the identification of a "particular aspect of a phenomenon ... [as] invariant or unaltered while the greater phenomenon undergoes certain specified transformations" (Mirowski, 1989, p. 13). Specifically, the search for conservation principles in economics is manifest as the identification of an invariant, that is, essential, source of value; it is economic value that remains unchanged while everything else is in flux. So a central supposition of neoclassical utility theory is that as an entity utility is conserved in any transaction (Mirowski, 1984b), while under Marx's value theory it is labor time that remains constant as it is passed from the worker to the commodity.

Mirowski (1990, p. 694) argues, however, that apart from being empirically untestable, all conservation principles are metaphorical; all appeal in one way or another to the root metaphor of a fixed identity (1989, p. 6). Furthermore, it is through these metaphorical appeals that essentialism in economics is maintained. Now, for Mirowski the principal source of those metaphors is physics (1989, p. 108). As argued above, the conservation of utility was taken from the mid-nineteenth-century idea of a field of force or energy, whereas the labor theory of value was distilled from a much earlier physicalist conception in which motion was conceived as "an embodied substance that is passed about from body to body by means of collision, but conserved as a whole for the world" (Mirowski, 1990, p. 697). The success of utility theory and the labor theory of value, therefore, was not because they were empirically true but because "they succeeded in appropriating the dominant physical metaphors of their epochs", and in doing so maintained an essentialist methodological stance (Mirowski, 1990, p. 699). For the reasons already given earlier in this chapter, however, both metaphors are inconsistent on their own terms. More generally, the very search for conservation principles will always fail because "no posited invariances hold without exceptions and qualifications. We live in a world of broken symmetries and partial invariances" (Mirowski, 1989, p. 387).

Mirowski attempts to offer another way, not one that eschews metaphors—they are inevitable—but one that eschews the inappropriate physicalist metaphors found in conservation principles. Furthermore, this way links to poststructuralism because it "den[ies] . . . any single fixed and stable referent[s]" (Mirowski, 1991, p. 565). The formal details of what Mirowski calls his postmodern or social value theory are intricate (Mirowski, 1981, 1990, 1991) and still inchoate, but it is useful at least to lay out the bare lineaments. The beginning point is Veblen's insight that economic transactions are "meant as a signification of a person's place in the culture's scheme of valuation" (Mirowski, 1990, p. 704). The implication is that

> in any valuation, the personal and the social are endlessly layered between acts of interpretation and signification. The buck stops nowhere, not in the neural context, not on the hard edges of the machine, not in biology, not in physics. Were someone to search for . . . the objective meaning of value, he or she would not be able to find it, because there would be no way of arriving at anything other than a transient common ground. (Mirowski, 1990, p. 705)

Mirowski's task then becomes to outline a framework for defining that "transient common ground."

Following Veblen, Mirowski argues that the key actors in the economy are social institutions, which by their very nature are contingent and historically specific. Nevertheless, they provide at least temporary stability, which is necessary for any consistent set of economic valuations. Specifically, social institutions within capitalism provide two preconditions for any workable price system. First, they allow something to be fixed and defined as a commodity. Recall that a problem noted above with neoclassical utility theory was that it assumed that commodities were defined by the physical attributes of the goods themselves. The difficulty is that those attributes vary massively even for supposedly the same type of good: some apples are red, others yellow; some have bruises; others are coated with insecticides; and so on. What, then, makes a generic commodity? For Mirowski (1990, p. 709), it is various kinds of social institutions, "ranging from the apprenticeships of the medieval guild to the enforced standardization of machinofacture to the modern cajolery of advertising," that narrow the potentially multifarious phenomenological characteristics of any physical good to only one or two. In this sense, commodities are socially constructed, given not by inherent physical attributes but by the network of institutional relations in which commodities and people are enmeshed. There is nothing natural about a commodity. Second, and related, institutions provide a system for measurement, again a necessary prerequisite for any system of exchange. Initially, those systems of measurement were different in different places—"the ell, the foot and even the pound were not standardized even for individuals" (Mirowski, 1990, p. 708)—but over time increasing uniformity was brought about by institutional mandate.

While these are the institutional preconditions for prices, they do not yet tell us the basis by which individuals compare different generic types of standardly measured goods and "how such comparisons can be reduced to a single common denominator or number" (Mirowski, 1990, p. 695). Mirowski believes that the common basis is money, which for him is yet another institutional construct. Specifically, money provides a metric for individuals to compare their gains and losses when engaging in exchange transactions over time and space. This does not imply that money is a new conservation principle because money "it[self] is socially instituted . . . continually shored up and reconstituted by further social institutions, such as accountants and banks and governments" (Mirowski, 1990, p. 712). At every turn, then, economic transactions are enmeshed in a series of overlapping contingent institutional networks, but at no point are they embedded in any kind of essential value entity. As Mirowski (1990, p. 716) puts it, "The entire system is like an archetypical Escher print, where stairs and pillars mutually buttress an elaborate interconnected edifice, but no part of the edifice ever touches the ground."

In sum, Mirowski's social value theory is still provisional, but it succeeds in eschewing physical conservation principles and in emphasizing the contingent, interpretive, and culturally fixed character of value. Ultimately the measure of value is not vested in any single invariance but in a shifting social, cultural, and economic matrix of institutional arrangements in which we and our commodities are caught.

Laclau and Mouffe and a Post-Marxist Value Theory

A final example of the attempt to develop a nonessentialist value theory is found in Laclau and Mouffe's post-Marxist *Hegemony and Socialist Strategy* (1985), a work that has generated a large amount of controversy and commentary (Geras, 1987; Laclau and Mouffe, 1987; Mouzelis, 1988; Corbridge, 1989; Landry and MacLean, 1991; Chilcote and Chilcote, 1992; Diskin and Sandler, 1993). Among the many things it attempts is a nonessentialist theory of the economy, society, and politics. In particular, following at least the spirit of Derrida (see Chapter Six), Laclau and Mouffe try to deconstruct various kinds of fixed conceptual identities within classical Marxism. Their central target is class, which they argue classical Marxists treat "as an essence to grant special subjects a theoretically and historically privileged location in society as bearers of socialism and to explain the movement of history itself from capitalism toward socialism" (Diskin and Sandler, 1993, pp. 28–29). Instead, for both theoretical and historical reasons, they argue that the essence of class should be abandoned and replaced by the idea of radical democracy, a notion implying multiple subject positions and context-specific struggles over powers and rights (Laclau and Mouffe, 1985, ch. 4). In this way the self-directed subject is partially restored as a theoretical entity, as are the interests of various groups, social movements, and social strata (Chilcote and Chilcote, 1992).

The theoretical basis of their argument is involved, but the crux is that Marxism has continually struggled to present a unified narrative—an "interior space" of necessary relations, as they put it. Over the hundred years of so of its existence, however, Marxism has been forced to cope with various "excluded exteriors," that is, elements that seem to lie outside the unified account but that nonetheless must be included. This is accomplished through a process of "suturing" such elements on to the main story. But those sutures remain weak points, and Laclau and Mouffe attempt to open them up through their deconstructive reading. Their goal is to show that there is no unity to the story, no foundation such as class on which a single narrative can rest. Rather, those excluded exteriors, principal of which are the social and the political, must be taken into account; they cannot be reduced to the one necessary logic of the economic.

In putting forward this position, Laclau and Mouffe also briefly discuss labor values, and it on this discussion that I will focus. For Laclau and Mouffe, the ultimate sanction for the privileged position of class in classical Marxism is derived from the economy; it is the "last redoubt of essentialism" (Laclau and Mouffe, 1985, p. 75). In order for the economy to constitute class subjects, three conditions must be met, the most important of which is that the economy's "laws of motion must be strictly endogenous and exclude all indeterminacy resulting from political or other external interventions—otherwise, the constitutive function could not refer exclusively to the economy" (Laclau and Mouffe, 1985, p. 76). Those laws of motion are represented by the development of the forces of production, a key component of which is labor power. Only by exploiting living labor can capitalists attain the wherewithal to invest and thereby push the forces of production ever forward. In this sense, class essentialism is predicated upon a second essentialism, the labor theory of value.

The problem, though, is that this classical Marxist story presumes that the mere hiring of labor will automatically generate value and hence fuel the forces of production. That is, it is assumed that labor is like any other commodity, its mere purchase immediately generating use value, in this case the production of abstract labor value. However, to obtain value from labor it must be purposely extracted in specific work conditions using particular kinds of organizational and institutional practices that always involve some form of domination. Once this is recognized, the very notion of "the development of the productive forces as a natural, spontaneously progressive phenomenon" is put into doubt because one can imagine times and places where that domination is resisted and struggled over (Laclau and Mouffe, 1985, p. 78).

The more general point here is that the political and the social cannot be excluded from the labor process and thus from the definition of labor values themselves. In terms of the earlier discussion, classical Marxism suggests that there is a necessary interior logic that connects the hiring of labor with the production of value. Laclau and Mouffe's point is that this logic is not necessary, and if it seems that way it is only because of the suturing that has occurred. Once those sutures are reopened, in this case by allowing for an institutionally organized process of value extraction, then it is clear that labor power is constituted not only by the economic but also by the political and the social. As in the case of Resnick and Wolff's analysis, labor values cannot be treated as pregiven essences but only emerge from a complex and contingent process of interaction among the economic, the social, and the political.

And Economic Geography?

What do these three different nonessentialist accounts of eonomic value have to do with economic geography? After all, geography is notable for its absence in each of them. This is not a fatal flaw, however. Because the three are nonessentialist theories, they possess the potential for integrating economic geography into their accounts without reducing it to something less than it is.

For example, it is clear that economic geographers could offer an important contribution to the analysis of the overdetermination of labor values that is presented in Resnick and Wolff's account. Sheppard (1990) has already shown that socially necessary labor time is overdetermined by transportation costs. This result has important consequences for Marxist economic theory because, as Sheppard analytically demonstrates, the inclusion of transportation costs within the definition of socially necessary labor produces negative exploitation rates in some places, even though the overall rate of exploitation is positive for the economy as a whole (Sheppard and Barnes, 1990, ch. 3). In Sheppard's portrayal, then, socially necessary labor time is not just some technical measure based upon the average productivity of the dominant production technology, but through transportation costs it is overdetermined by the very configuration of the system's economic geography. Moreover, as with Resnick and Wolff's original scheme, this is not a one-way flow, because that geographical configuration is in part determined by those very labor values that it (over)determines. This is only one example, but it illustrates that economic geographers have something to offer in working out an overdetermined value theory that shuns invariant entities.

Similarly, there is much that economic geographers could contribute to the various institutional relations and arrangements that form Mirowski's analysis of social value. For example, there is a growing economic geographical literature on the institutional processes shaping consumption and the very meaning of a commodity (Miller, 1991; Shields, 1992; Glennie and Thrift, 1992; Leslie, 1993). Likewise, there is a burgeoning body of work on the various institutions that bear upon money, taking cultural and social issues seriously (Corbridge, Thrift, and Martin, 1994). Futhermore, this kind of institutional bent is becoming increasingly theoretically sophisticated, in some ways more sophisticated than Mirowski's original contribution. For example, Thrift's work on money, space, and power draws upon the actor–network theory developed by Latour (1987, 1993), which is in many ways the intellectual successor of David Bloor's original sociology of science perspective on which Mirowski initially relied.

Finally, a considerable literature, particularly in industrial geography, discusses how the political and social overdetermine the nature of the labor process at particular locales. Moreover, that literature does not simply reduce the conflicts over labor process and work to class alone but allows other causes, such as gender, ethnicity, cultural politics, and so on. In many ways this was what the best of the studies within the locality project were all about (see Chapter One).

In sum, the examples I have given here are merely pointers to the ways in which economic geographers might contribute to one or more of the various nonessentialist value theories. That they can do so is precisely because such theories are nonessentialist; each allows and celebrates difference and variety and does not reduce things to a final cause. In making these suggestions, I'm not implying that economic geographers must choose one of them. Rather, they are only indications of what is geographically possible. In contrast, thirdhand conservation metaphors of dead physicists are geographically impossible.

CONCLUSION

It might appear paradoxical that two such ostensibly very different schemes, neoclassicism and Marxism, should both emerge out of a common nineteenth-century Western European intellectual context. That paradox disappears, however, if rather than looking for difference, we see the striking methodological similarities between the two schools. Historically both began by shunning religious dogmas and replacing them with a more compelling human logic. That logic involved taking "essential" human attributes and qualities and, through a process of logical derivation, making them the bedrock of complex theoretical statements about the economic and social condition (Gudeman, 1986, ch. 2). Where the difference between Marxist and neoclassical economics lay was in the selection of those essential attributes. For Marxism, the key code was the act of labor, the expenditure of human energy as humans wrested a living from a fickle nature. For neoclassical economics, in contrast, the foundation was the mind, the desires and mental agility of humans as they faced the world. The subsequent "grand theories" that were constructed explained everything because by definition their respective foundations were inviolable constants in human affairs. The difference between Marxist and neoclassical economics was only in the key selected, not the belief that there existed a key to begin with. Once the Marxist and neoclassical schemes were translated into a geographical context, the inevitable consequence was a monoplanar geographical landscape reduced to the chosen essence. It was inevitable because the foundation of inquiry—the theory of value—has no geographical component, and as such, geography must always be secondary.

The complexity and sophisticated nature of Marxist and neoclassical theory are seductive; the clean lines of determination provide clear answers to difficult questions. Since the 1940s, however, there has been increasing recognition, to use Mann's (1986, p. 4) phrase, that "societies are much messier than our theories of them." As such, a number of philosophers (Rorty, 1979, 1982; Bernstein, 1983), anthropologists (Geertz, 1973, 1983; Marcus and Fisher, 1986), and human geographers (Barnes and Curry, 1983; Thrift, 1983; Gregory, 1989a) have begun to argue that the world's messiness should be celebrated, not neatly packaged into grand theories and absolute conclusions. Economics has been the last of the social sciences to join this movement, albeit reluctantly and with many of its practitioners still actively resisting. But even economics cannot Canute-like forever resist the intellectual tide of the latter half of the twentieth century. Certainly, the 1980s have seen stirrings of change, often coming from those on the left, including those associated with institutional economics. The focus of much of this new discussion is on value theory and an attempt to eschew its historical legacy of essentialism by constructing a contextually based approach. Many of these attempts are still incomplete, but they show the desire to move away from the traditional economic lexicon that abounds in terms linked to necessity, universality, and uniformity toward one weighted toward terms related to contingency, particularity, and difference. Moreover, as I hinted, this new vocabulary is capable of accommodating a nonreductionist, nonessentialist view of space and place.

This transition from a nineteenth-century ironclad, rule-bound form of inquiry to a twentieth-century piecemeal approach that has no essential rules is, of course, difficult. But not to make that move is in effect to deny the variety that as geographers we seek to explain. If economists can begin to make that transition, then certainly economic geographers should be able to as well.

NOTES

1. For example, the so-called analytical Marxists (Roemer, 1982, 1986; Elster, 1985) explicitly reject the labor theory of value. But in so doing all they have done is to substitute the essentialism of labor values for the essentialism of the economic rationality postulate (see Chapter Three).

2. Although I focus on Rorty in this chapter, I want to emphasize that he is part of a wider antifoundationalist tradition represented by pragmatism and the even

broader movement of hermeneutics (see, for example, Bernstein, 1983, and Wachterhauser, 1986, and in human geography Curry, 1985a, and Gregory, 1989a). A central criticism of Rorty's work, though, is that it is not sensitive to power relationships. In particular, Rorty presumes a politically liberal democratic view of the "conversation" in which anyone can enter and have her or his voice heard (Rabinow, 1986; Weinstein, 1986). There exist, however, more radical versions of pragmatism that explicitly deal with power relations, for example, the work associated with Kenneth Burke (Lentricchia, 1983; Gunn, 1987). This critique of Rorty is clearly an important one (see also Bernstein, 1991, ch. 8). It does not, however, vitiate either Rorty's criticism of essentialism nor his view that theories are ways of coping with the world, which are the two issues I draw from his work in this chapter.

3. I emphasize again that this anti-essentialist critique of Marxist economic geography is limited to those who explicitly or implicitly make use of the labor theory of value. In fact, as I will suggest later in the chapter, there is a move by some Marxists away from an essentialist position (Resnick and Wolff, 1987; Wolff and Resnick, 1987). Also in human geography one might interpret Soja's (1980) pioneering paper on the socioeconomic dialectic as a contribution toward such an anti-essentialist Marxist geography (further reinforced by his later paper on Los Angeles; Soja, 1986). See also Graham's (1988, 1990) work that was discussed in Chapter One.

THREE

RATIONALITY AND RELATIVISM
An Interpretive Review of the Rational Choice Postulate in Economic Geography

Surely here is an opportunity to get rid of that great stick of a character *Homo economicus* and to replace him with someone real, like Madame Bovary.
—Donald McCloskey, *The Rhetoric of Economics*

Flaubert does not build up his characters, as did Balzac, by objective, external description; in fact, so careless is he of their outward appearance that on one occasion he gives Emma [Bovary] brown eyes, on another deep black eyes; and on another blue eyes.
—Enid Starkie, quoted in Julian Barnes, *Flaubert's Parrot*

Madame Bovary, c'est moi.
—Gustave Flaubert

Homo economicus[1] may have been lampooned more than any other character in the social sciences (Machlup, 1978). Marx called him "Mr. Moneybags," Thorstein Veblen (1919, p. 73) wrote that *Homo economicus* is nothing more than "a homogeneous globule of desire," and more recently the economic geographer John G. U. Adams (1981, p. 215) described economic man as "a nasty egoistical fellow . . . [of whom] most of us are thoroughly ashamed." If geographers are ashamed of economic man, however, it is not reflected in their work. For example, Couclelis (1986, p. 103) writes, "The continuing importance of rational models of choice . . . is hard to overestimate. . . . They still set the standards against which other models of decision and choice are measured."

Economic geographers, with their close links to economics, probably make greater use of the *Homo economicus* assumption than any other group in geography. Their usual justification for using the postulate is that it represents a behavioral norm against which they can compare "reality" (Abler, Adams, and Gould, 1972, p. 46). If the two do not coincide, the assumption is subsequently modified. But such a justification is scarcely compelling. It never makes clear on what grounds they make the rationality postulate the benchmark. Why not start with arationality or irrationality? Nor is it an accurate portrayal of how economic geographers actually use the assumption. Economic geographers usually either assume economic man throughout the analysis or never assume it at all—what they do not do is to begin with the assumption only to modify it later. Such a practice suggests that there is something about the wider framework in which the postulate is set—a framework that is rarely explicated—that makes the assumption indispensable. Finally, it presents a naive view of theory. As philosophers of science have recently made clear, theory is much more subtle than simply a mirror of the "real world" that is amended when its reflection is distorted (Feyerabend, 1978; Hesse, 1980). Rather, the nature of theory has as much to do with its designers' intentions, its audience, and the context of design as it does with the reality described (Curry, 1985b).

If we cannot easily justify the rationality postulate as a behavioral benchmark, then how can we justify it? If we turn to economics, we find that the justification there is couched in terms of a deeper epistemological grounding. An epistemological basis is provided that establishes on what grounds the *Homo economicus* assumption is making a claim to knowledge. Specifically, a set of logically consistent, unchanging, and universal rules and procedures is established that defines what counts as "true" knowledge; provided the rational choice postulated meets the criteria of such rules and procedures, its truthfulness is then guaranteed. This strategy seems more satisfying than simply tossing off *Homo economicus* as a behavioral norm, perhaps because it represents the avowal of what Curry (1985a) terms a "foolproof method." Once grasped, the right master key will reveal the truth. In this chapter I argue that the adherents of the *Homo economicus* assumption are implicitly making just such a claim; knowledge for them is grounded in a foolproof method, that of rational choice making.

Recently, however, the view that there exists some fundamental bedrock on which to ground our beliefs and knowledge of the world has been challenged in the so-called rationality-versus-relativism debate (Wilson, 1970; Benn and Mortimore, 1976; Geraets, 1979; Hollis and Lukes, 1982; Geertz, 1983, 1984; Breheny and Hooper, 1985; Curry, 1985a; Haynes and Stubbings, 1985). It is argued that there is no bedrock to knowledge; rather, humans make their own truth within their own particular place and time. Such a view is relativist; it avers that one cannot stand outside the context of which one is part. As such this view has been the point of departure for a number of sustained critiques of various "foolproof methods." Geertz (1973, 1983, 1984) has consistently attacked the view that there is some single form of rationality operating among different cultural groups; Feyerabend (1978) has criticized the idea that science is underlaid by a fixed and universal rational method; and Bloor (1983), following Wittgenstein, has taken on what is perhaps the pinnacle of rationality, mathematics, arguing that it can be understood only as a cultural construction (see Chapters Four and Six). In this light, my task in this chapter is to develop a relativist critique of the *Homo economicus* assumption in economic geography. The argument will be that *Homo economicus* fails not because of any intrinsic problems within the assumption itself; rather, its inconsistencies occur because of the broader methodological strategy employed to justify it.

Although my prime purpose here is to demonstrate the merits of relativism by example rather than in the abstract, a few general remarks about the relativist position are necessary. First, one should note the diversity of views that fall under the general rubric of relativism. In fact, a number of writers that I call "relativists" may well not be happy to be so labeled. Geertz (1984), for example, says that he is an anti-antirelativist; Bernstein (1983) wishes to go *beyond* "objectivism and relativism"; and Rorty (1982, p. 166) holds that "except for the occasional cooperative freshman . . . no one holds [a relativist] view." If by "relativism" is meant the idea that there are no grounds to choose between incompatible theories, then Rorty is surely right. In any case, this view of relativism is easily undermined: if all theories are as good as one another, then on what grounds should we accept the relativist position itself? In this chapter, however, I define "relativism" as the view that theories are grounded not in broader philosophical systems (such "grounding . . . [is] a wheel that plays no part in the mechanism"; Rorty, 1982, p. 167) but in a set of social practices of a given place and time. In choosing among theories, then, we must examine issues of context: the intellectual context in which theories are designed, the audience that they are designed for, the purposes of the theorists, and the context in which theories are applied. More broadly, because theories, interpretations, and models cannot be anchored in foolproof methods, their success depends upon their proponents' rhetoric (this is well argued for economics by McCloskey, 1985). As Rorty (1982,

p. 2) writes, theories do not succeed or fail on the basis of "antecedently plausible principles" but through the process of "prais[ing] our heroes and damn[ing] our villains by making invidious comparisons." This stricture must, of course, also apply to the relativist position itself. Relativism cannot be justified on any underlying epistemological grounds because it denies the whole project of epistemology altogether. Like any other approach within economic geography, the success of relativism will depend upon how it fares in academic practice. But by saying this, one is not claiming that the acceptance or rejection of relativism is somehow arbitrary or not important. Those people who put forward relativism have good reasons, as do those who deny it. If there is a resolution, it will be through debate according to the rules of the academy. Those who claim, though, that there is no reason for such debate, that such debate is resolved simply through an appeal to foundation, end up "killing the conversation" (Rorty, 1979).

This chapter is divided into five sections. In the next section I discuss the characteristics and use of the *Homo economicus* postulate in regional science and economic geography. I argue that the attraction of the *Homo economicus* assumption is in providing its users with an apparently foolproof method; the "fundamental postulate" allows economic geographers and regional scientists to discover the "real geographical order" submerged beneath an ostensibly chaotic economic landscape. In section three I assess the leading criticisms of *Homo economicus* that have been made by economic geographers and regional scientists. The argument here is that much of that criticism is ineffective because critics have focused on the "unrealism" of certain external attributes of the *Homo economicus* assumption rather than attacking the wider methodological position it exemplifies. More generally, critics of *Homo economicus* fail because they only want to establish a different foolproof method and not dispense with the notion of the foolproof method itself. In the fourth section I present a relativist critique of *Homo economicus*, arguing that it is more effective than the conventional criticisms discussed earlier. Specifically, I suggest that there is no firm bedrock in terms of a theory of knowledge that supports the rationality assumption. As such the postulate fails on its own terms. The truthfulness of the *Homo economicus* assumption is not sustainable because there is no secure bedrock of knowledge on which it is anchored. Finally, in section five I briefly sketch out some of the possibilities for economic geography and regional science that stem from a relativist perspective.

One final point is that this chapter is concerned only with economic rationality as embodied in the *Homo economicus* assumption. Clearly there are other views of rationality, such as that based upon the *process* of decision making (Liebenstein, 1966; Simon, 1976) or those stemming from a Marxist perspective (Godelier, 1972; Harvey, 1985a, 1985b; Carling, 1986).[2] These and other views of economic rationality are very important, but given the limitations of space, I focus on the best-articulated and most familiar of these approaches in economic geography: the *Homo economicus* postulate.

HOMO ECONOMICUS, NEOCLASSICAL ECONOMICS, AND ECONOMIC GEOGRAPHY

To appreciate the broader methodological position represented by *Homo economicus*, it is necessary to discuss briefly the intellectual tradition from which the postulate emerged. Jon Elster (1986, p. 26) argues that the view that human behavior is an outcome of rational choice "was born around 1870 . . . [with] the marginalist revolution in economic theory." Marginalist, or neoclassical, economics, as it became known, conceived the economic problem as the relationship between a fundamental psychological end, utility, and a set of scarce resources (Dobb, 1940, ch. 5). Although the hedonistic foundations of neoclassicism were subsequently sloughed off (Georgescu-Roegen, 1968b, 1973), the earlier definition of the economic problem couched in terms of means and ends remained (exemplified by the classic definition of the subject in Robbins, 1935, p. 16). One implication of the neoclassical vision, and one that is vital to the definition of economic rationality, is that in a world of scarce means but unlimited desires, individuals must make choices. The role of *Homo economicus* then becomes one of defining the "best" choices, that is, those that maximize an individual's ends given the limited means available. Neoclassical economists have subsequently shown that the problem of making the "best" choices reduces to a formal set of consistency conditions: completeness, reflexivity, transitivity of choice, and the condition that people always choose more of what they prefer over less (Senstat and Constantine, 1975; Hahn and Hollis, 1979). These four conditions formally define economic rationality in the sense that if any of them is violated, an incorrect choice is made and hence the action is irrational.

Although this formal definition of economic rationality is vital for theoretical work, it is less helpful in revealing the assumption's broader methodological characteristics; it is to these we now turn. The first is *reductionism*. Specifically, the use of *Homo economicus* represents a belief that social phenomena are explained only be reducing them to the mental states of individuals. This is because utility, the motivator of action, represents a psychological state. Boland (1982) calls this position "reductive psychological individualism." The consequence is that given a minimal set of initial facts—the psychological states of individuals, the resources available, and the rationality postulate that links the two—economists are able to derive all prices, quantities, and economic institutions for any given economy (this is readily seen in the attempt by Isard et al., 1969, to obtain a general equilibrium spatial model of economy and society). As a consequence, neoclassical economics is able to claim that its theoretical results, like those of other "hard" sciences, are derivable from a parsimonious use of assumptions.

A second feature of the rationality postulate is its *determinist* view of human behavior. As Rozen (1985, p. 665) writes, the assumption of economic rationality allows economists to make "claim[s] to precision and exact inference," but "once the anchor of strict optimizing behavior is cast away, economic science can only aimlessly drift, incapable of making useful predictions and with no way of ensuring internal consistency." In practical terms, neoclassical economics is able to model such determinant behavior by employing the mathematical technique of constrained maximization. By defining certain mathematical conditions that must hold for maximization to occur (in the case of utility, that the first partial derivative with respect to price is zero and the second negative), the neoclassical economist is able to deduce theoretically the economic consequences of rational behavior.

The third feature of the *Homo economicus* precept is that it is a *universal*; all acts in all places and in all times follow the strictures of economic rationality.[3] This is evidenced in the work of Becker and other members of the school of the new economics of the family (Becker, 1976; Crouch, 1979). (In economic geography this universality is seen in the attempt to apply utility maximization to a variety of geographical behaviors—commuting to work, shopping trips, recreational travel; Sheppard, 1980; Fischer and Nijkamp, 1985.) The charter for such work is that in all areas of our life, choices have to be made, and it is the rule of rationality that determines which choices are best. As Becker (1976, p. 14) writes,

> All human behavior is not compartmentalized. . . . Rather, all human behavior can be viewed as involving participants who maximize their utility from a stable set of preferences. . . . If this argument is correct, the economic approach provides a united framework for understanding behavior that has long been sought by and eluded Bentham, Comte, Marx, and others.

In trying to understand where the universality of *Homo economicus* comes from, Rosenberg has pointed to the very nature of the extremal mathematical technique in which the precept is expressed. Rosenberg (1979, p. 523) argues that by their very makeup, extremal theories "are all committed *to explain everything in their domains*. . . . The theory *ipso facto* provides the explanation of all of its subject's behavior, cites the determinant of all of its subject's states. There is no scope for treating . . . [extremal] theory as only a partial account of the behavior of objects in its domain."

Homo economicus, then, has two roles within neoclassicism. The first is theoretical. By defining the "best" choices, economic rationality allows the neoclassical vision of the economic problem, couched in terms of means and ends, to be realized. The second role is that of providing neoclassicism with a methodological agenda. It is an agenda based upon *reducing* the complexity of economic events at any time or place to the *universal* trait of rational choice making, a trait that because of its *determinist* nature is easily represented in a formal model. More generally, what tentatively emerges from this discussion of methodology is the link between the rationality postulate and a vision of the world given by natural science, especially physics. This link is explored more fully below.

Turning now to economic geography and regional science, we find that in its theoretical form at least, neoclassical economics and its associated rationality postulate are still a crucial component in theoretical research. Neoclassicism and *Homo economicus* are found in spatial equilibrium models whether at the regional (Lefeber, 1958; Isard and Ostroff, 1960; Harris and Nadji, 1985) or urban level (Brueckner, 1978; Sullivan, 1986); models of consumer choice in the city (Quigley, 1983; Brown, 1986); industrial location theory (reviews are given by Massey, 1979; Lever, 1985); microeconomic models of city populations in central place systems (Mulligan, 1983; Taylor, 1986); spatial interaction models (Sheppard, 1978; Niedercorn and Ammari, 1987); theories of contracts (Clark, 1983; Weber and Wiesmeth, 1987); and, finally, much of the discrete choice modeling literature (on this point see Richards, 1982, p. 341, and Fischer and Nijkamp, 1985, p. 533; examples of discrete choice modeling are found in Anas, 1982, and Pitfield, 1984).

To conclude this section, I will illustrate the role of the *Homo economicus* assumption in economic geography and regional science by giving a brief example, that of the new urban economic's model of household location in the city. Despite the careful review and critique of the new urban economics by Richardson, he does not mention the rationality postulate in his list of all the assumptions that the new urban economics makes (Richardson, 1977, ch. 3). It is almost as if economic rationality is so ingrained in economic theory that to single it out is superfluous. If, however, we go back to one of the first new urban economists, Alonso, we find he explicitly recognizes the importance of the assumption. In fact, Alonso (1964, p. 1) is almost apologetic: "The approach that will be followed in this study will be that of economics, and from this wealth of subject matter only a pallid skeleton will emerge. Both the Puerto Rican and Madison Avenue advertising man will be reduced to that uninteresting individual, economic man."

Uninteresting or not, *Homo economicus* is crucial to Alonso's scheme. For the purpose of his project is to determine the optimal location, size of land plot, and size of consumption bundle for individual households living in the city, where each household has certain tastes and a fixed income. Optimization is derived by first mapping out the locus of opportunities available to the consumer and then repeating the exercise with respect to consumer preferences. By comparing the map of opportunities to the map of preferences, we can easily determine optimality by using techniques of constrained maximization.

Both the theoretical and methodological roles of rationality discussed earlier are evident in Alonso's scheme. Theoretically, rationality allows geographically defined means—relative location of houses, land plot size, and consumption goods—to be linked to the end of utility maximization. The rationality postulate thus determines which are the best geographical choices. Methodologically, the model exhibits reductionism (people are "reduced to that uninteresting individual, economic man"), universalism (the model cuts across "both the Puerto Rican and Madison Avenue advertising man"), and determinism (the mathematical elegance of Alonso's model is realized by imposing determinativeness on households through the assumption of rationality).

Subsequent work by the new urban economists (Richardson, 1977) has clearly gone beyond Alonso's simple model. But as indicated by the reviews of the field by Harris (1985), and Muth (1985) the assumption of rationality still plays a pivotal role. Of course other views of rationality are found in urban economics, but there are good reasons why they are so infrequent. First, by dropping *Homo economicus* one is in effect also dropping the broader neoclassical framework, because (as already argued) economic rationality, by linking means and ends, is part of the glue that holds the neoclassical construction together. Second, when nonmaximizing behavior is assumed, solutions become increasingly complex and intractable (Isard and Dacey, 1962). This disturbs the elegance and simplicity on which the school prides itself. Third, there is a certain sociology to modeling. The infusion of neoclassicism into economic geography resulted in geographers' training within a particular tradition of modeling (Curry, 1985b, calls this the "workmanship of habit"). Having been so trained and taught to admire the qualities of simplicity, elegance, and determinativeness, geographers found it difficult to learn another type of craft that deals with different qualities such as those associated with nonmaximizing behavior.

In summary, because of its theoretical and methodological role, the rationality postulate is the tie that binds in neoclassical economics. Its absence would require a fundamental rethinking of how neoclassical theorizing should be carried out. When neoclassical economic theory is transferred to a space economy, all the hallmarks of the *Homo economicus* assumption are apparent. Through the lens of economic rationality, we see a determinant order to spatial arrangements, predicated upon reducing all behavior to the logic of rational location decisions. As such, economic rationality is a master gazetteer for the economic geographer; it renders comprehensible, and serves as a guide to, the apparent disorder of the economic landscape.

RATIONAL CHOICE: CRITICISMS AND COUNTERCRITICISMS

The rationality postulate has certainly not been without its critics either in economics or economic geography. The purpose of this section is to assess such criticism. To do so, however, one must be clear about what counts as a convincing critique. I follow the arguments of Lawrence Boland (1983), who suggests that the only effective criticism is one that is logically compelling. That is, criticism succeeds to the extent that it demonstrates that the theory's proponent must give up all or part of her or his aims, criteria, assumptions, and so forth if they are to be consistent with the criticism proposed.

Within the broader category of logically compelling criticism, one can recognize two types: external and internal (this distinction originates with Popper, 1945). External criticism represents the case of attacking one position from the tenets of another, usually by questioning the importance of the problem that a theory addresses, questioning individual objectives within the theory, or questioning the broader metaphysical doctrines on which the theory rests. Although such approaches are intent on providing logically compelling criticism—the critic claims that there is a contradiction between the theory's aims and the tenets of the critic's position—such criticism often generates more heat than light. The problem is that there is no agreeable basis on which to decide upon, for example, what constitutes an important problem, a significant objective, or an adequate metaphysical doctrine.

In contrast, internal criticism accepts the theorist's priorities, aims, metaphysical beliefs, and so on. The question then becomes whether a theory is consistent on its own terms. That is, are the various objectives of the theorist consistent with his or her own solution to the problem?[4] Wong (1978, p. 23) writes that "criticism of this type is the most devastating. The inconsistency of the objectives implies that the problem is unsolvable." In broader terms, internal criticism eliminates the difficulty of resolution implied in external criticism. In the case of external criticism, there are no agreed criteria between critic and the person criticized on which to accept an argument, thus leading to interminable disputes. In the case of internal criticism, the critic agrees to accept the criteria of the theorist criticized and yet still finds a logical contradiction. Because in this case criticism is in terms of the same frame of reference as the theory criticized, proponents of such a theory must accept the argument of the critic. If they did not, they would be inconsistent in terms of the theory that they themselves propounded. I contend that internal criticism is the only kind of argument that allows disputes to be permanently resolved.

It is generally argued that to meet the stringent definition of economic rationality, *Homo economicus* must possess a number of attributes: perfect knowledge, the ability and the desire to maximize, the pursuit of a single goal, egoism, and an independent set of preferences. Each one of these attributes has been criticized by economic geographers and regional scientists. I will argue here, however, that such criticisms are ineffective because they represent external critique. Specifically, each of these criticisms is motivated by a different vision of human behavior than that embodied by the *Homo economicus* assumption. But such criticism can never permanently convince proponents of the *Homo economicus* postulate because there are no agreed criteria on what constitutes an appropriate vision of human action. In terms of our earlier discussion, critics and proponents of *Homo economicus* are each proposing a foolproof method, and the argument is over which foolproof method is best.

Those who posit rational choice theory assume that a producer or consumer must have full knowledge of all potential choices and their outcomes (implying perfect foresight) if global maximization is to occur. Criticism of this postulate is widespread. Allen Pred (1967, p. 9) was an early critic, arguing that the assumption represents an "unwarranted departure from reality" because distance necessarily creates "spatial variations in information availability." Sayer (1976), citing Shackle's (1972) work, has attacked the perfect foresight assumption by arguing that a necessarily uncertain future denies the omnipotence of reason. More broadly, Pred and Sayer are suggesting that the perfect information assumption is inconsistent because an economic agent never knows whether she or he has obtained complete knowledge. This is because of either spatial barriers to information flow or the uncertainties of an unknowable future. Following Boland (1981), we might suggest that the problem with the arguments of both Pred and Sayer is that they only deny the feasibility of inductive knowledge when space and time are included, but they do not dispense with the inductive methodology itself. In fact, that methodology is essential to their argument. Pred and Sayer are saying that the only reason we need to worry about space and time is because they prevent us from inductively acquiring the "truth." But that means that the barriers of space and the uncertainties of time are important in the arguments of Pred and Sayer only if we take inductivism seriously to begin with. If, however, we deny the whole inductivist enterprise, which many have done (Boland, 1981), the arguments of Pred and Sayer have nothing on which to bite. In making this point, we are not denying that space and time affect information availability. Such an effect, however, undermines the perfect information postulate only if we assume inductivism is the sole method of acquiring knowledge. Because inductivism is not the one method of acquiring knowledge and because there are problems with the inductivist project itself, the perfect information postulate remains unscathed.

A second attribute ascribed to *Homo economicus* is the possession of both the incentive and the know-how to maximize. These two characteristics of economic man were criticized by Herbert Simon (1957), who argued that they should be replaced by the trait of "satisficing behavior." Economic geographers took up Simon's ideas and subsequently codified them within a "behavioral approach" to location (one of the earliest examples is Wolpert, 1964). Their justification was that "reality is arational", and could be explained only by satisficing behavior (Wolpert, 1964, p. 544). Boland (1981), however, again provides countercriticisms to this objection. First, it is extremely difficult to prove empirically whether someone is maximizing or only satisficing. Survey reports are highly suspect, and revealed preference theory that relies only on observed behavior has been criticized for its own logical inconsistencies (Wong, 1978). Second, there is a logical reason why one cannot distinguish between maximizers and satisficers. Maximizing theories are of the form "All consumers maximize something." But such a statement, as Boland (1981) notes, is neither verifiable nor refutable. It is not verifiable because one ultimately never knows whether all consumers are tested—the problem of induction. The statement is also not refutable because the "something" that consumers maximize varies from one individual to another. Thus even if it was found that two individuals were not behaving the same way, this would not refute the theory. The two individuals could be maximizing two different things. The upshot is that Simon's critique is not really a critique because on both empirical and logical grounds the maximizing thesis cannot be tested and therefore proved or disproved. A third criticism here, perhaps even more damaging to Simon's case, is that some have seen satisficing itself as a form of maximizing (Webber, 1972, ch. 5). Under this interpretation satisficing is equivalent to the maximization of the gains obtained from not maximizing. As such there is a logical contradiction in Simon's argument. He is attempting to criticize one concept by means of a second concept, but under scrutiny the latter turns out to be formally identical to the former.

The third feature attributed to *Homo economicus* is the pursuit of a single goal (see, for example, Wolpert, 1964, p. 537). Now, although many studies in economic geography have consumers and producers pursuing their single goals of utility and profits, at least in the case of utility that goal can incorporate a number of specific concrete ends. The so-called open utility function (McKenzie, 1978) allows anything to be included within it: from leisure to work, from income to savings, and from philanthropy to theft. The only requirement for inclusion of these specific ends is that they can be reduced to the common metric of utility. Furthermore, because producer profit in the neoclassical account is ultimately only valued for the utility it provides, the same argument applies. Thus producers may well wish to forge a compromise between the two concrete ends of attaining profits and cleaning up pollution.

The fourth characteristic of *Homo economicus* is egoism. This assumption has been criticized by Sheppard (1980, pp. 200–204), who argues that none of the usual justifications for the postulate—naturalistic, normative, and empirical—are convincing. Although Sheppard's criticisms are well taken, they do not logically undermine *Homo economicus* because ultimately the rationality assumption does not require egoism. Thus Machlup (1978b, p. 293) in reviewing the "egoism-versus-altruism" debate, argues that "it is quite irrelevant whether a decision-maker acts on the basis of a preference system that includes only his personal interests or also those of his family, his friends, his clients, his compatriots, or any *alteri*." That nonegoist behavior can be taken into account is a result of each of these different motives' being reduced to the neutrality of utility (Hollis, 1983, p. 250). As Sen (1979, p. 92) writes, providing the consistency requirements are met, "no matter whether you are a single-minded egoist or a raving altruist or a class conscious militant, you will appear to be maximizing your own utility in this enchanted world of definitions."

The final assumption within the *Homo economicus* postulate is that preferences are the actor's own. Such a condition is necessary, otherwise we might carry out actions that we think are in our best interests but that in fact are not. The criticism often made here, however, is that preferences are socially determined and influenced by advertising and the like.

There are at least two responses to this criticism. First, economists assume that the preferences of *Homo economicus* are given exogenously. Economists do not claim that they explain either how tastes are formed or what their broader social significance might be. If people want to interpret preferences in social term, then they can. Such an interpretation, however, does not undermine any of the economists' propositions about the origin of preferences because no such propositions are made. Second, in response to the argument that advertising and the like distort tastes, one can argue that on logical grounds such a contention is impossible to prove empirically. The difficulty is that to establish the effect of advertising, one would have to run two experiments for the same individual: one where the consumer is subject to advertising and the other where he or she is not. Since these experiments would have to be at two different periods of time, one would never be able to show conclusively that advertising led to the difference in tastes or whether tastes themselves changed in the intervening period.

In sum, all of the usual criticisms of *Homo economicus* focus on the assumption's external attributes. Such attributes are judged "unrealistic" in the sense that they do not conform to the alternative vision of behavior propounded by the critic. As was argued, however, such criticism is ultimately not compelling because there is no agreed-upon basis by which to compare different models of economic behavior.

AN INTERNAL CRITIQUE OF RATIONAL CHOICE

I argued in the previous section that the usual criticisms of *Homo economicus* do not stand up. Such a conclusion does not mean that the rationality postulate is invulnerable, only that the usual criticisms are not compelling. To provide a more convincing critique, we turn to internal criticism. This type of criticism is more damaging because it suggests that on its own terms *Homo economicus* is logically inconsistent. Specifically, it is argued that if we accept the external characteristics of *Homo economicus* (they can never be proved or disproved), there is nonetheless an internal inconsistency within the assumption itself. It is the contradiction between the claim to knowledge that *Homo economicus* makes and the lack of a convincing theory of knowledge that can support such a claim. Specifically, it is argued that on grounds of logical consistency each of the four common epistemological justifications that have historically been put forward by economists fails to provide a deeper grounding for *Homo economicus*. The consequence is that one is left with no firm bedrock on which to claim *Homo economicus* represents a foolproof method.

The first of the epistemologies used to justify the *Homo economicus* assumption as "true" knowledge is based on empiricism. This type of justification ranges from Hutchinson's (1938) so-called ultra-empiricism (Caldwell, 1982, chs. 6 and 7) to Samuelson's (1963, 1964) "operationalism" (Wong, 1973, 1978; Caldwell, 1982, ch. 9). The common claim of these positions is that rationality is justified only to the extent that it is empirically verified. This view has been attacked, however, because the way that the *Homo economicus* assumption is set up denies empirical testing. Specifically, rationality is protected from any direct falsification by means of its associated ceteris paribus clause (Hollis and Nell, 1975; Caldwell, 1982). The problem is that one can never refute the maximization hypothesis because if there is a disconfirming result, one never knows whether it is because the hypothesis is wrong or because the initial conditions have changed, thus violating ceteris paribus. As such the postulate is insulated from any empirical confirmation or refutation. Hollis and Nell (1975, p. 55) sum up the argument well:

> Rational economic man is not an actual man. He is, rather, any actual man who conforms to the model to be tested. So there is no question of testing an economic theory against the actual behavior of the rational producer or consumer. Producers and consumers are rational precisely insofar as they behave as predicted and the test shows only how rational they are.

The second type of justification stems from Milton Friedman's widely acclaimed essay "The Methodology of Positive Economics" (1953). Friedman's argument is that an assumption's realism is of no concern to the economic theorist because acceptance of a theory should be based only upon the accuracy of its predictions.

Although Friedman calls his position "positivist," commentators argue that a better label is "instrumentalist" (Wong, 1973; Boland, 1979). The instrumentalist position is characterized by the view that theory is no more than a tool; as a result, theory is neither true nor untrue but rather adequate or inadequate for the particular task. Its adequacy in turn is gauged by the theory's predictive power.

Although some have seen instrumentalism as unassailable (Boland, 1979), there are at least two criticisms of the position as a justification of *Homo economicus*. First, the instrumentalist cannot deal with the possibility that a different model of behavior may give as good a predictive result as *Homo economicus*. (For example, Becker, 1976, ch. 8, demonstrates that a downward sloping demand curve, usually justified by utility maximization, is also derivable from random behavior.) Friedman deals with this problem by using criteria such as "elegance" or "general applicability". But these kinds of concepts can have no place in his epistemological scheme because they are not derivable from predictions, the only source of guaranteed knowledge.

Another criticism is that the rationality postulate does not do very well in terms of prediction. In fact, it has been argued that it might be impossible to predict human behavior at all (Rosenberg, 1983). In that case Friedman's theory of knowledge fails because the very criteria on which it is based are unrealizable in the social world.

The third epistemological justification for *Homo economicus* is based upon a priori or self-evident truths. This kind of justification is associated with the writings of Robbins (1935) and Knight (1956). Both argue that neither controlled experiments nor historical evidence is sufficient grounds for the fundamental postulates of economics. Rather, such postulates are established by inspection of one's own behavior and experience. In more general terms, this methodological position, called a priorism (Blaug, 1980), asserts that economic theory is grounded on only a few intuitively obvious axioms.

At least two criticisms can be leveled at a priorism. First, there is the problem of the basis on which such a priori truths rest. Robbins's claim is that they are based on experience. But whose experience? Clearly it must be everyone's, or they would not be self-evident truths. But in turn this raises the question whether there is a universal economic experience. Economic anthropologists such as Polanyi (1968) and Sahlins (1972) would disagree. Furthermore, and perhaps more damaging, on what basis does the a priori method itself rest? Surely the method itself cannot also be a self-evident fact drawn from experience? If it was, we are led to an infinite regress where acknowledging the usefulness of our experience comes from past experience, and the usefulness of that past experience was discovered from yet a previous experience, and so on. But if we cannot justify a priorism in this way, how can we justify it, because by definition it is only everyday experience that is the basis for true knowledge?

A second criticism is that there are no criteria for distinguishing among competing a priorisms. For example, Hollis and Nell (1975) argue that economic theory should begin with the a priori truth that the economy is constantly reproducing itself. But how are we to choose between this a priorism and the one that Robbins suggests? After all, in trying to choose between a priorisms, we cannot use historical or empirical evidence.

The final justification of *Homo economicus* is based upon the methodology of ideal types. Thus Machlup (1978a), the best-known advocate of this methodology in economics, argues that to understand economic actors we must grasp their "meant meanings." The mental configurations that we construct of those meant meanings represent ideal types. Machlup makes it clear that ideal types need not be empirically correct. Rather, ideal types are either better or worse depending upon the situation. What improves them are the gradual changes to our ideal types that come with experience.

The problem with the ideal-type methodology, at least as presented by Machlup, is that it conflates two different epistemologies. Machlup argues that the role of *Homo economicus* as an ideal type is as a benchmark to examine economic phenomena. One compares real-world observations with those that would occur if behavior were rational. But to make such a comparison, one must assume that the ideal type, *Homo economicus*, has true knowledge. But this raises a logical contradiction. How can *Homo economicus*, who presumably uses ideal types in his own reasoning, obtain "true" knowledge when by definition the use of an ideal-type epistemology denies that such "truthfulness" can ever be obtained? Either there exists the possibility of obtaining true knowledge (the claim made by *Homo economicus*), in which case ideal types are redundant, or there is no possibility of true knowledge (the claim made by ideal types), in which case there is no room for a *Homo economicus* who embodies that assumption. We cannot have both.

RATIONALITY AND RELATIVISM

Each of the four epistemologies discussed represents a case of a belief in a foolproof method for acquiring knowledge. Specifically, empiricism asserts that the only legitimate type of knowledge is one that can be empirically observed; methodological instrumentalism claims that true knowledge comes only from a theory's predictive success; a priorism suggests that the only true facts are the facts of our everyday experience; and the ideal-type methodology avers that by referring only to the "meant meanings" of humans can the researcher "really" understand what is going on. Once these bedrocks are in place, *Homo economicus* becomes legitimate insofar as it is able to meet the criteria of knowledge that each of these different approaches holds.

In the last few years, foolproof methods have come increasingly under attack, thus undermining the broader legitimacy of the *Homo economicus* assumption. This criticism is seen in anthropology (Geertz, 1983, 1984), philosophy (Rorty, 1979, 1982), human geography (Barnes and Curry, 1983; Thrift, 1983), and even economic geography (Storper, 1985a). The central criticism is that it is wrong to suggest the existence of a bedrock to knowledge that reveals the essence of things. Rather, knowledge is acquired in many different ways; there is no single epistemology that reveals the "truth." To see how knowledge is acquired, we must examine the local context; that is, we must see how knowledge is obtained, used, and verified in a particular place and time. This view is relativist; there are no absolutes because one's knowledge is always "local" in origin.

In criticizing the four epistemologies above, we were in effect presenting a relativist argument. Each of the epistemologies examined tried to justify itself as a foolproof method for acquiring knowledge, thereby legitimating *Homo economicus*. But as Barnes and Bloor (1982) suggest, such a strategy must always fail on logical grounds. The problem is that in claiming to have found an absolute on which knowledge can rest, one is left with no justification of that absolute other than in terms of itself. This self-referentiality is manifest in the inability to provide an ironclad justification of *Homo economicus*. More specifically, each of the four epistemologies is involved in some sort of internal contradiction as it grapples with the problem of circularity. Thus although empiricism asserts that only empirical facts are a guarantor of knowledge, *Homo economicus* is defined in such a way that denies empirical testing. Methodological instrumentalism appeals to predictability as a criterion of veracity, but then it brings in criteria that cannot be predicted when distinguishing among competing assumptions. The a priorist approach resting on a belief that everyday experience is the arbiter of true knowledge is forced to assert that experience itself is an inadequate basis on which to rest the a priorist methodology. Finally, the construction of *Homo economicus* as an ideal type concerned with meant meanings appears incompatible with the *Homo economicus* assumption based upon perfect knowledge.

If these essentialist justifications are unconvincing, where does this leave *Homo economicus* as a postulate and the substantive question of how economic geographers are to do economic geography? In both cases guidance may be found from relativism. The central tenet of relativism is that human ideas and actions are only examinable within a particular social and cultural context. The implication of adopting this position for the questions raised above is twofold. First, to understand the idea of *Homo economicus*, we must see the assumption within the broader intellectual and social context out of which it emerged; second, to understand actual economic activity in a geographical setting, we must describe the local geographical context in which such activity takes place.

Taking the first issue, the social scientific activity of modeling takes place in a particular cultural and intellectual milieu. As a result the model comes to mirror the wider context of which it is part. Theorists have increasingly recognized that the context out of which the *Homo economicus* postulate was born lies in the methodology of nineteenth-century physics (Georgescu-Roegen, 1971; Thoben, 1982; Mirowski, 1989). Specifically, Mirowski (1989) argues that the rationality principle has its origins in the conservation principle of energy and its associated mathematical technique of constrained maximization. Within such a physical metaphor, early neoclassical economists substituted utility for energy in the constrained maximization equation of the physicists and made the rationality postulate equivalent to the physicist's principle of least action. Thus just as the technique of constrained maximization reveals the path of least action of any particle's movement, so the same technique is used to discover the most efficient (rational) actions of producers and consumers. If such arguments are correct, they go a long way toward clarifying the nature of *Homo economicus*: the concern with rigorous determination and causation in human affairs, the concern with universality (the principle applies everywhere and at every time), and the concern with reducing the world to fundamental principles and entities. Apart from the role of clarifying the nature of the rationality postulate, inquiring into the intellectual origin of *Homo economicus* also serves a critical function. Clearly the question that needs to be addressed is whether the physical metaphor is suitable for viewing human behavior (Barnes, 1987a). In that context it should be noted that other physical metaphors in economic geography, such as the potential and gravity models, have been criticized for their inability to deal with the social world (Lukermann, 1958; Lukermann and Porter, 1960).

In the case of the second question, a relativist perspective insists that to understand human behavior one must set it in its proper context—there are no universal rules of conduct the researcher can tap. For economic geographers, this involves explicating the local geographic context in which activity occurs. By definition such accounts must be synthetic because the relevant context itself is made up of a number of different features: the role of the state at all scales, the role of local culture and society, the influence of past and present events, the importance of both macro- and microeconomic processes, and so on. The point is to provide the texture and richness of the locale so that behavior there is understood. Because of the necessity of such a synthesis, perhaps the best way to describe and understand a particular economic activity is in terms of ethnography. Of course, there is a long tradition of ethnography in anthropology, but increasingly social scientists are recognizing that ethnographic studies can be applied to our own time and place (Willis, 1978; Marcus and Fisher, 1986; Gregory, 1989a, 1989b). Using an ethnographic account does not mean rejecting theory. Theory, however, must be informed by the details of the local study. In this sense, a relativist perspective does not correspond to the atheoretical idiographic approach of the 1950s. Certainly relativism celebrates geographical difference, but that difference is not portrayed as simply the spatial cluster of singular facts (Barnes and Curry, 1983). Rather, the areal differentiation that emerges is theoretically informed. That such an approach is possible in economic geography is evident, notwithstanding my remarks in Chapter One, in the recent work of number of researchers concerned with industrial restructuring (Murgatroyd and Urry, 1983; Soja, Morales, and Wolff, 1983; Massey 1984b; Morgan and Sayer, 1985; Soja, 1986). Each of them recognizes the specificity of place without abandoning theory. Now, of course, if some of the writers cited above believe that theirs is the only theory that grounds geographical difference, then we are back to foolproof methods. For the important point is that theorists be aware of what theories can and cannot do, as well as recognizing their own perspectives as theoreticians. It is against this critical awareness that we can then discuss the various theories that inform our view of any locale. To claim, however, that there is only one way to discuss the peculiarity of place is to cut the conversation short.

Massey's (1984b, ch. 5) work on south Wales provides a good example of an attempt to understand the broader geographical context in which acts are set. To comprehend that region's changing industrial landscape, Massey synthesizes a number of different features that have made that locale what it is. Thus Massey (1984b, ch. 5) interweaves the role of the state (in both the nationalized industries and in the provision of infrastructure), the local political situation (one dominated by the Labour Party and supported by trade unions), the importance of patriarchy in the region, the nature of the local class formation, and the broader national and international economic changes, such as the rise of the multinational corporation and the branch–plant economy. As such, Massey's account shows that viewing the recent changes in south Wales simply as a result of rational choice making misses both the nuances of behavior and the nuances of geography. In addition, her account is more than "mere description"; it is theoretically impregnated by the "geological metaphor" she employs (Warde, 1985). If the conversation is to be kept going, the next step is to discuss what that metaphor can and cannot do and the way in which it expresses Massey's broader concerns as a theorist.

CONCLUSION

In many ways the nineteenth century laid the foundations for "grand theory." Like its counterparts—Marxism, social Darwinism, positivism—neoclassical economics attempted to provide a rational basis for understanding all aspects of society. In so doing, it demystified the dogmas of religion that had previously dominated intellectual life and replaced them with a more compelling human logic. That logic involved making certain concepts universal and inviolable. Once in place, these "key codes" then formed the basis for deducing more complex theoretical statements.

The key code for neoclassical economics, and that part of economic geography that accepted its precepts, is rational choice making as embodied in *Homo economicus*. From such a position, all human activities no matter where and when they are performed are always reducible to the "lore of nicely calculated less or more." This theoretical stance is both powerful and in some ways attractive. By appealing to our (perhaps) ingrained ideas of universal humans traits, rational choice making provides the social scientist with an explanatory master key. The seductiveness of the *Homo economicus* assumption is further enhanced by its links to natural science. As a physical metaphor applied to the human world, carrying with it such qualities as predictability, rigor, and the potential for mathematicization, the rationality postulate is able to trade on the language, integrity, and above all prestige of science.

Despite the allure of the *Homo economicus* assumption, there are good reasons why economic geographers should be wary of it. The usual criticisms that focus on the "unrealism" of the assumption, however, are not very effective. A better line of attack is to follow a more general critique of all grand theories. Specifically, since the 1940s there has been a move to demystify the demystifiers. Grand theories, with their totalizing vision, their view that all the pieces of the world fit together rationally, are increasingly questioned. This critique originates from a number quarters: it is evident in Wittgenstein's later work (Curry, 1980, 1992a), it is seen in the German critical school of sociology (Adorno, 1967), and more recently it is found in proponents of the new pragmatism (Rorty, 1979, 1982). Certainly there are disagreements among these writers, but they are united on one point: the foolproof methods of the nineteenth century and their associated concepts, such as *Homo economicus*, involve turning away from the world. They reject the richness and diversity of human life by reducing it to some fundamental essence. In contrast, to understand why people do the things they do, one must see human action within the broader context in which it occurs.

Economic geographers are in as good a position to recognize and act upon the importance of context as any social scientist, concerned as they are with geographical diversity. That they have not done so until recently is at least in part a result of their own academic context, which awarded kudos for rigor, abstraction, and mathematical dexterity. Because of this legacy, it is unclear whether economic geographers can realign the discipline to emphasize context (although, as indicated, there are moves in that direction). Another related obstacle is the necessity of learning the new skills that a contextual approach demands. For example, once economic geographers are trained in the ways of quantitative methods, how easy is it for them to view the world from, say, an ethnographic perspective? Despite these difficulties, it is important to make the effort. The alternative is to deny the variety within the world that we seek to explain.

NOTES

1. Although I experimented with a variety of alternative gender-neutral terms for *Homo economicus*, they proved both clumsy and confusing (see also Billinge, 1986, p. 122). I think that the only way to avoid the sexist language of *Homo economicus* is to demonstrate that the concept is logically unsustainable, thereby

providing the grounds for expunging the notion from the lexicon of economic geography altogether. The purpose of this chapter is to contribute to that goal.

2. A recent approach in Marxist economics is the so-called rational choice Marxism (Carling, 1986) that accepts many of the characteristics of conventional *Homo economicus*. As such, the present chapter also bears upon this "analytical" turn in Marxist political economy (Roemer, 1986).

3. Interestingly, Clarke argues that it is the feature of universality that separates Max Weber's view of rationality from the neoclassical one. Although Weber accepts the importance of the means–end relationship and the rational action that links the two, his project is to account "for the historical origins of this form of rationality" (Clarke, 1982, p. 200). In this sense, Weber's work provides the sociological complement to marginalist economics.

4. There are many reasons why objectives and solutions might be inconsistent. A familiar example in human geography is where two or more logically incompatible theories are combined together to fulfill some objective. In this case the objective cannot be met because there are internal contradictions within the solution itself. Here we do not need to evaluate the two incompatible theories on external criteria; it is sufficient to show that they are mutually inconsistent, thereby undermining any objective that posits them as a solution.

PART III

MATHEMATICAL MODELS, METAPHORS, AND MUDDLES

FOUR

ENCOUNTERING EDINBURGH
Economic Geography and the Sociology of Scientific Knowledge

Strange to know nothing, never to be sure
Of what is true or right or real,
But forced to qualify *or so I feel,*
Or Well, it does seem so:
Someone must know.
                    —Philip Larkin, "Ignorance"

In retrospect the timing of Harvey's (1969) *Explanation in geography* could hardly have been worse. Instead of a manifesto for scientific geography, it quickly became an extended obituary for the scientific method. In all sorts of ways, *Explanation in Geography* remains a remarkable piece of work, but for at least two reasons it was the wrong book at the wrong time. First, the status of the scientific method within the social sciences from the late 1960s onward was increasingly besmirched. Human geographers, tired of mimicking economists who mimicked physicists, searched for approaches that spoke to the social part of the social sciences. Even Harvey (1973), in undertaking perhaps the most famous about-face in geography, followed suit, adopting a Marxist approach only four years after advocating the merits of the scientific method.[1] Second, the philosophy of science that Harvey espoused in *Explanation* was already looking dated by the late 1960s, but by the early to mid-1970s it was becoming almost antiquated. Within the span of a decade, following a series of withering assaults by critical philosophers, sociologists, and historians of science, many of the features that Harvey cherished in *Explanation*, such as the hypothetico-deductive (H-D) method, the existence of a neutral language of observation, and the sharp distinction between the practice of science and its method, were looking badly worn and, at worst, worn out.

My purpose in this chapter is to focus on the second of these mistimings. I will suggest that Harvey's dated account of the scientific method resulted in an inadequate hearing in geography for the "new" philosophy of science that came to succeed it. For not only was Harvey's review passé, but when he himself later came to dismiss those same ideas, it closed off debate within geography on the new work that was really occurring within the philosophy of science. Moreover, that work was compelling and germane to geographers (Bernstein, 1986, p. 151). Indeed, the various debates in this "new" philosophy of science foreshadowed many of the discussions that currently preoccupy human geography, including issues of writing and representation (Latour and Woolgar, 1979), power and authority (Rouse, 1987), and rationality and relativism (Bloor, 1976). In this sense, geographers took the long way to get to here from there. Or to pose it, perhaps unfairly, in more personal terms, had Harvey stayed with the philosophy of science, he might not have taken the twenty years to move from *Explanation* (1969) to *The Condition of Postmodernity* (1989).

One body of literature geographers never discussed because of this second mistiming originated in the late 1960s and early 1970s in Edinburgh with the "strong program" of the sociology of scientific knowledge (SSK). Frequently trained natural scientists themselves, the Edinburgh "new wavers" of SSK argued that the basis of knowledge claims in science was not in rationality but in a complex web of social relations. Scientific theories and facts reflected the contingent and contextual circumstances of their social origin. The practice of science was not about applying formal and universal rules of logic to a problem but was much messier, rooted in local historical and geographical conditions where scientists made things up as they went along, only later attempting to justify them. More generally, the new wavers of the sociology of science were epistemologically relativists, arguing that humans decided their own truth rather than having truth decided for them by the ineluctability of a universal scientific rationality.

The importance of the Edinburgh school for economic geography— which is the main focus of this chapter—is that its approach was used to offer a relativist alternative to the rationalism that continues to be found within the discipline. In stark terms, either one believes as a rationalist that there is a universal method that reveals the truth (or at least a method that reveals falsity), or one believes as a relativist that knowledge is contextual and contingent, where the best one can do is to fumble through by drawing upon local norms and ideas. The significance of Harvey's *Explanation* was that it formally codified a rationalist methodology within economic geography. When Harvey later came to disavow that earlier work, however, he rejected the traditional philosophy of science rather than rationalism per se. As a result, rationalism in economic geography continued unscathed. It is precisely such rationalism, though, that the Edinburgh school rejects, advocating instead a relativist alternative. That their relativism never made it onto the economic geographer's agenda was doubly unfortunate, however. The writings of the strong program would have provided an immanent critique of the continued rationalism in economic geography, and those same writings would have provided an exemplar for reconceiving the history of the discipline and the nature of its current practices. In this chapter I hope to make good on those two lost opportunities. In particular, from the perspective of the strong program, I will undertake first a criticism of economic geographers' rationalism and, second, a reconstruction along relativist lines of its past and present practices.

The chapter is divided into three main sections. By way of a benchmark, I begin by discussing the "received" view of the philosophy of science, which is the hypothetico-deductive system and the one that David Harvey espoused for geography. After discussing the criteria of theory choice embedded within the H-D model, I demonstrate the central role of rationalism to it. In the next section I review in detail the Edinburgh school's critiques of the traditional philosophy of science and the rationalist position that sustains it more generally. I also discuss their broader view of the practice of science. Finally, to demonstrate both the failures of rationalism as well as the merits of a relativist alternative, I attempt to write an alternative history of the scientific method in economic geography. I argue that the rationalist principles espoused by scientific geographers, and by implication others taking on different, later forms of rationalism, are belied by their practices. Rather, to make sense of those practices, one needs to know something about the local context and not overarching principles of rationality. This general argument is prosecuted through a series of individual vignettes of some of the key actors promoting geography's quantitative and theoretical revolution: William Warntz, Walter Isard, William Bunge, and Peter Haggett. In every case I argue that the theories and models that each advocates reflect only the local context in which they were propounded. In presenting my argument in terms of these vignettes, I show by example the value of the Edinburgh school's relativist epistemological position and their view of disciplinary practice.

THE HYPOTHETICO-DEDUCTIVE MODEL, VERIFICATION, AND RATIONALISM

The Hypothetico-deductive Model and the Philosophy of Science

From the 1920s to the late 1950s and early 1960s, the received view within the philosophy of science was the hypothetico-deductive model of explanation (Suppe, 1977). Before then the inductivist method prevailed. But because of a fatal logical flaw first recognized by David Hume—that an empirical regularity observed in the past need not logically continue into the future—inductivism was supplanted by a deductive model at the turn of the century (Alexander, 1964). It was not until 1948, though, that the H-D method was formally codified in a well-known paper by Hempel and Oppenheim (1948). They argued that all scientific explanation is characterized by the same logical structure, one combining hypothesized *laws* with the *deductive syllogism*. Although Harvey's *Explanation* uneasily bestrided both inductive and deductive traditions, ultimately he favored the H-D method as the basis for scientific explanation. It was "the standard model" (see also the review by Gale, 1972).

As a benchmark for the subsequent discussion, it is worth briefly reviewing the two components of that "standard model." A law is defined as the constant conjunction of two concepts, say, A and B, each of which possesses empirical instances. Formally, a law takes the form "If A, then B." Note first that the relationship between A and B is functional and does not necessarily depend upon temporal or spatial separation (Lewis, 1972, p. 160) and, second, that the law "If A, then B" holds for all times and for all places, and also for all instances of concepts A and B.[2] So defined, a law is then the basis on which scientific explanation and prediction proceed. This is best illustrated by recasting the discussion in terms of the following well-known scheme:

Law	If A, then B
Initial conditions	Existence of a (an instance of A)
Event	b (an instance of B)

An event is explained or predicted by being an instance of a broader concept about which there is a law. For example, an event b is an instance of concept B. Because concept B, of which b is an instance, occurs only if an instance of concept A also occurs, b is either explained or predicted by the occurrence of the law "If A, then B." Explanation is obtained by beginning with the event and then working backward to locate the appropriate initial conditions and law, whereas prediction is made by beginning with the law and locating the initial conditions under which they are realized. More broadly, in the H-D scheme "prediction and explanation are symmetrical, and [in both cases] deduction ensures the logical certainty of the conclusion" (Harvey, 1969, p. 37). One final point, not always recognized in the geographical literature, is that the laws that are part of this scheme are only *hypothesized* relationships and "are not themselves reducible to observations about events" (Blaug, 1980, p. 4). For this reason, one cannot tar hypothesized laws with the same brush used to criticize inductivism.

The second component of the H-D method is the logical syllogism. To use the previous example, an event *b*, which is an instance of concept *B*, is logically deduced in the H-D scheme by combining the major premise, that is, the law "If *A*, then *B*," with the minor premise, that is, the initial condition, which in this case is the presence of an instance of concept *A*. Thus, given the law "If *A*, then *B*" and the occurrence of an instance of *A*, event *b* is logically deduced. Here, as Harvey (1969, p. 36) notes, "the advantage of deduction as a form of inference is that if the premises are true then the conclusions are necessarily true."

Laws so far have been taken only as hypothesized relationships, but for the scientific method to be grounded, those laws must be empirically verified. As Caldwell (1982, p. 25) writes, "The [H-D] system gains empirical meaningfulness only when the system is given some empirical interpretation," and this occurs "when some of the sentences of the theory, usually the derived ones, are translated into the observation language." There was considerable debate over the nature of that "translation," but it was generally agreed that not every theoretical term within the H-D system requires an empirical counterpart (Hempel, 1958). Rather, the system as a whole is verified, not individual parts. In particular, verification occurs when the deduced consequence (predictions) of the model conform to real events in the world, where "conform" means a correspondence between the derived (translated) sentences of the H-D system and the neutral observation language in which empirical entities are described. At this point the laws found within that scheme are no longer simply hypothetical but are empirically verified.

One final point crucial to verification is the necessity for theoretical and observational terms to be independent of one another. If they are not independent, the very integrity of verification is jeopardized because one never knows whether the two "really" correspond or whether they correspond because the theoretical terms determine the meaning of the observational ones in such a way that congruence is attained.

In summary, the H-D model provides a set of prescriptive rules for achieving the truth. That truthfulness is guaranteed not only by the logical impeccability of the deductive syllogism but also by verification of the hypothesized law shown by the correspondence between theoretical prediction and a set of observations. Together these elements represent the basis of what Curry (1985a) terms a foolproof method. Provided that we are able to deduce logically, and predict successfully, we corner truth every time. For this reason, there is little choice among theories. Either a theory satisfies the two criteria of logicalness and verifiability, or it does not.

Rationalism and the Hypothetico-deductive Model

Although the H-D method stands on its own, it is part of a much broader approach to the acquisition of knowledge, an approach I term rationalism. Rationalism has been a dominant motif in Western philosophy ever since Descartes, and perhaps even before (Rorty, 1979). As a result, rationalism has been the inspiration for a series of different philosophies. But the important point is that although they differ, precisely because their intellectual origin is the same, such philosophies possess certain similarities. In particular, following the writings of a number of critical philosophers, historians, and sociologists of science, we can best represent rationalism as the conjunction of four interrelated beliefs (Bloor, 1976; Rorty, 1979; Hesse, 1980; Bernstein, 1983). By elaborating upon these four beliefs, I will try to delineate the precise links between the H-D method and rationalism.

Truth

Perhaps the most important of these beliefs is that the application of rationality leads to the *truth*. Although rationality is difficult to define, Bloor (1988, p. 69) provides a useful formulation: it is the view that "rules and meanings furnish us with invisible rails which reach ahead of behaviour giving guidance." Rationality, then, represents a set of rules and meanings that lie outside of us but when found lead us directly to the truth. Now, the exact nature of those rules and meanings varies historically, so the important issue is not their precise form but their existence. In this sense, as Bernstein (1983, pp. 22–23) points out, there is a strong link between rationality and foundationalism that also supposes that there exists some entity on which truth is predicated. But rationality makes an even stronger claim than foundationalism by insisting that there is something about the very rules and meanings of which it is constituted that makes one accept them; that is, they are compelling in and of themselves. Such characteristics are clearly present in the H-D model, which suggests that the rationality of rational rules and meanings induces us to follow them to the truth. In particular, scientific rationality involves following the rule of deductive syllogism and achieving a correspondence between theory and observations. With rationality so defined, growth, progress, and success in knowledge are ensured, because sooner or later the "invisible rails" will guide us to the truth.

Commensurability

Rationalism implies a common basis for resolving disputes. That is, the "invisible rails" of rationality ensure that everyone is on the same track. Following Kuhn's (1970) terminology, Rorty (1979) has called this facet of rationalism the assumption of *commensurability*. He writes:

> By "commensurable" I mean able to be brought under a set of rules which will tell us how rational agreement can be reached on what would settle the issue on every point where statements seem to conflict. These rules tell us how to construct ideal situations in which all residual disagreements will be seen to be "noncognitive" or merely verbal or else merely temporary—capable of being resolved by doing something further. (1979, p. 316)

Rorty's definition perfectly describes the H-D scheme, which provides a rigid set of rules for ensuring rational agreement. Those rules construct the "ideal situation" of scientific explanation. Provided that the logical syllogism is flawlessly followed and laws are conscientiously verified, there can be no disputes over theory choice. If there are, a human, not the method, has erred.

Reconstruction

Rationalism implies that there are rules and meanings that allow us retrospectively to understand progress in a discipline. Because rationality is the touchstone of correct theory choice, we are able to use it to *reconstruct both the successes and failures of past inquiries*. Once the methods and procedures necessary to carry out rational investigation are laid bare, intellectual historians are able to show why Galileo was right and Ptolemy wrong and why Curry's theorization of the gravity model was better than Carey's. More generally, by knowing such criteria and procedures, historians of science are able to provide, following Lakatos (1971), an "internal history of science" defined as a "congruence between scientific behaviour and a set of methodological rules derived from some chosen philosophy of science" (Bloor, 1988, p. 61). Furthermore, as Bloor suggests in some of his other writings, in laying out that rational reconstruction, rationalists feel no need to explain the reasons for scientists' following the rational method; rationality is its own justification. As Bloor (1988, p. 61) again writes, under rationalism "when a thinker does what is rational to do, we need enquire no further into the causes of his action, whereas when he does what is in fact irrational—even if he believes it to be rational—we require some further explanation." In this light, the H-D model is a prime example of a set of methodological rules derived from a broader philosophy of science that are then compared to actual behavior. For those scientists who follow such rules, we are able to derive a rational reconstruction of their successes, whereas for those who don't, we need to explain their mistakes by examining the causes of their foolhardiness.

Ineluctable Logic

Rationalists claim that there are rules and meanings that provide an *ineluctable logic of inquiry.* In its strong form that logic is explicitly assumed to be universal. But it does not have to be. As long as it is assumed that there are rules of theory choice that lie outside our social practices and that are deemed necessary to move forward, we adopt some form of this component of rationalism. In the case of the H-D model, it is the strong version that is proposed; there are universal a priori principles of procedure that, once followed, direct us to the truth. This is the importance of the H-D scheme presented above. It is a blueprint for scientific success. Once a law is verified, we effortlessly move along the groove of the deductive syllogism leading from major premise to conclusion, and hence to scientific explanation and prediction.

In summary, during the first part of this century, the H-D model represented the received view in the philosophy of science, and because of a historical overlap, as we shall see below, it was also taken up as the paragon method for economic geography. Drawing upon the broader principles of rationalism, the H-D method provided a template consisting of a set of rigorous rules and meanings that one could follow whatever the specific circumstances of application. By knowing those rules, one could find the truth, attain commensurability, understand past successes and failures, and be guided by an ineluctable method. More specifically, such rules provided an infallible algorithm of theory choice. In terms of the H-D model, those rules were to choose a theory that displayed the soundest logic and the best verified law. It was as simple as that.

THE EDINBURGH SCHOOL

Of course in retrospect it was too simple, and from the late 1950s onward, the H-D model was increasingly criticized by a new set of philosophers of science: Karl Popper, Imre Lakatos, Thomas Kuhn, and Paul Feyerabend. Given that the works of these four authors have already been thoroughly reviewed elsewhere, I will not repeat a similar survey here (see Hay, 1985; Marshall, 1985; Mair, 1986; Bird, 1989). For my purposes, it is enough to note that all four were a vital bridge for the Edinburgh school (even though it subsequently rejected many of their conclusions). In particular, as Bernstein (1983) elegantly argues, Popper, Lakatos, Kuhn, and Feyerabend, each to varying degrees, began selectively undermining the very rationalist undergirding of the scientific method as defined by beliefs in truth, commensurability, a rational reconstruction of history, and an ineluctable method. Of course there were differences among the four— Popper was clearly the most eager to retain some form of rationalism, Feyerabend the most ardent about vanquishing it—but this should not occlude the basic similarity, which was a dissatisfaction with the standard model and more generally, with the traditional account of scientific rationality.

In particular, the work stemming from these four writers increasingly led to a view of science as a series of local, historical practices rather than the unfolding of an abstract rational ideal. The very nature of the philosophy of science thus began to change, moving from formal logical expositions of scientific inquiry to case studies of actual scientists at work. As a result, as Richards (1987, p. 201) writes, there emerged "a new respect for scientists, not as impersonal automata, but simply as human individuals participating in a culture common to all." With this new respect, the philosophy of science and its history and sociology increasingly converged.

Once the initial critique of the standard model was made, new developments within the philosophy of science gradually arose from a group of sociologists of scientific knowledge based at Edinburgh.[3] In many ways it was not surprising that sociologists were so central in this movement to unsettle orthodoxy. As Hesse (1980, p. 30) notes, "The sociology of knowledge [has always been] . . . a notorious black spot for fatal accidents." In particular, the special contribution of the Edinburgh school was (1) to emphasize the critical role played by rationalism within the standard model and (2) to contest it with a relativist alternative worked through on the ground with specific case studies. In the remaining part of this section, I will attempt to detail both components of that contribution.

The Sociology of Scientific Knowledge

Karl Mannheim (1936) and Robert Merton (1973) were the pioneers of the sociology of scientific knowledge, although both were clearly influenced by Marx and Durkheim. In the early 1970s Mannheim and Merton were challenged by the Edinburgh new wavers, represented primarily by David Bloor (1976) and Barry Barnes (1974, 1977).[4] Merton was dismissed for failing to recognize that the very idea of science is a social construction, while Mannheim was attacked because he restricts sociological analysis only to false theories and not to correct ones (true theories by virtue of their very truthfulness require no further explanation). More generally, Bloor and Barnes attempted to widen the domain of sociological analysis by suggesting that the foundation of all knowledge claims in science was social, thereby eroding the rationalist underpinning of the traditional philosophy of science.

Motivating scientific practice for Bloor, whose work will be the main focus in this chapter, are broad social interests. To understand why scientists theorize in the way they do, one cannot turn for help to a set of abstract rules found within a particular philosophy of science. Rather, one must identify the specific *social* causes of belief, which are both time specific and place specific. Bloor (1984, pp. 299–302), for example, explains Robert Boyle's seventeenth-century air-pump experiments and his corpuscular philosophy of nature as a consequence of theological disputes between rival wings of the Puritans. More generally, Bloor (1982a), following Durkheim, argues that scientific theories are reflections of the wider organization of society. The social order through the practices of scientists becomes the natural order. Note also that Bloor's account implies the dissolution of the distinction often made in the traditional philosophy of science between the context of discovery and the context of justification. It is not simply that Boyle "discovered" his theory because he was living at a particular time and place, but that time and place entered into the very lineaments of the theory itself.

There are two principal foci of research within the strong program. First, there is a concern with critique, particularly of the received view of the philosophy of science but also the broader rationalist position that sustains it. And second, there is an interest in pursuing case studies of actual scientists at work. Such case studies are in turn taken to substantiate the strong program's relativist position, as well as providing a general exemplar for conceiving the nature of academic disciplines and the practices found within them. I will examine both foci in turn.

Criticisms of the Standard Model and Rationalism

All three components of the H-D model—deductive logic, laws, and verification—are critically scrutinized and found wanting by proponents of the strong program. First, Bloor (1982b) in a brilliantly terse account contests the logic of the deductive syllogism, claiming that it is only ever a post hoc rationalization for a conclusion already arrived at by other means. The problem is there is no independent justification for deduction. To make the move from the major and minor premises to the derivation, there needs to be a rule. But that rule can be justified only by appealing to the principles of deduction because deduction is the only foolproof means for making inferences, including inferences about deduction. Put simply, "the justification of deduction . . . presupposes deduction. [As a consequence, the argument] is circular because the[re is an] appeal to the very principles of inference that are in question" (Barnes and Bloor, 1982, p. 41). The implication is that logical deduction, one of the key components of the H-D method, cannot itself be logically deduced.

But if logic is not a set of ironclad rules for deriving ironclad conclusions, what is it? For Barnes and Bloor (1982, p. 45), like all academic knowledge,

> Logic is a learned body of scholarly lore, growing and varying over time. It is a mass of conventional routines, decisions, expedient reconstructions, dicta, maxims and ad hoc rules. The sheer *lack* of necessity in granting its assumptions or adopting its strange and elaborate definitions is the point that should strike any candid observer. . . . As a body of conventions and esoteric traditions the compelling character of logic, such as it is, derives from certain narrowly defined purposes, and from custom and institutionalized usage. Its authority is moral and social. . . . In particular, the credibility of logical conventions, just like the everyday practices which deviate from them, will be of an entirely local character.

Note that in making this argument, Barnes and Bloor are not saying deductive logic is without use. But it is useful only as ex post justification. Local practice always comes first.

Laws fare no better than deductive logic. According to the received view, laws summarize the recurring relationships that exist between observed facts, where those facts are instances of broader concepts. For the Edinburgh school, facts are socially constructed through the practice of science. As such, laws are not pure reflections of a brute reality but are manufactured by scientists themselves. This claim has resonances with the idea that facts are theory-laden, a notion that Popper, Lakatos, and Kuhn had all earlier recognized to varying degrees. Although those in the Edinburgh school acknowledge the legitimacy of these arguments they make an even stronger claim. Facts reflect the social and material circumstances of the particular local sites of their origin, which in the natural sciences is typically in the laboratory. This means the laboratory is not only a site of specific social relations but also the place of particular kinds of artifacts—equipment, chemicals, specimens—that are found only at that locus (see also Rouse 1987, 1992, on local knowledge). The pioneer work in this respect is Bruno Latour and Steve Woolgar's (1979) *Laboratory Life*. Prosecuting an ethnographical approach in which they attempt "to go native," Latour and Woolgar show over and over again the locally contingent nature of facticity (Knorr-Cetina, 1981). Facts begin as some form of literary inscription—an equation, a graph, a table. But then at some point an inversion is made. Rather than the text's producing the fact, the fact is made to produce the text. The blip on the printout is no longer a blip but the reality of a pulsar (Woolgar, 1988). Furthermore, all those steps involved in creating a fact are immediately forgotten, leaving only a new bit of brute reality. Specifically, such a process is manifest as scientists move down a hierarchy of "modalities," as Latour and Woolgar (1979, ch. 2) call them, that begin with highly qualified, speculative statements and end with no qualifiers at all. It is at this end point that a fact is born.

More generally, the creation of facts involves a process of continual negotiation. That negotiation, however, occurs only among scientists and their texts broadly conceived, not with the outside world, for it is the outside world and the laws that supposedly regulate it that are constructed in that very process of dickering. (Note that Pickering, 1993, prefers the verb "mangle" rather than "dicker" because there are always unexpected outcomes beyond the intentions of the participants.) More generally, as Woolgar (1988, p. 89) puts it, "nature and reality are the by-products rather than the predeterminants of scientific activity." The implication is that laws are not outside in the empirical world waiting to be found but are fabricated inside the local social world of the scientist.

Finally, there is the issue of verification and its twin, falsification, which have probably been the issues most discussed in this critical literature (Hesse, 1980; Knorr-Cetina, 1983; Richards, 1987). The problem of verification/falsification, following the Duhem–Quine thesis, developed in the first half of the twentieth century, is that it can be shown that any set of observations will always be theoretically underdetermined; that is, there is always more than one theory that will account for the same set of observations. As Hesse (1980, p. 32) writes, "Scientific theories are never logically determined by data, and . . . there are consequently always in principle alternative theories that fit the data more of less adequately." In particular, the Duhem–Quine thesis suggests that this is because theories are buttressed by auxiliary conditions and subsidiary assumptions (Harding, 1976). As a result, if a theory is, say, falsified, we never know whether that is because the theory itself is wrong or whether one of its auxiliary conditions has been violated. For example, the theory of economic rationality assumes ceteris paribus. While we may think we have falsified that theory, it is always possible that our result was only a consequence of ceteris not being paribus. Therefore, "it follows that a theory whose predictions do not materialize can always in principle be retained by making appropriate adjustments in the auxiliary hypotheses, if so desired. Conversely, it follows that there are in principle always alternative theories which are equally consistent with the evidence and which might reasonably by adopted by scientists" (Knorr-Cetina and Mulkay, 1983, p. 3). The broader implication is that cast-iron verifications or falsifications are impossible, with the result that some form of relativism is inescapable (Hesse, 1980). For if neither the data nor logic determines the theory, all that remains is a set of local, contingent factors.

In sum, each of these three criticisms made by the Edinburgh school go well beyond those that Popper, Lakatos, and even Kuhn made of the H-D model (see Bernstein's, 1983, review). In particular, the Edinburgh school is insistent that knowledge is irreducibly local. Thus, logic is not a universal calculus but locally produced; laws do not exist out in the world waiting to be found but are made up in socially specific locales such as the laboratory; and theory choice is not governed by a rational algorithm but is determined by the local standards of the practitioners themselves.

Apart from their attack on the components of the H-D view, the Edinburgh school also argues against the four precepts of rationalism. One constant argument is that rationality is an insufficient premise for deriving truth because rationality cannot justify itself as foundational. The problem is the same one that besets logical deduction: to justify rationality requires appealing to rational principles, for only they are guarantors of validity. But like all self-referential justifications, this argument necessarily stumbles on circular reasoning; rationality appeals for justification to the very principles that are in question. Instead, the Edinburgh school maintains, rationality should be the explanandum rather than the explananda. As Bloor (1988, pp. 69–70) puts it,

> Something does answer to th[is] term ["rationality"], but it has been misdescribed. Continuities of doctrine, the constraints furnished by correct meanings and implications, the feeling of reality speaking to us through the evidence, are all engendered and sustained by the behaviour of people around us. Like all divine and magical forces and queer mental processes, the force of reason . . . is the force of society misdirected.

Rationality, then, is not something that exists outside of us to explain the social, but it is something that is made within the social to explain the outside.

Second, the Edinburgh school attacks the idea of commensurability. To understand in particular Bloor's (1982a) argument, we must briefly discuss Mary Hesse's network model, on which Bloor relies. The gist of the network model is that knowledge is acquired through recognizing "family resemblances" among phenomena, that is, drawing similarities between something that is known and something that is not. In this sense, constructing family resemblances is an inherently metaphorical exercise, for it involves making the claim that one thing is like another. Or to use Hesse's (1980) term, it is a process of "metaphorical redescription." The similarities represented by such redescriptions, however, are not inherent in the phenomena themselves but are locally manufactured by researchers at a given time and place. For example, spatial interaction need not have been likened to the force of gravity, but there was something about the time and place—1950s America—that led many researchers to make that connection.

Through a continuing process of recognizing family resemblances, a web—or a network—of knowledge is eventually manufactured, its pieces connected one to another, however tenuously, through metaphorical redescription. Furthermore, all elements of that network have the potential to change once new family resemblances are recognized, causing in turn a ripple of change throughout the entire web. For example, the metaphorical recognition that spatial interaction may be more like entropy maximization rather than the force of gravity or that sites of industrial investment are more like strata of sedimentary rock (Massey, 1984b) than magnetic poles (Perroux, 1950) have the potential to be revolutionary, transforming the existing network of knowledge. Commensurability has no place in this scheme because at best there is only ever a partial basis of comparison among the new metaphors that are struck. For example, on what basis can Doreen Massey's metaphor that industrial sites are like geological strata be compared to François Perroux's metaphor of industrial sites as magnetic poles? For the nature of metaphorical redescription is to rearrange the bases of comparison, not establish similarities among those bases. To use Kuhn's own imagery, metaphor use is like a gestalt shift. You can see industrial sites as either like geological strata or like magnetic poles, but you cannot hold both metaphors simultaneously and establish commensurability, because holding one eclipses the other. In this view, incommensurability comes about because researchers are working with different sets of family resemblances, a result of holding particular central metaphors. It follows that to understand such differences will involve knowing something about the wider context of the participants, for example, that John Stewart, who popularized the gravity model, was an astronomer, and Alan Wilson, who pioneered entropy maximization, was a former nuclear physicist.

Third, Bloor in particular has been very critical of rational reconstructions of history. The problem is that proponents of the rational reconstruction view employ two different methods in accounting for history: one teleological and the other causal. As discussed earlier, rational reconstructionists suppose that there is no need to look for extra-rational factors to account for the success of rationality; it is its own explanation. This argument is teleological. It suggests that because rationality is a natural human goal and inclination, no reasons are necessary to explain our rational pursuits. In contrast, extra-rational *causes* are required to explain that some researchers go off the rails of rationality and make errors. For Bloor, this dualistic approach—a teleological account to explain rational researchers and a causal one to explain irrational ones—is inconsistent. For if on their own account traditional philosophers of science see the purpose of the sciences and social sciences as providing causal explanations, then they should explain rationality according to those same causal principles, not teleological ones. Rational reconstructionists are thus offering an asymmetrical explanation; they are upholding a method that they do not apply to themselves. In contrast, Bloor argues for "symmetry," seeing it as a necessary basis for consistent explanations within science.

Finally, the Edinburgh school argues that there can be no rational set of methodological rules that guarantee success. From her work on the history of science, Hesse (1980, p. x) concludes that "every set of metaphysical or regulative principles that have been suggested as necessary for science in the past has either been violated by acceptable science, or the principles concerned are such that we can see how plausible developments in our science would in fact violate them in the future." Bloor (1982b) provides a technical argument that supports Hesse's empirical conclusion, deriving his rationale from Wittgenstein's work. The problem with any rule-following procedure is that it leads to an infinite regress, where we need to establish rules for the rules, and then rules for the rules for the rules, and so on ad infinitum. This is not to deny the use of rules, only to say that we cannot either justify or derive them by appealing to some ultimate rule. In turn, for Bloor this argument provides a space for social practice. For if there is no ultimate rule such as rationality that justifies our methodological rules, then to understand why we do the things we do, we must turn to the local context. As Bloor (1988, p. 68) concludes, "There is . . . no essential doctrinal core that is being unfolded and whose content can guide those who work upon it. Nor do we possess any single, privileged touchstone of intellectual virtue that guides us when we must choose to enlarge our knowledge in that direction or that." In short, we have returned to a Ptolemaic universe, where the center point of inquiry must be humans themselves.

In sum, the strong program's critique of rationalism emphasizes again the importance of the locally constructed nature of knowledge and thereby the significance of the wider relativist position. It is to the task of clarifying this relativism that I now turn.

The Edinburgh School and Relativism

The relativism espoused by the strong program is certainly not the naive one that all beliefs are equally true or equally false. Either of these two variants, as Bloor and Barnes recognize, is self-refuting. Rather, Bloor and Barnes (1982, p. 23) define relativism as the view that "all beliefs are on par with one another with respect to the cause of their credibility." Note that this definition is in effect a variant of Bloor's symmetry postulate; there are no self-justificatory beliefs because all beliefs have some social cause. In turn, this formulation of relativism provided the basis for the Edinburgh school's substantive case studies that typically are historical. For the sake of brevity, those studies cannot be reviewed in any detail here. It is enough to say that their common purpose is to attempt to locate the sociological causes of credibility: why Robert Boyle held on to a corpuscular theory of nature (Shapin and Schaffer, 1985); why nineteenth-century scientists believed in phrenology (Shapin, 1975); and why physicists in the Weimar Republic argued for the antiscientific *Lebensforum*, which maintained a philosophy that attempted to dispense with the very idea of causality (Forman, 1971). More generally, such work shows that credibility is determined neither by rational rules nor the facts but is the result of specific local conditions that take the form of particular metaphors and analogues and various vested social interests.

The role of metaphors and analogues has already been briefly discussed with respect to Hesse's network model. Their significance for the Edinburgh school's examination of local knowledge is that they are the basis of actual scientific practice on the ground. Specifically, from the strong program's historical studies, Bloor concludes that scientists proceed by moving from "case to case mediated by complex judgments of similarity and difference, and informed at all points by the local purposes of the concept users" (Bloor, 1991, p. 164). In this view, metaphors are the means by which scientists move from "case to case" and are the vehicles by which "judgments of similarity and difference" are made. The pivotal role of metaphors in scientific practice was first emphasized by Kuhn (1970) and Hesse (1963). Kuhn in particular argued that theoretical relationships are inferred neither deductively nor inductively but by metaphorical leaps. Certain established relationships become exemplars that are then metaphorically applied to new circumstances. For example, in the development of spatial interaction theory, there was first the recognition of a potential analogy of interacting humans with Newton's model of interacting planetary masses—the gravity model. Given the success of this metaphor, the gravity model then became an exemplar for exploring the metaphorical applicability of other of Newton's ideas, from his potential model to his work on light. This was yet further developed by searching for other (non-Newtonian) physical theories that would serve as metaphors, for example, entropy. Interaction theories are therefore not derived from any general deductive logic but are generated on an ad hoc basis as researchers move from one case to another metaphorically.

Bloor later generalized Kuhn's insight, calling this general strategy of theory development "finitism." This is the idea that "meaning is created by acts of use. Like a town, it is constructed as we go along. Use determines meaning; meaning does not determine use" (Bloor, 1983, p. 25). What this means is that metaphorical meaning is ever shifting in response to new practices. In terms of the previous spatial interaction example, although Newton's gravity model provides the initial metaphorical leap, once it is placed within a geographical context it takes on new meanings, where those meanings are defined by the model's present users. Initially there may be an attempt to hold on to established meanings (for example, early proponents of the gravity model were reluctant to change Newton's original equational exponents), but this position rarely lasts as new meanings are constructed in response to particular local contexts (for more detail, see Chapter Five).

Pertinent for this discussion is that the metaphors scientists deploy in their practices are a reflection of the local conditions in which the scientists are embedded. For example, that Doreen Massey uses a geological metaphor in constructing an alternative theory of industrial location becomes partly understandable when we know that her own training was in geography, a discipline that has a long tradition of using physical metaphors; that as an English Marxist writing about the UK during the depression of the early 1980s, she wanted to accommodate both historical change (such as the rise and fall of industrial northern England) and spatial differentiation (such as the prosperity of the southeast and the privations of the north), both signaled by a sedimentary geological metaphor; and that as an industrial geographer she was critically responding to three decades of work carried out mainly by regional scientists but also Marxists such as Harvey, which had progressively effaced the specificity of place. It is in this sense that the localness of Massey's own context is found in her geological metaphor. I don't mean to suggest that there is some ironclad determinacy here. All I intend to imply is that within that local context, the sedimentary metaphor became an appealing one. (As an aside, it is interesting also to note that this metaphor did not take root among economic geographers in North America. Something about the local context there mitigated against its use.)

The second way in which local conditions bear upon knowledge is through the vested social interests of different actors. For example, Shapin (1975), in his now classic account of the phrenology debate in early nineteenth-century Edinburgh, showed how different theories of the brain reflected the specific sets of social interests of those groups proposing them. On the one side of the debate was an elite group of university teachers who maintained a belief in the social hierarchy as a unified system, while on the other were the mercantile middle classes who viewed society as a republic of different but equal groups. Without going into the details, we can note that the particular theories of the brain suggested by each of these two factions reflected their particular social interest—university anatomists viewed the brain as unified, whereas the merchant phrenologists saw it as composed of a series of separate faculties, each on a par with one another. In this way nature was being put to social use by each group such that it seemed to justify their respective views of society and their role within it. Although perhaps an exotic example, the same general issue pervades the academy. Academic reputations are based upon a theory's success, and in this sense the inventor of the theory has a vested interest in its survival. Vested interests, however, are generally created in opposing pairs. "Whenever someone's reputation will suffer if a theory is discarded, someone else's will be enhanced" (Bloor, 1988, p. 67). As a result, the academy is constantly beset by competing social interests. In making this argument, the Edinburgh school is not claiming that vested interests are bad. Rather, they are inevitable given the social nature of knowledge acquisition. For theories are socially collective works. As Bloor (1988, p. 68) puts it, "The point is *not* that scientists attend to these [social] considerations *rather than* the experience of nature. The claim is that these and similar factors are intrinsic to the collective apparatus that they must create and use to give that experience a shared structure and meaning."

More generally, the vested social interests that shape theory are locally constituted both temporally and spatially. Thus, social interests often clump both historically along generational lines and also geographically between distinct schools of thought in particular places. An example of the first is the dispute during the late 1950s and 1960s between the rising young Turks of the new geography and the old guard of regional geography (see Taylor, 1976). Each side mobilized the social resources at its disposal: new journals were created, specialty groups were formed, editorial boards were tussled over, and hirings and promotions were fought tooth and nail. All of this was an attempt by the one side to hold on to power and by the other to wrest it away. An example of the second kind of social interests, those defined geographically, is the clash over issues of industrial flexibility between a number of British industrial geographers and an American group at Los Angeles (see Chapter One). One reading of this controversy is in terms of the very different local conditions found in those two places: the optimism of the Los Angeles school in its celebration of flexibility is simply alien to British researchers who lived their lives in an era of national and regional industrial decline.

In both examples the more general point is that the social interests that lie behind knowledge acquisition are locally formed (see also Gertler's [1992] insightful comments about the geography of the flexible production idea).

In summary, the criticisms of the Edinburgh school undermine both the received view of science and the fundamental tenets of rationalism. In its place is an approach that begins and ends with local practice. Since the early 1980s there have been other writers and other schools of thought, including splinters of the Edinburgh school, various factions having taken similar methodological positions (see Pickering, 1992, 1993; Rouse, 1992; Bassett, 1994). These approaches are certainly as important as those of the original Edinburgh school and make up for some of the lapses in its discussion. Apart from the reason of brevity, there are two virtues in concentrating only on the Edinburgh school here. First, they present an internal critique of science and rationalism; that is, they use the very logic of rationalism to undermine its own tenets. In this sense, they are engaged in a deconstructive enterprise in which the H-D model and rationalism are shown to unwind from within. Second, their ideas are grounded in actual case studies, and so the wider position of relativism that they propose becomes historically palpable through their substantive work. Moreover, in providing those case studies, the proponents of the Edinburgh school are in effect offering exemplars for those in other disciplines to follow. It is to this task that I will turn by constructing in the final section of this chapter an alternative history of scientific economic geography.

RIGHTING A NARRATIVE, WRITING A COUNTERNARRATIVE

Ironically, at the same time that Popper, Lakatos, Kuhn, and Feyerabend began criticizing the traditional philosophy of science, economic geographers began to espouse its virtues. The subsequent story of the rise of the scientific method in economic geography is told in the same way by proponents and critics alike (Chisholm, 1975; Gregory, 1978, p. 32; Johnston, 1991). From the publication of Schaefer's (1953) pioneering article through Bunge's (1962, 1966) and Haggett's (1965b) works, economic geographers in the course of two decades progressively reached a fuller understanding of the scientific method. That understanding reaches its apogee with Harvey's (1969) *Explanation in Geography*, and its celebration of the H-D model. Furthermore, as Harvey argued, that part of geography that had already moved farthest in the direction of the H-D method was economic geography, which, through "location theory, . . . ha[d] been especially concerned with the development of the theoretical deductive method" (Harvey, 1969, p. 118).

In this section I oppose this progressive history of economic geography in two ways. First, in general terms, I will suggest that in spite of the rhetoric, few economic geographers understood or practiced the scientific method. Second, by focusing on a set of specific individuals who promoted the scientific method in geography, I argue that in every case their work flouted the most basic tenets of that method. Instead, following the Edinburgh school, we might best view their work as the consequence of a set of locally derived metaphors and social interests. In making both these claims, I am not derogating the abilities or imagination of those involved in spatial science. Latour and Woolgar (1979, p. 31) say about science that "we don't deny that [it] is a highly creative activity. It is just that the precise nature of this creativity is misunderstood." The same applies to my critical comments about spatial science below. I am not suggesting that those who were involved in such practices were uncreative or unimaginative, only that they and subsequent commentators were unclear about the ways in which they were creative.

Righting a Narrative

Livingstone (1992, p. 7) argues that much of the history of geography is presented in Whiggish terms in that it "amounts to little more than a timeless ransacking of the documents of history in the hunt for what are variously called 'anticipations,' 'premonitions' and 'foreshadowing' of current wisdom." This certainly holds for most accounts of the rise of the scientific method in economic geography, which typically read back from Harvey's *Explanation* (for example, Chisholm, 1975). Before the publication of that book, runs the traditional narrative, some economic geographers had recognized a few of the components of the H-D scheme. For example, Schaefer (1953, p. 227) had realized that: "human geography has to be conceived as the science concerned with the formulation of . . . laws." Or again, Haggett had discerned that "in the long run the quality of geography in this century will be judged less by its sophisticated techniques or its exhaustive detail, than by the strength of its logical reasoning" (1965b, p. 310). No one, though, had brought these various parts together. This was the brilliant accomplishment of Harvey, who combined systematically these "anticipatory" elements within the single H-D scheme.

Even if history happened this way, which is very doubtful, a major problem with the account is its supposition that economic geographers behaved according to the strictures of the H-D scheme once they were explicated. From any cursory examination it is clear that much of what went on in the name of the scientific method in geography violated virtually all of its methodological rules. As a result, there was an enormous gap between the practice of science and its philosophical ideal. This is well exemplified by the quantitative and theoretical "revolutions" that for many were the very basis of the scientific method in geography and for some remain so even now (see Getis, 1993).

The quantitative revolution first announced by Ian Burton in 1963 consisted of a set of both descriptive and Neyman–Pearson inferential statistics. These were added to during the decade and became increasingly more sophisticated and powerful, although they remained within the Neyman–Pearson tradition. The main use of such statistics, however, was not for verifying laws through prediction but either numerical description or the testing of ad hoc hypotheses. Furthermore, because of their origin in the Neyman–Pearson inferential tradition, such techniques prompted inductive forms of reasoning. Now, it is possible to verify both statistical laws within the H-D scheme (see note 1) and deductive laws using quantitative methods, but there is little evidence that this is what economic geographers did. Instead, as Gregory (1978, p. 37) suggests, "The quantitative revolution continued—some . . . would say strengthened—the hold of inductivism." Cox (1989, p. 205) goes further, saying that the way geographers used quantitative techniques represented a "continuity with the style of 'traditional' (for example regional) geograph[y]." For this reason it was wrong for some geographers to imply that quantitative methods and the scientific method were synonymous (for example, Burton, 1963, p. 156; or French, 1971, p. 4). As already suggested, even by the turn of the twentieth century, inductivism was disavowed as a *scientific* form of explanation.

Second, the other revolution, and perhaps the more important, was the theoretical one, and it, too, flaunted the assumptions of the standard model. A theory in the H-D scheme is the combination of a set of laws that are explained (theorems) and a set of laws that do the explaining (axioms) (Sack, 1972, p. 65). The "theoretical revolution" in economic geography, though, did not consist of logically working through and later empirically verifying these axioms and theorems. Instead, it frequently involved importing off-the-peg theories from other disciplines, principally from neoclassical economics and functional sociology (Gregory, 1978). Such an importation was often illegitimate, however, because already existing axioms and theorems involve precisely defined concepts that are characterized by limited domains. This implies that the laws that are the basis of any set of theorems and axioms are constrained in their application; only those events that exactly fall within the concepts of a theory or axiom are subject to the law in question. For this reason, the axioms and theorems on which theories are predicated cannot necessarily be transferred to fields such as geography. So as with the quantitative revolution, the theoretical revolution provided geographers with only the semblance of the scientific method but not the real thing as embodied in the H-D model. No wonder, then, that Richard Morrill (1993, p. 443) "never met a positivist." In terms of actual practice, there were none.

Of course, the argument of the Edinburgh school is that because of inconsistencies within the standard model, and rationalism more generally, positivism in the form of the standard model could never have been attained anyway. So even if economic geographers had been scrupulous in their reading of traditional philosophers of science (Johnston, 1991, ch. 3, claims that they were not), it would not have made any difference. The disjuncture between scientific theory and practice was logical, not pragmatic. The irony, though, is that when in the mid-1970s geographers began abandoning the scientific method, it was not because of this disjuncture but because the scientific method could not capture certain fundamental truths about the social world (for example, the persistence of social injustice). Even if this claim were true, it neither undermines the scientific method on its own terms nor, more important, does it challenge the critical role of rationalism. The result of this at best incomplete critique was that alternative approaches to the standard model often continued to be based upon some form of rationalism (see Chapter One). The broader point is that had economic geographers attended to the disjuncture between the practices and the ideals of the scientific method, they would likely have been led to questioning the very consistency of the rationalist position. In this sense, philosophy of science was dispensed for the wrong reasons and led only to the continuation of the problem rather than its final resolution. This gap between practice and methodological ideal is even more evident as we now look at specific individuals.

Writing a Counternarrative

The seeming paradox of the Edinburgh school is that despite its incisive critique of scientism and its celebration of practice, it offers no alternative to current scientific practice. To suppose that it should, however, is to mistake the target of the Edinburgh school's attack. It is not the practice per se of scientists that is critiqued but those who think about that practice in rationalist terms. The same applies here to economic geography. Economic geographers will continue to do economic geography in the way that they always have done, that is, by creatively drawing upon existing ideas and beliefs and responding—sometimes with great originality and imagination, other times with less of each—to the concerns of their own local context. The usefulness of the Edinburgh school is in pointing out that this is all there is to practice. There is no foolproof method directing inquiry. Certainly we may think we are following the dictates of omnipotent rationality, but on closer inspection it turns out that we are manufacturing yet another piece of local knowledge. For this reason, we must necessarily lift the veil of rationalist justifications and establish the locally constructed nature of knowledge that lies behind.

By constructing what I will call a counternarrative, I intend to undertake both these tasks. In particular, following Rorty's (1979) sense of hermeneutics, I will argue that the first practitioners of the scientific method within economic geography were engaged in a hermeneutical project rather than an epistemological one (for a more detailed discussion of that distinction, see Chapter Five). By that I mean that they were clearly casting around for a new vocabulary that would help them to cope more effectively. In retrospect one can recognize four kinds of new vocabulary: William Warntz's use of physical analogies (along with J. Q. Stewart, the Princeton astronomer); Walter Isard's working through of neoclassical economic theory for a space economy; William Bunge's drawings upon geometry (an outgrowth of Schaefer's pioneering search for morphological laws); and Peter Haggett's delineation of a model-based approach (often worked out in collaboration with Richard Chorley). While all of those works appealed to the common rhetoric of rationalism and were all later folded under the umbrella term of "scientific method," I will argue that precisely because they were hermeneutical projects, their local origins always disrupted their rationalist scientific claims. Specifically, following the Edinburgh school, I will suggest that the "new" geography promoted by these individuals was nothing more than the embodiment of a diverse set of locally constituted social interests and the application of a local set of metaphors. That is, the new geography was not new at all; it was just another piece of local knowledge.

Constructing a counternarrative based upon the assumption that all knowledge is local knowledge poses a number of problems, however. First, much of what is written, including personal recollections, is framed in terms of the canons that the counternarrative attempts to displace; in this sense, a counternarrative is always going against the grain of the textual evidence that it seeks to use (an exception here is Hanson's [1993] subversive account of the quantitative revolution, which by way of contrast should be compared to Berry, 1993). For this reason, a counternarrative must try to read between the lines and focus on the footnotes, the prefaces, and the asides, for that is where the interesting story, the story about practice, is told. Second, there needs to be a fine balance in recognizing the significance of events outside of the academy and those within it. Typically, the accounts that actors themselves provide dwell only on internal, disciplinary factors. But as Rouse (1992, p. 13) notes, "Scientific work continually draws upon and is influenced by culture 'outside.' The traffic in this direction involves, among other things, scientists seeking or acquiring significant material and financial resources, recruiting, meaningful and significant questions and problems to investigate, a vocabulary and the metaphors and analogies it incorporates, allies, and much more." The difficulty, though, is in bringing the external and the internal together. Finally, there is a problem of representation. A counternarrative is still a narrative, and this implies continuity. But the arguments made above suggest the opposite, that scientific practice is discontinuous, ruptured, and fractured. How can such characteristics be represented even by a counternarrative? The tack taken here is to present a series of discrete vignettes, with no attempt to link them under a single narrative structure. Clearly, this is not a perfect solution, nor are the strategies I employ to deal with these other problems. Perhaps the key point, though, is in recognizing the importance of writing a counternarrative in the first place.

William Warntz

In reflecting on his life, William Warntz (1922–1988) portrays himself as working at the margins of geography (Warntz, 1984). For he was not trained as a geographer, did not hold any positions within professional geographical societies, and was not even a member of a geography department until the last third of his professional life. Warntz's self-assessment is slightly disingenuous, however, in that much of his early career was spent as a research associate at the American Geographical Society and, following that, as professor of theoretical geography at Harvard University. One reason Warntz portrays his life as he does is because rhetorically it provides him the justification for making the claim that he sees better than most the isomorphisms between geography and the other disciplines in which he has worked. Establishing this isomorphism is his larger project. As he writes, the "full advancement of human welfare . . . [requires the] search for isomorphism. This means to exhibit each well organized discipline as possessing important item to item correspondence—concept to concept, and process to process—with each other" (Warntz, 1984, p. 146).

Rather than seeing this project as inherently metaphorical, Warntz views it as fulfilling the mandate of science; that is, all disciplines are "but mutually related isomorphic examples of one generalized logic" (1984, p. 144). But which logic is that? If we focus on Warntz's early work on potential models, which is his claim to celebrity within the quantitative and theoretical revolutions, we find that his logic is certainly not the pure one found in the standard model. Instead, it is very much a hybrid, reflecting the local nature of Warntz's own theorizing as he engaged in both metaphorical redescription and the promotion of a particular set of social interests.

Let us begin with Warntz's metaphors, the prime source of which derived from his experience during World War II, when he was a navigator in the U.S. Air Force. One of the required books for his training was J. Q. Stewart's *Waves and Weather*, which included an "exotic chapter describing potential of population and its sociological importance" (Warntz, 1984, p. 141). After completing his wartime service, he returned to the University of Pennsylvania as a doctoral student in economics, and it was there that he brought together the physical and meteorological metaphors, indirectly learned from Stewart, in his published dissertation, *Toward a Geography of Price* (1959).

It is important to recognize that Warntz's dissertation and later his even more well known *Macrogeography and Income Fronts* (1965) employed two quite separate sets of metaphors, although he often seemed to assume that they bleed into one another. The first was the Newtonian potential model. The potential model, unlike the gravity model, which is restricted to only two interacting points, represents a measure of general interaction across an entire system of points. Specifically, the potential of, say, a population at a point *i* is equal to the sum of the population at each point within the system divided by the distance between that point and *i*. What this means is that "each center is simultaneously under the influence of *all* centers and simultaneously exerts an influence upon all centers, as well as *all points* located within the boundaries of the system." In this way "a field is created . . . [which serves as] a functionally integrated and interdependent whole" (Coffey, 1988, p. 19). Potentials can be calculated for all manner of variables that vary over space, including prices, commodity flows, and income. In each case the potential measured at a given point provides an indication of the degree of interaction or accessibility between that point and all others within the system.

The second metaphor was meteorological, based upon air masses, fronts, and pressure systems. Its purpose was to facilitate forecasting and prediction, especially with respect to income and population. In particular, Warntz draws the analogy between temperature and income on the one hand and pressure and income density on the other. In meteorological terms, a front exists between two air masses of different temperatures, where pressure differences between the two are negligible. Likewise income fronts for Warntz occur on the border between two different income regions, for example, the western United States and the southern United States, where income density is roughly equal for both. Now, just as it is possible to predict the movement of weather fronts given knowledge of pressure and temperature, so, according to Warntz, it is possible to predict the movement of income fronts given knowledge of income levels and densities. By utilizing large amounts of empirical data on incomes and income densities for different time periods, Warntz traces out the movement of income fronts, concluding that "the major income fronts in the United States are dissipating" (1965, p. 50).

Even if we accept the effectiveness of the meteorological analogy for predictive purposes, the relationship between the two metaphors Warntz employs remains problematic. In *Macrogeography and Income Fronts* (1965, pp. 23–25), he does try to derive logically the link between them by invoking Boyle's law. But he soon gives up the attempt, saying that "the complete details of the agreements and disagreements involved in the analogy . . . need not be included here" (Warntz, 1965, p. 26). In any case, Warntz (1965, p. 26) later writes, "The phenomenon now labelled income front was discovered independently, with no a priori definition." By recognizing this, Warntz in effect admits that there is no necessary relationship between the meteorological and potential models. The only link is serendipitous: they both appeared in Stewart's book, which Warntz happened to read as a trainee navigator.

That metaphors rather than the rationalism of "science" lay behind Warntz's work we can see even more acutely if we critically examine Warntz's methodology (and here I follow Lukermann's [1958] prescient critique; see also Chapter Nine). The problem is that on at least two related counts Warntz contravenes the tenets of traditional scientific explanation. So like many of those in the new geography, he mobilized the lexicon of science but did not practice its principles.

Warntz's first error derives from his confused notion of scientific explanation. He seems to think that because a model ostensibly explains observations in one discipline, that same explanatory success isomorphically applies to another discipline. Now, the scientific method certainly allows one to transfer models across disciplines, but it does not allow one to transfer specific laws, because by definition they are restricted to a given class of events. This point formed the core of Lukermann's early critique of Warntz. The laws that Warntz brings wholesale from other disciplines cannot apply to a geographical world because those laws from the outset contain no geographical assumptions or data. Or to put it in the terms used earlier, the classes of events to which Warntz's borrowed laws apply are not geographical ones, and so such laws can never explain the geographical world. As Lukermann (1958, p. 4) writes, "The question of principle we wish to raise is not whether the answers given by this section of the scientific school are wrong, but rather whether the questions which they have undoubtedly answered correctly are not the wrong questions. To be blunt: are they not questions beside the point; are they not non-geographical questions . . . ?" This does not mean that Warntz was wrong to use physical metaphors, but it does mean that he cannot use the particular metaphors he did and still claim to be doing science.

Warntz's second mistake, seen most clearly in his work on the potential model, is his failure to understand that the "standard model" proceeds by isolating distinct causal relations and requires a testing of its predictions against an independent set of observations. First, the explanatory framework that Warntz employs is not the H-D one, but because of the very physical metaphor he uses, the potential model, it ends up as some form of structural functionalism. I give details in Chapter Nine, but the gist is that by employing a potential model that assumes a "field" of attractions and resistances to interaction, Warntz necessarily treats space, time, and mass as simultaneously working together to position the individual parts within the whole system. The implication is that there is no distinct causal chain or isolation of determinate causes that link explanans with the explanandum. Instead, everything explains everything else. As Lukermann and Porter (1960, p. 502) write, in potential models space, time, and mass "are mutually and simultaneously determining. Thus, there is no causal nexus, but there is no possible isolation or determination of cause and effect. There is no analysis of process; there can be no explanation." Second, even if a consistent theory could be worked out on this basis, it would undermine the possibility of independent testing. This is because there is a circularity in the testing procedure. The statistical surface against which the potential model is tested is derived from the very model itself. According to Lukermann and Porter (1960, p. 502), "The contours of the potential maps [against which Warntz thinks he can test his models] have no specific denotation. They are statistical 'surfaces' which have no reference to events/places on the earth's surface represented by the map on which the potentials are conformed." If this is a correct interpretation, then Warntz's procedure clearly violates a fundamental tenet of scientific verification.

The upshot is that whatever Warntz was doing, it was not the scientific method as conventionally conceived. Rather, he did what most others do, muddling through using a limited set of metaphors as a guide. Where Warntz was fortunate, though, was in making use of a set of metaphors that increasingly chimed with the times. This is seen by the considerable discussion that Warntz's work generated (see Janelle and Janelle's [1988] essay on citations) and the way in which it garnered institutional support. For example, he was offered a post as research associate at the American Geographical Society in New York and lectured both at Princeton and the fledgling department of regional science at the University of Pennsylvania under Walter Isard's directorship.

More generally, the success of Warntz's enterprise reflects its congruence with some powerful social interests at the time, interests that were backed up by important and resource-rich institutions. Warntz's program offered overtures to researchers in other disciplines, thereby possibly garnering alliances in a range of different settings (Latour, 1987; Curry,

1992b). Potential colleagues were in physics, meteorology, economics, planning, regional science, and of course geography. All might contribute. In the particular case of geography, Warntz's work was exactly right for legitimating the emerging new geography that combined scientific theory with statistical techniques. The form of his work also accorded well with the broader intellectual sentiments of the time: while his research invoked the prestige of physics and the credibility of mathematics and necessitated the use of emerging computer technology (it was for these last talents rather than theoretical geography per se that Warntz was offered the professorship at Harvard), it was also part of the social sciences, a set of disciplines that burgeoned in 1950s and 1960s America (King, 1993). Furthermore, Warntz's empirical work offered a soothing political message: disparities of any sort would correct themselves through the natural movements in income potential fronts.

In sum, Warntz was the right man at the right time and place. It did not matter that he mixed metaphors, failed to understand or implement traditional canons of scientific explanation, or even come up with good predictions. His importance was symbolic, and for that reason he has become either a venerated pioneer or evil incarnate, depending upon the Whig history to which one subscribes. It would be far better, though, to see him as just a man of his times who, through luck, accident, imagination, and doggedness, was able to dominate the geographical conversation slightly longer than most.

Walter Isard

Like Warntz, Walter Isard (1919–) was trained as an economist. But unlike Warntz, Isard has been continuously able to garner and maintain the institutional support to promote his vision. While Warntz ended his career as professor of geography at the University of Western Ontario, Isard still exerts considerable control in two major departments in Ivy League universities, Cornell and at the Wharton School of the University of Pennsylvania.

The shaping of that vision began at Harvard, where as a graduate student in the early 1940s, Isard was supervised by Abbot Usher, an economist with an unlikely interest in the location of economic activities. Under Abbot's tutorship and because of Isard's ability to read German (a result of his Dutch Reform Quaker roots), Isard was strongly influenced by the writings of the German location school that included von Thunen, Weber, Losch, and Predohl. This close reading in turn provided the basis for Isard's classic *Location and Space Economy* (1956), which contains both an assault on the traditional economic assumption of a spaceless economy and a constructive theoretical approach to the "space economy" based upon a revamped version of the German locational school. In particular, by adding transportation inputs to economic models, Isard added a spatial plane to the hitherto "wonderland of no dimensions" (1956, p. 25). The book, though, was part of a much wider institutional agenda. In December 1954 Isard convened in the Sky Room at the Hotel Tuller in Detroit the first meeting of the Regional Science Association, which has subsequently met annually not only in North America but across the world (there are now twenty separate regional congresses). The ensuing *Papers and Proceedings of the Regional Science Association* was published in 1955 and was quickly followed by the *Journal of Regional Science* in 1959. With this momentum, the first Ph.D. program in regional science was established in 1956 at the University of Pennsylvania, and two years later at the same university the first regional science department was set up, with Isard as head.

From this account, it is clear that the institutionalization of regional science was quite an unusual process; it was the product of the vision, control, and extraordinary energy of one man, Walter Isard (Smith, 1990, p. 1). That said, we can see that the broader context of 1950s America was also conducive to Isard's project. As Chatterji (1990, p. 342), one of Isard's many students, writes, "Regional science was born in an auspicious time." It was auspicious in many ways: it was a time of expansion in postsecondary education and the emergence of a number of new academic specializations (King, 1993); it was an era of kudos for things economic— after all, economists seemed to have shown how to cure recessions and to build growing economies—and it was a period of Panglossian optimism about science and technology and instrumental rationality more generally. In such an environment regional science could hardly fail.

It was also in 1950s America that the first stirrings of a scientific economic geography arose, and as a result there was always cross-pollinization between the two disciplines. Economic geographers attended regional science meetings, contributed to regional science journals, and obtained postgraduate degrees from regional science departments. As a result, economic geography both in terms of theory and method during the 1960s and early 1970s increasingly took on a regional science complexion. The flow, however, was one-sided—regional science took little from traditional economic geography. In fact, in marking out the turf of regional science, Isard has always been careful not to concede much to economic geographers (Isard, 1990, pp. 304–305). Their role for him is only as hewers and bearers of data for the models of pure regional scientists. The reason for Isard's reluctance to recognize economic geography again seems more fully an institutional one: it was too much like the project that he himself wanted to pursue.

Although "science" is part of the name Isard invented for his new discipline, he shows little understanding of traditional scientific explanation. In his most explicit statement, Isard says that " 'science' expresses the intention to apply concerns of rigorous techniques of investigation to analysis and to develop theoretical structures and concepts of general applicability" (Isard and Reiner, 1966, p. 1). At best this statement is vague and at worst a series of tautologies (surely all rigorous techniques are analytical, and all theoretical structures general?). Rather than the scientific method, Isard's major contribution to economic geography was a central metaphor based upon substitution. This metaphor in turn provided economic geographers with a doorway into neoclassical economics and its attendant scientific credibility.

Isard begins by arguing for "the development of a more adequate general theory of location and space economy" that "seeks to bring the separate location theories into one general doctrine" (Isard, 1956, pp. viii, 23). Following Predohl, Isard suggests that such a general theory is derivable from the "substitution framework," that is, the notion that "location analysis reduces to a consideration of substitution between transport inputs" (1956, p. 36). The idea is that space in the form of a transportation input is in effect a fourth factor of production, along with capital, labor, and land. Just as it is possible, say, to substitute capital for labor, it is also possible to substitute space in the form of transportation inputs for any other factors of production. To use Isard's own example, farmers may decide to increase output by extending spatially the margin of their cultivation by employing more transportation inputs rather than using greater amounts of capital to cultivate more intensely existing sites. In this way space is substituting for capital. Isard's wider purpose here is clearly to establish the applicability to a space economy of traditional neoclassical production theory based upon substitutability of inputs. To this end Isard employs exactly the same apparatus of transformation curves and iso-outlay lines as neoclassical production theory in determining locational optimality.

As was quickly pointed out, there are all kinds of problems with Isard's position and for those economic geographers that followed him. First, in spite of Isard's earlier fulminations against marginal economics, it is exactly with their position that he finishes: space itself becomes one of the things that he adjusts at the margin. Regional science is not really a new social science after all but only neoclassical economics in a different garb. This also raises questions about his interpretation of the German locational school, many of whose proponents were steeped in a historical and institutional tradition that was antithetical to neoclassicism (in that light see Gregory's [1981] rereading of Weber, and Barnbrock's [1976] reinterpretation of von Thunen). Second—and a fundamental issue— there is something about the nature of space when used in conjunction with the substitution metaphor that makes it incompatible with the neoclassical agenda.

These arguments have been well rehearsed elsewhere (Massey, 1973) and need only brief recapitulation here. The problem is that for substitution to occur, space itself must be able to be treated in terms of marginal increments in the same way as capital, land, and labor. Many argue, however, that a certain "lumpiness" to space brought about by indivisibilities of production and agglomeration economies mitigates against using the substitution model and its associated optimization techniques of constrained maximization. As Boventer (1970, p. 327) wrote in an early critique, "if [indivisibilities and agglomeration economies] are included, the substitution principle, if it is applied at the margin, loses much of its force and becomes useless in finding the optimal spatial structure." If Boventer is right, economic geographers cannot use the substitution framework or the techniques of constrained maximization in general to make the connection to neoclassical economics and its supposed scientific status.

These difficulties with the substitution metaphor were later implicitly recognized by Isard himself (and explicitly by his students; see Moses, 1958). Eventuating, though, was not a more streamlined, logically consistent scientific model but if anything a more local one composed of a hybrid of metaphors in response to shifting social interests. There remained the old neoclassical goals, but articulating with them were a series of physical and biological metaphors and a variety of ad hoc operational techniques. Rather than the spatial counterpart to neoclassicism's supposed universal logic, regional science became a very local project.

Let us examine these three components in turn. First, Isard follows an extreme neoclassical position in setting as his goal the explanation and representation of all aspects of social life. There are hints of this stance in his discussion of "general theory" in *Location and Space Economy*, but four years later, in his collective tome *Methods in Regional Science*, he is more explicit:

> There is the need for a much more comprehensive general theory which not only covers equilibrium with respect to location, trade, price and production . . . but also treats the fundamental interactions of political, social and economic forces as these interactions affect the values of society, condition its behavior patterns and goal setting processes, and lead to concrete decisions and policies. (Isard et al., 1960, p. xi)

Furthermore, Isard has subsequently made his general theory even more general by increasingly broadening the subject matter that he thinks can be modeled—ecological relationships, social problems, war and peace (culminating in the kindred discipline of peace science), and the intricacies and interactions of the world as a whole. As Kuenne (1990, p. 8) writes, "The term 'large scale modelling' does not adequately convey the Isardian view of a seamless, monistic universe. About the only topic left in this category that Walter [Isard] is not known to have researched is the providential integration of relations between Heaven and earth. And there are rumors even there!" Certainly, Kuenne is right to point to the all-encompassing nature of Isard's project, but it is not seamless. For in attempting to construct the world in his model, Isard has combined a disparate array of physical and biological metaphors that disrupt and puncture any continuous analysis. This contrasts to pure neoclassical economics that does maintain a seamless view of the world (seen, for example, in Gary Becker's [1976] work) precisely because it pursues only a single metaphor (see Chapters Two and Three).

Second, the diversity of the metaphors Isard mobilizes is staggering. At various time he bases his regional science models on field theory, general relativity, waves, ripples, optics, magnetic fields, life cycles, gravity, and crystallography. Isard is the great eclectic, or, as Kuenne (1990, p. 9) put it in a tribute to him, "Scholarly sclerosis has never been symptomatic in Walter's academic journey." From this list, however, it is clear that the only metaphors that interest Isard are physical or biological ones. This led Edgar Hoover (1963, p. 11) in an early Regional Science Association presidential address to note that although "all kinds of social scientists . . . make use of [physical] analogies . . . I think the possibilities are especially manifold in the case of regional science." There is no intrinsic reason, though, why there would be greater possibilities for employing physical metaphors in regional science than in any other social science. Rather, as the Edinburgh school makes clear, the strategy of metaphorically redescribing social relationships as natural is age-old. In this sense, Isard is doing what everyone else, including neoclassical economists, is doing (Mirowski, 1989). His metaphorical practices, like his broader goal, are just more extreme than most.

Third, the reason for this extremism is in part a result of the combination of Isard's normative and technical–interventionist leanings. On the one hand, Isard thinks there are values to follow that would make society a better place. On the other hand, those values can be realized only if we know how to intervene successfully in the world, which in turn is possible only providing we can predict and control. This normative–interventionist stance was there from the beginning. Isard (1990, p. 293) says himself that regional science arose after the end of World War II precisely out of the desire to intervene and cure ailing regions and cities in the United States. This same sentiment carries through to his later work on ecological issues, peace studies, and even world modeling. In each case

Isard presumes that if we can predict and control events, we can then improve reality by, say, attaining a clean environment, achieving peace, and living harmoniously in an integrated world. Several related points follow. For one, prediction requires a bevy of operational techniques (first systematically compiled in *Methods of Regional Analysis;*, Isard et al., 1960). For another, and related, given Isard's desire for prediction and control, it is not surprising that he was drawn to those physical and biological metaphors that had historically been successful at those two tasks. That said, in trying to control and predict the whole world, Isard was also driven to find more and more metaphors to complete his project. One or even a handful of metaphors was never going to be enough as Isard strove to represent the entire globe. Finally, Isard's focus on prediction and control helps explain why Isard is not concerned with explanatory methods as such. For prediction and control do not necessarily require explanation (Caldwell, 1982, ch. 8).

In sum, like Warntz, Isard in his practices did not proceed by following the H-D scheme. Rather, his was a local model. Certainly it began with neoclassical economics, but early on it was clear that those precepts could not operate in the spatial world Isard wanted to portray. The resulting hybrid scheme reflected a variety of interests, both personal and societal. His concern for social problems was in part a reflection of his Quaker background, but it was also part of the contemporary American society in which he lived, as was his belief in the technocratic solution. This is well illustrated by William Garrison in another presidential speech to the Regional Science Association. Garrison saw the early success of the discipline bound up with the social values of the country as a whole. He writes that his "main conclusion is that the values of regional science are great and that they largely stem from its contributions to new technology and from its contributions to the solution of social problems" (Garrison, 1964, p. 7). In short, regional science was the American way.

If it is right to see regional science as a peculiarly American project of a particular period, one can perhaps begin to understand an extraordinary statement Isard recently made in an essay specially written for a volume of his collected essays. Isard (1990, p. 322) writes, "Sooner or later [regional science will] be surpassed in the social science arena. Why? In part, because of it already becoming institutionalized . . . [and] approaching a dead end—from an overspecialization that becomes fruitless and obsolete. . . . To conclude, let us guard against the dangers of institutionalization, overspecialization, and overmathematization." Isard makes nothing of the irony that he was primarily responsible for all of the things that he now says regional science should guard against. Nor does he provide any critical analysis of his apparent about-face. That reversal, however, is understandable if we see it as an indication of the changing local context in which Isard operates. For over the past forty years Isard's postwar verities on which regional science was constructed have become clichés in a world of new "post"-isms: postindustrialism, postmodernism, post-Reaganism, and post-cold war. Because Isard's America is not what it was, regional science cannot be what it was either.

William Bunge

William Bunge (1928–) has always been a revolutionary in geography. His rebelliousness begins with *Theoretical Geography* (1962, 1966), the first booklength argument for a scientifically based discipline; continues with *Fitzgerald* (1971), an intensely personal study of an inner-city Detroit neighborhood; and ends with *The Nuclear War Atlas* (1988). Throughout all these very different works, Bunge remains committed to rationalism, and science in particular. In *Fitzgerald*, for example, after railing against the "rotten rich," he concludes his autobiographical insert by writing, "I believe in science; in the powers of the rational thought in the midst of seeming chaos; in our ability through reason to achieve a just, humane, and natural order for all, the only stable order. Science, not policemen, created what order man has achieved" (Bunge, 1971, p. 137).

Bunge's rationalist hero (and intellectual model) was Fred K. Schaefer, who, as a scientific socialist, believed in both social justice and science. Indeed, Schaefer followed Engel's argument in the preface to *Anti-Dühring*, that achieving the justice of socialism historically went hand in glove with the maturing of natural science. That same faith in scientific socialism is also the thread that connects the various parts of Bunge's intellectual life. But Bunge's life cannot be understood without first knowing something more about Schaefer's.

After becoming involved in the German trade union movement and the Social Democratic Party in Berlin during the early 1920s, Schaefer later undertook postgraduate research in economics and political geography at the University of Berlin (Bunge, 1979a, pp. 128–129). With the rise of nazism, Schaefer, already a marked man because of his links to the Left, fled Germany in 1933 as a political refugee, finding sanctuary first in England and later in the United States, where he eventually attained a position in the Department of Geography at the University of Iowa (Bunge, 1979a). Schaefer's interest in both economic theory and mathematics and statistics led him, like Isard, to the German locational school. But unlike Isard, Schaefer was also concerned with issues of scientific explanation, in part prompted by the presence at Iowa of Gustav Bergman, also a political refugee and one of the original members of the Vienna circle of positivist philosophers. The result of Schaefer's "seven years of intense work" at Iowa was, according to

Bunge (1979a, p. 132), "one great work," the article "Exceptionalism in Geography: A Methodological Examination," which was published posthumously in the *Annals, AAG* in 1953. Its greatness was as much symbolic as anything (certainly Hartshorne, 1955, eviscerated any of Schaefer's claims to historical scholarship). For what it introduced for the first time in human geography was the rhetoric of twentieth-century scientific method. In particular, following the H-D model, Schaefer argued that explanation proceeded by identifying empirical facts as instances of broader laws. As Schaefer (1953, p. 227) writes, "Description, even if followed by classification, does not explain the manner in which the phenomena are distributed over the world. To explain the phenomena one has described means always to recognize them as instances of laws." In particular, for Schaefer pure geographical laws are morphological laws, that is, recurring spatial patterns: if spatial distribution A, then spatial distribution B.

Where Schaefer leaves off, Bunge begins. Under Schaefer's scheme pure geographical laws are static, "containing no reference to time and change" (Schaefer, 1953, p. 243). Bunge, however, wants to go beyond stasis and deal with process in the form of spatial movement. Specifically, Bunge conceives of spatial movement and spatial structure ("defined most sharply . . . as geometrical"; Bunge, 1966, p. 212) as duals of one another. As he writes, "Whatever the type of movement it leaves its mark on the face of the earth. That is, it produces the geometry. In turn, the geometry produces the movements. Thus geometry and movement are the inseparable duals of geographic theory" (1966, p. 200). To explain both types of spatial relations (movement and geometry), he points to a single set of principles, those of Euclidean geometry. According to Bunge, geometry is "one of the most promising [areas] for geographers. After all, it should hardly be surprising that the genius and energy that have gone into the abstract analysis of space would prove of great utility in helping geographers to order their spatial understanding of the humanly significant phenomena abounding on the earth's surface" (1966, p. 223).

As with both Warntz's and Isard's work, Bunge's rhetorical claims about scientific method are belied by his practice. In a brilliant internal critique, Sack (1972) shows that Bunge's goal of an independent scientific geography based upon geometry is unrealizable. The problem is that by definition "time or change is not a term in synthetic geometry" (Sack, 1972, p. 72). As a result, it is impossible for Bunge to explain spatial relations—the dual between movement and geometry—in terms of the axioms of Euclidean geometry. Even Bunge implicitly recognizes this problem, because he provides a second argument for the link between process and pattern, one based upon "parsimony." Bunge writes:

> Another argument is available to unify patterns with movement. The argument arises from the fact that the actual substantive work of geographers seems to lead to a problem that is repeated over and over in aspects of geography as varied as climatology and economic geography—the nearness problem. The problem takes the form of finding the spatial arrangement of interacting objects, often of different dimensions, and placing these objects as near to each other on the earth's surface as possible. (1966, pp. 210–211)

Again, as Sack (1972) incisively argues, this second position is also inadequate because there is no such principle as "parsimony" in geometry; parsimony is simply an ad hoc device Bunge uses to buttress an already inconsistent argument.

If Bunge is not following the traditional scientific methodology, what is he doing? Certainly one element of his work is metaphorical redescription, for Bunge is on a continual quest for analogues between geometrical patterns associated with one process and patterns associated with another. In this sense, Bunge's project is deeply metaphorical, seeing one pattern and process as like another. In many ways he realizes this himself and speaks about "spatial cross fertilization" (1966, p. 27):

> For instance, are not animals located according to central place principles with the animal food chains providing the hierarchy? Why cannot portions of Ullman's concepts dealing with exotric and dioric streams be applied to highways? . . . [And] is not the problem of raking the lawn similar to the problem of urban arrangement? Leaf piles can be identified with minor cities, compost piles with major cities, areas of leaves with market areas, etc.

The broader point is that "geography lends great efficiency to spatial studies precisely because of the repetitive spatial situations found in the observable world" (1966, pp. 32–33).

The problem with Bunge's attempt at metaphorical redescription is his assumption that those analogues can be scientifically explained (for further discussion, see Chapter Five). Specifically, we can think of Bunge's project as having two parts: First he identifies geometrical and processal isomorphisms across different phenomena—the pattern of a highway is like the pattern of a river, migration flows are like heat flows, and the distribution of cities is like the distribution of floating magnets in a bowl (Bunge, 1966, pp. 29–30, 119, 283). Then, having recognized such isomorphisms, he tries to explain them scientifically using one of two variables, either geometrical axioms or principles of parsimony. The trouble is that these two explanatory variables are incompatible. Although geometry can be used to identify analogous patterns and principles of parsimony can be used to identify analogous processes, for the reasons already given, neither can be employed to explain *both* pattern *and* process. The upshot is that although many things shine through in Bunge's *Theoretical Geography*, consistent scientific explanation is not one of them.

Instead, it is better to see his project as a local one, cobbled together from a number of disparate local sources. Thus, the idea of parsimony Bunge takes from Schaefer via the German locational school—Losch, for example, heavily uses "lex parsimonae" in his construction of central place theory; Bunge's use of geometry, and mathematics more generally, emerges from ideas that were up and coming in human geography, especially at the University of Washington, where Bunge was a graduate student (on the importance of the University of Washington as an intellectual environment, and especially the role played by Donald Hudson, the former chair, see Berry, 1993; Getis, 1993; and Taffe, 1993); and, finally, his focus on isomorphic geometrical patterns and processes had already been established as part of Warntz's social physics project—it is interesting to note here that Warntz and Bunge planned to write a book together, "Geography: The Innocent Science," that was never published. None of this is to cast aspersions on Bunge's abilities or originality; it is just to say that he was doing what all creative economic geographers do: responding to his local context as best he could.

If Bunge in his earlier work attempts to mimic, albeit unsuccessfully, the scientific part of Schaefer's scientific socialism, in his later work it is the socialism that is more prominent and also more effective. In a semiautobiographical essay that begins by asking, "What is the logic of life?" Bunge (1979b) points to both the beginning of the American bombing of Vietnam and following a few days later the events in Selma, Alabama, as cusps in his own political education. Ironically, just as the second edition of *Theoretical Geography* was published, in 1966, Bunge began pursuing a directly applied geography following his involvement with both the peace and civil rights movements. After leading a series of "geographical expeditions" into Detroit's inner city (Bunge, 1977), he became involved in the community politics of his own African American neighborhood of Fitzgerald. But throughout he remained stoutly loyal to scientific precepts and the goal of a unified geography. He was thus obviously genuinely confused when Marxists in geography, such as Harvey, began "to purge the quantitative-theoretical gains of the sixties" (1973b, p. 333). For Bunge, scientific methods were the way to achieve socialist aims, and if they had not done so yet in geography, it was only because they had been misapplied, not because they reflected any "intrinsic inhuman quality of [such] work" (Bunge, 1973b, p. 332; see also Bunge, 1973a, p. 324).

Bunge's broader argument here, following Schaefer's scientific social-ism, is that science can be a progressive social force. In making this claim, Bunge is establishing a sharp demarcation between method and practice; scientific method can be progressive if it is in the right hands. This is why his retrospective "Perspective on Theoretical Geography" still includes commendations of Christaller and von Thunen and a reiteration of one of the basic claims of his 1962 book: "all theoretical geography starts with flows and ends with the patterns these flows etch on the human landscape" (1979, p. 171).

In sum, there is certainly a logic to Bill Bunge's life, but it is not the logic of the deductive syllogism; rather, it is that of a local modeler who was intensively influenced by the broader context of his early life and readings and never wavered from them. That local setting—his admiration for Schaefer, his graduate education at the University of Washington, his appointment at Wayne State University in inner-city Detroit, and the turbulent events of late 1960s and early 1970s America—were not mere background conditions but entered into the very sinews of the models, theories, and explanatory accounts he offered. There is perhaps no better example than Bunge's work on the conflation of the contexts of discovery and justification, and thus also no better example of the inappropriateness of the standard model for understanding scientific practice, Bunge's own claims notwithstanding.

Peter Haggett

Peter Haggett (1933–), one of the "terrible twins" of British geography of the 1960s (along with Richard Chorley), shares Bunge's fascination with spatial structure and movement and is similarly captivated as much by the aesthetics as by the intellectual challenge of the resulting geometries. He concludes his semiautobiographical monograph, *The Geographer's Art* (1990, p. 184), by noting:

> But for me the basic puzzle and riddles of geographical structure remain enduring. The structural symmetry of the planet as viewed from outer space, the sequence of atolls in a Pacific island chain or the terraced flights of irrigated fields on a Philippine hillside continue to be awesomely beautiful. When the time dimension is added, then changing structures take on added gleam. Diffusion waves become an interweaving dance of trajectories in multidimensional space.

Haggett's main contributions to analyzing scientifically that multidi-mensional space derive from his book *Locational Analysis in Human Geography* (1965b) and two volumes he edited with Richard Chorley,

Frontiers in Geographical Teaching (1965) and *Models in Geography* (1967). In many ways *Locational Analysis* follows the geometrical template of Bunge's *Theoretical Geography*, with Haggett dividing his text into sections on movement, networks, nodes, hierarchies, and surfaces. Unlike Bunge, however, Haggett does recognize the importance of nongeometrical approaches to geographical thought. For Haggett, it is only because the geometrical tradition has received short shrift that a greater emphasis on it is now required.

Another difference between Haggett's and Bunge's work is style. While Bunge is assertive and cocky ("The book [*Theoretical Geography*] is difficult to the geographer who is not familiar with . . . modern mathematical geography"; 1966, p. xi), Haggett is demure and self-deprecating (*Locational Analysis*, he writes in the preface, emerged "somewhat haltingly [from] a course of lectures which tried to set out what I thought was happening in locational research"; 1965a, p. v). While Bunge shouts his message, Haggett politely asks for your ear. And while Bunge knows the answer ("geography is a strict science"; 1966, p. x), Haggett knows only the questions ("Most of the fundamental questions in human geography have no single answer"; 1965b, p. 2). This dissimilarity in style is in part a result of cultural and personality differences (see Thrift, 1995), but it also stems from the distinct purposes of each. Bunge is the evangelist, trying to convert geography all of a piece to Schaefer's new science of geometrical relations, whereas Haggett's book, as he himself describes it, is "a report from an active battlefront" (Haggett, 1965b, p. vii). Haggett is the foreign correspondent interpreting the events of elsewhere. As he says later, "There was very little of my own research reported in [*Locational Analysis*]. . . . It is mainly a description of work which was going on in the United States and the continent" (Browning, 1982, p. 47).

Haggett, then, unlike the other three writers examined here, does not present his own theory as such. Rather, his influence is through his interpretation of the works of others. Central to that interpretation is the idea of theoretical models. For Haggett, theoretical models are the very stuff of science. With Chorley he writes:

> We cannot but recognize the importance of the construction of theoretical models, wherein aspects of geographical reality are presented together in some organic structural relationship, the juxtaposition of which leads one to comprehend, at least, more than might appear from the information presented piecemeal and, at most, to apprehend general principles which may have much wider application than merely to the information from which they were derived. (Haggett and Chorley, 1965, pp. 360–361)

The problem with Haggett's emphasis on models is that there is little agreement on the importance of modeling within the traditional (H-D) scientific method, and insofar as there is agreement, it suggests that the models Haggett promotes are not legitimate. In this sense, there is again a disjuncture between the scientific ideals to which Haggett aspires and his practice.

In the traditional account, for example, that of Nagel (1961) or Braithwaite (1960), a scientific model must possess the same formal structure as the theory, or part of the theory, that it represents. As Braithwaite (1960, p. 225) puts it, "A model for a theory T is another theory M which corresponds to the theory T in respect of its deductive structure." Nagel (1961, p. 96) elaborates on this view, adding that the prime function of a model is to provide an interpretation of theory "in the sense that every sentence occurring in the theory is then a meaningful statement." In other words, a model takes a set of abstract principles that constitute a theory, or part of a theory, and reproduces them in a more familiar domain in order to understand better the nature of the relationship among those principles. In this view, then, models are quite different from theories in that, first, they do not necessarily embody the full set of relationships within the theory that they represent and, second, the empirical domain of the models is often quite different from the empirical domain of the theory represented.

This definition of models is at odds with the one adopted by Haggett, which is of "an idealized representation of reality in order to demonstrate certain of its properties" (Haggett, 1965a, p. 106). But this definition misses the point, for what is represented in a model is not reality but theory, and it is not the properties of "reality" that are demonstrated but again the properties of theory. A similar misunderstanding is seen in the introduction to *Models in Geography*: "A model can be a theory or a law of an hypothesis or a structured idea. It can be a role, a relation or an equation. It can be a synthesis of data" (Haggett and Chorley, 1967, p. 21). Again, under the traditional approach to models, this view is misleading, for the point is never made clear that a model must bear some formal isomorphic relationship to the theory. It is obvious that Haggett's approach to modeling is outside the traditional scientific explanatory framework. For him, almost anything can be a model, provided the model is like the thing that is represented. This hints at the relationship between Haggett's view of models and metaphors; in fact, he recognizes this link: "because models are different from the real world they are analogies" (Haggett and Chorley, 1967, p. 23).

Now, some philosophers and historians of science (Black, 1962; Hesse, 1963) have linked models with metaphors, but this work lies outside the canons of traditional scientific explanation. It is easy to see why. In the H-D scheme the sentences of the theory must connect up with observational terms. But metaphors do not operate like this. They are, to use Kuhn's analogy, like "gestalt shifts"; we see the world all of a piece in very different terms after the metaphorical redescription; there is no item-by-item correspondence. Haggett, however, while entertaining analogies, still dabbles in the more traditional method, hankering after the old kind of correspondence. This ambiguity is also seen in his portrayal of Kuhn's work. In some places Haggett and Chorley recognize Kuhn's radical implications—for example, the way in which he says order is "subjectively" created rather than objectively found (Haggett and Chorley, 1967, pp. 20–21)—but in other places they portray Kuhn as a hard-line positivist who believes paradigms are nothing but "super-models" that facilitate "determination of significant facts" and "the matching of facts with theory" (Haggett and Chorley, 1967, pp. 26, 35).

Rather than following the scientific method, Haggett relies on local modeling, an unexplicated attempt to engage in metaphorical reasoning under the guise of the scientific method. Particularly important in determining the metaphors that Haggett takes up is the influence of his early education; it is a theme to which he often returns (see also Thrift, 1995). Both at grammar school in Somerset and later at Cambridge, he was "always on the cusp of physical science" (Browning, 1982, p. 41). In fact, at Cambridge at least half of his degree was in physical geography. In particular, his "original interests were in landforms and geomorphology" (Browning, 1982, p. 47). Furthermore, one of the early books he read even before entering university was D'Arcy Thompson's (1917) *On Growth and Form*, which showed that "many subjects found common ground in morphology" (Haggett, 1965a, p. 109). The result, as Haggett relates, was that when in *Locational Analysis* "I looked at the socio-economic landscape [it was] in terms of its morphology, trying to see what its structural components were. In a sense, although I had done a considerable amount of reading in economics I was much more interested in looking at parallel developments in physical geography" (Browning, 1982, p. 47). One can thus interpret *Locational Analysis* as one giant metaphor or, in Haggett's terms, a model; the socioeconomic landscape is like physical morphology. It is no wonder that the book is divided into sections based upon different kinds of form: nodes, hierarchies, surfaces, networks. The only section that does not fit this pattern is that on movement, but for Haggett movement is always channeled along preexisting forms. In this way Haggett avoids Bunge's problem, because for him there is only one-way causation—form determines process.

His emphasis on form and metaphor, as well as the analytical techniques he deployed, were strengthened by Haggett's collaboration with Richard Chorley at Cambridge during the late 1950s and 1960s (see

Chorley, 1995). Chorley was a geomorphologist and had written a paper on analogues (Chorley, 1964). However, whereas Chorley's work increasingly drifted toward systems theory, Haggett resisted any overarching theory. He was always more interested in the resemblances among the forms rather than setting them within a wider explanatory framework. As he reflects, "It's probably a lower order kind of technical work which has interested me most and I think the broader theories of the subject are not something I can cope with as easily. . . . Essentially one has to go back to my broader concern with form and morphology; I feel most happy as a sculptor in dealing with physical forms of this kind" (Browning, 1982, p. 54).

Such a statement, like so many of the remarks Haggett makes about himself and his work, is unduly modest (see also Thrift, 1995). After all, more than any other figure of the 1960s, Haggett is associated with the theoretical revolution. His success is in part due to his manifold abilities and good timing. But there are also sociological factors, including his various institutional linkages. Moving from Cambridge University to University College, London, back to Cambridge, and finally to Bristol University all within ten years during the late 1950s and early 1960s meant that Haggett was, as Thrift (1995, p. 380) says, at the center

> of a web of contacts. . . . He was a member of a group of Cambridge undergraduates, many of whom went on to outstanding academic careers. He was part of a generation of Cambridge postgraduates who were to go on to colonize British and North American geography. Finally, he became a member of a group of academic staff at UCL and Cambridge who were, or who would become, the cream of British geography. It is this membership of a multiple geographical elite that accounts for the success of . . . [Haggett's] ideas. He was able to mount an assault on the then geographic establishment in part because he was so firmly located within it. This meant that the geographical establishment could less easily identify him as a foe and, in turn, its younger members acted as willing conductors for his ideas.

Now, while the difficulties of mounting that assault shouldn't be underestimated (Stoddart's recollections of Haggett's trying to persuade members of the Royal Geographical Society of the virtues of multiple-regression equations make for particularly interesting reading; Thrift, 1995, pp. 380–381), there is surely something to Thrift's argument that the importance of Haggett's standing and contacts within geography made the 1960s theoretical revolution in geography happen. Of course, as Thrift (1995) also recognizes, Haggett built upon those contacts at the international level as well. By the time of the publication of *Locational Analysis in Human Geography*, Haggett had already visited the United States on several occasions, "gate-crashing" his first regional science meeting at Berkeley in 1962. In addition, he widened his network by making contacts with Hagerstrand in Sweden and later with geographers in Australia and New Zealand. In a discipline as small as geography, the "personal touch" was extremely important in spreading the word.

In summary, Haggett in all of his works has been driven by the urge to make metaphorical connections among spatial forms. He is captivated by geographical pattern. Given this context, models became the way to establish scientifically the relationship among those different forms. But at least in the conventional view of science, the use of models as metaphors is illegitimate. None of this is to deny the importance and lasting impact of Haggett's work, though. In fact, it is ironic that while Bunge's writings are the more evangelical, Haggett's works likely had much more general influence. In particular, Haggett and Chorley penetrated deep into the institutional structures of geographical education in England and Wales. Their Maddingly Hall lecture series, out of which both *Frontiers in Geographical Teaching* and *Models in Geography* originated, were directed primarily to "specialist teachers of the subject in Training Colleges, Grammar Schools and similar institutions" (Hickson, Foreword to Chorley and Haggett, 1965). So although British geographers were less involved than their North American counterparts in laying down the foundations for the "new geography," the influence of that movement was in some ways deeper there because of the early institutional linkages forged by Haggett, Chorley, and others (see Haggett and Chorley, 1989; Chorley, 1995). As such, it is yet another illustration of the power of institutions not only to shape the limits of knowledge but knowledge itself.

CONCLUSION

My specific task in this chapter was to argue that economic geographers missed out by not staying with the philosophy of science, or in a few cases by staying only with the old philosophy of science and not changing with it. Had they followed the new philosophy of science, and the Edinburgh school in particular, they might have avoided the continuation of flawed rationalist explanations and Whig interpretations of the discipline. By way of showing what is possible, I attempted to provide a reinterpretation of the quantitative revolution, using as a guide David Bloor's work.

Despite the length of this chapter, the arguments presented here are far from comprehensive and certainly not final. For example, I have said nothing about the gendered nature of economic geographical discourse and the very nature of the academy in which it sits; it is not a coincidence that all four of my case studies involved male scholars. Likewise, I have not problematized the fact that this discourse is Western, and more particularly Anglo. These are significant omissions, and ones that I would hope to rectify in trying to move beyond what is at best a preliminary study.

In spite of its tentative and partial nature, I hope that I have at least indicated in this chapter that the very posture of the new philosophy of science is one of incredulity toward any comprehensive and definitive statements. The result, as Woolgar (1988, p. 13) notes, is that SSK is "a project which is neither safe nor very comfortable. It raises fundamental questions which persistently rebound upon the questioner and prompt awkward doubts about the cool, clinical relationship sometimes imagined to exist between social scientists and the object of study." Facing up to this problem of what is in effect the issue of reflexivity is not confined to the new philosophies of science, of course. The recognition of reflexivity and strategies for dealing with it have a long lineage beginning at least with Nietzsche and through him to Heidegger and most recently Derrida (Lawson, 1985). So in calling for the use of new philosophies of science in economic geography, I in effect call upon a distinct line of European, continental thought, which has been particularly important in the recent discussions about various kinds of "post"-prefixed theory (see Chapter One).

By situating the argument in these terms, I have tried to make clear that this chapter is just part of a broader effort to rethink some of the established ideas of economic geography. For example, in Chapter One I noted how feminists have challenged the male-gendered subject matter and the phallocentric assumptions in the method of economic geography. Another example is the way in which the colonial past of economic geography has been confronted from a postcolonial perspective. And yet a final example is how some have disputed the very focus on the economic, arguing that the study of the economy necessarily involves an examination of the wider social and cultural practices in which it is embedded, including racialization and patriarchy. All of these critiques of economic geography are vital and, I would argue, complementary to the arguments about rationalism and relativism raised here. For in each case the main point is that our theories are not distillations of rationalist thought but very much reflect the bias of those who have social power and authority. Once we have such an awareness, the academic task becomes one of revealing how such biases lead to the formulation of particular theories, and the political task becomes one of trying to unthink those biases so as to provide for a more acceptable politics. This doesn't mean that biases will go away, but at least they will be recognized for what they are rather than as the product of some invincible rational logic.

NOTES

1. Gregory (1994, p. 350) has recently argued that in prosecuting a classical Marxism in the early 1970s, Harvey was also out of step with his time. In particular, the events of May 1968 were a repudiation of the traditional Marxism he advocated in *Social Justice and the City*.

2. If the law "If *A*, then *B*" applies to all instances of concepts *A* and *B*, then the argument is determinist. It is quite possible, however, to make probabilistic statements and still hold on to the H-D scheme of explanation. In this case, a "statistical law [would] state that if each member of a class of objects has the character *A*, then a certain proportion p $(0 < p < 1)$ of the objects have the character *B*" (Golledge and Amadeo, 1968, p. 771). Admittedly, as Sack (1972, p. 65) writes, "The means of confirming [such] statistical . . . [laws] raises very difficult problems." But as he later adds, "these difficulties do not create or warrant a different conception of explanation."

3. There has been an enormous amount of critical discussion around the Edinburgh school and the sociology of scientific knowledge in general. For the sake of both brevity and continuity, I will not refer to much of that literature here. Bloor's (1991) postscript to the second edition of his *Knowledge and Social Imagery* provides a review of his critics and also a set of counterarguments. In addition to the Edinburgh school, other approaches to the sociology of scientific knowledge include the Bath school of constructivist–relativists, discourse analysis, ethnographical laboratory science, actor–network theory, and cultural studies of science (for reviews and extended bibliographies, see Pickering 1992, 1993, and Rouse, 1992). In geography some of the differences among these various approaches are discussed in Barnes (1993, 1994) and Bassett (1994).

4. A difficult issue here is delineating the membership of the Edinburgh school. The founding members are David Bloor and Barry Barnes, and historically other members have included Harry Collins, David Edge, Steven Shapin, Steve Woolgar, Trevor Pinch, and Michael Mulkay. Not everyone in this last group would align himself with the strong program now, though. More on the fringes have been Bruno Latour, Kristine Knorr-Cetina, Andrew Pickering, and Mary Hesse, who, although sympathetic to the relativism of the strong program, have some reservations. What links all these writers—and this takes us to the heart of the strong part of the strong program—is that they are critical of rationalism and believe that knowledge is a product of particular times and places. Beyond these two characteristics not much more can be said. When I use the term "the Edinburgh school," then, I always mean Barnes's and Bloor's work, but at other times it will also refer to the wider group. Rather than offering a review of the diversity of positions within the Edinburgh school and the sociology of science, I have tried, for good or bad, to present a consistent argument.

FIVE

METAPHORS AND CONVERSATIONS IN ECONOMIC GEOGRAPHY
Richard Rorty and the Gravity Model

Universal history is the history of the different intonations given a handful of metaphors.
                                        —Jorge Luis Borges, *Labyrinths*

In his essay "On the Fearful Sphere of Pascal," the Argentinian writer Borges (1964) explores the different metaphorical intonations various cosmologists have given to the sphere over the past three millennia. For Xenophanes, the sphere is God, the most perfect of figures. But for Pascal, the sphere is the abyss, "a fearful sphere, whose center is everywhere and whose circumference is nowhere" (Borges, 1964, p. 192). The intonation changes, but the metaphor remains the same.

In effect, this chapter comprises footnotes to Borges, but footnotes that are drawn from the works of the philosopher Richard Rorty. For there is in Rorty's writings a persistent recognition of the centrality of metaphorical intonations. Furthermore, in his recent works Rorty (1987, 1989, 1991a) provides a systematic and what he terms a nonfoundational account of metaphor, one that is at variance with traditional theories. My purpose in this chapter is to utilize Rorty's account of metaphor to explore the recent history of economic geography, focusing in particular on the development of the gravity model. I will first suggest that that history is indeed the history of a handful of metaphors and that we need to interrogate that history with a set of critical questions that illuminate such metaphorical practices.

In undertaking these tasks, I will first discuss metaphors in general; second, scrutinize Rorty's own metaphors in particular; third, outline Rorty's theory of metaphor; and finally, bring such discussion to bear on the history of economic geography, and in particular that of the gravity model.

It should be noted that for the most part I do not make use of the admittedly small geographical literature on metaphor (an exception is Buttimer's, 1982, work). This is for two reasons. Such writings (for example, Tuan, 1978) are often concerned with literary metaphors or, as Barnes and Curry (1992) term them, the "small" metaphors that pepper individual sentences and that contribute to writing style. In contrast, I am concerned here with the role of "big" metaphors that shape whole research agendas and schools of thought (for an example in economics, see Mirowski, 1989). And when geographers have turned to "big" metaphors (for example, Livingstone and Harrison, 1981), they tend to use theories of metaphor that are incompatible with the Rortyan position elaborated upon here.

ON METAPHOR

Debate and controversy over metaphor has continued since at least Plato (Johnson, 1981). On the one hand, metaphor is viewed as at best frivolous and ornamental and at worst obfuscatory and logically perverted (Cohen, 1979, p. 1). Thus, Plato himself writes that metaphors can "make trifles seem important and important points trifles" (*Phaedrus* 267a–b; quoted in Johnson, 1981, p. 5); likewise Hobbes (1914, p. 13) says that "when [we] use words metaphorically . . . [we] thereby deceive others"; and more recently, David Harvey (1967, p. 551) avers that "the form in which . . . metaphors are cast seems to hinder objective judgment."

On the other hand, there has always been a strong undercurrent celebrating the centrality of metaphor. It is found in Aristotle, who provides the seminal definition: "Metaphor consists in giving the thing a name that belongs to something else"; it is also there in Vico's work and Nietzsche's (truth, Nietzsche writes, is "a mobile army of metaphors"). In the twentieth century, I. A. Richards's work has been central; he writes that rather than "a sort of happy extra trick with words," metaphor is "the omnipresent principle of language" (1936, pp. 90, 92). Richards's work in turn sparked interest in others, including Max Black (1962) and, through him, Mary Hesse (1963).

It has been particularly in Hesse's field of the history and philosophy of science that much of the innovative work on metaphor has been developed and applied since the 1970s (Cameron, 1983), and that work has influenced Rorty. Such research stemmed directly from the critique mounted within the philosophy of science on what Bernstein (1983) calls "objectivism." For objectivism was almost exclusively concerned with validation, that is, developing procedures to check the correspondence between theory and the real world. However, it became increasingly clear in the philosophy of science—at least following the Duhem–Quine thesis in particular (Hesse, 1980) and writings by Kuhn, Feyerabend, and Lakatos more generally—that one cannot express the real world in its own terms but only in theoretical ones (Bernstein, 1983). Thus, it makes no sense to check theory against some neutral outside world because the outside world itself is apprehended through theory. Interest, therefore, switched from concerns about validation to concerns about how theories themselves were formulated and developed, that is, concerns about the *practice* of science. Science was thus seen "less as an inert body of positive knowledge and more as an on-going activity" (Cameron, 1983, p. 263). To understand that activity of theorizing, a number of people turned to metaphor, claiming that it is an intrinsic part of the everyday practices of scientists as they cope theoretically with the world.

Although there is much controversy over the meaning of metaphor, Aristotle's definition, couched in terms of the similarity between two or more different things, is generally accepted. For example, the sphere is God. Here, one thing, the sphere, is metaphorically redescribed in terms of a frame of reference with which it is not usually associated, God. In general, the coexistence of different frames of reference can result in all manner of effects: incredulity, a smirk, a pithy essay in a well-known collection by an Argentinian author, or eventually even a chapter in a book (about economics). Of course, in most cases the metaphor is simply forgotten, but occasionally the bringing together of two hitherto unrelated things is the spark for something more. As Buttimer (1982, p. 90) writes, "Metaphor . . . touches a deep level of understanding . . . for it points to the process of learning and discovery—to those analogical leaps from the familiar to the unfamiliar which rally imagination as well as the intellect." In this sense, metaphor provides a bridge for understanding the development and formulation of theory.

RORTY'S METAPHORS

Underlying the central arguments of Rorty's work are strong claims about the power of metaphor. Rorty (1979, p. 12) writes, "It is pictures rather than propositions, metaphors rather than statements, which determine most of our philosophical convictions." Specifically, Rorty's argument is that the Greek ocular metaphors that hitherto have dominated Western philosophy are not coping well; they need to be replaced by others, in particular by metaphors of conversation. Note that Rorty is not dismissing ocular metaphors because they are metaphors but simply because they are not useful in getting things done.

"Our glassy essence" and "the mirror of nature" are the two ocular metaphors that Rorty (1979) identifies as having been central in Western philosophy. Very crudely, by "our glassy essence" Rorty means the philosophical belief that separating us from the animals is our inner mind's eye that sees general truths (that two parallel lines will never cross) as well as particular truths (that it will snow in Sweden in the winter). By the "mirror of nature," Rorty means the belief that our glassy essence can perfectly reflect nature as it really is, in its own terms. Philosophers having accepted such tropes, the history of Western philosophy is then the history of these two ocular metaphors as they direct the philosopher's vision. On the one hand, they lead to discussions about "mind stuff," as Rorty puts it—about the nature of our glassy essence and its location—and on the other hand to discussions about theories of knowledge—about the kinds of things that can be reflected in our mind's eye and are therefore knowable.

For Rorty, the main consequence of adopting such ocular metaphors is that knowledge is equated with accurate representation; mind is the mirror of nature. Furthermore, such a view then "lends itself naturally to the notion that certain sorts of representations, certain expressions, certain processes are 'basic,' 'privileged' and 'foundational' " (Rorty, 1979, pp. 318–319). That is, the mind's eye brings into focus—clearly represents— only that which is central. Unfortunately, different people focus on different things. For example, Marx sees the process of class conflict as basic, Freud views the tension between id and ego as privileged, and Darwin perceives natural selection as foundational. In each case by favoring certain sorts of processes, the respective theorist knows which representations are accurate and which are askew. Marx knows that Ricardo's theory is distorted because Ricardo says nothing interesting about class conflict; Freud is certain that the view of the associationist psychologists is clouded because they do not even mention id and ego; and Darwin is convinced that the creationists are blinded because there is no place for natural selection in their static view. More generally, through the gaze of ocular metaphors, philosophers saw the essence of humans as one of discovering essences, of finding a "universe . . . made up of very simple, clearly and distinctly knowable things, knowledge of whose essences provide the master vocabulary" (Rorty, 1979, p. 357). In this way the ocular metaphors provide a vision of philosophy as foundational, as providing criteria for discerning the good, the true, and the beautiful.

Rorty's purpose is to deny the usefulness of the ocular metaphors, to claim that they are more trouble than they are worth. He does this in part by showing that the questions arising from ocular metaphors are not very interesting questions (for example, those about truth: "truth is not the sort of thing one should expect to have a philosophically interesting theory about"; Rorty, 1982, p. xiii); in part by showing that when answers have been given to such questions, they are not very good answers (for example, Descartes's answer to the question of where our glassy essence is found); and in part by showing that both better questions and better answers are obtainable by discarding the ocular metaphors altogether and turning to others based on the metaphor of conversation. In prosecuting this argument, Rorty knows that there can be no final knockdown arguments that will convince others; to say so would be like saying that Galileo could have convinced Cardinal Bellarmine of a heliocentric universe by invoking the legitimacy of science. For at the time it was that very legitimacy that was being hammered out. Likewise, Rorty is in the very process of trying to legitimate metaphors of conversation; all he can do to convince others is to show the difference that they might make to our practices, telling us the kinds of things that we can now do if our vocabulary is couched in terms of conversation metaphors rather than ocular ones.

Briefly, the conversation metaphor that Rorty wants to substitute for the ocular one "sees the relation between various discourses a[s] those of strands in a possible conversation, a conversation which presupposes no disciplinary matrix which unites the speakers, but where the hope of agreement is never lost so long as the conversation lasts" (Rorty, 1979, p. 318). There are two points to note here. First, although there is no single grid that ensures commensurability among the different speakers, there will be times and places when we understand perfectly well what is going on in the conversation and in fact will want "to codify it in order to extend, or strengthen, or teach, or 'ground' it" (Rorty, 1979, p. 319). In such cases Rorty says we are epistemological. This does not mean that we have discovered something about the true nature of human knowledge, only that for the time being we have a set of agreed-upon social practices. Such practices are not correct because they correspond to some ideal of accurate representation; they are deemed correct because they are accepted. In other cases the conversation will elude us. Someone will turn a new metaphor, coin a new phrase, invent a new term, make a withering remark or an ironic snipe, and the conversation begins to go over our heads. In this case "when we do not understand what is happening but are honest enough to admit it . . . we must be hermeneutical" (Rorty, 1979, p. 321). Note that being "hermeneutical is not having a special method, but simply casting about for a vocabulary which might help" (Rorty, 1982, p. 200). What it certainly does not involve is stopping the conversation by bringing it back to basics or foundations or certainties, for there are none to be found when inquiry is seen in conversational terms.

Second, Rorty pursues the conversation metaphor because it is the best means to attain what Dewey calls a "working harmony among diverse desires" (quoted in Rorty, 1982, p. 207), that is, the liberal hope of realizing community and solidarity. Here we should note a marked contrast with another antifoundationalist, Foucault. Both writers want to deny that there lies something outside of us—Truth, Rationality, Science, God—that can save humankind. But for Foucault, who believes that society upholds metaphors of incarceration, repression, and constraint, evil always wins out. In contrast, Rorty's pursuit of conversation metaphors allows "room for unjustifiable hope, and an ungroundable but vital sense of human solidarity" (Rorty, 1982, p. 208). Evil might always win out, but through conversation there always remains the possibility of a kind of hope that need not be buttressed by transcendental beliefs.

RORTY ON METAPHOR

Implicit within Rorty's writings is the idea that the resolution to many of the problems of philosophy lies in a metaphorical revolution. In a recent exchange with Mary Hesse (Rorty, 1987; Hesse, 1987) and in his latest books (1989, ch. 1; 1991a), Rorty makes explicit how that might be done by presenting a nonfoundational theory of metaphor, albeit one indebted to the philosopher Donald Davidson (1979).

Before Davidson, there were two main theories of metaphor: the substitution view and the interaction view. The substitution view suggests that when we use a metaphor we are in effect substituting the characteristics of the object of metaphorical comparison for literal characteristics of the object itself. For example, when we say "God is a sphere" we are really saying that God is like a sphere in terms of the following characteristics: possession of a perfect form, a center that is everywhere, a circumference that is nowhere, and so on. In contrast, the interaction view suggests that every metaphor possesses both a principal and subsidiary referent (Black, 1962). The meanings associated with each referent, though, are not indelibly fixed but change through a process of interaction, thereby producing a new meaning. For example, because of all manner of associations and kindred concepts, the meaning of God, the principal referent, can be changed through its metaphorical interaction with the subsidiary referent, the sphere, to produce a third meaning that is equivalent to neither God nor the sphere.

For Rorty, the problem with these traditional theories is that they suggest metaphors can be used to make truth claims, that metaphors have a cognitive status. In the case of the substitution view, a metaphor's claim to truth rests on its ability to be checked against literal characteristics of the world. In the interaction view metaphors have a cognitive content because of their presumed ability to create a new meaning, a meaning that cannot be derived through any other means (Black, 1962, p. 42). In one sense, the two traditional theories are very different, but in another sense they offer a common view, one that Rorty rejects. For both claim that metaphors work because they can be grounded in something that guarantees knowledge (the literal or new metaphorical meaning, respectively).

In contrast, Rorty, following Davidson, argues that a metaphor has no meaning other than a literal one, which is "usually a patent falsehood or an absurd truth" (Davidson, 1979, p. 41). This does not mean that metaphors are not helpful but just that one cannot speak about them sensibly in cognitive terms because by their very definition they are outside agreed-upon canons of meaning. As Davidson (1979, p. 41) writes, "What distinguishes metaphor is not meaning but use." And that use is in changing our beliefs through the jolt, the *frisson*, that a novel metaphor can produce. As Rorty writes about Davidson, he "lets us see metaphors on the model of unfamiliar events in the natural world—*causes* of changing beliefs and desires—rather than on the model of *representations* of unfamiliar worlds" (Rorty, 1987, p. 284). Metaphors, precisely because they are patently false and absurd, cause us to stop and think and thereby possibly lead us to do different things than we have done in the past. Furthermore, the reason that metaphors surprise us is not because they have some special cognitive status but because they have none at all; if they had that status, they would not be surprising. As Rorty (1991a, p. 13) writes, "A metaphor is, so to speak, a voice from outside logical space."

For Rorty, the importance of metaphors is that they change the conversation in interesting ways. Coining a new metaphor—for example, that people interact over space as planets do in the celestial system or thinking of the landscape as a palimpsest—can produce vivacious talk, an interesting turn in the dialogue. But to account for that vivacity, one cannot draw upon traditional theories of metaphor. For they suppose that "reactions to metaphors a[re] dictated by rules, or conventions," whereas for Rorty asking how metaphors work is like asking " 'What is the nature of the unexpected?' or 'How do surprises work?' " (Rorty, 1987, p. 289).

One of the consequences of continuing the conversation by coining new metaphors is that eventually those live metaphors become dead ones; the initial murkiness of the metaphor is cleaned up as it is systematized, unpacked, and grounded. As a result, metaphors in the end become equivalent to the literal. Or to use Quine's (1979, p. 160) own incisive metaphor, "The neatly worked inner stretches of science are an open space in the tropical jungle, created by clearing tropes away." In Rorty's terms, of course, all that happens as we move from live metaphors to dead ones is that we shift from hermeneutics to epistemology. By agreeing that the metaphor is useful, is coping well, we can use it to talk to one another without causing any consternation. It is only when the metaphor is still alive that we must be hermeneutical, holding back our objections until we see how it fares. Furthermore, by being hermeneutical here we are also being liberal. For the liberal aspiration

> amounts to the hope that every new metaphor will have its chance for self-sacrifice, a chance to become a dead metaphor by having been literalized into the language. More specifically, it is the hope that what Dewey calls "the crust of convention" will be as superficial as possible, . . . that things will go better for everybody if every new metaphor is given a hearing. (Rorty, 1991a, p. 18)

The twin liberal hopes of democracy and social change thus come together in those open-ended conversations where new metaphors are coined and are given the chance to prove their mettle.

ECONOMIC GEOGRAPHY AND METAPHOR: THE CASE OF THE GRAVITY MODEL

What does such this examination of metaphors have to do with economic geography? In one sense everything, but in another sense nothing. Everything because as we think about even the recent history of the discipline, it is the history of different metaphors—places are points of mass that interact (Stewart and Warntz, 1958), places are maps that we store in our heads (Gould and White, 1974), places are deposits of dead labor time secreted from the circular flow of capital (Harvey, 1982), places are geological strata of past investments (Massey, 1984b), places are poles of flexible linkages (Storper and Scott, 1988). For each of these metaphors there has been an initial period of hermeneutics during which some people criticize, others reserve judgment, and yet others enthuse. This is followed by another period during which people become epistemological—distance decay parameters are measured for the nth time, mental maps make their way into textbooks, David Harvey receives medals of achievement from the king of Sweden and the Association of American Geographers, the journal *Environment and Planning A* (1990) devotes a whole issue to locality studies, and very large sums of money are spent on conferences around the world to discuss the reality of flexible specialization. More broadly, what is happening is that live metaphors are becoming dead ones;

the initial metaphors are being equated with the literal. Of course not all metaphors go through this complete process. Many metaphors do not even pass to the hermeneutical stage; they are simply ignored. In this sense, we might also say the history of economic geography is the history of armfuls of forgotten metaphors.

Where Rorty's metaphorical talk has nothing to offer economic geography is with respect to the social practices in which economic geographers' metaphors are necessarily embedded. In other words, Rorty does not say much that is interesting about process. Why is it that some metaphors, such as gravity models, are accepted, while others, such as Lukermann's (1966) circulation manifold, are all but ignored? Why is it that some metaphors, such as core and periphery, are very fruitful, while others, such as travel as light refraction (Warntz, 1957), appear as dead ends? Why is it that some metaphors are repeated with different intonations, such as life cycle, while others are confined only to one main use, such as "dummy" variable? And why is it that metaphorical redescription often takes so long—for example, the 300 years that it took before human geographers metaphorically employed Newton's *Principia*? These types of questions, though, are the most interesting for economic geographers. In one sense, because he was a nonfoundationalist, we can perhaps understand Rorty's silence here. Having settled the issue of the cognitive status of metaphor, he had nothing more to say. But for economic geographers, there remains everything to say.

In particular, there are at least three broad issues that should be considered when scrutinizing the use of metaphors within the actual practice of economic geography. To illustrate them, we turn to the example of the gravity model. For to say that $I_{ij} = P_i P_j d_{ij}^{-\alpha}$ is *like* the process of traveling to work or to shops or to holiday resorts is to make a metaphorical claim (Barnes, 1989a).

First, following Rorty's nonfoundational approach, we must show that the importance of the metaphor is not in its meaning but in its use. To demonstrate that the metaphor has no intrinsic meaning, it is necessary to show that it does not represent some essential truth, that the gravity model is not somehow, as Galileo put it in referring to mathematics, "nature's own language." To do so requires disputing the kinds of justifications put forward for the gravity model, of which there have been two: an empirical one—the empirical world naturally expresses itself in terms of the relationships represented by the gravity model; and a rationalist one—the gravity model is true because it is rooted in a set of logically consistent axioms expressed in mathematical terms.

The empirical justification is often made on the grounds of the model's high predictive ability. But such predictability and the very estimation methods used have been criticized on a number of grounds.

For one, prediction is not the same as explanation, with the consequence that the model is overidentified (Olsson, 1970) and therefore cannot be the one true representation of reality. Second, the very methods used to obtain prediction are frequently technically inaccurate and misspecified, implying that it is impossible to test unambiguously whether interaction really conforms to the inverse distance law (for a lucid review of such problems, see Sheppard, 1984). Finally, even the predictive power of the gravity model itself is questionable given the need to recalibrate it for each new study. Furthermore, the results obtained are often directly counter to the expectations of the model, for example, the finding of positive distance exponents (for this and other anomalous results, see Fotheringham, 1981). The upshot is that it is hard to justify the gravity model empirically when its very nature mitigates direct and unequivocal testing and produces empirical results that undermine the model itself.

The rationalist justification of the gravity model, in contrast, is couched in terms of the abstract calculus of rational choice theory (Sheppard, 1978; Fotheringham and O'Kelly, 1989). In this view, spatial interaction is the consequence of someone's *choosing* to travel to maximize utility, where the gravity model represents the aggregate of all those individual travel choices. By beginning with the axioms of rational choice theory, an explanation (as opposed to description) of spatial interaction is provided, but there remain both technical and conceptual problems. Of the three choice-theoretical approaches that have been used to justify the gravity model, Sheppard (1978) formally demonstrates the logical inconsistencies of deterministic utility theory and models of probabilistic choice with constant utility, while Fotheringham and O'Kelly (1989, pp. 74–76) do the same for the third approach, rational choice with stochastic utilities. Furthermore, even if these technical difficulties and problems of logic were resolved, the interaction theorist would still only be left with the *Homo economicus* assumption, an assumption that I've already argued is riddled with problems of internal consistency (Chapters Two and Three; Hindess, 1988). In short, a rationalist justification of the gravity model based upon logical impeccability has yet to be realized, and if the critics of rational choice theory are to be believed, it will never be realized.

To then demonstrate that the metaphor's meaning is in its use, we must in addition show that it allows people to do things that they could never have done before. In particular, we can see the move toward the gravity model in economic geography as a reaction against an old and entrenched vocabulary that limited questions about, for example, explanation and prediction, to a half-formed new one that at the time promised great things. For this reason, it is not surprising that there was so much enthusiasm, even an evangelical zeal, in that early literature on the gravity model (Gould, 1979). People like Stewart, Warntz, and Carrothers had not only been innovative but lucky. By metaphorically redescribing geographical things in terms of physical models, they found that they could use statistical methods, make predictions, publish in scientific journals, speak authoritatively about scientific explanation, and more besides. The more general point is that in hindsight the gravity model metaphor was pragmatic, not cognitive. It did not reveal the Truth, but it enabled economic geographers to look at the world in a different way and do many things that they could not have done before.

The second broad issue is that there is a history, sociology, and even geography to metaphor use that needs to be explored. Metaphors do not just suddenly emerge but are a response to the context in which academics live and work. In the previous chapter I described that context for Warntz. In addition, the metaphor can become a rallying cry for new communities within a discipline, where the formation and maintenance of such communities has its own sociology; that is, the sociology of moving from hermeneutics to epistemology. Taylor (1976) describes such a process well for the case of the quantitative revolution in geography in general and the use of theoretical models, such as the gravity model, in particular: during the early 1960s, through their vocabulary, their new journals, and their rapid rise in academic institutions, the young Turks were able to wrest power from an old guard, thereby reshaping the discipline along the lines of the new metaphors. In this sense, Harvey's (1969) aphorism was misconceived; it should have been "by our metaphors you shall know us." Discussions of the context of metaphorical redescription are important here in at least two ways. They show why people were persuaded to adopt the new metaphor in their academic conversations. That is, such discussions speak to the rhetorical power of metaphors. For example, there was something about the broader context of society, especially the institution of human geography, that made gravity equations convincing in the 1950s but make them less so now. But they also show why metaphors come out the way they do. Thus, that Stewart (1958, p. 153) was a physicist made a difference in how he conceived, for example, the mass and distance exponents of the gravity model; he wanted them to be set to one because for him space, time, and mass were fundamental physical dimensions, constants that were the same whether in geography or in physics (Lukermann and Porter, 1960, pp. 496–501; Olsson, 1965, p. 55).

If the context of metaphorical description is important for the two reasons given, then it becomes hard to sustain the distinction sometimes made in the philosophy of science between the context of discovery and the context of justification. This is an important point because it is sometimes argued that metaphors are useful only in initially generating an idea (the context of discovery), but once the idea is generated, science (the context of justification) supersedes. Thus, Alan Wilson (1969, p. 159) writes that "though part of the study may proceed through analogy, in the end the analogy must be thrown away." The position taken here, however, is that metaphor is central for both discovery *and* justification in science. Apart from the fact that science itself from the outset is metaphorically ingrained (Cameron, 1983; Arib and Hesse, 1986), it is also clear that the context of metaphorical redescription shapes the very nature of the justification process. For example, because of the different contexts, the physical metaphor of gravity was justified in a very different way in the late 1950s than, say, the physical metaphor of sedimentary rocks put forward by Doreen Massey (1984b) in the mid-1980s. The former was in the grip of science and used rigorous and formalized methods for justification; the latter was in the grip of politics and used arguments about power and social equity for justification.

Finally, there is a critical, even emancipatory, purpose in exploring metaphors. When metaphors die, it is easy to forget that they were once alive, initially surrounded by qualifications, hesitations, and reservations. As a consequence, while the first generation recognizes some of the limitations within a metaphor, the second generation often does not; caution can become stridency. For example, in his early review of gravity and potential models, Carrothers (1956, p. 99) is careful to delineate the differences between the physical and the social worlds, arguing that "a fundamental difficulty arises from the different nature of the two basic units involved: the individual human being can make decisions with respect to his actions, while the individual molecule presumably cannot" (for other examples, see Pfouts, 1958, p. 157, and Schneider, 1959, pp. 51–52). Such qualifications are conspicuous by their absence in later work. Furthermore, there are many cases where even initial proponents of the metaphor are not aware of all the intellectual freight it carries and that it therefore needs to be critically disinterred. Here Gunnar Olsson's (1980) early work is instructive. Within a decade Olsson moved from equating the gravity model with the literal to exhuming the metaphor that underlay it. In so doing, he brought to light implications that were hitherto hidden, implications that were epistemologically revealing and politically unsettling. Moreover, this critical disinterment of metaphors is not just an intellectual exercise, affecting only a few academics. Metaphors such as the gravity model have also had tremendous practical consequences as they were taken up by planners in Europe and North America after World War II and used to transform the lived landscapes of the everyday. In a very real sense, there is nothing trifling about a metaphor. The more general point is that we must continually think critically about the metaphors we use—where they came from, why they were proposed, whose interest they represent, and the nature of their implications. Not to do so can lead us to be the slaves of some defunct maker of metaphors.

CONCLUSION

In summary, my purpose in this chapter was to argue for taking metaphor seriously. In presenting that argument I turned to the work of Richard Rorty. For Rorty is doubly serious about metaphor. First, he sees the problems of his own discipline of philosophy as a result of inappropriate metaphor use and therefore solvable only through a metaphorical revolution; second, he offers a distinctive theory of metaphor that sees them not in foundational terms but rather as "unfamiliar uses of noises and marks . . . [that then] make us get busy developing a new theory" (Rorty, 1989, p. 17). But Rorty says nothing about the actual process by which metaphors are accepted, developed, and often disappear. Such issues, however, are generally the most interesting ones, and I addressed them in the latter part of this chapter.

Rorty's position, it should be noted, has been criticized, particularly by those on the political left (although even there he has some admirers; Resnick and Wolf, 1987; Graham, 1990). It is certainly true that Rorty pays insufficient attention to relations of power and the material conditions that sustain them. More broadly, he fails to recognize that the conversation can become a monologue. Nonetheless, the aspiration of a free-flowing debate where every metaphor has a chance at least to be heard is surely accepted by those on the left. Rorty's liberal hope is that this aspiration will become the reality, but even Rorty (1991b, p. fn. 29) recognizes that hope is sometimes thwarted. With the recent history of economic geography, the irony, given Rorty's anti-Marxist stance, is that his liberal hope may well depend upon critics from the left who continually undermine orthodoxy by inventing new metaphors and thereby prod the conversation in new and interesting directions.

Finally, in raising these issues about metaphors, I am neither trying to denigrate their use nor to say that there is another way out. They are just something that we are stuck with and stuck to. We can, though, try to be self-conscious about them. And for us as geographers, this means also that we need to be self-conscious about the nature of geography, for we require metaphors that illuminate the geographical imagination, not the imagination of sociology, economics, or physics.

SIX

PROBABLE WRITING
Derrida, Deconstruction,
and the Quantitative Revolution
in Economic Geography

The innocuous-sounding demand that there should be some
demonstration that mathematics formed a complete and consistent
whole . . . open[s] up a Pandora's box of problems. In one sense,
mathematical propositions . . . seem as true as anything could
possibly be true; in another, they appear as no more than marks on
paper.

—Andrew Hodges, *Alan Turing: The Enigma*

In his article "Mathematics and Geography," written at the height of the
quantitative revolution in geography, Cole (1969, p. 160) contrasted by
example the "verbal 'uncertainties' " of traditional regional geographical
writing with the precision afforded by mathematics.[1] The text he works
over is an extended passage (of which only a small extract is cited below)
taken from Stamp and Beaver's (1947) *British Isles* that discusses the
geography of wheat cultivation. Cole's comments on Stamp and Beaver's
original passage are in parentheses: "Broadly speaking (vague), it may be
said that the possible (vague) limits (limits) of cultivation of any crop are
determined by geographical (vague), primarily by climatic, conditions.
The limits so determined (how?) may be described (definition) as the
ultimate (vague) or the geographical (vague) limits" (Cole, 1969, p. 160).

He then compares this extract to his own rigorously derived summa-
rizing figure of the same phenomenon. Whereas Stamp and Beaver's
description is full of "imprecise verbal statements" and is characterized

by a "neglect of . . . meaning" (Cole, 1969, p. 163), Cole is scrupulous in both his precision and meaning. As a result, the British Isles are now divided into distinct subscripted spaces (S_i; $i = 1, \ldots, 5$); boundaries and limits are definitively marked; and although he does not carry out the project, Cole urges "the application of a standard correlation procedure" in order to counter Stamp's and Beaver's "tentative" conclusions that "leave the reader still wondering why wheat is grown where it is" (1969, p. 163). Cole (1969, p. 163) rhetorically concludes: "The reader is left to decide for himself to what extent the lengthy verbal description quoted above achieves what it sets out to do."

In this chapter, by drawing upon Derrida's idea of deconstruction, I want to raise precisely this same question about Cole's own mathematical approach. Can mathematics achieve all it sets out to do? The argument here is that it cannot. Cole's text, based upon formal logic and mathematical symbols, is no better in revealing the truth than Stamp and Beaver's. For as in all forms of writing, submerged beneath the ostensible clarity and precision of mathematics is a series of tropes, and rhetorical moves that subvert its central claims. Deconstruction is the means of subversion, where deconstruction is defined as the attempt "to reverse the imposing tapestry [of a text] in order to expose in all its unglamorously dishevelled tangle the threads constituting the well-heeled image it presents to the world" (Eagleton, 1986, p. 80).

For the purposes of this chapter, the texts to be deconstructed are some of the programmatic ones that formed the basis of the quantitative revolution in geography. My argument will be that those texts by reason of an inconsistency that lies at their heart cannot meet the ends that they assert. It should be noted that this type of criticism is different from that adopted during the 1970s by opponents of the quantitative revolution, primarily Marxist and humanistic geographers. Then, much of the criticism was not about the internal coherence of mathematics as a body of knowledge but rather its applicability in, for example, rendering political and social conflicts or representing the affective traits of humans. In contrast, my focus is on mathematics itself as a structured system of knowledge and its own *internal* aporias, blind spots, and dead ends. The external uses to which mathematics is put are thus secondary.

In carrying out this deconstruction, I also draw upon some of the recent literature on the sociology of mathematics. This is a necessary addition to Derrida's account, for as Bernstein (1991, p. 225) writes, Derrida's analyses "need to be *supplemented* by the theoretical and empirical study of societal institutions and practices . . . [because] his own understanding of society and politics . . . [is] rather 'thin.' " In particular, by augmenting it with institutional and historical details about the practices of mathematicians, we make Derridean deconstruction thicker in the sense that we begin to understand how mathematicians come to believe the things that they do and the authority by which those beliefs are sustained. More generally, by including institutional practices, we are able to follow the processes by which the instability of meaning is transformed into something that is fixed and stable.

The chapter is divided into four sections. First, I discuss Derrida and deconstruction. Second, I review the various reasons geographers have cited for employing mathematics in geography. I will suggest that those factors are in Derrida's terms "presences" that form the basis of the attempt to create a logocentric system based on mathematics. Third, I take a first cut at deconstruction by arguing that such "presences" are not attainable, and this is reflected in the contradictions found within the very presences that are asserted. In making this argument, I rely heavily on the literature of the sociology of mathematical knowledge, and in particular Bloor's (1983, 1991) work and his reading of Wittgenstein. Such an addition, I argue, provides the institutional focus that is absent from Derrida's scheme. Finally, I take a second cut at deconstruction by examining the failure of inferential statistics in geography. The argument is that lying behind inferential statistics is not some final presence but a particular metaphor, in this case one based upon eugenics. Even leaving aside the potential internal problems within this metaphor, I will suggest that its importation into geography proved a failure because it came into contradiction with other metaphors traditionally used to define the discipline.

DERRIDA AND DECONSTRUCTION

Writing about Derrida is unsettling because his aim is to question the very project of writing, including writing about him. For this reason, as Lawson (1985, p. 92) suggests, "Many who have tried to give an account of Derrida have begun with a consideration of how to begin, or of how the account itself should be read." The resulting self-consciousness, which will also be found here, is therefore not simply academic pretentiousness or tediousness (although it may also be that) but reflects Derrida's central concerns.

That self-consciousness is certainly evident in the discussions that surround the term "deconstruction." Although it is the central theme of this chapter, defining the word is difficult. Even Derrida is doubtful. He writes, "Deconstruction loses nothing from admitting that it is impossible" (Derrida, 1991, p. 209); or again, "deconstruction" is "a word I have never liked and one whose fortune has disagreeably surprised me" (Derrida, 1983, p. 44). This said, since the early 1980s or so a small cottage industry has grown up around interpreting the term. There have been two main strategies: either writing in nontraditional ways (often about the works of others) to show deconstruction by example, thereby circumscribing the necessity of a definitive definition (in geography this strategy is seen in Olsson, 1991, and Doel, 1993); or beginning with a clear definition, realizing that it is potentially subject to later deconstruction (this is best found in the work of Culler, 1983, and also Lawson, 1985, and Norris, 1987). I will follow the second route, although there is a point when the two strategies must necessarily converge. For even the most outlandish writing will need to make its meaning clear if it is not to be simply ink marks on a page, and even the most limpid writing must eventually become turgid if it is, to use Rorty's (1989, p. 124, fn. 6) phrase, "to eff the ineffable."

Logocentrism, Presence, and Deconstruction

One of Derrida's persistent themes is the philosopher's hankering for oral communication over its written form. The reason for this hankering is the belief that speech is a more direct means for representing the world than is written language. The underlying assumption is that spoken words are directly linked to the moment of experience, that is, they are contemporaneous with the events themselves and are therefore their most accurate representation. This contrasts with the kind of world that emerges from writing, which is hopelessly mired in the various tropes—metaphors, similes, puns, metonyms, oxymorons, and so on—that constitute written language. Thus, while written language distorts, obfuscates, and corrupts reality, the spoken word is translucent and transparent, providing immediate access to experience. Given the historical quest for clarity and certainty in Western philosophy, it follows that whatever philosophy is, it cannot be a kind of writing (Rorty, 1982, ch. 6). As Culler (1983, p. 92) writes, "Philosophy defines itself as what transcends writing, and by identifying certain aspects of the functioning of language with writing, tries to rid itself of these problems by setting writing aside as simply an artificial substitute for speech."

This impulse to privilege speech over writing is part of an even more fundamental project by philosophers that Derrida terms logocentrism. This is the assertion that the world is fundamentally ordered, that at bottom there is some foundation to knowledge beyond which we need not go, such as rationality, logic, truth, or the spoken word. As Rorty (1991a, p. 89) puts it, "The dream at the heart of philosophy . . . [is] the hope for a language which can receive no gloss, requires no interpretation, cannot be distanced, cannot be sneered at by later generations. It is the hope for a vocabulary which is intrinsically and self-evidently final." Now, different philosophies privilege different things in formulating that final vocabulary (*logos*), but the strategy of constructing the resulting logocentric system is the same: to create a "metaphysics of presence." By that term Derrida means that in order to assert their claims about knowledge, philosophers "rel[y] on the assumption of an immediately available arena of certainty. This origin and foundation of their theories is presence" (Lawson, 1985, p. 96). So behind any word or concept or theory (signifiers) is some bedrock presence that is constant and unmediated. For example, this might be direct experience, as in phenomenology, or pieces of the factual world, as in positivism. The broader point is that any logocentric system gains its power by linking its knowledge claims to a particular presence or origin point.

The problem, though, as Derrida argues, is that we are unable to gain access to that presence, and as a result all logocentric systems are without foundations. Ultimately this is because we are unable to escape language and thus locate some final presence that lies outside of it. Language and the tropes and rhetorical devices contained therein continually frustrate us. It is here that deconstruction is so important because it is the means by which the disruptive effects of language on any logocentric project are revealed.

Specifically, deconstruction breaks the link between presence and the logocentric system by showing that the presence that is asserted is undermined by other definitions within the logocentric system itself. A useful illustration is Culler's (1983, pp. 85–89) example of cause and effect, which in turn comes from Nietzsche. Much of science rests on the assertion that causes precede effects. In this sense, the logocentric system of science rests on the presence of causality. As Nietzsche argued, however, that sequence rests upon a particular tropological operation within language. Suppose we feel a pain in our arm. That then leads us to look for a cause, say, a pinprick. However, instead of repeating this perceptual order—pain (effect) then pinprick (cause)—we reverse the logic and say pinprick then pain. In order to make that switch, what we have done is to engage in metonymy by substituting the cause for the effect. But if the cause–effect nexus rests on a rhetorical move, then in what sense are cause and effect fundamentally present?

There are two points to note about this example. First, the questioning of the presence of causality is carried out from within the system of causality itself, in this case by raising doubts about the original hierarchical ordering of the two central terms. As a result, "deconstruction appeals to no higher logical principle or superior reason but uses the very principle it deconstructs" (Culler, 1983, p. 87). Deconstruction, then, represents an acute form of reflexive criticism, one that uses the meaning of a term to disrupt that meaning. Second, that disruption is made by showing that relationships we thought were somehow outside of language are in fact inside language. In the above example, cause and effect are produced by the trope of metonymy.

This is only one example, but it is reflective of the strategy of deconstruction in general: to isolate pivotal distinctions, distinctions that provide the basis of presences for the entire logocentric system, and then showing that they are inconsistent and paradoxical because of the rhetorical moves that are necessary to construct them. In this way "the text is seen to fall by its own criteria—the standards or definitions which the text sets up are used reflexively to unsettle and shatter the original distinctions" (Lawson, 1985, p. 93).

But why is this possible? For Derrida, it is because presences can never be unambiguously identified. This is so for two reasons. First, the meaning of words and concepts (signifiers) can never be directly tied to particular things (signifieds). As Derrida shows in his writings, the meaning of a signifier is never fully determined. For meaning is derived from a signifier's position with respect to *all* other signifiers in the system. According to Harland (1987, p. 135), "In Derrida's conception, one signifier points away to another signifier, which in turn points away to another signifier, which in turn points away to another signifier, and so on *ad infinitum*." There is no anchor of some final presence or some ultimate origin point of meaning. Meaning, rather, is always produced through displacement and deferral, shaped as much by what is absent as by what is present. To describe this process, Derrida employs a variety of terms such as "*différance*," "trace," and "supplement." Each has a particular role within Derrida's scheme, but they all point to the unstable production of meaning. Turning to the second related issue, if meaning comes only from orchestration of signifiers, which are not tied to signifieds, then that system of signifiers is inescapable. Derrida (1976, p. 158) writes that we

> cannot legitimately transgress the text toward something other than it, toward the referent (a reality that is metaphysical, historical, psychobiographical, etc.) or toward a signified outside the text whose content could take place, could have taken place outside of language, that is to say, in the sense that we give here to that word outside of writing in general. . . . There is nothing outside of the text.

The consequence of both these arguments is to deny identification of an unimpeachable presence. For if there is no ultimate signified and only a shifting system of signifiers that is inescapable, there can only ever be the flux of meaning and no constant presence. But if there is no presence, there can never be any consistent logocentric systems. It is precisely this "(im)possibility" that deconstruction seeks to reveal.

Reflexivity and the Other

If these are the details of Derrida's work, what are some of its broader features? The first is reflexivity, an issue that haunts Derrida as well as anyone who writes about his work. As Rorty (1991a) argues, Derrida is always trying to name the unnamable, to say something about logocentric systems without invoking another logocentric system. This is the reason for his neologisms such as *différance*,[2] or his puns or his attempts at erasure through crossing out words that already exist on the page. They are his way of trying to construct a scheme that is not a scheme, because as soon as it is a scheme then all he is giving us is yet another bankrupt logocentric system. But can Derrida maintain this reflexivity? Some such as Lawson (1985) and Norris (1987) think that he can through a continual deconstruction of his deconstructions. Rorty, however, is less sanguine, at least about Derrida's early work, which "sometimes goes in for word magic" (Rorty, 1989, p. 124, fn. 6). Even Rorty, though, admits that Derrida's later writings are more successful because he "creat[es] a style rather than . . . inventing neologisms" (Rorty, 1989, p. 124, fn. 6). By that Rorty means that Derrida now writes in a way that is unique, that cannot be copied; it is a system without a system. The implication, though, is that there can be no writing based upon Derrida's work as such (including this chapter) because that would imply that Derrida has provided some kind of logocentric system on which a text could be based. There is no escape from this dilemma, and Derrida recognizes that even he is not exempt. This is why he says paradoxically that deconstruction is impossible. All we can do is point to the impossibility of closure, while recognizing the closure implied in that very claim. In this sense, it is the warning rather than the solution that is perhaps most important (Bernstein, 1991, ch. 6).

Second, Derrida's antipathy to any final closure makes his work both anti-essentialist and antifoundationalist. But he is not therefore an idealist; in fact, he ironically calls himself a "radical empiricist." His claim is that we can never have direct access to things in and of themselves. This is because in order to understand those terms, they must already be expressed in language. But if they are part of language, then their meaningfulness only comes about through a play of difference among signifiers, which, as Derrida has already shown, exclude any fundamental signifieds or presences. As Lawson (1985, p. 100) writes, "All we have is a collection of meanings, and even then there are no fixed meanings. There is no independent signified, the signified being always merely part of the play of the signifiers." So it is not that Derrida disbelieves in the empirical word but rather that he believes in it so much that he does not imbue it with characteristics that it can never possess, such as signifying itself in its own terms.

Finally, and this is also goes against any charges of philosophical idealism, Bernstein (1991) argues that Derrida is passionately concerned with ethics and politics, and in particular the fate of the Other, the exiled, and the disenfranchised. In Bernstein's (1991, p. 184) terms, "Few contemporary thinkers have been so alert and perceptive about the temptations and dangers of violently crushing or silencing differences, otherness or alterity—in 'others' or even the 'other' in ourselves"—hence, as we have already seen, Derrida's suspicion of presence or a final vocabulary or a single meaning. These are all examples of trying to master the world. But Derrida's task is always to raise questions about such mastery: presences depend upon absences, meaning depends upon difference, and final vocabularies are never final.

Missing from these accounts of the suppression of otherness, however, is little sense of on-the-ground, institutional practice. Bernstein accounts for this "lacuna" by pointing to Derrida's lack of engagement with the social sciences and their institutional analysis of power and authority. Adding an emphasis on institutional practice to Derrida's work would help not only in understanding the fate of the Other, but also in comprehending how meaning is fixed more generally. For although there may not be any single presence underlying meaning, much of social life is carried out on the conviction that it is. Still, lying behind those convictions are often ingrained institutional practices, practices that need critical inspection. By examining the use of mathematics in geography, I attempt in the remainder of this chapter both to carry out a deconstructive critique and to fill in the institutional lacuna.

THE FINAL VOCABULARY OF ECONOMIC GEOGRAPHY: THE QUANTITATIVE REVOLUTION

The broad lineaments of human geography's quantitative revolution are well known (Gregory, 1978; Cloke, Philo, and Sadler, 1991; Johnston, 1991). The quantitative movement began in earnest in human geography with the use of bivariate statistics in the late 1950s, flourished through the 1960s, but from the early 1970s onward waned, and by the 1980s, in spite of some revisionist readings (for example, Wrigley and Bennett, 1981) was increasingly marginalized (see Cox, 1989, p. 205 for a slightly different interpretation). That marginalization, however, was primarily in terms of its power to shape the discipline. As a set of practical techniques, quantitative methods continue to be widely used, and for some scholars they are still the object of research.[3] So although down, quantitative methods are not yet out (in fact, quantitative methods remain the path to salvation for some; see Getis, 1993, and Casetti, 1993). Following Derrida, I argue in this section that the attraction of quantitative methods for many human geographers was, and for some continues to be, that they offer a final vocabulary.

Before examining the basis of that final vocabulary, I should clarify two points. First, I include within the term "quantitative methods" both pure and applied forms of mathematics, as well as geometry and formal logic. This wide definition simply reflects the breadth of usage of the term by its practitioners (exceptions, though, are Bunge's, 1966, specific plea for geometry, and Wilson's, 1972, special advocacy of pure mathematics). Second, although there is a clear intellectual overlap between quantitative methods and the more general tenets of spatial science, the two are not identical. As a result, my critique is limited only to those specific arguments within spatial science that are predicated upon quantification and mathematicization.

In reading the programmatic statements of the early quantitative geographers, we can see that their aim was to construct a logocentric system. The basis of the application of mathematics was the supposition that its order fundamentally mirrored the order of the world. Furthermore, mathematics offered the prospect of being the most logocentric system of all because it virtually dispensed with writing altogether. This is the upshot of Cole's article cited above. As he writes, mathematical methods provide an "economy of space or conciseness" (Cole, 1969, p. 155). More generally, echoing the philosophers, Cole saw written language as fundamentally obfuscatory. This was the reason he annotated Stamp and Beaver's work with all those disparaging adjectives. His task was to extirpate any ambiguity or uncertainty by using quantitative methods. Cole, of course, was not alone in these views, and from his writings and those of others, it is possible to identify five underlying features that provided mathematics with the certainty required to be a final vocabulary.

Universal Truth

It was contended that mathematics possessed a *universal truth*. Harvey (1969, p. 179) wrote that mathematical "systems provide an objective and universal language for discussing geographical problems." Or as Garrison (1956, p. 428) noted, "Statistical methods are written in the universal language of mathematics." Such an assertion was often followed by the claim that this universality allowed the different branches of geography to be united under one vocabulary, therefore permitting it to share its results with other disciplines that were similarly mathematically inclined (Gregory, 1971, p. 32). Anuchin (1973, p. 54), for example, wrote that "mathematics is being transformed into the 'esperanto' of scientists, [with the result that] the formalization of problems increases the mutual understanding amongst geographers of quite different branches, and this secures a better knowledge of the whole discipline." Bunge (1966, p. 201) goes further and even redefines the internal structure of geography in terms of the mathematics of geometry. Historical, social, and economic geography were to be replaced by the geographies of lines, points, and surfaces. This was possible because mathematics was a universal language that cut across the subject matter of all disciplines and subdisciplines.

Logical Inference

Another feature of quantitative method is its role in developing consistent theory through *logical inference*. The premise here is that if mathematics is based on sound logic, then the reasoning of its users would be, too. As Gregory (1971, p. 30) put it, the function of the quantitative approach "is to facilitate thinking according to a certain internally-coherent logic rather than sitting, waiting for inspiration to arrive from on high." Or as Bunge (1966, p. 36) wrote, "The essential point is that mathematics provides the logical framework on which we can build theory." It was Peter Haggett, though, who was most optimistic about the potential of logic. He concluded his seminal *Locational Analysis in Human Geography* by remarking, "Although we may intuitively shy from a system which threatens to reduce 'Ophelia loves Hamlet' to H → O, the rigour of the axiomatic method has a powerful attraction. . . . In the long run the quality of geography in this century will be judged less by its sophisticated techniques or its exhaustive detail, than by the strength of its logical reasoning" (Haggett, 1965b, p. 310). In particular, that logic was seen as necessary in order to avoid inconsistencies and to derive ironclad deductions from a set of premises (Burton, 1963, p. 157). In turn both these features of logic were a necessary complement to the successful application of the hypothetico-deductive method, touted as the primary vehicle for attaining scientific theory at the time (Harvey, 1969).

Objectivity

Mathematics is *objective* in the sense that its users were prevented from smuggling into their work subjective views or those that were value-laden (Burton, 1963, p. 157). One could therefore be confident that there was neither self-deception nor the deception of others. This is because the rules of mathematical inference were not only correct but public, in the sense that anyone could repeat the same operations and arrive at an identical result. This was not so with ordinary language. As Gregory (1971, p. 26), wrote: "Any particular conclusion on interpretation arrived at [by personalized assessment] . . . may well be perfectly correct and one hundred per cent valid—it may equally be utterly wrong and one hundred per cent invalid, but no one can prove this one way or the other, for it depends upon personal inference." Mathematics, because it is open to all, avoids such personalization.

Simplification of Reality

Mathematics allows for the *simplification of reality*, making it understandable. Wilson (1972, p. 32) wrote, for example, "In the case of some complicated systems, explanation can only be adequately achieved with the help of mathematical language." Or as Anuchin (1973, p. 55) suggested, "Mathematics can, and should, be used in all cases when the questions facing one are sufficiently complex to demand the creation of their own mathematical symbolism and specialized sequence of solutions (algorithms)." The rationale is that there is a clarity and logic to mathematics that imposes an order that is immediately graspable, an order that is lost in the quagmire of the vernacular.

Precision, Conciseness, and Efficiency

A final feature, and probably the one most often cited, is couched in such terms as *"precision," "conciseness,"* and *"efficiency."* This, of course, was Cole's main objection to Stamp and Beaver's work. He writes, "A difference between everyday language and mathematics is the need for precise definitions, rather than approximate ones. The distinction is between the emotional and the factual" (Cole, 1969, p. 154). Or as Gregory (1971, p. 30) noted, mathematics "can help remove the vagueness and the imprecision that has characterized much of geography of the past by allowing concepts to be presented in an unambiguous form" (see also Bunge 1966, p. 2, and Harvey, 1969, p. 189). Mathematics is the most exact of vocabularies, written language the most inexact.

These five characteristics of mathematics—universality, logicalness, objectivity, simplification, and precision—formed the basis of the geographer's final vocabulary. In Derrida's terms, they were the presences—the claims to foundational security—on which the logocentric systems were constructed. By following the spirit if not the word of Derrida, I will try to show that such presences rest upon certain internal contradictions, aporias, that prevent them from being ultimately realized as full and complete, thereby disrupting the quantitative logocentric project. Such contradictions were not recognized, at least until much later, because of deep-seated institutional practices. This point applies both to mathematics in general (which is examined in the next section) and more specifically to users of quantitative methods within geography (examined in the last section).

A FIRST CUT AT DECONSTRUCTION: MATHEMATICAL WRITING IN GENERAL

If the five features of mathematics discussed above are fundamental presences in the sense used by Derrida, then it should be possible to deconstruct them by turning their definitions against themselves. It is with this task that I am concerned in this section.

To assert that mathematics is a universal vocabulary implies that it holds for all times and places. Given this definition, however, it is difficult to imagine that anyone could assert universality with any warrant. For the person making such a claim is necessarily restricted in both time and place and therefore unable to know unequivocally if her or his claims possess universal validity. Mathematicians deal with this seeming contradiction by drawing upon one of two kinds of justification, each of which in turn rests upon a particular metaphor. The first is Platonism (or realism, Bloor, 1973, p. 176), which is based on the metaphor of a "hidden world," and the second is logicism or formalism, predicated upon the metaphor of a "foundation" (Davis and Hersh, 1980, pp. 330–338).

Platonists argue that mathematics is universal in the sense that its logic and rules exist outside of human practices, in another world; we then simply observe that world, writing down what we see (Bloor, 1983, pp. 83–89). As the mathematician G. H. Hardy (1967, pp. 123–124, quoted in Bloor, 1983, p. 84) wrote, "I believe that mathematical reality lies outside us, that our function is to discover or *observe* it, and then the theorems which we prove, and which we describe grandiloquently as our 'creations' are simply our notes of our observations." The metaphor Hardy draws upon here is that of a preexisting hidden world that becomes observable when we carry out the operations of mathematics (Bloor, 1973, p. 177). Thus, 4 + 4 = 8 because it is already inscribed in the hidden world; all we have done is to "trace out what was already faintly written down" (Bloor, 1983, p. 85). Such a metaphor, though, fails on its own terms because it presumes that we already know that this hidden world is the right hidden world. Wittgenstein (1964, pt. 1, para. 3), in his *Remarks on the Foundations of Mathematics*, makes this critique by using as an example the rule "add 2" to form the progressive series 2, 4, 6, 8, ... For Platonists, this series already exists, and we simply copy its outline. But Wittgenstein asks, How do we know that we are following the right series when using the "add 2" rule unless we already know the correct answer? More generally, the trouble with the hidden-world metaphor is that it is predicated upon circular reasoning: to know whether the hidden world provides correct answers, we must already know what the correct answers are, but it was those correct answers that the hidden world was supposed to reveal.

Formalists and logicists fare no better. David Hilbert representing the former and Bertrand Russell the latter both attempted to show that mathematics could be constructed upon the universal foundation of logic. In metaphorical terms logic is the bedrock, the necessary foundation, of any true mathematical claims. Specifically, Russell claimed that all true mathematical propositions could be derived from set theory, which in turn could be reduced to elementary logical propositions, while Hilbert argued that "every 'correct proof' of a classical theorem could be represented by a formal determination, starting from axioms, with each step mechanically checkable" (Davis and Hersh, 1980, p. 335). The use of the foundation metaphor, however, was soon shown to be inappropriate. Russell himself established various contradictions within set theory (the best known of which is the "Russell paradox"[4]; Davis and Hersh, 1980, p. 332), and Hilbert's formalist project was denied by Gödel's incompleteness theorem. That theorem states that "given any set of axioms for a system strong enough to express arithmetic, there exists sentences true in arithmetic which are *formally* underivable from that system" (Mirowski, 1986b, p. 184). In both cases, then, logic was not a sufficient foundation to assert universality. There are always some mathematical statements that are not derivable from logical propositions. In Derrida's terms, logic fails as a final metaphysics of presence because it does not produce a closed logocentric system; there is always a residue of meaning that cannot be accounted for by those supposed foundations.

The upshot of both these sets of criticism, as Kline (1980, p. 6) writes, is "that the concept of a universally accepted, infallible body of reasoning—the majestic mathematics of 1800 and the pride of man—is a grand illusion." Rather than believing that mathematics is a logocentric system based upon a presence such as universality, we would do better to view it as a set of local institutional practices that arose historically and cannot be formulated under a single system. This is Wittgenstein's position (Bloor, 1983, ch. 5). Rather than forming all of a piece, derived from a single origin point, mathematics proceeds finitely, step by step. Wittgenstein believes that "mathematical conviction might be [thus] put in the form, 'I recognize this as analogous to that' . . . [where "recognize" means] the acceptance of a convention" (Wittgenstein, 1976, pp. 62–63, quoted in Bloor, 1983, p. 95). Wittgenstein uses the terms "analogy" and "convention" to signal that mathematics is not preformed and inexorable but is something that humans have made up. As a result, there is no unfolding of a single ineluctable mathematical logic; instead, the mathematical truths we hold are simply institutionalized but not yet questioned. Mathematical proofs are not proofs in any universal sense but are accepted only because they are endorsed by the prevailing institutional standards, rules, and authorities of the time. As Bloor (1983, p. 92) writes,

> The compelling force of mathematic[s] . . . derive[s] . . . from being accepted and used by a group of people. The procedures are not accepted because they are correct, or correspond to an ideal; they are deemed correct because they are accepted. Mathematical truth, said Wittgenstein, is . . . established . . . because we agree that "we lay it down as a rule, and put it in the archives."

The second feature of mathematics is its supposed logical rigor, which in turn allows its users to derive consistent theories. Again, as with the idea of universality, there is a contradiction within the very system of logical deduction: there is no logical compulsion to be logical. That is, there is nothing within logic itself that compels us to move logically from one statement to another. That we think otherwise is only because we believe that there is no alternative within the language we are using. As Bloor (1983, p. 112) puts it, "The *must* of logic is a track laid down in language."

There have been a number of justifications proposed for the use of logic, but according to Bloor (1983, p. 118), "all of them fail." For brevity's sake, only two justifications are examined and criticized here (see Bloor, 1983, ch. 6, for the full blow-by-blow analysis and critique). First, there is an appeal to the principles of logical deduction. Logic is justified by the claim that it is the best means for making logical inferences, including inferences about logic. So the move from the major and minor premises to the conclusion within a logical syllogism is justified on the grounds that it is the logical thing to do. This, however, is a circular argument. For in this case "the justification of deduction . . . presuppose[s] deduction . . . [by] appeal[ing] to the very principles of inference that are in question" (Barnes and Bloor, 1982, p. 41). The second justification is based upon appealing to some rule that is not based upon logical deduction. The problem here, though, is one of an infinite regress. As Wittgenstein showed, once we establish any rule-based inquiry we are left with the problem of needing a rule for the rule, then a rule for the rule for the rule, and so on. In sum, both these arguments indicate that there is no compelling reason for making logical deductions in a scheme of logical deduction; deduction fails by its own criteria.

If logic is not a set of ironclad rules for deriving ironclad conclusions, then what is it, and why do we feel compelled to follow its track? For Wittgenstein, logic is simply the steps in the argument that are not questioned: "Isn't it like this: so long as one thinks it can't be otherwise, one draws logical conclusions" (Wittgenstein, 1964, pt. 1, p. 155, quoted in Bloor, 1983, p. 112). The reason "one thinks it can't be otherwise" is, in Derrida's account at least, because of the persuasive force of language, which is riddled with various kinds of tropes. However, such tropes are never stable enough to support some final metaphysics of presence. They always unravel in ways already seen. That such tropes are so deeply embedded is a result of institutional support and authority. In this sense, we follow logic because of ingrained institutional habits. As Barnes and Bloor (1982, p. 45) conclude,

> Logic is a learned body of scholarly lore, growing and varying over time. It is a mass of conventional routines, decisions, expedient reconstructions, dicta, maxims and *ad hoc* rules. The sheer *lack* of necessity in granting its assumptions or adopting its strange and elaborate definitions is the point that should strike any candid observer. . . . As a body of conventions and esoteric traditions the compelling character of logic, such as it is, derives from certain narrowly defined purposes, and from custom and institutionalized usage. Its authority is moral and social. . . . In particular, the credibility of logical conventions, just like the everyday practices which deviate from them, will be of an entirely local character.

The third issue is objectivity, which is typically presented as a contrast between subjective and objective statements. So mathematics is an objective inquiry in the sense that individual numbers do not depend upon individual subjective states because if they did, there would be as many meanings of, say, the number nine as there were individuals—clearly an absurdity. It is not clear, however, that this is the important dividing line between proponents and critics of mathematical objectivity. Deconstructionists, for example, would readily admit that ordinary language is above all social; it is *not* a result of individual subjective predilections. Similarly, Wittgenstein provided a series of devastating arguments against the existence of any kind of private language (Bloor, 1983, pp. 54–64). In this sense, ordinary language is as objective as mathematics if by what is meant by "objective" is a set of meanings that do not depend upon individual subjective states.

There is another interpretation of "subjective," however, which means something like ideological bias or cultural judgment. Under this interpretation the argument of the objectivists is that mathematics is nonideological and outside of culture (the best known proponent of this claim was Mannheim, 1936, who saw ideology all around him except in the sciences and mathematics). From the outset, though, there is a problem with this position: anyone claiming a nonideological viewpoint is adopting an ideology. Like Hemmingway's nonstyle, it is a style of its own.

The problem with such a position is seen most clearly in the work of the late-nineteenth- and early-twentieth-century mathematician Gottlob Frege, who tried to argue for the objectivity of mathematics (this illustration comes from Bloor, 1991, pp. 92–99). Frege claimed that mathematical objects such as numbers were neither psychological constructs nor material ones but were derivative of reason and hence were objective. Thus for Frege (1959, p. 35, quoted in Bloor, 1991, p. 96), "The axis of the earth is objective, so is the center of mass of the solar system, but I would not call them actual in the way the earth itself is so. We often speak of the equator as an imaginary line; but . . . it is not a creature of thought, . . . but is only recognized or apprehended by thought." So it is not the physical presence of an entity, such as the equator or the center of the solar system, that makes it objective; it is that it was derived by dint of our reason. The problem here is that what is taken as reasonable and objective has varied tremendously both historically and geographically. To take Frege's own example, it has only been over the past few hundred years that consensus has existed about the center of the solar system. Does that then mean that everyone before Kepler was unreasonable? Or does it more likely mean that what is considered reasonable is linked to a whole host of culturally specific conventions, conjectures, and background assumptions? If so, then objectivity is not the precipitate of pure reason but is simply that which is agreed upon at the time, given existing cultural norms and assumptions.

The important point for this chapter is that such norms and assumptions are just as important in mathematics as in any other line of inquiry. Again, Bloor (1991, ch. 6) provides a series of illustrative examples, of which only one will be given here, the case of the square root of 2. For the ancient Greeks, the peculiarities of the square root of two meant that it was simply not a number. The result was a sharp separation for them between pure numbers on the one hand and magnitude or arithmetic on the other (Bloor, 1991, pp. 122–125). In contrast, in contemporary mathematics the division between pure numbers and arithmetic is not made. Root 2 is a number, albeit an irrational one. But as Bloor (1991, pp. 123–124) argues, there is no mathematical argument that demonstrates that the Greek's view of root 2 is any better or worse than the modern one. Rather, the view that is accepted depends upon a set of background assumptions informed by the broader culture. Bloor (1991, p. 124) writes, "Certain conditions have to obtain before a computation has any meaning. These conditions are social in the sense that they reside in the collectively held system of classifications and meanings of a culture. Consequently they will vary and as they vary so will the meaning of pieces of mathematics." More generally, cultural "bias" is not something that can be eradicated from mathematics; it is part of the necessary background conditions that make mathematics possible in the first place.

The fourth issue concerns the need for the simplicity of mathematics in facing the complexity of the world. Or to put it in slightly different terms, for advocates of quantitative methods, ordinary language only mirrors the complexity it finds, whereas mathematics simplifies and thereby makes sense of it. The key terms here are "simplicity" and "complexity," and as defined by believers in quantitative methods, they are often value-loaded. Complexity is bad, simplicity is good (a possible exception, though, is in the mathematics of chaos theory). Even leaving aside the irony of such value-ladenness, the paradox of this formulation is that to demonstrate the simplicity of mathematics requires an immense amount of complexity. For only those who are able to master the complexities of mathematics can appreciate its simplicity. For example, Cole suggests it would have been much simpler for Stamp and Beaver to have carried out a regression analysis on the geographical distribution of wheat in Britain than to have provided an account in the vernacular. But just how simple is regression analysis? It must first be learned and understood, which itself involves knowing other statistical terms and theorems and even more general mathematical precepts. It then requires a careful scrutiny of the specific conditions of its application. And finally the results must be assessed and interpreted in terms of the specific substantive case (part of which paradoxically involves taking into account the complexities of ordinary language again). In short, there is nothing simple about r^2 (a fact borne out by, if nothing else, its tortuous 200-year history; Pearson, 1970).

People can argue that mathematics is simple only because they have been institutionalized in such a tradition. That is, something is simple only because it has become an established institutional norm, convention, and belief. It is only for this reason that Alan Wilson (1972) could make the claim cited in the previous section above about mathematics and geography. Because he was a trained nuclear physicist, the complexity that Wilson saw within the urban system could only be rendered understandable to him—simplified—only by being translated into the logic of mathematics, and the mathematics of entropy maximization in particular. But for many geographers who had not been institutionalized in nuclear physics, the equations of entropy maximization were far more complex than the complexities of the urban system that they were meant to represent.

The final claim about mathematics by the quantifiers is that it is precise and unambiguous. The paradox here is that the only means of sorting out those standards of precision and unambiguity is by using ordinary language. For precision and unambiguity are not inherent in mathematics but are criteria that are applied after the fact and are thus debated and discussed in the vernacular. This point raises the broader issue of whether mathematics can ever be separated from ordinary language at all. Wittgenstein (1922, p. 169) implies as much when he writes, "We use mathematical propositions *only* in order to infer from propositions which do not belong to mathematics to others which equally do not belong to mathematics." Wittgenstein's point is that for mathematical propositions to make any sense to us, we must translate them into ordinary language. As a result, there can never be any sharp separation between the vernacular and mathematics (Dennis, 1982). As Mirowski (1986b, p. 199) writes, "Mathematical models constitute a subsystem of notations which, by necessity, remain embedded within a framework of conventional language." He adds (and this remark seems just as pertinent to geographers as to the economists he writes about), "Since economists are so rarely first rate mathematicians, most of the contributions economists can reasonably aspire to make to their chosen discipline must come in the twilight zone of *semantical* interpretation of previously developed mathematical structures" (1986b, p. 200; my emphasis). In sum, the argument made about precision and unambiguity by quantifiers does not hold because mathematics cannot be divorced from ordinary language.

In summary, in this section I have argued that none of the features attributed to mathematics by its geographical proponents holds. In each case there is a contradiction that undermines the final effectiveness: universality rests on a local claim, logic is unable to justify the use of logic, the assertion of objectivity is itself a value-laden claim, simplicity can be obtained only through complexity, and the precision of mathematics is expressible only by using the imprecision of ordinary language. Such contradictions are not ones that we can escape. Nevertheless, by probing such contradictions we can recognize how they are maintained by distinct sets of institutional practices and authorities. It is in part to this task that we now turn by examining the use of one kind of mathematics in human geography, inferential statistics.

A SECOND CUT AT DECONSTRUCTION: ECONOMIC GEOGRAPHERS AND INFERENTIAL STATISTICS

For reasons already given, the development of inferential statistics was not, and could not have been, predicated upon the working out of some final presence. This raises twin questions: On what basis did it develop, and what sustained the various claims it made? Following the earlier arguments, in this section I will suggest that like much of mathematics, inferential statistics emerged piecemeal, through a series of discrete metaphorical moves that were sanctioned by powerful institutional forces. Those metaphors, however, were not "innocent," but carried with them all kinds of often unexamined assumptions that derived from wider social practices and beliefs. More generally, it was institutional practices and authorities that consolidated the meaning of inferential statistics, and not the unfurling of a unitary logic.

The metaphor that underlay inferential statistics, and on which much of human geography's quantitative revolution rested, came from heredity and eugenics: inferential statistics was metaphorically like the inheritance of biological characteristics (Hilts, 1973; MacKenzie, 1981; Porter, 1986). Although many questions, especially political and moral ones, are raised by this metaphor, the focus here will be on the difficulties that emerged when it was imported into geography. For the eugenics metaphor clashed with other, preexisting geographical metaphors, thus rendering it problematic. Those difficulties, it should be noted, were subsequently recognized by some of the users of quantitative methods (Gould, 1970; Bennett, 1981, 1985, 1986). Bennett (1986, p. 214), for example, writes that "it is now clear that emphasizing inference *per se* produced numerous difficulties." However, such problems were typically seen as one-of-a-kind, ad hoc hindrances, with the result that geographers simply switched from inferential statistics to other kinds, for example, Bayesian. The argument here, though, following the general precepts of deconstruction, is that such switching could never be a final solution because every branch of statistics faces the same problem: all are constructed upon a set of metaphorical moves that bring with them hidden assumptions that ultimately make their claims to finality problematic.

Clearly these are very large claims, and given the need for brevity, none of them is satisfactorily demonstrated in the following discussion, which focuses narrowly on the early development of inferential statistics, in particular on correlation and regression analysis. This section, then, is as much an agenda for future work as it is completed argument.

Historians of the discipline generally agree that the foundations of inferential statistics were laid at the turn of the century in Britain by two men, Francis Galton and Karl Pearson (MacKenzie, 1981; Porter, 1986; Stigler, 1986). Certainly, there were others who followed and made significant contributions, such as Fisher, Pearson's son Egon, and Neyman, but in many ways they simply continued down the track that was laid earlier (MacKenzie, 1981).

Galton was the first. A Victorian private scholar, he was interested in issues of heredity and eugenics even as an undergraduate (Porter, 1986). Statistics became important because they provided a means for representing the dependence of the characteristics of offspring on the characteristics of their parents. Specifically, it was Galton who devised the first correlation and regression (initially "reversion") coefficients. Admittedly, a form of the correlation coefficient was in existence, but it had been developed in physics and astronomy as part of "error theory" (MacKenzie, 1981, pp. 68–72). There the problem was one of *correcting* for variations ("errors") among variables. But for Galton, it was precisely this variation that was so significant and that required further exploration. Thus the very fact that Galton was a eugenicist made a crucial difference in the way in which he constructed correlation and regression coefficients. As MacKenzie (1979, pp. 43–44) writes,

> Galton's concepts were a revolutionary breakthrough from . . . the mathematicians interested in the treatment of observational errors. There is no reason to suppose that workers in this earlier tradition would eventually have developed the concepts of regression and correlation. Some "error theorists" [such as Bravais and Schols] did produce similar mathematical formalisms: but they handled and interpreted these quite differently. For the error theorists, statistical variation was error: it was to be eliminated. For Galton, the eugenicist, it was the source of racial progress. For Bravais and Schols, statistical dependence . . . was a nuisance. . . . For Galton, statistical dependence . . . was what made eugenics possible. Thus Galton, because he was a eugenicist, worked in a different framework of meanings and assumptions from his predecessors: he developed the theory of statistics in ways that would have seemed pointless to them.

Inferential statistics, therefore, did not develop out of pure reason or logic but from very specific concerns of a particular time and place—late-nineteenth-century England, where issues of eugenics were politically rampant (Searle, 1976). In fact, Galton explicitly conceived the method of correlation "not as an abstract technique of numerical analysis, but as a statistical law of heredity" (Porter, 1986, p. 270). More generally, it seems unlikely that inferential statistics would have emerged in the form it has taken without the prior influence of eugenics; it was the overwhelming presence when late-nineteenth- and early-twentieth-century British statisticians "took up their pencils to write down formulae" (MacKenzie, 1979, p. 43).

Galton's work was subsequently developed and institutionalized as an academic discipline at the turn of the century by Pearson at University College, London. Like Galton, Pearson was a strong believer in eugenics (MacKenzie, 1981, ch. 4), and that conviction informed, as had Galton's, the very nature of the statistical theory that he developed. MacKenzie (1981, ch. 7) provides one example, that of measuring the degree of association among nominal-scale variables. To this end Pearson developed what he termed the "tetrachoric coefficient of correlation." It was analogous to the standard correlation coefficient associated with interval-scale data, allowing the two to be directly comparable. For MacKenzie (1979, pp. 44–47), this comparability, which was built into Pearson's statistical design, was essential because it allowed him to compare the strength of heredity for nominal-scale variables, such as intelligence (the Binet interval scale of intelligence had yet to be invented) to interval-scale data, such as height. If the two values were roughly comparable, he could then conclude that because, say, height is only a result of heredity, then intelligence must also be caused by the same factor. In contrast, other measures of nominal-scale data, such as Yule's, were unacceptable because they could not ensure comparability (MacKenzie, 1981, pp. 164–175). Thus, just like Galton's, Pearson's statistics were made to fulfill particular tasks within the wider agenda of eugenics.

The consequence of this wider context was that inferential statistics took on a set of particular hallmarks. First, the studies involved large samples but samples that nonetheless were still only a very small proportion of the total population (for example, Pearson's major study of human heredity sampled over 4,000 pairs of siblings; MacKenzie, 1981, p. 115). Second, there tended to be a preoccupation with normal distributions. The normal distribution in the form of the so-called error law had been well established in physics and astronomy. By metaphorical extension, Galton argued that human traits (for example, characteristics such as height or intelligence) took on that same distributional form. But rather than seeing variations about the mean as "errors," theorists changed the terminology and very meaning of the normal curve to fit the new application (Bloor, 1983, pp. 103–109). Pearson replaced "error law" with the term "normal distribution" and "probable error" with the term "standard deviation." So by 1920 Pearson could write that "the following assumption . . . lies at the basis of our present treatment of heredity. The variation of any organ in a sufficiently large population . . . is closely defined by a normal distribution curve" (quoted in Seal, 1970, p. 220). Third, there was the concern with prediction and control. If the political mandate of eugenics was to be fulfilled, it was necessary to know the consequences of breeding particular individuals. To do so required testing by controlled experiments. For this reason, it was essential that the studies of biometricians were both repeatable and open to confirmation by others. Finally, there was the assumption of independent sampling (Chang, 1976). To demonstrate that heredity is the principal factor determining a characteristic such as intelligence, samples must be independent of one another. If they are not, critics could claim that it was the nature of a particular sample chosen, not heredity, that determined intelligence; they could say, for example, that the results were a product of restricting the sample to a particular kind of environment.

The problem with these assumptions is that when geographers applied them to their work they frequently came into conflict with other postulates that traditionally defined their discipline. For one, given geographers' inclination to examine local, place-bound issues, statistical populations are often small and equal to the sample. In this case using inferential statistics to infer characteristics of a population from a sample is of no help at all. For another, the diverse kind of phenomena geographers examined were more varied than hereditary traits and were often not normally distributed. Certainly, they could be transformed into a normal distribution, but the effect of that transformation was to alter completely the existing relationship (Gould, 1970). Then, too, given the nature of the traditional human geographical study, which is not conducted in a laboratory, there can be no controlled repeatable experiments. The consequence is that error terms should be included for both the dependent and independent variables, which in turn makes operationalizing inferential statistics, particularly regression analysis, very difficult (Gould, 1970). Finally, the assumption of random independent sampling is in effect unsustainable in a *geographical* world. Because of difficulties of the map-pattern effect, spatial autocorrelations, and the modifiable areal unit problem, samples are rarely independent from one another (Gould, 1970; Unwin, 1978; Bennett, 1985).

That it took geographers at least a decade to identify the problems of inferential statistics was again a consequence of institutionalization (Taylor, 1976). To achieve success, at least during the crucial early years, the quantitative revolution required unity among the revolutionaries. Moreover, the academic payoffs to proponents of the quantitative revolution were significant once they arrived—new chairs were established, new journals published, and attractive job offers forthcoming. There was an incentive, therefore, to stay with the success that inferential statistics seemed to provide. Finally, even if there was the inclination to disavow what one had learned, it was always going to take time to mount such an internal critique given the momentum of inferential statistics, which by the late 1960s included the emergence of several textbooks slanted toward that approach (for example, Gregory, 1963; Cole and King, 1968).

In sum, the inferential statistics initially at the core of the quantitative revolution was not based upon any final presences but instead on a biometric metaphor that was sustained by a host of institutional authorities, (for a general discussion of those authorities at least in Britain, see Irvine and Miles, 1979, and Shaw and Miles, 1979). That this was not recognized until recently in human geography (Livingstone, 1992) was in part the result of the power of logocentric thought. With logocentrism undermined, however, the issue of the kinds of historical practices responsible for institutionalizing inferential statistics becomes central. From this perspective we can then understand why inferential statistics has had such difficulties within human geography. The type of assumptions necessary to complete the eugenics project on which inferential statistics was constructed conflicted with traditional geographical assumptions. In this sense, the problems of inferential statistics within human geography were the result of disciplinary institutional disjunctures, not disjunctures in logic.

CONCLUSION

As Derrida readily recognizes, all of us, including Derrida, are implicated in logocentric projects. They are our historical and geographical legacy. We can struggle against them, but we can never completely overthrow them. The best we can do is to maintain a state of "perpetual uneasiness." Deconstruction is one means to that end; it is a way of decentering, or throwing out of kilter, any all-encompassing project that claims certainty, finality, and determinateness. Furthermore, insofar as such projects also embody similarly all-encompassing ethical and political positions—ones that privilege a particular gender, race, and class—deconstruction underscores the silencing of the Other that inheres within those logocentric schemes.

I argued in this chapter that mathematics is a prime example of logocentrism. For it is above all an attempt to impose order on the world. But I also tried to show that order neither inheres in mathematics nor the world as such but only in the local institutional authorities that control mathematical practices. Of course, there have been attempts to justify those practices as something more than practices—for example, the claim that mathematics is universal or that statistics is a foolproof method for making inferences. But such justifications always unravel, as I have sought to demonstrate here. They unravel because at bottom they assert that there is a realm of certainty that lies beyond language. It is here that the arguments of deconstructionists are so valuable. For they show that there is nothing outside the text; our truths are only those that we write to ourselves.

Some may suggest that we do not need deconstructionists to tell us this or for that matter to make the kind of critique provided here of the use of mathematics in geography. There is something to this argument. Certainly, I did not explore the political silencing of the Other that Galton's and Pearson's work implied, nor did I provide the kind of detailed institutional analysis of logocentric closure that I promised. That I failed to deliver all that I implied at the outset of this chapter is in part a result of the undoubted clumsiness of the deconstructive effort I undertook here, if it was even that. However, its clumsiness comes about in part because of the very processes of institutionalization that I emphasized. It is difficult to write against the grain of logocentrism when, as Olsson (1992, p. 87) puts it, one has gone to bed and woken up with it for most of one's life. In this sense, perhaps deconstructionists' most insistent claim is that we should not roll over and go back to sleep. If we do, only a bad dream, and not the dream of philosophy, awaits us.

NOTES

1. In this chapter I've rhetorically constructed my critique of the application of quantitative methods in human geography around Cole's (1969) article. This is certainly not because it is somehow inferior; quite the reverse. Ironically, Cole's paper is useful for my purposes precisely because its arguments are expressed so clearly. There is also another irony in that I'm trying to do to Cole what he tries to do to a yet earlier generation of geographers (which will likely be my own fate).

2. Technically, *différance* is a neographism rather than a neologism. For while in French it sounds the same as *différence*, it clearly is not the same once it is written down on a page. This difference emerges only when written is Derrida's way of once more poking irony at the metaphysics of presence and its privileging of speech. I owe this point to Matt Sparke.

3. A distinction might be made here between those users of quantitative techniques who believe in logocentric projects and those who don't but who nonetheless continue to use mathematics in their work. Sibley's (1981 and no date) work is one example, and my work is another (for example, Sheppard and Barnes, 1990). In my own case, I would justify the use of mathematics on the basis of the prior recognition that mathematics is a language like any other, and as long as one is willing to scrutinize it critically in the same way as one scrutinizes critically other areas of language, then it will be at least no more harmful than alternative forms of writing (Barnes, 1989a). Again, it is the warning rather than the solution that is perhaps most important.

4. The Russell paradox is about a potential contradiction within class (or set) membership. Most classes are not members of themselves—for example, a class of objects is not an object. There are some sets, however, that are members of themselves; for example, the class of comprehensible statements is a member of itself because that class is a comprehensible statement itself. A problem arises, though, with the class of those classes that are not members of themselves. Is that class a member of itself or not? If it is, then it is not one of those classes that are not members of themselves. But if it is not a member of itself, then it is a member of the classes not members of themselves, and so is a member of itself after all. Hence the paradox.

PART IV

THREE EXEMPLARS

SEVEN

THE MASK OF JANUS
Looking toward Formalism and Contextualism with Piero Sraffa

Wittgenstein once remarked to Rush Rhees that the most
important thing that he gained from talking to Sraffa was an
"anthropological" way of looking at philosophical problems.
—Ray Monk, *Ludwig Wittgenstein: The Duty of Genius*

Of the well-known Cambridge economists, Piero Sraffa is probably the
least known. In fact, in many ways he is an éminence grise, the ghost in
the well-oiled machine of Cambridge economics. But this status, or lack
thereof, is peculiar given his accomplishments. He explicitly or implicitly
provided devastating critiques of at least three core economic ideas:
Marshall's theory of the firm, the neoclassical marginal productivity
theory of capital and income distribution, and the Marxist labor theory
of value. He paved the way for the establishment of at least two major
schools of research in economics, on imperfect competition and neo-Ricardianism. He was friend and intellectual interlocutor to: the political
theorist Antonio Gramsci—Sraffa supplied the imprisoned Gramsci with
books and made repeated efforts to have him released (Napolitano,
1984–1985); the philosopher Ludwig Wittgenstein—Sraffa was instrumental in convincing Wittgenstein to abandon his earlier views in the
Tractatus and to replace them with those of the *Philosophical Investiga-
tions* (Davis, 1988); and the economist John Maynard Keynes—Sraffa
organized the so-called Cambridge circus to discuss Keynes's *Treatise on
Money*, the precursor to the *General Theory*. Finally, he succeeded in one
of the most important pieces of detective work in economics by finding

in a tin box at the Raheny estate in county Dublin Ricardo's long lost, uncompleted final manuscript, "On Absolute and Exchangeable Value," an essay that subsequently became key to Sraffa's famous introduction to his definitive eleven-volume edited set of the *Works and Correspondence of David Ricardo* (1951–1973) (Pollitt, 1988).

This said, Sraffa's curriculum vitae is remarkably slim for a man who lived until his mid-eighties (he was born in 1898 and died in 1983) and whom his intellectual foes now call a genius (Samuelson, 1987, p. 460). His twenty-two publications (Roncaglia, 1978, pp. 151–153) include only one book, and that is fewer than 100 pages. That monograph, *Production of Commodities by Means of Commodities*, was greeted with puzzlement and even amusement, though. Paul Samuelson tells the story that when he first obtained Sraffa's book he showed it to Robert Solow and they joked about whether an assistant professor from North Texas State would get tenure with such a meager offering. Samuelson's joke was both terribly wrong and terribly right. It is wrong in that, as Samuelson (1987) now recognizes, through pure brain power and not technical mastery over mathematics Sraffa's book provides some of the most trenchant critique and creative reconstruction by any economist of this century. Samuelson is right, though, in that North Texas State would probably not have given Sraffa tenure. North American economics departments, and those European economics departments over which its pall is cast, remain peculiarly resistant to Sraffa's ideas. And it is symptomatic that one of the best-known articles on Sraffa written by a North American (Levine, 1974) is entitled "This Age of Leontieff . . . and Who?" The who, of course, is Sraffa.

The thesis I want to develop in this chapter is that Sraffa is Janus-like in the possibilities that he offers economic geography and regional science. It is not to both past and future that Sraffa looks, however, but rather toward formalism and contextualism. In this sense, he has something to say both to regional scientists, who traditionally engage in abstract, rigorous theorizing, and to economic geographers, who traditionally have their feet planted on the ground. As a vehicle to discuss these two features of Sraffa's work, I will focus on urban modeling broadly conceived. I will develop both a formal model of the urban economy using Sraffa's work as a starting point and also discuss his contextual position by examining the recent work of Allen Scott on Los Angeles. Before undertaking these two tasks, I will provide a sketch of Sraffa's life and works, seeing as the connecting thread his interest in the theory of economic value. I do so because such intellectual biographical details are directly relevant to the later part of the chapter, where I put Sraffa's formalism and contextualism to work. In particular, I will argue that the charter for both these types of study lies precisely in Sraffa's own value theory. In doing so, I will connect this chapter to the earlier one on theories of economic value and their relationship to essentialism and contextualism (Chapter Two).

SRAFFA AND THE THEORY OF ECONOMIC VALUE

Strictly speaking, a theory of value is simply a theory of price determination and is usually presented in formal terms. But as Gunnar Myrdal argues (1969, p. 15), value theory also has a broader epistemological significance in that it is made "the starting point for all economic analysis which really tries to probe the surface." Myrdal is suggesting here that if economists "really" want to *know* what it going on, that is, to probe rather than merely to describe the surface of events, they must begin from the epistemological bedrock of economic value; a failure to rest analysis on such a foundation undermines any prospect of doing economics. In this light, I will argue that Sraffa's writings explicitly demonstrate in formal terms that traditional value theories are logically inconsistent, thereby implicitly demonstrating that the whole notion of value theory as an epistemological enterprise is misconceived. Under this interpretation, Sraffa's central constructive task then becomes one of developing a non–value theory, a value theory that does not rest on any ultimate foundation but is nonetheless formally consistent. I will argue that he achieves this goal in his book *Production of Commodities by Means of Commodities* and in so doing Sraffa also points to the two directions of formalism and contextualism simultaneously. Let me flesh out these claims by turning to Sraffa himself.

After completing his undergraduate degree in 1920 at the University of Turin (where he first met Gramsci), Sraffa continued his interest in monetary theory and banking and incurred Mussolini's wrath for attacking the Italian financial elite and their close relationship with the state (Eatwell and Panico, 1987). By the mid-1920s Sraffa was already turning his attention to value theory. In two articles, one appearing in Italian in *Annali di Economia* (1925) and the other in English in the *Economic Journal* (1926), Sraffa provided a penetrating critique of the Marshallian theory of the firm under conditions of perfect competition and partial equilibrium. At bottom his criticism was an attempt to undermine the "modern theory of value" that posited that "the essential causes determining ... price ... are the forces of supply and those of demand" (Sraffa, 1926, p. 535). Sraffa's argument is that the U-shaped cost curve of a firm, representing first increasing and then diminishing returns and from which an industry's supply curve is derived, is flawed in terms of both its intellectual history and its logic. With respect to intellectual history, increasing and diminishing returns originated in two entirely different contexts: the former in Adam Smith's examination of accumulation through the relationship between extending the market and increasing the division of labor, and the latter in David Ricardo's work on extensive differential rent. For this reason, there was never historically an intellectual symmetry between the two types of return as implied in Marshall's portrayal. With respect to the second issue of logical consistency, neither decreasing nor increasing returns are compatible with price determination under partial equilibrium and perfect competition. Diminishing returns are incompatible because where there is a constant amount of a factor, an increase in the output by one firm not only affects its own costs but every other firms' costs as well. Because of these "collateral" effects, as Sraffa called them, Marshall's ceteris paribus clause essential for partial equilibrium is violated. Increasing returns fare no better. Internal economies of scale, as even Marshall recognized, are incompatible with perfect competition, and external economies are subject to the same problem as diminishing returns: changes in the output of one firm produce collateral effects on all others, thereby undermining partial equilibrium. The wider consequence of Sraffa's critique is that the traditional supply curve derived from Marshall's theory of the firm is "unable to support the weight imposed upon it," thereby calling into question modern value theory that represents price as "a pair of intersecting curves of collective demand and supply" (Sraffa, 1926, pp. 536, 535).

In his articles Sraffa suggests three solutions to the task of reconstructing value theory. The first is to assume constant returns to scale. In that way neither perfect competition nor ceteris paribus is violated. Although advocating this approach in the 1925 article, by the 1926 paper he recognized that such an assumption could be at best only a first approximation. This led him to the second alternative, which was to abandon the assumption of perfect competition altogether. This is what he suggests in the 1926 article, which then became the propaedeutic for future work on imperfect competition, quickly taken up by Joan Robinson and Edward Chamberlain. But by 1930 Sraffa decided that the second alternative was also unsatisfactory (Bharadwaj, 1988). The reason is not hard to find. For the theory of imperfect competition that developed after Sraffa's articles was quickly absorbed by neoclassical economics, and rather than providing a new value theory, it became just a special case of the old one. This paved the way for Sraffa's third alternative: to allow for simultaneous equilibrium in numerous industries where no assumptions are made about returns to scale at all. In fact, he recognized this solution in the 1926 paper but did not take it up on grounds of the complexity of such a task. That complexity was great indeed, because Sraffa (whom Keynes once described as a man "from whom nothing is hid") took over thirty years to provide an eventual solution in his *Production of Commodities by Means of Commodities.*

In the interim period between the 1926 paper and his 1960 book, however, Sraffa was not idle. In 1927, under Keynes's invitation, Sraffa left the University of Cagliari and came to Cambridge to take up the post of lecturer. But the strain of elaborating in English his attack on Marshall's work (he lectured on value theory) was too taxing, and in 1930 he gave up lecturing for good. Through Keynes's good offices, he took over in the same year the editorship of the Royal Economic Society's edition of *The Works and Correspondence of David Ricardo*. Despite Keynes's optimism that Ricardo's *Works* would be published in 1933, it was not until forty years later that Volume 11, the general index, was finally completed. The disproportionate time taken to finish was partly due to Sraffa's brilliant piece of sleuthing in Eire (mentioned above), which required the total reorganization of the collection even though six of the volumes were already at the galley proof stage (Eatwell and Panico, 1987). But the main reason for the delay was Sraffa's perfectionism, which one commentator said "paralysed his capacity to expound via the printed word both his own lines of thought and those of Ricardo" (Pollitt, 1988, p. 55) Two especially recalcitrant sections for Sraffa were the general preface for the whole edition and the introduction to Volume 1, *The Principles of Political Economy and Taxation*. It was only with the help of Maurice Dobb, the well-known Cambridge Marxist economist, that in 1948 Sraffa's writing block was finally broken. Through a process in which Sraffa dictated notes to Dobb and Dobb wrote them up and took them back to Sraffa for further revision, the preface and the introduction were completed (Pollitt, 1988). Most economists would say that the time and intellectual anguish expended were worth it and that Sraffa's edition of Ricardo's *Works and Correspondence* represents a scholarly masterpiece. As George Stigler (1953, p. 586) wrote in reviewing the first nine volumes, "Ricardo was a fortunate man. He lived in a period . . . when an untutored genius could still remake economic science. . . . And now, 130 years after his death, he is as fortunate as ever: he has been befriended by Sraffa—who has been befriended by Dobb."

During this prolonged intellectual excursion into the early-nineteenth-century world of Ricardo, Sraffa maintained his interest in the issue of economic value. In fact, his introduction to the *Principles* in part showed that Ricardo cannot be interpreted as an early forerunner to the neoclassical supply-and-demand theorists, which was Marshall's reading. This was the crucial significance of Ricardo's essay "On Absolute and Exchangeable Value." It showed that until his dying day Ricardo had no truck with a supply-and-demand framework but consistently maintained the view that prices were determined by costs of production.

With the bulk of Ricardo's *Works* completed, Sraffa (1960, p. vi) turned to piecing together the "mass of old notes" that had accumulated since the 1920s. But these were not any old notes. They even included a formal proof of the Perron–Frobenius theorems of nonnegative square matrices that had been scribbled on a postcard and sent to Sraffa by the Cambridge mathematician Besicovitch while the latter was on holiday (Eatwell and Panico, 1987). Finally, in 1960 *Production of Commodities by Means of Commodities* was published.

As might be expected, Sraffa's book is unusual even for economics. There is no introduction nor conclusion, no institutions nor social actors. All we are given is a set of simultaneous production equations. As Joan Robinson (1965, p. 7) wrote in an early review, "Addicts of pure economic logic have here a double distilled elixir that they can enjoy drop by drop for many a day." But this logic had mixed effects on its audience. Harry Johnson (1974, p. 25) said the book was "an apparently purely scientific rallying point for . . . anti-Americanism," while Robert Wolff (1982, pp. 230–231) likened it to "a Gregorian plainsong of the middle ages," that engendered "a deeply moving experience."

Although Sraffa's terseness has been interpreted as just a quirk of his writing style, another interpretation is that in some sense what Sraffa leaves out is more important than what he includes. This is true in two ways. The first is evident when we recall the book's subtitle: *Prelude to a Critique of Political Economy*. Sraffa is not offering the critique itself but rather offering the wherewithal for others to carry out that critique. Specifically, *Production of Commodities by Means of Commodities* implicitly contains logical criticisms of both neoclassical and Marxian value theories, elaborated upon, respectively, in the "capital" (Harcourt, 1972) and "value" (Steedman and Sweezy, 1981) controversies. These objections are couched in terms of formal mathematical consistency and show that neither "capital" in the neoclassical aggregate production function nor "labor values" in Marxian economics can be treated on grounds of logical consistency as fundamental constants on which to determine prices or values. In this sense, there is a unity of purpose between Sraffa's criticisms of Marshall's work in the 1920s and his *Prelude to a Critique* thirty years later: in both cases he means to demonstrate that in terms of the very assumptions of either neoclassical or Marxian economics one cannot logically posit some bedrock entity that is the basis of value.

The second issue suggested by Sraffa's reticence is tied to the constructive function of his book. The problem for Sraffa is that if one rejects fundamental entities such as the supply curve, capital, or labor values as a basis for price determination, what does one put in their place? To discuss Sraffa's solution to this problem, I need to turn to the substance of his book, and in particular I will interpret it in light of evidence that links Sraffa with Wittgenstein's later philosophy (Roncaglia, 1978; Davis, 1988). For what characterizes Wittgenstein's later work is an abandonment of a foundational theory of knowledge (Curry, 1980). There are no golden rules for acquiring knowledge; to understand how we acquire, use, and verify knowledge, we must examine the particular practices at hand. Under this interpretation, what links Sraffa and Wittgenstein "is that both in different ways expose and criticize the Western habit of constructing models which purport to have an ultimate foundation in given and isolable features" (Gudeman, 1986, p. 35). If Sraffa adopts contextualism, it then explains his laconism. For under a contextual position, nothing can be said a priori; we have to wait until we examine the context at hand before we make more complete statements. To establish this claim, let me discuss Sraffa's book.

Sraffa portrays an economy where inputs, which are themselves commodities, produce other commodities. The process is circular: the output in one production period is used as input for the next production period. Sraffa begins this discussion with the case of a subsistence economy. What is produced at the end of the production period is just sufficient to replace the inputs used up. In most economies, however, there is a surplus left over even when all inputs are replaced. Thus we might imagine that in a feudal economy most of the surplus goes to the lord of the manor, whereas in modern capitalism it is divided between workers and capitalists. Sraffa then demonstrates that regardless of whether there is simple reproduction or reproduction with a surplus, it is always possible to derive a unique system of prices consonant with the reproduction of that system.

Figure 7.1 allows us to see more clearly Sraffa's system and the way in which it is compatible with contextualism. At the end of the production period, there is a certain level of output. That output serves two purposes: first, it is used as an input for the next round of production. If outputs are less than inputs for the next round of production, then the economy is not reproducible. If, however, outputs exceed necessary inputs, there is a "surplus" available to distribute as income to members of society. How

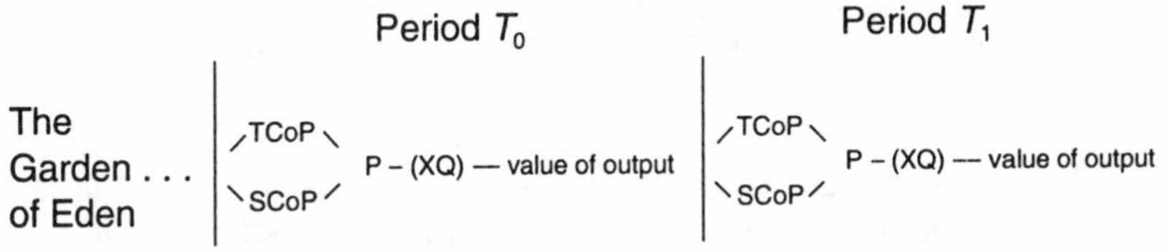

[*Note*. TCoP = technical conditions of production; SCoP = social conditions of production; P = prices of production; Q = physical quantities of commodities produced.]

Figure 7.1. Sraffa's production of commodities by means of commodities.

inputs are used (the technical conditions of production) and how the surplus is divided up (the social conditions of distribution) technically establish the level of prices and thereby the level of output measured in money terms. The technical conditions of production are defined here as the prevailing technology used within a given sector. It is formally represented by a series of input–output coefficients specifying the kinds and amounts of commodities required to produce one unit of output. The social conditions of distribution, in contrast, are defined by the way in which the "surplus" is distributed among members of society.

An immediate thing to note about Sraffa's model is that there are no absolute sources of value determining prices. Prices of commodities are determined both by the division of the surplus between wages and profits (social conditions of production) and by prices of inputs (technical conditions of production). But both the current value of the surplus and prices of inputs were established by prices in the previous production period. Those past prices, however, were set by the social and technical conditions of production prevailing in that period. And the value of both the surplus and prices of inputs that made up those social and technical conditions were established in yet a previous production period, and so on. In short, determination of prices and the social and technical conditions of production are interdependent. As a result, there is no bedrock; there are only the ceaseless interconnected movement of prices, the changing methods humans have employed to produce things, and the changing patterns of dividing what humans have produced among themselves. The important implication is that for Sraffa there are no fundamental constant, supply curves, capital, or labor values underlying prices. As Gudeman (1986, p. 68) writes,

> Sraffa's model does not rest on a foundation in nature. For him, prices are not derived from "given" features of the real world, such as land, labor or equipment. Rather, the prices of labor and capital are shown to be interdependent, the question of their ultimate determination being left to one side. In the Sraffa model there is no reference to a final level or feature that, once located, provides the key to the remainder. . . . For Sraffa there is no derivation from ultimate features.

The result is a crucial difference between neoclassical and Marxist approaches and approaches based on Sraffa's model. Whereas the neoclassical concern for the exchange and consumption of goods is defined in terms of fundamental entities of value, Sraffa is concerned only with the production of "things." The word "thing" is used deliberately because it implies no valuation; "things" take on meanings only when they are embedded in a particular context.

That context for Sraffa involves the technical conditions of production and the social conditions of distribution. These, however, are not controlling essences, because Sraffa does not ground them in anything. There is simply no Sraffan theory of what determines income distribution (it might be the rules of potlatch or the rules of the market) or what sets technical conditions (it might be the desire to exchange "kula" or the desire to make profit). Rather, Sraffa leaves these questions open; they can be closed only by examining the context at hand.

A similar position is put forward by Napoleoni (1978, pp. 75–76), who also recognizes Sraffa's focus on things when he writes, "A re-reading of *Production of Commodities by Means of Commodities* has confirmed my initial impression that it is 'things' rather than 'subjects' which move around in Sraffa's construction." This leads Napoleoni to suggest that Sraffa leaves us with a theoretical tabula rasa. It is in this sense that Sraffa presents a contextual value theory. As Napoleoni (1978, p. 77) says, Sraffa "forces us to take everything back to the beginning. True, he gives us no suggestions with which to begin again: he would not, I think, wish to give any; and I am not sure he would be able to."

We are now in a better position to understand what Sraffa thinks one can say about an economy and what he thinks one must be silent about. At the most fundamental level, Sraffa outlines the physical conditions necessary for an economy to reproduce itself, that is, for the economy to have enough output to at least replace all inputs. Furthermore, Sraffa shows the price conditions necessary for that sustainability. He does this without any reference to metaphysical values. Rather, to establish prices, one must examine the broader context of distribution and technical conditions of production. But in examining that context, Sraffa provides no theory about social classes, human nature, preferences, the origin of technical change, the forces affecting income distribution, the progress of history, resource endowments, and, most important of all, value. This is not because there is nothing we can say; rather, we have to wait and determine what is appropriate for that time and place.

This is a fundamental point because it is Sraffa's silences that have been most criticized. Such criticism is voluminous, and it is not possible to discuss that literature here (for a sample, see Roosevelt, 1974; Shaikh, 1981; and Howard, 1987). Nonetheless, Sraffa's critics generally suppose that his silences imply that he is against, for example, a materialist interpretation of history or the efficiency of the free market. Sraffa simply does not want to discuss these issues, but by not discussing them, he is not saying that they are unimportant nor that they must go unanswered. Rather, Sraffa does not say anything because to do so would be to fall into an essentialist position. In this sense, it is quite conceivable that Sraffa's work is compatible with theories drawn from either neoclassical or

Marxian economics. Such theories cannot be applied a priori, though. One must scrutinize the context and examine whether it is compatible.

For some, the very absence of an all-encompassing theory may be even more troubling than having the wrong theory. Sraffa, however, is not rejecting theory per se but objecting to the kind of theory that provides answers before questions are even posed. Instead, he is suggesting that we must sort through the bag of theoretical concepts at our disposal, take from it what we can, and modify, fashion, and invent in accordance to the particular context at hand. Thus, it is not theory itself that is the issue but the assumptions made by its users with respect to its applicability.

Hausman (1981, pp. 183–184) reaches a similar conclusion:

> Sraffa does not take economics to be a separate science with its own distinctive laws and causes. . . . Its laws are not necessarily individual-istic or psychological, although some may be. In seeking to explain given economic phenomena one should draw freely upon the results of other social studies. No special set of causal factors is predominantly respon-sible for all major economic phenomena. In each given problem situ-ation, the economist must isolate the major causal factors by empirical investigation and theoretical ingenuity. Occasionally these may coincide with the factors [that neoclassical or Marxist] theorists pick out as primitives. Often there will be no such coincidence. Economists should seek many different (but mutually consistent) explanations at different levels of detail.

In summary, I argued here that the connecting thread among Sraffa's three most significant works—the articles from the 1920s, the introduc-tion to Ricardo's *Principles*, and his book—is a rejection of any founda-tional value theory. Instead, Sraffa provides in the *Production of Com-modities by Means of Commodities* a non–value theory, a theory couched in formal terms but open to context. Furthermore, and returning to the theme I raised in the introduction to this chapter, it is precisely at the juncture between his abstract rigor and non–value theory that Sraffa is Janus-like, simultaneously pointing to formalism and contextualism. For on the one hand, Sraffa provides the raw materials to construct formal models. His linear production equations and the relationship among prices, capital, wages, profits, and rent that he derives from them can be taken up and, as I will show, fruitfully deployed in a space economy. On the other hand, by the very nature of his work, such formal models can never be complete; at best, they only show what is possible. To close Sraffa's formal model, it is necessary to embed it within a broader social, historical, and geographical context. In this sense, Sraffa also looks toward contextualism. I will now briefly illustrate both these faces of Sraffa first by presenting a formal model of the urban economy that draws upon some joint work completed with Eric Sheppard (Sheppard and Barnes, 1990, ch. 7) and second by presenting a contextualized account of Sraffa's model by drawing upon Allen Scott's work on Los Angeles.

A SRAFFAN FORMAL MODEL OF THE URBAN ECONOMY

By bringing together the two components of Sraffa's model—the conditions of production and distribution—I will now outline a formal model of the urban economy. For brevity's sake, I will provide neither rigorous proofs nor discuss all the potential elaborations of the model (for the full details, see Sheppard and Barnes, 1990, ch. 7). I will present the Sraffan approach to the city in two stages: I outline the basic model; and I deal with issues of housing, consumer services, and residential distribution.

The Basic Model

First, assume a set of P basic production establishments (in Lowry's sense) that produce N goods. Let that city in which production occurs be divided into J land parcels, on which no more than one basic sector establishment can be located ($N < P < J$). The technology for producing the N goods is known and is represented by a set of fixed input coefficients a_{ij}^{mn}, where a_{ij}^{mn} is the amount of good m produced in location i required to produce a unit of good n produced in location j. Assume also that there is a single market at the center of the city through which all finished and intermediate goods are sold. Also let money wage and profits be equalized.

The theoretical task is to define the profit-maximizing intra-urban location pattern for the P basic sector establishments, which requires a simultaneous determination of location, spatial interdependencies among producers, market prices, and land rents charged on the J plots of land. For purposes of exposition, this task is carried out in two stages: first, excluding land rents; second, with rents included.

First, arbitrarily assign the P sector establishments to the J land parcels. For any assignment of establishment n on parcel j, the market price is equal to

$$p_j^n = [\sum_m a_{ij}^{mn} p_i^m + (\sum_m T_{Cj}^m + T_{jC}^n) p_C^t] (1 + r) \qquad (1)$$

where:

p_j^n is the market price of good n produced at location j.

a_{ij}^{mn} is the technical coefficient of production representing the amount of

m locally produced at location i required to produce a unit of n at location j (including wage goods consumed by labor).

T^m_{Cj} is the amount of transport services required to ship a unit of m from the central market C to location j.

T^n_{jC} is the amount of transport services required to ship a unit of good n from location j to the central market.

p^t_C is the production price of transport produced at the central market.

r is the rate of profit.

Equation 1 states that the market price for good n produced at location j is equal to the cost of intermediate and wage goods purchased at the market, plus the transport cost of shipping the intermediate inputs from the market to the production site j where n is produced, plus the transport cost of shipping the finished good n back to the market where it is sold. This sum is then incremented by the rate of profit.

Another equation must be added to Equation 1 specifying the price of transport:

$$p^t_C = \left(\sum_m a^{mC}_{it} p^m_i + \sum_M a^{MC}_{It} p^M_I \right) (1 + r) \qquad (2)$$

It is assumed that because transport services are produced at the city center they do not directly require any transport services in their own production.

There are in total $P + 1$ price equations—P equations of the form given in Equation 1, and Equation 2 specifying the price of transport—and $P + 2$ unknowns (P prices of produced goods, the price of transport, and the profit rate). By letting one of the prices equal one as a numeraire, we can demonstrate that the resulting set of determined prices is positive and unique (Pasinetti, 1977).

Having solved for prices and the profit rate for one particular assignment of basic sector activities to land zones, we must establish which one of the total $\binom{J}{P} . P! / (P_1! P_2! \ldots P_N!)$ assignments is optimal, where P_i is the number of sites occupied by each sector i ($\sum P_i = P$). In previous work I have shown how such an optimal locational assignment problem can be solved (Sheppard and Barnes, 1986). For each potential locational assignment, draw the associated so-called wage–profit frontier. Such a frontier describes the various combinations of wages and profit rates that are possible for a given location pattern (Figure 7.2). Under our assumptions, the frontier will always be negatively sloped, thus indicating the potential economic and political conflict between workers and capitalists; an increase in the share of one group decreases the share for the other. Graphically, by superimposing the wage–profit frontiers for all the different assignments on a single diagram, we then define the profit-maximizing location pattern by the outermost frontier for a given wage level. Although always downward sloping, the shape of each frontier is unrestricted, thereby allowing curves to cross one another. As a result, different locational assignments are profit-maximizing at different wage rates. For example, location pattern A is profit-maximizing at any wage rate below w_1, but pattern B is profit maximizing at wage rates above w_1 but below w_3 (for example, w_2). There is also a form of "reswitching" in that the same location pattern is optimal for at least two separate wage rates—pattern A is profit-maximizing at wage levels below w_1 and above w_3. More broadly, the intra-urban geography of production depends upon the conflict between the two classes, workers and capitalists, in establishing the wage rate. In this sense, the economic geography of the city is predicated upon "social, and moreover institutionally and historically relative changing and changeable conditions" (Dobb, 1973, p. 261) that affect the power relations among urban social classes.

As set up, the model suggests that the same goods produced in different places will have different market prices because of the differential effect of transport costs. Such price differences, however, cannot persist if

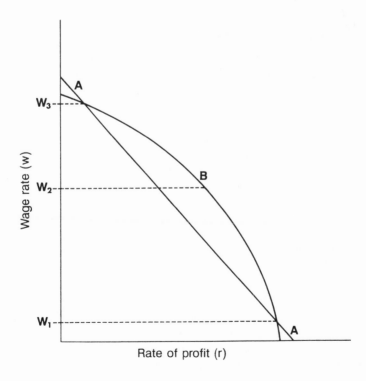

Figure 7.2. Two wage–profit frontiers for two different location patterns.

equal prices are enforced at the central market. As a result, land rents come into existence reflecting the resulting locational advantage. To incorporate land rents into the model, we assume that there is a single market price for each good that is given by the most expensive, marginal supplier.

With land rents included, the new price equation for good n produced on land zone j is given by

$$p_j^n = [\sum_m a_{ij}^{mn} p_i^m + \sum_m a_{Ij}^{Mn} p_I^M + \tag{3}$$

$$(\sum_m T_{Cj}^m + \sum_M T_{Cj}^M + T_{jC}^n) p_C^t + Q_j^n R_j^n] (1 + r)$$

where all terms are as before. Q_j^n is the quantity of land required to produce a unit of good n at location j, and R_j^n is the land rent charged per unit of land.

Again as demonstrated elsewhere (Sheppard and Barnes, 1986), it is possible to calculate rents from a price equation of the form found in Equation 3. That procedure, which I will not repeat here, involves identifying the marginal land for each commodity type and also one global marginal land for all commodity types. By changing both assignments of users to lands and the marginal lands themselves, then comparing wage–profit frontiers, one can determine the optimal spatial arrangement of producers within the city, together with the rents paid at each location.

In constructing this model of land rent, we assume that the same good is produced by the same technology in different plants, thereby deriving extensive differential rent. By relaxing this assumption or assuming that the transportation sector itself is composed of different techniques of production, we can calculate various forms of intensive rent (Sheppard and Barnes, 1986; 1990, ch. 7). Furthermore, absolute or monopoly rent can also be readily incorporated into the model following Harvey's (1974) suggestions. In addition, the rent on fixed capital—on shops, factories, and houses—can also be calculated by following Sraffa's suggestions about joint production (see Sheppard and Barnes, 1990, ch. 7).

Population, Retailing, Housing, and Real Wages

The model constructed so far at best deals with only half of the urban economy. Questions about the spatial distribution and size of the urban population; the spatial distribution of consumer service activities; the cost, construction, and geographical pattern of the housing sector; and potential spatial variability of the real wages have all been ignored. One solution is to make use of some type of analytical Garin–Lowry model. As is well known, by beginning with a set of exogenously given basic industries and employment levels, where each industry is located in a discrete zone within the city, the Garin–Lowry model estimates the spatial distribution of total population and service employment.

A major difficulty with the Garin–Lowry model, as Webber (1984, p. 160) notes, is that it "contains no motor to make things happen." But linking it to the Sraffan model already constructed in effect supplies such a motor. It is then the dynamics of the production system along with the division of the surplus among classes that drives the Garin–Lowry model. Thus, instead of starting with an exogenously given set of basic industries and employment levels as does the Garin–Lowry model, the beginning point is with the set of profit-maximizing locations, land uses, and rents (including building rents) that were endogenously determined within the Sraffan framework.

For brevity's sake, I cannot present the details of linking the Sraffan and Garin–Lowry models. The gist is that with levels and locations of basic sector employment determined endogenously, the expected geographical distribution of workers' residences can be determined for a given level of cost-minimizing behavior using a type of trip distribution model that assigns workers to residential zones on the basis of the price of land and housing costs, commuting costs, and the retail cost of consumption goods. Each one of those costs can be derived endogenously within the model. Housing is an item of fixed capital whose price and rental costs are determined in the manner of other types of fixed capital. Commuting costs are easily calculated once workers' residential locations are known along with the derived price of transportation. And retail costs are also easily worked out if production prices are known and if locations of retail sites can be determined on the basis of the population in each zone. Furthermore, because such costs are spatially variable, different workers likely receive different real wages. The potential result is intraclass conflict as lower-paid workers demand remuneration from capitalists comparable to those workers at the higher end of the wage scale. Higher-paid workers, however, may themselves resist such demands, wishing to keep differentials in place, thereby precipitating intraclass conflict.

In summary, by drawing upon Sraffa's work, I outlined here the bare lineaments of a formal model of the urban economy. Taking the technical conditions of production and the social conditions of distribution, I derived the profit-maximizing intra-urban location pattern for set of P basic industries, one that explicitly includes a variety of forms of rent. Furthermore, by linking Sraffa's model with Garin–Lowry issues of population and residential distribution, we can address housing, commuting, differential wage rates, and social conflict. One function the model serves is in challenging certain conclusions of the new urban economics, for example, the view that social conflict is somehow peripheral to analysis. Another is that of clarifying existing ideas and honing new ones. Nonetheless, because the model is couched at a formal level, ultimately it can represent only possibilities, not actualities. By its very construction, Sraffa's model is necessarily open to the case study. To establish closure Sraffa's work must be embedded in a particular historical, cultural, social, and geographical context. It it to this issue that I now turn by reviewing Scott's recent work on Los Angeles.

A SRAFFAN CONTEXTUAL URBAN MODEL: LOS ANGELES

By embedding technical conditions of production and the social conditions of distribution in late-twentieth-century North American metropolitan development, Allen Scott provides the geographical context to discuss Sraffa's work. In providing such a context, Scott is in effect closing Sraffa's open system. That is, by examining the particularities of place and time, Scott tries to answer the questions that Sraffa, and the formal model derived from his work, deliberately leaves unanswered.

That said, I should also note that in earlier chapters I criticized Scott's work for its ambiguity toward essentialism, whereas my argument here is that Sraffa is not ambiguous at all; he is vehement in his anti-essentialism. In this sense, there is a potential contradiction in using Scott's work to illustrate Sraffa's theory. My intention here, however, is to emphasize only the contextual part of Scott's work that exemplifies Sraffa's anti-essentialism. I recognize that this is not everything within Scott's work, nor is it necessarily an interpretation with which he would agree (I suspect he wouldn't).

Scott's initial theoretical interest in Sraffa was expressed in a pioneering paper linking Sraffa's formal production equations with a von Thunen model of land use (Scott, 1976). In the ensuing years this initial spartan presentation has been enriched by Scott's "empirical investigation[s]" and "theoretical ingenuity" (Hausman, 1981, p. 184). Specifically, by drawing upon a number of diverse theorists and focusing on the particularities of Los Angeles, Scott has sought to provide an explanation of the late-twentieth-century North American city. At the basis of that account are the twin components of the technical conditions of production and the social conditions of distribution that Sraffa emphasizes. As Scott (1985, p. 479) writes, "These arguments are all in one way or another elaborations out of a single underlying thesis, namely, that the spatial character and dynamics of cities and regions in capitalist society grow out of the *social* and *technical* relations of commodity production" (my emphasis).

The technical conditions of production in Sraffa's scheme are translated in Scott's work as the spatial input–output linkages among firms in the city. By drawing upon the work of Coase, Stigler, and Williamson, Scott further argues that these linkages take on a clear spatial intra-urban pattern. Labor-intensive manufacturing activities and office activities alike require inputs from, and provide outputs to, similar kinds of firms. The upshot is spatial clustering, as firms minimize transaction costs. Furthermore, because of both the nature of the input–output linkages and the nature of the labor market, such clustering is found downtown. Scott terms these specific technical conditions of production vertical disintegration. In contrast, "capital-intensive" firms are able to locate independently of other firms, usually in the suburbs, where land costs are low. Such conditions of production are called vertical integration. In addition to input–output linkages, Scott (1979; 1986b, p. 31) also discusses technological change. Here Scott emphasizes the effects of "reswitching" on urban land use patterns. The notion of reswitching comes directly from Sraffa's work, and for Scott it represents the effects of changing wage and profit rates on technical choice, and hence the spatial pattern of production.

Scott discusses the social conditions of distribution in terms of the reproduction of labor. There are two interconnected issues here: establishing the level of wages and providing a full account of the broader urban context in which such reproduction is secured. Taking the first issue, Scott recognizes a fundamental antagonism between labor and capital in setting wage rates (justified by Sraffa's demonstration of a negative relationship between wage and profit rates, noted above). Nonetheless, like Sraffa, Scott does not identify a single mechanism to explain the outcome of the "wage bargain." Scott has pointed to a range of influences: commuting time, levels of unionization, gender, and ethnicity. A second facet of labor reproduction is the spatial outcome represented by the creation of residential space. The idea here is that in securing the wage bargain, "emergent effects . . . are set in motion as the [working] population sets about the task of occupying a residential space" (Scott, 1986b, p. 29). Specifically, "the useful reproductive capacities of intraurban space become fully appropriable for specified factions of the labour force only when that space is also reconstructed (through the housing choices of individuals) as a system of quasi-homogeneous neighborhoods" (Scott, 1986b, p. 33). Neighborhoods as places are therefore integral to labor reproduction. Furthermore, as neighborhoods acquire a distinctive "politics of place" (Scott and Storper, 1987), they play an active role in shaping both the city and the broader production system in which it is enmeshed. In this way place is not passive but makes a difference.

Through this brief and baldly stated account of Scott's work we see some of the features embodied in Sraffa's contextual approach. First, there is no attempt to provide a single theory that accounts for everything. In trying to understand a particular context, Scott has drawn upon a number of theorists from quite different traditions: from the avowedly neoclassical George Stigler to the avowedly neo-Ricardian Ian Steedman. In this sense, Scott is offering a piecemeal approach. Providing, however, that the elements are mutually consistent, such a practice fulfills the mandate of contextualism, sensitive to the context and not slave to a single theory. In this way the charges of eclecticism that Amin and Robbins (1990) and Lovering (1990) in particular level at Scott's work maybe misplaced. Once interpreted as anti-essentialist, Scott's eclecticism should be seen as a virtue rather than a sin (see also Scott and Storper's, 1992, comments about the triad of different influences on their work—Weberian location theory, institutional or evolutionary economics, and regulationist theory).

Second, Scott eschews essentialism. The twin ideas of the social and technical conditions of production are not unchanging, universal entities. Rather, they take on meaning only when placed within a particular context. Technical conditions of production vary historically (vertically integrated production units are relatively recent; Scott, 1982), while the social conditions of production are different in different places (inner-city ethnic neighborhoods in Los Angeles provide "pools of cheap and malleable labor" for the vertically disintegrated production units close by, while the suburban landscape of the Santa Clara valley is the complement of proximal vertically integrated plants; Scott, 1986a, p. 34).

Finally, Scott is concerned with context. Although contending that there are broad features of capitalist urbanization, Scott (1986b, p. 32) argues that "each different city is marked by a specific local history, [one] that is shot through with the particularities of place and locale."

CONCLUSION

In conclusion, as an intellectual Sraffa was very much a man of the twentieth century, a period when nothing is taken for granted and there is a deep suspicion of any absolute theory and any absolute conclusion. As nineteenth-century thinkers such as Marx, Darwin, and Comte demystified religious dogma, twentieth-century thinkers such as Wittgenstein, Foucault, and Sraffa demystified the theory that the demystifiers erected in the place of dogma. In this chapter I argued that this twentieth-century project is manifest in Sraffa's particular work on value theory. From the late 1920s onward, Sraffa was concerned to show in formal terms that prevailing value theories which posit some foundation for economic life are logically inconsistent on their own terms. His constructive task then becomes one of developing a value theory that is formally consistent but that makes no reference to underlying bedrocks. I believe that this is the central contribution of the *Production of Commodities by Means of Commodities*. In this work Sraffa simultaneously points to mathematical abstraction and concrete contexts—directions, I argued, that can be fruitfully explored by both regional scientists and economic geographers.

More fundamentally, Sraffa is holding out the prospect of bringing economics into the twentieth century. He also holds out the same possibility for economic geography and regional science, should we choose to accept it.

EIGHT

HAROLD A. INNIS
Local Hero

I am always appalled at some of the work done in geography.
In many cases it is bad descriptive economics.

—Harold A. Innis

Harold A. Innis (1894–1952), part of Canada's revered intellectual troika along with Northrop Frye and Marshall McLuhan, was a lifelong member of the Department of Political Economy at the University of Toronto. Such institutional bounds, however, never bound Innis. As he prosecuted (often at the same time) economic history, economic geography, communication theory, political economy, and cultural criticism, Innis was above all a public intellectual, someone continually engaged with the political and moral sensibilities of his own place and period. Perhaps for this reason the university was his perfect refuge. As Innis said, "I once had to choose between going into university work, and going into politics and I decided to go into politics" (quoted in Watson, 1977, p. 45).

The lineaments of that "university work" are easily enough described (Creighton, 1957). After completing undergraduate and M.A. degrees at McMaster University, Innis went to the University of Chicago in 1918 to complete a Ph.D. in economics. Although Thorstein Veblen, the American institutional economist, had already left, his intellectual legacy was still potent. The completion of Innis's doctoral thesis on the history of the Canadian Pacific Railway led in 1920 to his appointment at the University of Toronto. His subsequent career there can be divided roughly into two phases: the first was the elaboration of the staples thesis, the idea that the history of Canadian economic and institutional development was bound up with the export of a series of primary resources; and the second, beginning in the latter part of the 1930s, was centered on communication studies. Many argue, however, that it is wrong to see these two phases as distinct (Easterbrook, 1953; Parker, 1977). Linking them is a strong geographical theme, spaces of power. In the case of staples, each commodity type and its form of production create a particular spatial configuration that tends either to centralization and the relative power of the metropole or to decentralization and the relative powerlessness of the periphery. In the communications work, Innis metaphorically extended his original staples idea (McLuhan, 1953; Wernick, 1986; Patterson, 1990). By substituting types of knowledge for types of staples and the form of communication for the form of production, he argued that knowledge and its form of communication lean toward either a spatial bias that creates territorial "empires" or a temporal bias that leads to local "monopolies of knowledge" (Wernick, 1986). More generally, the shift in Innis's work from staples to communications was a movement in degree rather than in kind. As Marshall McLuhan (1953, p. 385) put it in his obituary, Innis "shifted his attention from the trade routes of the external world to the trade routes of the mind." The common geographical metaphor is the critical point, and my main purpose in this chapter is to clarify that geography.

Innis's geography is generally not recognized by geographers, however. In fact, for the most part they all but ignore Innis. He would have enjoyed the irony, particularly because during his formative years he even referred to himself as associate professor of economic geography (Dunbar, 1985). That he is not now much read by geographers (nor by most other social scientists) is perhaps more understandable when we look at how he wrote and at the details of what he wrote.

"Enigmatic," "cryptic," and "aphoristic" are some of the euphemisms applied to his prose. More bluntly, his writing style is frequently dense, almost brutal, making for headache-inducing reading. Furthermore, the contents of his books appear to have, at best, an antiquarian interest for contemporary economic geographers and, at worst, none at all. For example, his early historical writings on staples seem of little relevance to the current Canadian economy in which most workers are no longer tillers of soil or hewers of wood. His later works are even more oblique. Of what interest to modern social scientists are Phoenician scrolls, Egyptian hieroglyphs, or Babylonian tablets, the focus of his communication studies?

The argument of this chapter, however, is that Innis's work is intensely relevant to economic geographers. If his prose appears awkward, it is not because he cannot write but because he had good reasons for writing the way he did, reasons that are as important now as when he was alive. Likewise, if he wrote about the fur trade or cod fisheries as staples, or the inscriptions of ancient Phoenicians, Egyptians, and Babylonians, then it was not because of an archaic bent but because they were the catalysts to theorizing about such fundamental issues as the nature of power, empire, and technology, and especially space and time.

In this chapter I will argue that linking these seemingly disparate aspects of Innis's work is his attempt at what I will call local modeling. A full discussion of this term is given below, but in brief it means the inventive construction of models that from their very conception are designed to cope with the events of a particular time and place. In the case of Innis, he was always interested in working out ideas that would help make sense of the particular local formation of Canada. In so doing, he necessarily eschewed appeal to universal principles, for they were only the misnamed ideas of metropolitan powers and had been foisted upon the colonies. As Carey (1978, p. 149) puts it, "American and British scholarship was based, [Innis] thought, on a conceit: it pretended to discover Universal Truth, to proclaim Universal Laws, and to describe a Universal Man. . . . Imperial powers, so it seems, seek to create not only economic and political clients, but intellectual clients as well."

Innis's position that there are no universal models but only local ones leads to a major problem, though. For on what basis could he assert the plausibility of his own local model, other than through the circularity of appealing to his own local circumstances? Innis recognized this problem and termed it "bias," but it is perhaps better expressed as reflexivity. That is, local models by their very construction bend back, as it were, and question their own legitimacy. In this case there is seemingly no justification of local models other than in terms of their own localness. I will argue that Innis was acutely aware of the problems that attend reflexivity and that one purpose of his later work on communications is an attempt to deal with such problems.

In making this argument, I divide this chapter into four main sections. First, I discuss the nature of local and universal models. Second, I argue that Innis was attracted to local models because of both his position as a colonial intellectual and his sympathy with the American school of institutional economics, which through its links to the philosophy of pragmatism provided the intellectual wherewithal for his project. Third, I present Innis's staples approach and discuss the features that make it a local model. I also emphasize that unlike most universal models, Innis's work on staples by its very construction includes an explicit geography and history. In the last section I briefly review Innis's work on communications, arguing that one of its ends was to deal with issues of reflexivity arising from the original staples model. Furthermore, it was a reflexive account that explicitly incorporated space and time.

LOCAL AND UNIVERSAL MODELS

Although the general idea of a local model can be traced back to Vico, the particular conception of it used in this chapter derives from Gudeman and Penn (1982), who contrast it with the notion of a universal model.

For Gudeman and Penn, a universal model is defined by a particular "core" language that represents the essential features of the phenomena investigated. By "essential features" is meant those inviolable characteristics that define a phenomenon. If there is no reference to such features, then the model is simply not a model of that entity or event. In turn the core language possesses four properties (Gudeman and Penn, 1982, pp. 91–93). First, because universal models have their origin in the Galilean–Cartesian intellectual tradition, they tend to portray the relationship among elements of the core language in mathematical terms, which is presented as a final vocabulary. Second, the core language consists of a set of both systematically defined terms and concepts as well as inference rules. This in turn allows relationships among phenomena to be represented as necessary truths that are deductively derived "rather than expressions of the fortuitous occurrence of specific causal factors" (Gudeman and Penn, 1982, p. 91). Third, the core language represents a bedrock on which to base explanation. In spite of the ostensible complexity and variegation of surface events, they are always reducible to, and thereby understood by, the invariant relationships embodied in the core language. Note that if those invariant relationships do not include space or time, then space and time themselves will also be so reduced (see Chapter Two). Finally, the relationship between the model and reality is typically portrayed in one of two ways. Rationalists maintain that the core language possesses a logic of its own, and it is this logic that enables us to see and understand the significance of empirical facts. In contrast, the empiricists see the core language as somehow derived from the facts themselves. Irrespective of these differences, the important point is that both rationalists and empiricists view the relationship between the model and the real world as objective. The modeler's role is passively to connect the two by applying a formal set of rules and concepts derived from either rationalism or empiricism. As a result, the context in which the modelers work does not affect the relationship between the model and the modelers.

A prime example of a universal model, one that will be relevant in my later discussion of Innis's work, is neoclassical economics and its assumption of rational choice (see Chapters Two and Three). In terms of the four characteristics outlined by Gudeman and Penn, it is first a model expressed in mathematical terms, usually in differential calculus. Second, its core language consists of a set of formal definitions and inference rules such as rationality, perfect competition, the firm, prices, and so on. From those definitions deductive claims are made about various elements within the system, such as individual behavior. Third, its core language is invariant. Rational behavior supposedly holds for all times and places (seen, for example, in the so-called formalist school of economic anthropology; Burling, 1962). In fact, even time and place are reduced to rationality. Time is not history but logical time manifest as a rationally derived equilibrium point where history has stopped (Hicks, 1976; Robinson, 1979), and place is not geography but rather a dimensionless point at which producers rationally derive the greatest gap between revenue and costs. Finally, the relationship between the core language and reality tends to be portrayed either in rationalist terms (as found in von Mises, 1963, or Machlup, 1978a and 1978b) or in empiricist terms (as found in the work of Hutchinson, 1938, and more recently Samuelson 1963, 1964).

The wider vision that grounds the idea of universal models has increasingly come under attack. I will not rehearse all those criticisms again (see Chapters Two, Three, and Four), but the central point is that it is wrong to suggest that there is a bedrock to knowledge that reveals the essence of things. Rather, knowledge can be acquired in many different ways. But to see how it is acquired, we must examine the local context, that is, we must see how knowledge is obtained, used, and verified in the practices of people living in particular places and times.

A local model is the antithesis of a universal one. Rather than making universal and essentialist claims, it makes local and contextual ones. In particular, a local model is designed in order to understand the events at a particular time and place. It is thus local in that it refers to a specific context, not that it is necessarily restricted to a limited geographical area.

The four features that characterize local models are the antonyms of those that define universal ones. First, there is no single accurate language of representation such as mathematics. As I argued in Chapter Six, mathematics is not a final vocabulary but is shot full of contradictions, hidden assumptions, and various aporia. More generally, local modelers are attuned to the problematic nature of writing in any form. For once one abandons the notion that meaning stems from foundational essences, the very idea of writing an "accurate representation" is called into question (Barnes and Duncan, 1992).

Second, local models typically shun definitive definitions and linear deductive logic. It is recognized that knowledge is acquired in all kinds of ways, not just through the deductive syllogism (that is, if knowledge is ever acquired that way at all; see Chapter Four). Rather, anything can be used as a model, and frequently is. In particular, many models (as I already argued in a number of previous chapters) are extended metaphors. Knowledge is then derived from the internal logic of the metaphor itself, which tends to be nonlinear and based upon the jolt of pattern recognition rather than item-by-item correspondence predicated upon logical deduction.

Third, local modelers reject the idea that there is a single bedrock on which explanation of the supposed variability of the world is based. Apart from problems of justifying these essences (see Chapter Three), such a strategy is deeply reductionist. Instead, local modelers celebrate the messiness of social life by building particularity into their very models through deployment of disparate metaphors and codes. In this way geography and history are retained and not reduced to logical constructs.

Finally, local modelers deny the idea that reality and the model are separate entities and that some grand method such as empiricism or rationalism is needed to join the two objectively. Instead, reality is created by the practice of modeling itself. Modelling is as much a constitutive activity as a representational one. The modeler is not passive but active. It is for this reason that reflexivity is such an important issue in local modeling. For local models (reflexively) say as much about the process of constructing a model as the world that the model represents.

INNIS, COLONIALISM, AND INSTITUTIONAL ECONOMICS

Innis once said that "one cannot be a social scientist without a sense of humour in Canada, and one is in constant danger of dying with laughter" (quoted in Berger, 1976, p. 193). In this as in many of his aphorisms, Innis's meaning is not immediately apparent. Certainly there are few side-splitting jokes in his writings. But Innis's prose is spattered with biting ironic asides that at least raise a bleak smile. If it is to the humor of irony that he points, then his maxim begins to make more sense. For to be ironic is to recognize self-consciously the near impossibility of what you are trying to do but to do it anyway. In this sense, irony is born out of constraint and limitation.

As a "colonial intellectual," Innis felt constrained and limited principally by "the dominant and myopic paradigms in research set by metropolitan institutions and intellectuals" (Watson, 1977, p. 45). For in the 1920s and 1930s, much of Canadian intellectual life was dominated by British academics (Drache, 1983, p. 39). In attempting to resist that hegemony, Innis turned to local modeling, the eventual result of which was the staples model (Drache, 1983, p. 39). Furthermore, Innis was not alone in his attempt to break free. As Berger (1976, p. 9) notes, there was a concerted effort by many Canadian intellectuals, artists, and writers during this same period to strive for "more authentic, indigenous . . . [forms of representation that were] freed from the bondage of

European paradigms." Perhaps the best-known example is the Group of Seven.

In trying to escape his bondage, Innis was ultimately engaged in a subversive enterprise: to challenge, confront, and combat colonial orthodoxy. Wernick (1986, p. 130) writes that Innis had a "wild side," and "like other foes of empire and dominant culture, [he] hid out in history." In Innis's (1956a, p. 3) specific case, history was so important because it "becomes . . . a tool by which the economic theory of the old countries can be amended. . . . [That is,] the only escape [from old economic theory] can come from an intensive study of Canadian economic problems and from the development of a philosophy of economic history or an economic theory suited to Canadian economic needs."

The economic theory of the old countries was the universal model of neoclassical economics, and Innis's amendment to it, through his intensive study of Canadian economic history, was the staples model. The details of his staples model are given in the next section, but it is clear that even in his earliest writings he saw neoclassical economics as not just inappropriate to Canada but pernicious. As Innis (1956a, p. 3) wrote, the dominance of neoclassical thought meant that "Canadians are obliged . . . to fit their analysis of new economic facts into an old background. The handicaps of this process are obvious, . . . resulting in a new form of exploitation with dangerous consequences."

The "old background" of neoclassical economics was first articulated in Europe in the 1870s by Jevons in Britain and Walras and Menger on the Continent. The basic tenets of the neoclassical scheme have already been adumbrated in Chapters Two and Three. For the particular case of Canada, neoclassicism would contend that by rationally trading in the resource commodities in which the country possesses a comparative advantage, the efficiency of the competitive free market mechanism would ensure that markets would clear, diversification would follow, and long-run equilibrium be attained.

At least when Innis first began publishing in the early 1920s, no one had yet undertaken an explicit neoclassical analysis of the Canadian economy. By the late 1920s, however, a contemporary of Innis, W. A. Mackintosh, adopted a form of neoclassicism by arguing that Canada's staples trade would eventually produce equilibrium once the country's geographical hindrances were overcome (see especially Drache, 1976, p. 4, but also Drache, 1982; Laxer, 1991; Clement and Williams, 1989). By the time Innis died, explicit, full-blown neoclassical analyses were completed (for example, Baldwin, 1956; Buckley, 1958). Furthermore, as "Canadian economics became a branch plant of US economics" (Watkins, 1982, p. 17) following the end of World War II, the frequency of such analyses increased. In fact, by the 1950s "the shift in western economics towards econometrics ... , [meant that] mathematics and deduction [had] replaced historical inquiry" (Laxer, 1991, p. xv). So when he warned about a "new form of exploitation" in 1929, Innis was as prescient as he was looking to his own time.

I argued above that general neoclassical theory displays the four features of a universal model, and those characteristics are certainly evident in the neoclassical equilibrium analyses of markets, trade, and investment that were subsequently applied to Canada (see, for example, Caves, 1960). For Innis, however, there was nothing universal about them at all. In presenting a general critique and in formulating his alternative local model, he implicitly drew upon the American institutionalists, primarily Veblen, whom he saw as carrying out a parallel project (seen, for example, in Veblen's attempt recognition of the dangers inherent in a "final economic theory"; Innis, 1956c, p. 26). Without going into the details, I will say simply that the institutionalists presented a very different conception of science from the Galilean–Cartesian view embodied in universal models and thereby a very different type of economics, one conducive to the construction of local models (Wilber and Harrison, 1978; Mirowski, 1988). In particular, as Mirowski (1988, p. 113) argues, institutionalists drew directly upon the leading American pragmatist philosophers—Charles Sanders Peirce, John Dewey, and William James. For these pragmatist philosophers, there are no fundamental essences to be represented, foolproof methods to be found, or final vocabularies that were indubitably final (Dugger, 1992, p. 25). Rather, truth is made, not found; it emerges out of particular practices and communities of inquiry, both of which are historically and geographically variable (Rorty, 1982, pp. 160–169; Bernstein, 1983, pp. 197–207). Consequently, pragmatism celebrated the variability of belief and practice and was attuned to the need for an interpretive and a historically and geographically sensitive approach. As Dewey (1939, p. 246) had written, "philosophy as a concrete existence is historical, having temporal passage and a diversity of local habitations." Economics needed to be similarly concrete, historical, and local, at least so the institutionalists argued (Dugger, 1992).

With these intellectual antecedents, the American institutional school prosecuted a very different kind of economics from neoclassicism (Dugger, 1979). First, it rejected abstract mathematical theorizing (albeit not quantitative methods as such; Seckler, 1975, p. 6). This is because "formalist models simply cannot handle the range of variables, the specificity of institutions, and the non-generality of behavior" (Wilber and Harrison, 1978, p. 72). Instead, "institutional methodology stresses historical realism at the expense of mathematical rigor" and is thus "messy and tentative rather than abstract and definitive" (Dugger, 1992, p. 55). One topic where the methodological differences between neoclassicism and institutionalism are particularly acute is with respect to the approach of each to markets and price setting. For institutionalists, market activity is made possible by a host of institutional norms, expectations, and conventions, all of which are historically and geographically relative (Hodgson, 1988, ch. 8). As Hodgson (1988) argues, those institutional norms affect both what and how much consumers buy, the quantity firms produce and their methods of production, and the final set of prices that are charged. Such detail and variability, however, cannot be presented by a neoclassical framework that employs the universal and homogenizing mathematics of supply-and-demand functions (which, taken to its extreme, is an exercise only in mathematics, seen in Debreau's, 1959, Nobel-award-winning work on neoclassical value theory). For those mathematical functions squash flat difference, making nonmarket institutions appear as "fictitious or ephemeral in nature" rather than the concrete and enduring phenomena that institutionalists consider them to be (Rotstein, 1977, p. 27).

Second, modeling those institutional relations in terms of deductive logic is generally unsatisfactory. For there is no invariant logic across institutions. Institutions evolve historically and are the crystallization of certain habits, customs, and instincts. (Veblen, 1919, p. 239, defined them as "settled habits of thought.") By definition, habits, customs, and in- stincts are not amenable to deductive logic. Rather, a very different kind of analysis is needed, one institutionalists term the "pattern model" (Wilber and Harrison, 1978; Dugger, 1979). In this model, as Ruth Benedict shows in *Patterns of Culture*, individual acts and events are linked to some broader institutional complex of meaning (see Chapter One). This pattern cannot be deduced from first principles, nor do individuals themselves logically derive it when undertaking their actions. Rather, the pattern evolves over time and forms the necessary background for any intelligible action at all. The kind of method needed to understand such patterns is ethnographical and historical not logical and mathemati- cal. In this sense, as Dugger (1992, p. xxviii) writes, "institutionalism is cultural economics." The classic example is Veblen's study of "conspicu- ous consumption." Such behavior cannot be rationally deduced; the ostentatious waste of money, time, resources, and effort is not logical. But to those elite who were socialized into the wider pattern of culture of late-nineteenth-century America, wasteful consumption was the norm, the expected pattern. Veblen's analysis was therefore as much ethnographic and anthropological as it was economic (see also Diggins, 1978).

Third, institutionalists have an antipathy toward the rationality postulate. Veblen (1919, p. 73) satirically portrays "economic man" as a "homogeneous globule of desire . . . [with] neither antecedent nor conse- quent. He is an isolated, definitive human datum, in stable equilibrium except for the buffets of the impinging forces that displace him in one direction or another." Again, this view fails for the institutionalists because it does not acknowledge the broader cultural matrix in which action occurs, including its history and geography. Individuals act not in an institutional vacuum but in a rich and messy context. As Veblen (1919, pp. 242–243) writes, "The wants and desires, the end and aim, the ways and means, the amplitude and drift of the individual's conduct are functions of an institutional variable that is of a highly complex and wholly unstable character." The rigidity of the rationality postulate denies both that complexity and instability, and so the task of institutional economics becomes one of moving "beyond the bounds of the . . . ratiocinations of the individual into the meanings and institutions of culture" (Dugger, 1992, p. xxvii).

Finally, there is evidence, albeit somewhat controversial, that Veblen, at least, questions the idea of an objective theorizing and recognizes the importance of reflexivity. In a well-known passage, Veblen writes, "A discussion of the scientific point of view which avowedly proceeds from this point of view has necessarily the appearance of an argument in a circle; and such in great part is the character of what here follows" (1919, p. 32). On the basis of this passage and others, Samuels (1990, p. 707) concludes that Veblen "applied his own theory of preconceptions to his own preconceptions, that is his analysis was self-consciously self-referential." For example, Mayhew (1988, p. 27) suggests that Veblen at least implicitly recognized that his mode of analysis, intent on presenting economic life as "an unbroken sequence of cumulative change," was itself reflective of the machine process that for him constituted the very economic life he was studying.

In sum, rather than attempting to construct a universal model of the economy in the Galilean–Cartesian tradition, the American institutionalists followed the pragmatists in allowing for cultural difference. Both particularity and relativity are introduced through the recognition of institutional variability and diversity manifest in space and time. Innis was drawn to these features by his own antipathy toward the universal model of neoclassical economics and his desire to construct a made-in-Canada alternative. The result was the staples model, which not only pointed to the political and material consequences that result from "the discrepancy between the center and the margin of Western civilization" but also self-consciously recognized the particularity of the Canadian social formation, including its geography and history.

INNIS'S LOCAL MODEL: STAPLES THEORY

The central idea of Innis's staples model is that to understand Canadian economy and society we must begin with the export of a series of minimally processed primary resources: staples. For staples function as "the leading sector of the economy, and set the pace for economic growth" (Watkins, 1963, p. 144). That growth, though, is continually frustrated and never comes to fruition in the form of equilibrium development. For a staples economy always becomes ensnared in a staples trap (Williams, 1983). That is, diversification is blocked because of such reasons as an export mentality among producers, the domination of the economy by a few large and often foreign-owned multinational corporations, and a truncated industrial branch–plant structure that minimizes the development of higher-order control and research functions (Britton and Gilmour, 1978). The result, to use Innis's terminology, is that staples-producing regions become hinterland economies whose fates are strongly tied to events in more powerful foreign metropoles.

Innis identified four principal connections between the nature of staples production and the economic instability and dependency found within staples regions. First, the market for staple commodities much more approximates perfect competition than the market for manufactured goods. As such, staples regions are price-takers in a market where price volatility is the norm. In particular, the bulk and crude exports that are the basis of most staples regions tend to be very vulnerable to demand shifts in markets that are both highly competitive and price-elastic. Second, because domestic sales of staples are relatively small, international market volatility has direct and strong impacts, thereby producing the characteristic boom-and-bust economy of resource-producing regions. Third, for a variety of reasons (technological advances that reduce resource inputs for production, the growth of synthetic substitutes, and low long-run income elasticities of demand), the terms of trade for primary commodities are increasingly less favorable to staples-producing areas. Finally, resource production tends to be undertaken by big, often foreign-owned multinational corporations. Spry (1981) argues that this is a direct consequence of the large capital expenditures and production indivisibilities associated with staples. However, the presence of foreign multinational firms in staples regions creates a number of potential problems, including appropriation of large economic rents because of the undervaluing of resources by the local state; the inhibition of resource upgrading prior to export because the resource extraction subsidiaries are only one part of a vertically integrated corporation where processing is often carried out elsewhere; very low levels of technological development; lack of local control; and a weakened ability to control trade through explicit policy because of the high degree of intracorporate transfers.

In sum, there is a direct relationship between the type of trade in which a staples region engages and its level of social and economic development. Note that this is not a connection that neoclassical economics would ever make. It would say that through the free workings of the market, staples nations such as Canada would eventually achieve equilibrium industrial development by initially specializing and trading in those commodities for which it has a comparative advantage, primary resources. It was this view that Innis (1956a, p. 3) dubbed "a new form of exploitation."

To circumscribe such exploitation, Innis developed his staples theory in such a way that it was peculiarly suited to the local facts. That theory brought together three types of concerns: geographical/ecological, technological, and institutional. This triad in turn became the basis for a theory of staples accumulation.

By geography, the first leg of the triad, Innis had at least two things in mind: the natural environment of an area and broad spatial relationships. Specifically, the conjunction of particular ecological conditions with a given physical geography creates at least one of two spatial patterns of settlement and economy. Centripetal forces culminate in local metropoles in which distribution and processing occur, while centrifugal ones produce a periphery of scattered resource communities. More broadly, each type of staple is associated with a particular space–time "bias" toward either centralization or decentralization, making the Canadian economic landscape a patchwork quilt of different staple geographies. Such biases are not innocent, though; they give shape to the very nature of regionalism within Canada.

Technology, the second component, has been seen by some as the most important. Watkins (1963, p. 141), for example, concludes that "methodologically, Innis's staple approach was more technological history writ large than a theory of economic growth in the conventional sense." Certainly, technology has been a critical issue in Canadian intellectual thought (Kroker, 1984). In Innis's model the dominant technology affects both how (and if) staples are produced and, through its manifestation in the form of transportation, the very space–time biases inherent in each resource commodity. Nonetheless, Watkins's claim is exaggerated. Geography and technology work hand in hand, and furthermore, this interaction can occur only provided that the third leg of the triad, an appropriate institutional structure is also present. Investing in staples production in the periphery requires large amounts of capital expenditure because of the high "minimum indivisible cost[s] that must be met if production is to be undertaken at all" (Spry, 1981, pp. 155–156). Only two institutional forms are capable of raising sufficient funds to cover such costs: the state, which provides basic infrastructure, and large corporations, often foreign owned, which meet the immediate costs of plant and capital equipment.

Finally, when the right geography comes together with the right technology and the right institutional structure, the result is accumulation of "cyclonic" frenzy. In this way virgin resource regions are transformed and enveloped within the produced spaces of the capitalist periphery. Such intense accumulation, however, never lasts, and because of the very instabilities of staples production, sooner rather than later investment shifts to yet other staples regions, leaving in its wake abandoned resource sites and communities.

Staples Theory as a Local Model

Given this compressed account, we can nonetheless begin to see the local nature of Innis's work and its link with the American institutionalists. Following the general characteristics of local models, Innis shuns mathematical formalization in his work. He writes that one "must resist the fatal attraction of analogies with the physical sciences and particularly with the possibilities of mathematics" (Innis, 1935, p. 284). This is in part because of the difficulty (certainly in his time and even now) of representing the unstable, noncompetitive, and nonequilibrium conditions that characterize Canadian resource production. But it is also because, following the institutionalists, Innis recognizes the need to include noneconomic variables in understanding, for example, markets, and such variables cannot be reduced to the homogeneity of supply-and-demand functions. As Drache (1992, p. 4) puts it, Innis realized "that markets had to be organized and economic space defined. Culture was a key determinant because markets reflected historical practices, geography, technological change and social custom. These made structures and institutions the powerful foundation of economics rather than [any] abstract laws" (also see Melody, 1981, p. 9).

It was not only the traditional neoclassical mathematical vocabulary of markets that Innis avoided, however. He was also increasingly leery of any conventional forms of representation that used existing theories, models and concepts. This wariness came about in part because on intellectual grounds he saw such conventions as ossifying thinking, creating "grooves which determined the channels of thought of readers and later writers" (Innis, 1951, p. 11; also see Brebner, 1953, pp. 14–15, and Carey, 1967, pp. 6–7 fn. 1). But Innis also believed such modes of thought often bore the stamp of the colonial powers from which they originated. To counter such "bias," Innis necessarily invented his own vocabulary and style. Hence, his various terms such as "space–time bias," "cyclonics," "centrifugal and centripetal forces," and "metropole and margin" (Drache, 1982, p. 55, fn. 6). Such a vocabulary not only bespoke Canadian localness but also countered the "new forms of exploitation" by breaking from a hegemonic lexicon. It is here that we begin to understand Innis's alleged travails with written English. It was not that he could not write but that he wrote in the way he did because of his definite views about politics and the intellectual.

Second, Innis eschews deductive logic and formal reasoning. As Brebner (1953, p. 15) notes, Innis specialized in "draw[ing] sufficient conclusions from what appeared to be insufficient premises." More generally, like the institutionalists, Innis is more interested in establishing the broader pattern, a pattern in his case made up of the triad of institutions, technology, and geography. The disparate nature of these elements, along with Innis's desire to signal their shifting meaning and importance, meant that the static and homogenizing deductive syllogism was of little help. Instead, as Brebner (1953, p. 18) argues, Innis favored a narrative in which institutions, technology, and geography could be "woven . . . into . . . a vivid and variegated and tough fabric of explanatory exposition." Because Innis had such leanings, Brebner (1953) further argues, his model took on traits of nonlinearity, displaying analogical rather than deductive modes of reasoning. This argument is supported by Patterson (1990, p. 32), who writes that Innis was constantly moving between "idea[s] from one medium or frame of reference to another and . . . he did not do so by logical connection but by way of analogy. . . . He was engaged in 'pattern recognition.' " An example is his use of the climatic metaphor of the cyclone: it captured the instability, intensity, unpredictability, speed, and sometimes devastating effects of staples production (Berger, 1976, p. 97). In applying this metaphor, Innis was certainly not concerned with logical derivation; rather, its role was rhetorical and heuristic, drawing attention to the similarities between a dramatic natural event and a dramatic social event (see also Parker's [1988, p. 66] insightful comments on Innis's meteorological metaphor).

Third, Innis sided with Veblen against the rationality postulate (Innis, 1956c). His main reason is that the postulate is the basis of a "standardized, static economics," whereas for him economics should be intent on "outlin[ing] . . . dynamic change and . . . work[ing] out a theory not only of dynamics but of cyclonics" (Innis, 1956c, p. 26). More generally, Innis's staples model emphasizes flux and uncertainty—price fluctuations, unstable market demand, new technological developments, and changing knowledge about resource supplies. Such uncertainty is difficult to square with the assumption of omnipotent knowledge and incorrigible decisiveness associated with economic rationality. As Neill (1991, p. 134) suggests, Innis "was too conscious of the consequences of objective irrationality, that is 'unpredictablness', to think that much could be learned about historical outcomes from . . . [applying] subjective rationality" (see also Parker, 1985, p. 84).

More generally, Innis's skepticism about *Homo economicus* was part of his wider anti-essentialist view. For him, specificity and particularity could not be reduced to something more fundamental; they were fundamental in and of themselves. This is why he was concerned to include a disparate collage of codes in his work: of politics and economics, of technology, and of geography and ecology. Although Carey (1988, p. 150) calls this "a made-in-the-kitchen" approach, it is nonetheless central given Innis's goal of maintaining diversity and difference. For Innis recognized that "variations in history and geography demand in scholarship concomitant variations in social theory and cultural meaning" (Carey, 1988, p. 150).

Finally, and this point will be taken up below, Innis became increasingly distrustful of claims to objectivity. This was because Innis (1935, p. 280) believed social scientists were necessarily biased as a consequence of their being both observers and observed; "their practices were bound up with the very social complex they sought to analyze" (Berger, 1976, p. 105). Thus there is no point of detachment. The resulting bias then insinuates itself into the models of social science and is eventually institutionalized. The pervasiveness of bias does not imply that we should abandon social science, though. Implicitly following the pragmatist line, Innis suggests that we should engage in a reflexive project; that is, we need to understand our understanding by directly studying those biases. As Innis (1946, p. 83) writes, "We need a sociology or a philosophy of the social sciences and particularly of economics, an economic history of knowledge or any economic history of economic history."

In sum, following the American institutionalists and through them a pragmatist philosophy, Innis's work on the staples model "made thinkable a de-dogmatising re-arrangement of the local intellectual field" (Wernick, 1986, p. 137). Innis eschewed the universal model of neoclassical economics and the Galilean–Cartesian assumptions on which it ultimately rested in favor of a local alternative. Furthermore, this alternative emphasized both space and time in contrast to the neoclassical account in which economic events happen on the end of a pin and history is stalled in permanent equilibrium. Let me conclude by briefly explicating that geography and history.

Space, Time, and Staples

Harvey (1986, p. 142) notes that the introduction of geography and history have "a numbing effect on the central propositions of *any* social theory." While this may be true for the social theory embodied in universal models, it does not necessarily apply to local models. Local models, precisely because their localness is defined by a distinct geography and history, often incorporate space and time into their analyses from the beginning. This claim is borne out by Innis's staples model.

The geography of the staples model stems directly from the staple commodity itself, which, once produced, creates a distinct web of spatial relations (Wernick, 1986, p. 140). In crude terms, those relations tend toward either decentralization and the geographical margin or centralization and the metropole. Note that in both cases the space is neither neutral nor homogeneous.

First, as Innis's terminology implies, both spaces disclose a political and material inequality and dependence brought about by staples production itself. In this sense, the geography of staples is as much a geography of power and control as it is of physical distance. Not that physical distance is unimportant, as Innis's (1956b) discussions of transportation make clear. But it is a space that has already been thoroughly socialized within the process of staples accumulation.

Second, both the margin and metropole are internally differentiated. On the one hand, the margin consists of a myriad but finite number of sites of staples extraction, the resource communities. Each is defined by a particular physical geography, a particular kind of technology of production (typically characterized by large amounts of indivisible fixed capital), and a particular institutional structure (the "company town" controlled by outside investors; Lucas, 1971). That geography, investment, and institutional structure, however, make such places inherently unstable. Sooner rather than later, as a result of resource problems (for example, depletion), difficulties associated with production indivisibilities (for example, excess output or debt load), or new corporate strategy (for example, internationalization of investment), such places are abandoned as the cyclone of resource extraction moves on. In Innis's conception, then, the very individuality of place, as represented by a specific ensemble of features, determines both its initial existence and longevity. Yet the places of the metropole, although much fewer in number, are primarily the sites of economic and political control and physical distribution. Also characterized by large amounts of fixed capital, the investment is often public rather than private and not directed toward production as such but concentrated in infrastructure, particularly transportation. Although both more homogeneous and stable than single-industry communities, metropoles are not all identical. There are different specializations among them, and the hierarchy of metropoles changes over time in response to the rise and fall of different "empires" and their demand for staple goods (for example, the relative shift in positions of Quebec City, Toronto, and Vancouver as the empires of the Old World, New World, and Pacific, respectively, have waxed and waned).

This internal geographical differentiation of margin and metropole produces a complex landscape, but it is made even more complex because over time new sets of metropole/margin relations are overlaid on old ones as fresh staples are introduced. For each staple will bring its own unique set of relations of centralization and decentralization. As a result, as Brodie (1989, p. 144) writes,

> It is as if Canadian history c[an] be represented as a series of transparencies, each representing a different matrix of economic growth and political organization, laid on geographical space on top of one another, as the international political economy change[s]. Each staple le[a]d[s] to different geographical configurations that [are] unstable across time. Boundaries—whether national or regional—are not 'in the land' but rather tied to the pattern of staples exploitation.

There are clearly resonances here between Brodie's interpretation of Innis and Massey's (1984b) more contemporary work on spatial divisions of labor. Whereas for Massey economic space is constructed by the layering of past and present manufacturing investment in response to local labor markets, in Innis's scheme it is constructed by the layering of past and present rounds of staples accumulation, each in response to the triad of geography, technology, and institutions. Drawing out this similarity should also indicate that Innis's geography is not simply a crude core–periphery model; its internal geographical differentiation is a necessary explanatory part of the wider model. For Massey and Innis alike, geography matters.

Time also matters. Innis incorporates time into his model by ensuring that there are continual forces of instability that prevent the realization of equilibrium. For equilibrium by definition is a time when there is no time. As Hicks (1976, p. 140) writes, "The use of the equilibrium concept is a signal that time, in some respect, has been put to one side." In an equilibrium world there is no instability because by definition one day is exactly like another. In contrast, the forces of instability that Innis includes mean that every day will be quite different.

Specifically, the forces of instability, and thus the forces of time, derive from the triad of factors that propel the cyclone of accumulation. First there is the instability that derives from technological change. Changes in production methods or transportation techniques, for example, will "disrupt inherited societal structures and relationships, with significant long term consequences" (Melody, 1981, p. 8). Second, changes in geographical factors and their economic expression cause instability. Nonrenewable resources run out, cheaper supplies are found elsewhere, and lower prices on international commodity markets make current production sites unfeasible. Finally, there are instabilities associated with institutional structure. The oligopolistic character of many staples firms necessary for the large capital expenditures produces financial and production "rigidities" that cause disequilibrium (Drache, 1982). Financial rigidity follows from the large debt load under which such firms place themselves to meet the minimum indivisible investment required for resource extraction and processing. Apart from the costs of servicing the debt, the firm ties up large amounts of capital that cannot be used again, possibly for decades. Under such conditions, the firm is vulnerable to the outside change so characteristic of the staples sector. Production rigidities follow from the inelastic production capacity associated with such investment projects. There is little scope for changing the nature of the product, and it is difficult to adjust output smoothly to meet changed demand conditions (Spry, 1981; Parker, 1985).

In sum, as a local modeler Innis is sensitive to the incorporation of space and time into his work. Indeed, those variations in space and time make up his object of inquiry. As he writes, economic "history is not a seamless web but rather a web in which the warp and weave are space and time, woven in a very uneven fashion and producing distorted patterns" (Innis, 1951, p. xvii). Universal models are of no help here. For in order for models to be universal, space and time must be conceived as the same in every place and every period within them. But for Innis it is precisely the differences in places and periods that are the basis of his study.

KNOWING WHERE YOU STAND: THE BIAS OF COMMUNICATION

The argument made so far is that Innis, because of his anticolonialist sentiments as well as the influence of the American institutionalists, constructed a local model of the Canadian scene that directly incorporated space and time. In this final section I want to argue that one purpose of Innis's later work on communications, which came to eclipse his writings on staples, was to provide a reflexive account of that earlier work. In making this argument, I am not denying that Innis's studies in communications had other ends, only that one end was addressing the problem of reflexivity. To make my argument, I divide this section into two parts: in the first I elaborate on the problem of bias and reflexivity, and in the second I demonstrate that Innis's communication studies provide a way of dealing with that problem, one in which, as in the staples model, space and time figure prominently.

Bias and Reflexivity

The term "local model" has so far meant a model of particular local context. There is, however, a second meaning that refers to the practice of modeling as a particular kind of activity. This second sense of the term implies that the model itself reflects its own local context. That is, modeling, the social scientific activity, takes place in a specific cultural and intellectual milieu with the result that the model comes to mirror the local context of which it is part. The implication is that if we want to understand others through our models, then we also need to understand something about ourselves, because our models are as much about us as they are about anyone else. For this reason, local modeling is by necessity a reflexive activity that requires an analysis of our analysis (Berger, 1976, p. 105).

Note that reflexivity is not a problem raised by universal modelers. For they believe in some universal bedrock entity—principally empiricism and rationalism—that always justifies the truthfulness of its representation of the world. Local modelers, however, shun such universal bedrocks. In so doing, they see the justification for the model as lying only within the context of the modelers themselves.

Through his reading of Veblen, Innis must have soon been aware of this general problem of reflexivity. Innis's first explicit writings on the topic, however, did not appear until the mid-1930s in the context of a debate about objectivity in economics following the publication of Lionel Robbins's (1935) seminal *Essay on the Nature and Significance of Economic Science* (Neill, 1991, pp. 134–135). Specifically, Innis's (1935) paper "The Role of Intelligence: Some Further Notes" first outlines the problem of "bias" and, in turn, as Neill (1991, p. 135) notes, marked "the beginning of his departure from Canadian economic history for the history of communication."

The argument of the 1935 paper is that a "social scientist cannot be 'scientific' or 'objective' " because the observer is also the observed (Innis, 1935, pp. 283, 280). This does not make social science impossible, though. Rather, required is a reflexive analysis of the sources of bias, that is, comprehension of why we believe the things that we do. This type of analysis is possible because bias is not simply subjective, a result of mere whim and fancy, but is part of the structure of our own society and culture and is cemented in the "cumulative bias of [our] institutions" (Innis, 1935, p. 29). Because of this institutionalization of bias and its constancy, one can undertake a systematic and intensive analysis of it. This is not to suppose that we can ever make that bias disappear, but through a reflexive account "the social scientist . . . can learn of his numerous limitations" (Innis, 1935, p. 283) and thereby achieve a kind of freedom. In Innis's case this meant acknowledging the biases of traditional economic theory and thereby gaining the freedom to provide an alternative account. In this way "the innumerable difficulties of the social scientist are paradoxically his own salvation" (Innis, 1935, p. 283).

Those "innumerable difficulties," though, are particularly intractable. For in general terms, Innis had "encountered the methodological problem (the hermeneutical dilemma) of discovering an 'epistemological' strategy by which we might think outside of the 'bias of communication' within which we are trapped" (Kroker, 1984, p. 109). Like Derrida (see Chapter Six), Innis responds to this dilemma in part through a particular writing style that is, as already noted, ironic, self-conscious, metaphorical, aphoristic, and nonlinear. For Innis knows that he is pursuing an impossible but necessary task: to claim knowledge about the world while recognizing that such knowledge is impossible to obtain. Of course, this unorthodox writing style does not solve such problems in any definitive way, but it does signal that there is no sense in pursuing definitiveness. As Berger (1976, p. 108) puts it, Innis was always "conscious that the things that he wanted to say simply could not be said in a style that itself implied completeness and finality." So to dismiss Innis's work on the basis of his writing style—because it is only a series of random jottings—is to miss the point; for random jottings are the best that he, or any other social scientist, could do.

But Innis had another way of approaching the issue of reflexivity, one that involved turning away from his work on staples and undertaking research on a seemingly very different topic, communication studies (Berger, 1976, p. 188).

A Theory of Communications

Although Innis never completed these communication studies because of his relatively early death (at fifty-nine), one of his main purposes was to examine bias (Berger, 1976, p. 88), that is, to provide an "economic history of economic history" (Innis, 1946, p. 83). In particular, Innis investigated the spread and institutionalization of knowledge through various media of communications. This was not, however, a mere mechanical tracing of bits of information and data but, as with staples, intimately bound up with structures of power and empire.

Innis's (1951, p. 33) main argument is that the "medium of communication has an important influence on the dissemination of knowledge over space and time." Here "medium of communication" is "broadly used to include all modes of symbolic representation," embracing everything from speech to pictorials, from soap-box oratory to e-mail (Carey, 1967, p. 7). The justification for making the communication medium central, following Carey (1967, p. 8), is that it "influences the kinds of human associations that can develop in any period," and thus the way humans think and what they think about. Indeed for Carey (1967, pp. 7–8), "consciousness is built on these human associations," and, in this sense, "communication media . . . are literally extensions of the mind."

The term "human associations" does not imply just physical interaction among people, though. Rather, the argument is that through the influence of the media of communication on institutional structures, structures in which human associations are formed, particular kinds of knowledge are legitimated and given authority. Or to put it in Innis's terms, the media of communication facilitate "monopolies of knowledge." As Carey (1967, p. 12) writes, "Innis wanted to know what, in general, determines the location of ultimate authority in society and what will be recognized as authorative knowledge. His answer was this: That media of communication . . . confer monopolies of authority and knowledge." By using the term "monopoly," Innis indicates that there is a politics to knowledge, that those who control communications also control "both consciousness and social organization" (Carey, 1967, p. 8).

In the course of his historical studies, Innis recognized two main types of communication media, each associated with a particular set of institutional forms that in turn control distinctive monopolies of knowledge. First, "light" communication media (such as papyrus, paper, and later electronic media), because of their ease of transmission across large distances are associated with the institutions of empire, such as the state and the military and in the twentieth century the multinational corporation. The kind of knowledge (bias) these media foster tends to be instrumental, secular, and presentist (Carey, 1967, p. 10). Second, in contrast, "hard" media of communication (such as stone or clay tablets) are much more difficult to transport and lead to locally circumscribed monopolies of knowledge. The central institutions in this case have a "concern with history and tradition, have little capacity for expansion of secular activity, and thus favor the growth of religion, or hierarchical organization, and of constrictionist [activities]" (Carey, 1967, p. 9). According to Innis, the kind of knowledge cultivated under these circumstances tends to focus on the sacred, the moral, and the historical.

As with the case of staples, Innis directly incorporates space and time into his communication studies and thereby his examination of "bias." For every communication medium is "biased" toward either space—light communication media favor spatially expansive empires—or time—heavy communication media favor local historical traditions. Notice that Innis uses "bias" in two senses here. There is epistemological bias, which is his concern in the 1935 article and there is the "dimensional" bias toward either space or time inherent in any medium of communication. At some point the two meanings of "bias" converge, however. For the bias in the communication media engenders a specific kind of institutional knowledge, which then becomes an epistemological bias.

More generally, Innis conceived of Western history as a clash between the biases toward either space or time that inhere in any medium of communication. Over the long run, Innis thought, communications favoring the bias of space and its particular institutional structures and knowledge would win out over those favoring time; that is, empires, not localities, and instrumental, not moral knowledge would predominate. In particular, Innis foresaw the "tragedy of modern culture" as deriving from the intrinsic tendency for the media of communication to reduce space "to the service of a calculus of commercialism and expansionism" (Carey, 1978, p. 135). Such a prognosis seems particularly prescient given the revolution in telecommunications since the 1980s. With "communication systems that transmit messages at the extremes of the laws of physics" (Carey, 1978, p. 170), empires now stretch worldwide. Indeed, the bias toward space seems so complete that geographical barriers have all but disappeared (Harvey, 1989).

At this point we can begin to understand how Innis's work on communications fits within his reflexive project. For his communication studies are above all a theory of the history and geography of knowledge. Monopolies of knowledge are the outcome of certain institutional structures and the power relations that inhere within them, which in turn are shaped by the dominant media of communication and their spatial and temporal biases. It is thus a theory of what people know in particular times and places and why they know those things. Such a theory of course reflexively applies itself to Innis's own work. In fact, in the preface to *Empire and Communications* (1950) he writes that "all written works, including this one, have dangerous implications." There is no escape here; Innis is implicated in empire in just the same way as everyone else. The important point, though, is to be aware of theory's limitations and consequently one's own. In short, Innis is arguing that social scientists should know where they stand.

CONCLUSION

Economic geographers perhaps more than any other group should know where they stand. Innis himself recognized their potential contribution, although his enthusiasm waned as they produced only "bad descriptive economics" (quoted in Dunbar, 1985, p. 160). He would likely have been even less enthusiastic about the turn to spatial science in the late 1950s, which not only continued the former empiricism but also strove to emulate the universal models of science. For the reasons given in this chapter, Innis thought that such claims to universality were not only impossible to realize but frequently masked wider ideological projects such as colonialism. His responses were, first, to engage in the construction of local models that were peculiarly attuned to the specific context of study and thus avoided the imperialism of the universal; and, second, to seek to become more reflexive, to think about his thinking. Moreover, he thought such reflexivity could be undertaken systematically by examining the institutional frameworks and their biases in space and time that are the consequence of the very media of communication, in which knowledge is constructed. Because of his illness and subsequent early death, he never completed the last part of his project to his satisfaction. Nonetheless, his work is pregnant with hints and possibilities for a more satisfactory economic geography. Insofar as those cues have recently been taken up by economic geographers through their interest in localness and difference, power and knowledge, culture and communication, and the production of space and time, geographers may now finally be able to appreciate the significance of Innis and thereby realize his own initial faith in the discipline.

NINE

LUKERMANN ON LOCATION

While the answers change, the questions always remain the same.
—Fred Lukermann

The Minnesotan geographer Fred Lukermann shares a number of characteristics with both Piero Sraffa and Harold Innis. He, too, is an academic gadfly, often at odds with orthodoxy; his writing, too, is dense and complex, inviting varied interpretations; and he, too, is an iconoclast, inventing his own vocabulary and method as he goes along. But perhaps most important, like Sraffa and Innis, Lukermann has an abiding interest in the local and an abiding suspicion of the universal.

Unlike the other two, however, Fred Lukermann is still alive and remains active (he recently retired from the University of Minnesota). This makes writing about him different from writing about either Innis or Sraffa, whose final corpus of work is known. It is also different because I was a graduate student of Lukermann, and took a number of courses from him. This means any critical judgments are difficult for me to make. Apart from our student–teacher relationship, my approach to critical judgments (including those about a mentor) was influenced by Lukermann's writings and especially his teachings.

This marks yet another difference between Lukermann and the other two. Lukermann's influence stems as much from his role as a teacher as it does from his role as an author. In contrast, Sraffa found lecturing in English torturous and reputedly on one occasion gave a lecture course of only one lecture. Similarly, Innis struggled with lecturing throughout his life, speaking as much to the floor and ceiling as to his students. Taking a course with Lukermann, however, always meant being part of an event. As graduate students, we said that everything about Lukermann's performance in class was done on cue, scripted as if on a movie set.

Furthermore, to continue the analogy, Lukermann's courses were always extravagant epics, telling stirring stories of how we came to be. They typically began in the American Midwest with tales of Hartshorne and Schaefer, frequently ended in Königsberg with Kant, and in between embraced a host of supporting characters and locations including Kroeber and Sauer in Berkeley, Boas and Benedict in New York, Veblen and Meade in Chicago, Dilthey and Windelband in Germany, and Aristotle and Strabo in Greece. With Lukermann's prop of the equilateral triangle, carefully drawn on the blackboard at the beginning of each class and used as an intellectual pegboard, it was riveting drama.

A central theme of Lukermann's teaching and writing was the relation between geographical pattern and process, which in turn often led to his further exploration of the relation between the whole and its constituent parts. He pursued this line of inquiry often by examining parallel issues in other disciplines such as physics (through Heisenberg's findings), anthropology (through Benedict's work on the pattern of culture), and sociology (through C. Wright Mills's notion of the sociological imagination).

My purpose in this final chapter is to take up the theme of pattern and process, the whole and its parts, and to examine it in the context of some of Lukermann's early empirical writings on the issue of location in economic geography. His methodological debate with Brian Berry in the late 1950s on the geography part of economic geography is well known (Lukermann, 1958; Berry, 1959), revolving as it does around issues of essentialism and universalism in spatial science (Barnes, 1987a). But during that same period Lukermann also published a little-known series of substantive papers on industrial location: one set dealt with flour milling (Lukermann, 1959a—1959g), another with cement (Lukermann, 1960a, 1960b). These papers, I should add, are less known simply because of where they were published, in the weekly Minnesota trade magazine *The Northwestern Miller* and in the Polish journal *Przeglad Geograficzny*. If their places of publication were slightly eccentric, the substantive arguments they made about geographical location were not. Apart from containing some of Lukermann's finest prose—lucid, smooth, and even elegiac—both studies represent a constructive attempt to link substantively pattern and process, whole and parts, in economic geography without invoking the essentialism and universalism found in the models of spatial science.

Any discussion of these two empirical studies of location, however, cannot be undertaken without a corresponding review of Lukermann's broader methodological writings. As Lukermann himself wrote, "Geographers cannot avoid their methodology or lack of it. One cannot do substantive research without knowing how one explains, and how one explains is methodology" (Lukermann, 1961, p. 5). For this reason, it is necessary to read Lukermann's case studies of flour and cement mills in tandem with his methodological works written around the same time or shortly thereafter. In this way the broader purpose of this chapter is to grope toward the typical Lukermannesque project of finding a wider pattern within the individual pieces, where in this case the pieces are Lukermann's own writings.

The chapter is divided into four sections: first, I very briefly lay out the two ways in which aggregate location patterns and processes were connected by early spatial scientists in economic geography, against which Lukermann was reacting in his substantive studies; second, I discuss Lukermann's flour and cement milling articles, interpreting them both as an implicit critique of spatial science and as a first attempt at an alternative approach; third, by reading these studies in light of Lukermann's methodological writing of the early and mid-1960s, I examine Lukermann's own changing methodological attempts at resolving the pattern–process, and whole–part dualisms, without drawing upon essentialism or universalism; finally, in an extended conclusion I try to locate intellectually Lukermann's anti-essentialist and anti-universalist stance by drawing, in particular, upon David Bloor's (1983) work.

PATTERN AND PROCESS
IN ECONOMIC GEOGRAPHY

When Lukermann was writing on flour and cement in the late 1950s, he was reacting against two recent attempts to link geographical pattern and process. In making that connection, each of these different approaches also provided a particular kind of resolution to the whole–part conundrum, each resolution resting upon two already established philosophical positions.

First, there is the locational theory that draws upon neoclassical economics and is exemplified for Lukermann by Isard's (1956) work on industrial location. Isard's problem is to define an optimal set of locations for industrialists, where "optimal" means the location associated with the lowest manufacturing costs and hence the greatest profit. For Isard, this locational problem "reduces to a consideration of substitution between transport inputs" (Isard, 1956, p. 36). By this Isard means that the geographically separated factors of production that industrialists need to bring together in order to produce output at a given location can always be expressed in the common metric of transportation inputs, defined as the in situ costs of a factor of production plus the transportation cost of bringing it to the location site. By notionally substituting one transportation input so defined for another, we can find the site that minimizes total costs and can thus establish the optimal industrial location. More specifically, under the assumption that all industrialists are rational economic agents, the least-cost location is derived using the calculus of constrained maximization (Isard, 1956, pp. 222–230). Furthermore, that same technique also establishes an equilibrium pattern defined as the set of locational points from which no industrialist has an incentive to move.

In Isard's neoclassical landscape the ordering of optimal locations is a result only of the individual rationality of economic agents. That is, the wider pattern is reduced to individual rational decisions, the whole explained by its parts. In philosophical terms, this relationship between pattern and process is known as methodological individualism. Under this scheme, explanations of any social and economic phenomena are reducible to the properties and relations of individuals and only individuals (Przeworski, 1985; Levine, Sober, and Wright, 1987).

For reasons that will be clear later, it is useful to cast this use of methodological individualism in terms of an even more general philosophical position, the covering law model of human behavior. The covering law model attempts to express human behavior in terms of the hypothetico-deductive model of scientific explanation discussed in Chapter Four. Specifically, any action is explained deductively from a major premise (the "covering law") and a minor one. In the case of Isard's industrial location theory, the major premise is that all industrialists are rational decision makers bent on maximizing profits by reducing location costs, whereas the minor premise is a statement about the specific industrialist and location choices from which they must choose. By combining the two, we can explain or predict the locational choice of any industrialist and hence the resulting locational pattern.

By casting the methodological individualism of Isard's approach in terms of the covering law model, we can make yet one more claim. The neoclassical covering law that all individuals are rational is (as already discussed in Chapters Two and Three) based upon a physical metaphor appropriated by neoclassical economists at the turn of the nineteenth century. Specifically, as Mirowski (1989) demonstrates, the covering law "All capitalists maximize profits" is the direct analogue of the law of the conservation of energy. The interesting consequence is that because the law of the conservation of energy is predicated upon mechanical causality, so is the economic analogue. As a result, when this physical metaphor is applied to a space-economy through the covering law, optimal location patterns are simply the mechanical–causal consequences of individual rationality; their rational nature causes individuals to make the right locational choices (see also Rosenberg, 1976).

The second location theory, social physics or macrogeography, is more difficult to characterize. Nevertheless, it was the one that most preoccupied Lukermann's critical attention. As described in Chapter Five, macrogeography was codified in the 1950s by the work of the Princeton physicist John Stewart and the economic geographer William Warntz. They contended that aggregate human interaction over space can be explained and predicted using physical theories and laws.

The best examples are the gravity and potential models. Analogous to Newton's law of gravity, the gravity model assumes that humans interact over space as heavenly bodies do in the celestial system. In this formulation interaction between two places is directly proportional to the product of their respective masses (usually measured by population size) and inversely proportional to some function of the distance between them. The pattern in this case is a series of interactions among pairs of discrete places. Stewart and Warntz later showed, however, that these results could be generalized over continuous space for a complete set of simultaneously interacting points by using a second model, based on potential. For in the potential model, as Coffey (1988, p. 19) writes, "Each center is simultaneously under the influence of *all* other centers and simultaneously exerts an influence upon all other centers, as well as upon *all points* located within the boundaries of the system. Thus, a field is created." The postulated processes at work here, as with the gravity model, rest on the assumption of presumed forces and resistances associated with aggregate entities (population).

In terms of the relation between the whole and its parts, macrogeographers implicitly rested their argument on a form of methodological holism; the whole explains the parts. As Lukermann (1965b, p. 192) wrote, in any potential model "the position of the parts is analytically determined from the *whole.*" This is because in order to make the analogy with physics, macrogeographers were required to assume a space continuum; without it they could not logically invoke the idea of a force of resistance field associated with aggregate entities. But once assumed, a space continuum determines the value, usually measured as the potential for accessibility, of every location within it.

Just as Isard's methodological individualism can be connected to a mechanistic causality, the methodological holism of social physics can be connected to structural functionalism. For in invoking the physical analogy of a force of resistance field, Stewart and Warntz necessarily commit themselves to an explanation in which the structure of the whole, the combined interaction of all aggregate entities, functionally accounts for all its individual elements, the values ascribed to any individual site. As a result, and in direct contrast to methodological individualism, it is the broader sociospatial system itself that does the explaining, not the individual parts within it.

There is one final point. *Insofar as* a structural functionalist methodology is predicated upon a self-regulating system in which the whole ensures that the parts function in such a way to reproduce the wider system, then some notion of equilibrium is invoked by social physics. Note that not all holistic systems are necessarily self-regulating (for example, Marx's), but Warntz's (1959, p. 104) task was to make, in particular, his potential model also an equilibrium model by explicitly linking it to neoclassical price theory, the very embodiment of a self-regulating mechanism. Specifically, the purpose of Warntz's (1959, p. 104) *Toward a Geography of Price* was to show that through the price mechanism population demand potential and space supply potential were regulated at equilibrium levels.

In summary, the two up-and-coming location theories in economic geography during the late 1950s were based on neoclassical economics and macrogeography, respectively. In some ways it is curious that the two came to be linked under the common rubric of regional science (see Chapter Four) because each offered a very different mode of explanation. While neoclassical economics is rooted in methodological individualism and associated with the mechanistic causality of its covering law, the foundation of macrogeography is in methodological holism, which proffered a structural functionalist mode of explanation. Of course, the tie that bound was the knot of science, and for sociological reasons within the academy this link was more significant than any intellectual difference that might separate them.

BAGGING FLOUR AND CEMENT

It was against this intellectual backdrop that Lukermann undertook his case studies of flour and cement. The seven articles on flour milling that appeared in winter and spring issues of *The Northwestern Miller* in 1959 consist of extended commentaries on a series of maps of flour milling capacity and location. The earliest map is for 1879, the latest for 1958. From those maps the main empirical trends found for this eighty-year period were (1) a striking decline in the number of a mills, particularly smaller ones; (2) the rise of multiplant milling corporations that typically refined flour in very large plants; (3) as a result of these first two trends, a growing locational concentration of mills; (4) a historically shifting regional pattern of location—at different times the flour milling centers of the East Coast, the upper Midwest, the lower Great Lakes, the central southern states, and the Pacific Northwest variously rode the crest of a boom or wallowed in a recessionary trough; and (5) a discordance between broad regional locational trends and the contemporaneous locational decisions of large individual corporations.

Although Lukermann's ostensible purpose in these articles is empirical, he also creates a critical subtext that forms the basis of a critique of the two strains of regional science identified above, including an attack on their solution to the pattern–process, whole–part question. Lukermann's criticisms, it should be noted, were remarkably prescient and sophisticated given that regional science was itself nascent. Indeed, the marshaling of the full panoply of arguments against regional science, leading eventually to its marginalization within human geography, was still at least a decade and a half away.

Lukermann's first general point is that a location pattern cannot be separated from history. Any map of location patterns is only a snapshot. To be really understood, a map needs to be set within a third dimension that extends at right angles to the other two, "with the past behind it, and the future in front" (Robinson, 1979, p. 52). In this sense, location maps are never really about the present but always about the past. As Lukermann (1959e, p. 12), writes: "A single map makes 'sense' only if it is recognized as an accumulation of past cause and effect—of inertia and momentum." This is a problem for both neoclassical and macrogeographical accounts that are cast in an equilibrium analysis. For equilibrium is set in logical not historical time, allowing movement backward into the past with the same facility as moving forward into the future (Curry and Barnes, 1988). In real historical time, however, this shunting to and fro between the past and the future is impossible; once choices are made, they are irrevocable and lead to consequences that are often impossible to alter.

For this reason, Lukermann thinks that the very idea of locational equilibrium that both neoclassical and macrogeographers aver is misconceived. The decisions on which eventual map patterns are based are always made in historical rather than logical time, with the result that there cannot be a return to some former point of equilibrium; we are always caught in the Heraclitean flux. According to Lukermann (1959g, p. 14), "There has never been any equilibrium in the [flour milling] industry from a locational standpoint. . . . An explanation of any given locational distribution may be found more readily in the historical circumstances of the industry."

The upshot is that much of traditional location theory—von Thunen's rings, Weber's triangles, Losch's hexagons, and even Warntz's isopleth maps—is inapplicable (see also Gregory's, 1982, comments about frozen geometries). These geometrical solutions are all final positions and hence static. But what is needed is an explanation that simultaneously brings together both geography *and* history, that is, both pattern *and* process.

Lukermann's observation is that if locational equilibrium is suspect, then so, too, is optimal location. Locational optimality theoretically implies that for any given case one can always work out where a firm should best locate. This is possible regardless of circumstances because rational capitalists follow the same logic of choice given by the covering law: choose a site that always provides the most for the least. But through his maps Lukermann shows over and over again that the geographical world is far too messy to be put into a constrained maximization equation or a single variable isopleth map. Geographical variability in all forms continually defeats the likes of Isard and Stewart and Warntz. Lukermann (1959g, pp. 15–16) writes, "At any one moment in any one area the conditions affecting location are not the same. There are no stable, natural or economic conditions applicable to all areas simultaneously nor, for that matter, similar conditions affecting all of the other economic enterprises in an area at one time."

Finally, Lukermann turns his criticism to the applicability of the methodological strategies neoclassicism and macrogeography employ in connecting the whole and its parts. The whole in this case is the general pattern of flour mill location, and the parts are the location decisions of individual owners. Basing his argument on the empirical evidence he has collected on these mills, Lukermann rejects both methodological individualism and methodological holism. On the one hand, methodological holism fails because the whole is unable to explain its parts. As Lukermann (1959f, p. 16) writes, "Somehow in analyzing or breaking down the total we do not account for all the parts. Somewhere deep in the pile of statistics are some human decisions still lost in the sum." On the other hand, methodological individualism fails because when we examine the locational decisions of the largest and most important firms, firms that we would expect to be the most rational, they produce patterns that are incongruent with the broader one (Lukermann, 1959f, 1959g). That is, the parts do not add up to the whole.

Having rejected the two leading theories of location, Lukermann is left with providing an alternative account. In the flour milling papers, at least, he advocates some form of contextual solution that attempts to understand individual location decisions on the basis of a series of ad hoc locational factors such as market size and accessibility, sources of supply, and transportation costs. This is clearly no Weberian triangle nor Isardian corruption of it. Apart from the lack of formalism, Lukermann is not integrating these factors into a single theory, "they do not combine in a fixed relationship for any given location" (1959d, p. 13). Instead, we need to wait and establish contextually whether any or all of these factors operate in particular times and places. Although this position may be defensible for one particular case study, it is clearly inadequate as a general resolution to locational problems, and in particular to the pattern–process, whole–part dilemma.

Lukermann moves further toward that general resolution in his next study focusing on cement mills. Here Lukermann's approach is slightly different. He separates out an explicit methodological discussion of cement mill location, published in the *Professional Geographer* (1960b), from historical description, found in the *Przeglad Geograficzny* (1960a). As with flour milling, he undertakes a historical approach to location, the basis of which is again a series of maps, eight in all, charting the changing patterns of cement mill location in North America from 1818 to 1958. By constructing for that whole period a set of graphs that illustrate number of plants, production levels, capacity, and so on, he selects eight periods "by degree of homogeneity and boundary coincidence" (Lukermann 1960b, p. 537). He notes, however, that carrying out this chronological ordering implies neither "a cyclical (recurrent) process nor evolutionary (necessary order) stages."

As with flour milling, the regional location pattern of cement mills slips and slides over time. Initially concentrated on the East Coast, cement mills subsequently "moved west and south delineating as have other industries the migration and penetration of the new eras of social change" (Lukermann 1960a, p. 559). In examining these changing patterns, Lukermann is again keen to work out the relationship between aggregate regional pattern and individual location. To that end he restates, and elaborates upon, the methodological position that he had begun to develop in the flour milling papers. There is again the centrality of context and history but also the beginnings of its elaboration into what he later called a discourse-level narrative (explained below) concerned with recognizing the peculiar general stamp of a specific period, the way in which its multifarious elements form a distinct whole. Such an approach was not equivalent to structural functionalism, however, because Lukermann made no attempt to explain individual elements in terms of their functional position with respect to the whole. Instead, Lukermann seemed to suggest that elements could be connected by some kind of unique internal relationship with one another that was neither functional nor based upon a covering law.

This suggestion, however, was still preliminary, and it was several more years before the final version was worked out. Before we get to that version in the next section, however, we should note that Lukermann's cement study continued his earlier critique of spatial science. In fact, Lukermann is increasingly exasperated with economic geographers' infatuation with formal location models, particularly neoclassical ones. Such models prioritized one or some combination of three location factors: raw materials, the market, and transport. Within this framework each factor was assigned a quantitative weight, the size of which determined the final optimal location. One immediate problem with such a locational logic was its exclusion of nonquantifiable factors that were typically historical, such as technological change, inertia, and personal quirks (Lukermann, 1960b, p. 5). More broadly, the flaw in such models was that they began with answers rather than questions. It was not that markets, transportation costs, or raw materials were unimportant, only that it was not possible a priori to devise a single theory based upon some fixed relationship among them. This was because by definition such an approach left out what was most important in a geographical explanation: the variability of location itself, cloaked as it was in the models of spatial science under the colorless blanket of a covering law or holistic functional relationship (Lukermann, 1960b, p. 5).

In summary, Lukermann's work on flour mills and cement mills represents a rejection of neoclassical and macrogeography locational models and their postulated connection between pattern and process, whole and parts. Pattern is not reducible to individual locations, nor are individual locations all there is to the pattern. There needs to be a different way, one that begins with the geographical and historical contexts rather than ending with them. Lukermann's studies of flour and cement milling were first-cut attempts at beginning with geography and history. But further argumentation was clearly needed, and Lukermann provided that as he increasingly turned away from his empirical work to concentrate on methodological issues.

LOCATING LUKERMANN

Lukermann begins that work on methodology by attempting to define geography. In his view geography is primarily defined by the questions it asks. Lukermann (1964a, p. 167) writes, "Geography is a catalogue of questions, and the questions—not the phenomena, not the facts, not the method—are geographic." For Lukermann the ultimate geographical question is, "Why is the world—or why do we see the world—divided up into places or regions?" (1964a, p. 167). To answer that question we need concepts—means of looking at and knowing the world. Such concepts break into the continuum of the world and provide an understandable order for the knowing subject. Of all the concepts geographers have used to address the geographical question, the most important is location. "Historically, it is the most consistent theme running through the literature of the field" (Lukermann 1964a, p. 169).

Lukermann emphasizes two facets of the concept location. Location as a concept necessarily implies a relationship to other concepts, of which there are two mains kinds. First, location is always relative to other locations; that is, "the location of place is not completely defined for the geographer until it is described in relation to all other interacting places" (Lukermann, 1964b, p. 170). Second, location is also relative to its past and the pasts of other places. Lukermann (1964b, p. 170) writes, "It is difficult to speak of locating something, or the location of some place, without necessarily becoming involved in the antecedent distributional conditions of the place under study. . . . It follows that complementary to the geographic concept of relative location is a concept of *age and area*—the interaction of place and period."

The second facet he stresses is that although location is an abstraction, it does not necessarily imply generalization and the effacing of individuality (see Entrikin, 1991, pp. 95–96, and also Sayer, 1984, who emphasizes the same point). Now, it is obvious that some abstractions do imply generalization, and certainly some geographers have offered this interpretation of location, but in Lukermann's hands location refers to a unique coherence and indivisibility (see also Oakes, 1986). In particular, that singular coherence and indivisibility is best expressed in the idea of place, defined as a unique combination (ensemble) of different elements that cleave at a given location. In his two studies, for example, those elements might include items such as flour mills, cement mills, wheat pools, portland cement pits, and so on. Each location or place will have a peculiar arrangement of these and other elements, where the resulting ensemble is quite different from any other.

Lukermann then argues that both these facets of location connote two separate implications for geographical inquiry. First, doing geography for Lukermann must involve examining the two relationships that inhere within location itself, space and time. Through empirical analysis and classification it is necessary to link locational sites together both geographically and historically, and in this way a locational system, or pattern, is constructed. Such geographical ordering is exemplified by Lukermann's maps that accompany the flour and cement industry studies. He includes them because this geographical ordering is the first step in practicing any geography at all, as it is implicit in the very notion of location. Lukermann (1964b, p. 169) writes, "The meaning of location to the geographer—the relative distributional condition of the area under study—is the first conceptual criterion of doing geography. If the geographer fails to conceive of his research as involving this step it seems difficult to accept such study as either explanatory or descriptive in any geographical sense."

Second, because location is relational, it follows that there is necessarily interdependence among the various ensembles of elements—locations or places—within the broader pattern or system. That is, each ensemble is dependent upon some other—both now and in the past. In more general terms, as Lukermann (1965a, p. 130) writes,

> every event in the world is conditioned by every other event in the world. . . . Practically then, any event is the result of a number of causal chains intersecting at some point in time and space. The event is caused, but nevertheless not determined; rather it is contingent on the indispensable but fortuitous intersection in time/space of multiple chains of causation.

There are several points to note here. Although there are causes in Lukermann's scheme, there are no preordained final determinations but only contingent or probable ones. This is because in a concatenating world characterized by chains of causation across different locations, one can never identify a final cause; in fact, the whole vocabulary of determination is inappropriate. Rather, the occurrence of individual locational events is only ever contingent. As Lukermann (1965a, p. 133) explains, "To be contingent is to be probable. To be probable is to be conditional. To be conditional is to be dependent. But to be dependent does not mean to be determinate. For to be determinate each individual event would have to be lawful, and we know by experience that this is not so."

Following from this previous point, there can be no determinate laws of single locational events because of the very singularity of those events. As we saw in Chapter Four, under the "standard model" of scientific explanation, laws take the form of a constant conjunction between one class of events and another: "If A then B." It follows that to apply a law to a single event, one must be able to identify commonalities among events sufficient to constitute a homogeneous class. This is denied by Lukermann's conception of locational events. Any locational event is necessarily causally connected in a unique way both to other places and to other times. This makes the event singular and thus impossible to collapse into some uniform class of events. Lukermann (1965a, p. 133) thus writes, "Events by their individuality extend beyond the boundaries of any class in which they may be classified." Instead, following Entrikin's (1991, ch. 7) discussion, Lukermann's work fits better within a historical form of explanation that emphasizes single causes.

The gist of this form of explanation is that one can refer to causes without necessarily referring to causal laws. So it is legitimate both to invoke causation, as Lukermann does, and to say, as he also does, that causal laws cannot explain locational events. Note that in calling this the single-cause view, proponents are not suggesting that there is only one cause at work; what they highlight is only the singularity of a cause or complex of causes. In fact, Entrikin refers to a distinct "process" of cause and effect. He writes (1991, pp. 121–122):

Events must be understood in terms of a whole or a sequential process. The description of this process . . . offers a form of causal explanation. Within these descriptions, the end point of the processes becomes the "effect," which is preceded by its "causes." Thus, . . . cause becomes a continuous process and the description of the process . . . provides the basis for the claim . . . [of] causal explanations.

The singularity here, then, is in the uniqueness of the causal process—the particular combination of causes that forms the processal chain.

Finally, the consequence of "saying that all events are caused but not determined, and, therefore, not lawful [is that] we [must] leave the explanation of individual events and plans to empirical description, not to deductive science. The latter is not causal and explanatory of individual events" (Lukermann, 1965a, p. 134). Lukermann's point here is that by their very constitution scientific-based models are inappropriate to geographical inquiry, which is by definition concerned with individual places. Scientific models applied to geography do not explain the world but only their own hypotheses. This is because the general assumptions of those models, based upon homogeneous classes of events, are inapplicable, and as a result they give back only their own internal logic, not anything useful about the world. Lukermann's alternative is empirical description. Only this kind of description provides the unique "sequential process" of singular causal change (see also Entrikin, 1991, pp. 121-123). Note that Lukermann uses the term "description" here not to mean a mere listing of events either chronologically or geographically but an account that imposes some necessity. As Entrikin (1991, p. 24), following Ricoeur, puts it, it is description not of one thing following another but description of one thing because of another. In other words, it is an account of the "process" of cause and effect, one that captures the unique combination of causes operating as a chain on a particular event.

Given this brief discussion, we can now better understand why Lukermann's industrial studies came out the way they did. Both were about location, and this implied, by the very meaning of that term, a need to examine the relationships among places and across time. Hence the centrality of historical maps. The maps represent the very "description of the geographic phenomena and associations so arranged and ordered" (Lukermann 1958, p. 9).

Moreover, because one needs to understand history in order to comprehend location, it makes sense that Lukermann so forcefully rejects the idea of locational equilibrium in both sets of works; equilibrium is a time when there is no time. There is a second aspect of equilibrium that is also at odds with Lukermann's broader vision and that also explains his opposition, namely, its teleological character, its determined end point.

But as argued, Lukermann shies away from all forms of determination, teleological or otherwise. It is also for this reason that Lukermann eschews in his studies the neoclassical idea of optimality and those location models that rest upon that concept.

Given his general view of geography, we can also understand his skepticism toward any scientific-based model, such as those that were entering economic geography through regional science. Couched in terms of the "standard model" of the philosophy of science and its associated covering-law model of explanation in the human sciences, the resulting assumptions of timeless laws, determinate deductive logic, and universal characteristics were clearly at odds with Lukermann's conception based upon uniqueness, historical process, and contingency.

Finally, we better understand Lukermann's descriptive case study approach. To grasp the complex chain of causal processes at work for any given firm, we must describe the specific case at hand, which is what he does in the last of his flour milling articles by scrutinizing the locational choices of such specific multiplant firms as General Mills and Centennial Mills.

All this said, lacking in both the case studies is any general methodological resolution to the connection between pattern and process, whole and parts. There are hints and suggestions but no explicit statements. In effect, there are two levels to Lukermann's account. One is of large-scale patterns across space and time, patterns discerned through empirical analysis and classification. The other is at the scale of individual events, which are multiply caused but not determined. But how are the two levels linked? What is the relationship between the macropattern and microprocesses, the whole and its parts?

Certainly, the relationship cannot be one of methodological individualism. After all, Lukermann believes individual events are contingent, and so one cannot deterministically reduce the whole to its parts. What about methodological holism? The problem here, as Lukermann deftly demonstrated in his attacks on Stewart and Warntz during the same period, was that in their hands, at least, methodological holism cannot recognize the individuality of particular places. Lukermann and Porter (1960, p. 495) write:

> The potential model . . . aggregates linear distances and mass points into a functional whole, i.e., it *abstracts* discrete observations into a mathematical continuum. . . . [But] being whole it no longer comprehends limited variables but only universals. . . . [As a consequence,] Warntz . . . has carefully reduced to zero all "specifically limited variables" such as climate, soil fertility, and cultural variations, which might account for "differences among parts of the country."

In other words, the methodological holism of macrogeography fails for Lukermann because it squashes flat the very locational difference that is for him the geographer's central question. Macrogeography is so pure as a theory that it never once besmirches the world.

Where does that leave him? Is there a third way between methodological individualism and methodological holism that would allow pattern and process, whole and parts, to be consistently integrated and also avoid the pitfalls of equilibrium, optimality, and the standard scientific account? It seems to me that much of Lukermann's later work during the 1960s moves hesitantly toward that third alternative. Along the way he suggests a number of possibilities.

His earliest suggestion is to combine elements of both a contextual description of the pattern and a model-based explanation of the process. He writes that "description . . . has as its culminating study the investigation of process, and geographic research thus defined would prescribe a synoptic as well as an analystic approach" (1958, p. 10). But he never explicitly addresses the issue of the consistent integration of these two approaches, and insofar as he continues to accept the potential relevance of traditional model building and theory, he presumably still holds to the attendant positions of methodological individualism or holism, as well as their assumptions about equilibrium, universal laws, and the like.

A second alternative is a revamped methodological holist approach, best seen in his *East Lakes Geographer* (1966) article, "Empirical Expressions of Nodality and Hierarchy in a Circulation Manifold." By beginning with a series of historical maps of the U.S. urban system, he tries to provide geographical and historical specificity in a way the macrogeographers did not. Although he does retain the notion of the indeterminateness of individual events, it is the broader system "that has the decision-making power. It creates its own environment. It pulls in towns that fit. It adapts from a population of potential aspirants those that have a situational advantage, given the system" (Lukermann, 1966, p. 43). This is clearly methodological holism, and Lukermann's use of such terms as system "adapting" and "fitting" suggests that it also relies on some kind of structural functionalist argument. Through his historical approach and the use of maps, Lukermann does attempt to introduce a geography to this holistic system. But again, given his scathing remarks about macrogeography, it is not clear that he can still use its method and simultaneously escape its pitfalls. Even Lukermann seems dissatisfied, writing at the end of the paper that "this article has offered questions, not answers" (Lukermann, 1966, p. 43).

Finally, he offers a third possibility of connecting the two through what he calls a "discourse-level" narrative, which he mentions at the end of his 1965 Minnesota Academy of Science paper, "Geography: De Facto or De Jure." This is the approach he seems to have pursued most often in his later work. Briefly, a discourse-level narrative transcends both object-level description, the extreme pursuit of which is ultimately enervating, and a model-based explanation, which is determinate and thus inadequate in the contingent world of geography. In contrast, the discourse-level narrative "alone integrates our categorized subject matter into the scope of human experience" (Lukermann 1965b, p. 194).

That word "integration" is central. By it Lukermann means that our account of pattern and process, the whole and the parts, should be seamless. It perhaps best corresponds to the sociologist Sorokin's (1937–1941, p. 19) idea of "logico-meaningful integration," defined as "integration in its extreme form . . . because in such instances each part, when set in its designated position, is no longer noticeable as a part, but all the parts together form, as it were, a seamless garment." This is the reason Lukermann later became so interested in the work of ethnographers. They were trying to characterize, to integrate, a diverse range of distinct phenomena into a single account. In this sense, Lukermann's goal is an ethnographic account of economic location. More generally, the seamlessness that Lukermann strives to achieve is possible, he thinks, through the device of narrative or, as Ricoeur calls it, "emplotment." Emplotment, following Entrikin (1991, p. 125), "is a way of ordering experience by drawing events into a structured whole and giving them meaning. It overcomes the chaotic conception of events as they occur in the world both successively and simultaneously and 'configures' them into stories." Through this kind of configuration within a narrative, Lukermann is offering the possibility of connecting the parts to the whole, processes to patterns.

Narrative configuration is possible, though, only by imposing a "central principle (the reasons) which permeate[s] all the components, giving sense and significance to each of them" (Sorokin, 1937–1941, p. 32). It is here that we can link together the idea of emplotment and a process of cause and effect. For emplotment involves finding that central reason that allows us to narrate a consistent story through the telling of the process of cause and effect. And in a world of multiple causes and effects, we need to make decisions about those that are most significant, those that allow us to give meaning, direction and understanding to the heterogeneous phenomena we study. We make such a decision by the kinds of emplotments we use. In this sense, causal configurations do not emerge out of the facts themselves but are created through the emplotments we employ. Furthermore, the use of such emplotments requires human creativity, inspiration, and flair; just as there can be bad metaphors or puns or metonyms, there can be bad narratives. In particular, good narratives are those that allow us to understand the broader significance of a set of disparate events—not one thing after another but one thing because of another.

At this point we can begin to see how a discourse-level narrative resolves some of the issues that preoccupied Lukermann in his work on location. As an integrative account, narrative allows the connection of geography and history, but it does not impose any final determination because the (single) process of causes portrayed is not part of a wider set of laws. Rather, these causes are specific to a particular set of events. Furthermore, in a narrative the causal process is conveyed through description, through telling a story, not through formal models. Finally, the configuration of the narrative links the whole and its parts without either reducing one to the other or making one functionally dependent on the other.

One final issue never resolved in Lukermann's writings, is the extent to which in pursuing a discourse-level narrative he concluded that the very distinction between pattern and process, whole and parts, that initially motivated him is in some sense irrelevant. For these are dualistic conceptions, whereas the narrative Lukermann seems to seek is always integrative. As Sorokin (1937–1941, p. 22) puts it, in an integrative narrative "there is strictly speaking neither cause nor effect, neither variable nor function. . . . In fact, th[is] whole method . . . is simply inappropriate." In this way Lukermann may have come to the realization that even thinking about events in terms of wholes and parts, patterns and processes, was to concede too much to the scientific method and the models that it spawned in economic geography.

What does all this mean for studies of location in economic geography? It means an integrative account where—although there is specialized information about a factory, a firm, or an industry—there need to be links to a wider set of events and patterns. And the best form for portraying those links is through narrative. This was what Lukermann was hinting at with respect to the location of the cement industry: that we need to see it in the light of a much wider set of processes going on in North American society associated with the changing nature of the urban frontier. This is not just economic, but social, cultural, and political. The changing nature of the urban frontier becomes, as it were, his central integrative thread in constructing the narrative; it keeps the individuality of specific events such as the mill closings and openings but provides a wider configuration that makes sense of it all. But the urban frontier itself must be seen in terms of the experiences of generations of Americans as they initially move west and, when the West runs out, increasingly congregate within the new frontier of urbanization and industrialization.

CONCLUSION

In summary, my immediate purpose in this chapter was to provide an interpretation of Lukermann's early industrial studies on flour and cement by setting them within the context of his other methodological works. I did this in part to show that there are connections among the different facets of Lukermann's work and in part because I wanted to make a statement about Lukermann's broader vision of geography, one that takes in some of the current work in economic geography. Let me conclude by painting in wide brush strokes the nature of that broader vision.

The sociologist of science David Bloor (1983) would, I think, call Lukermann's view conservative (see also Chapter One). Using this epithet to characterize Wittgenstein's later philosophy, Bloor argues conservatism represents a counterideology to the Enlightenment. It is marked by an appeal to history rather than a belief in progress; an assertion of the importance of tradition rather than individual reason; a stress on our dependence on culture, nation, and institution rather than on individual rights; a belief in the complexity of social reality rather than a desire to clarify and simplify; and an emphasis on the variability of our needs and the importance of local interests rather than on universal requirements of humankind.

All of these traits, I would argue, are found in Lukermann's writings. Moreover, in a brief passage in his unpublished "Geography Among the Sciences" (1964a), Lukermann in effect recognizes the same distinction as Bloor and attempts to work through the implications of the Enlightenment and conservative views for economic geography. The view from the Enlightenment—a belief in progress, the individual, simplicity, and universalism—is clearly embodied in the location models of early theoretical economic geography and regional science. In broad terms, such models suggest that entrepreneurs "in selecting places of production or distribution *adapted* themselves to the natural and economic conditions, and chose that place of maximum economic return" (Lukermann, 1964a, p. 50). The crucial point for Lukermann was that such a portrayal assumed that "the world was given and man's success was the result of an objective appraisal or ferreting out of nature's secrets. The world had order, man had only to find it" (Lukermann, 1964a, p. 50).

In contrast, the conservative view is much more pessimistic about the power of reason and far "less sure of nature and certainly less sure of societal laws" (Lukermann, 1964a, p. 50). Nature, in this view, is no longer a "problem to be solved, a secret to be discovered, but a continuing sequence of events and experiences to be worked out. The world is contingent not given, a continually changing complex, not a given order but an evolving order, a system which is made by no one of us, but by all of us" (Lukermann, 1964a, p. 50).

It is Lukermann's position with respect to each of these different views that, I think, provides the rationale for at least the two facets of Lukermann's writings that I described in this chapter. First, as a critic of the Enlightenment view, crystallized in his attack on locational modeling, Lukermann over and over again made the point that nature does not have a single secret, an inherent order. Rather, that order is constantly changing. This is very explicit even in his earliest writings. In one of the flour milling essays, for example, Lukermann (1959d, p. 13) writes, "No individual location has had, or ever will have, a natural advantage if by that phrase is meant a permanent or stable value through time and space. Each advantage is relative to changing social, political, economic and technological conditions, all of which are relative to each other." Second, as a conservative thinker, Lukermann is also concerned with working out the lineaments of the nature-as-contingent view for geographical location. This means recognizing that humans need to be placed at the center of things, that we create our own world, our own patterns, and to understand them we must look at ourselves, not to a "single, omnipotent 'secret' of nature, the one answer for all time" (Lukermann, 1964a, p. 51). This is another reason he stresses the importance of history. We constantly make and remake our future in different and complex ways. To say "probable" is the best we can do.

Lukermann has always been an irritant within orthodox geography, if not an outright rebel. Ironically, however, since the early 1980s orthodoxy has increasingly come to meet him. For conservatism, in the sense Bloor meant, has become more dominant in the social sciences—seen in Rorty in philosophy, Geertz in anthropology, McCloskey in economics, and the various moves in human geography toward postmodernism and cultural critique. Even economic geography has undergone change. Ever since Doreen Massey's (1984b) *Spatial Divisions of Labour,* there has been an attempt to place location within a broader social, cultural, and historical context, which was the sort of thing Lukermann was calling for twenty-five years earlier. This turn of events contrasts markedly with Lukermann's grim prognostications about economic geography in the early 1960s, which he saw as increasingly returning to the seventeenth century. Insofar as economic geography is now wrestling with the intellectual issues of the twentieth century, Lukermann, like many great film directors, points to a happy ending, despite some scary parts in the beginning and middle.

TEN

CONCLUSION

In the preface I spoke about my Jekyll-and-Hyde existence as an under-graduate, as I was torn between my public obligation and my private inclination. I feel the same way in setting out this conclusion. Originally, I had not planned to write one. In the sense that an author strives in a concluding chapter to draw everything together and point to the way ahead, I thought it would be antithetical to the main argument of my book. When the referees' comments came in on the manuscript, however, the one major change they wanted was the addition of a summary; they wanted a statement that brought everything together. So, in the spirit of the Beatles' song "Come Together," here goes.

I've already said that relatively early on I abandoned any attempt either to summarize the whole field or to reconstruct it all of a piece. The best I could do was to practice a logic of dislocation. That logic has three main components, each of which is defined by the different meanings of the term "dislocation." Furthermore, as I will argue in this conclusion, those meanings parallel my purposes in the book's various sections.

The first definition means something like the disruption of a pre-viously established order, as in, for example, the dislocation of Europe following World War I. Such a definition is germane because much of the book was an attempt at unraveling the tight-knit order found in various schemes of economic geography proposed since the 1960s. My argument was that what held those schemes together internally—that is, what established the order inside each—was the provision of some kind of unimpeachable assumption; an assumption that once found was self-evi-dent and once accepted brought with it a particular logic for organizing all other aspects of inquiry. I called this general belief in unimpeachable assumptions essentialist or rationalist, and in the first three chapters of the book I argued that it has been a pervasive practice within economic geography in the recent past. As I described, at various times labor values, utility, the rationality postulate, the necessity of necessary relations, the logic of spatial divisions of labor, and the regime and mode of production have all been proposed as bedrock notions, each bringing with it an immanent spatial logic when applied to the geographical world.

The purpose of those first three chapters, however, was not to celebrate the resulting closed disciplinary order but to dislocate it by raising questions about those supposed unimpeachable assumptions and logic. By turning rationalist and essentialist claims against themselves, that is, by showing that on their own terms they did not meet their criteria of impeccability, I argued there is neither a single origin point for inquiry nor a single logic, spatial or otherwise. The best we can hope for are shards and fragments; there is not one economic geography but many economic geographies, not one complete story but a set of fragmented stories. For this reason, the project of constructing a unified, complete, and seamless discipline should be abandoned. More specifically, rather than pretending to do something that we can never do, we should instead concentrate on what we do do, that is, our practices.

It is here that the second meaning of "dislocation" comes into play. That meaning is roughly equivalent to displacement and is the process by which an established body of ideas, people, or things gives way to another. In this case, as I argued in Chapters Four, Five, and Six, the recent history of economic geography is one of continual intellectual dislocation in which one set of ideas gives way to another, newer set almost as soon as it is established. While there are certain parallels between the process I described in those chapters and Kuhn's notion of paradigm change, there are differences as well. By drawing upon the Edinburgh school and other later approaches within the sociology of science, I emphasized the importance of social power and social interests, dimensions virtually absent in Kuhn's work. Specifically, my argument was that from the moment we enter the academy, we are socialized into preexisting networks of knowledge and power that, whether we are conscious of them or not, come with various sets of vested interests. Those networks of power/knowledge are not fixed for all time, however. They change as new power alliances and interests are formed along with accompanying changes in knowledge itself.

One, but certainly not the only form, in which those interests and power positions are played out is through competing metaphors. Sometimes this is a benign challenge—gravity versus entropy models—while at other times the stakes are higher—physical versus biological metaphors as a basis for representing rationality within the economic system (Barnes, 1992). Yet at still other times metaphorical challenges are made at the highest epistemological level, questioning the very nature of knowledge itself. This is perhaps an interpretation of the rise of "post"-prefixed theories. Proponents are suggesting that the old epistemological ocular metaphors (philosophy as the "mirror of nature") that have been a staple of Western thought should be changed to new ones, such as, say, conversation (Rorty) or the body (Haraway) or the subaltern (Spivak). In these latter cases it is recognized that the advocation of metaphorical redescription is a difficult process fraught with both material and political interests. Metaphorical redescription is revolutionary.

The final meaning of "dislocation" takes up the medical definition, which revolves around the idea of a discontinuity or an "unnatural" break—for example, when bones normally connected to one another are no longer joined. Far from a painful event requiring immediate remedy, I argued in the final three chapters that dislocation within economic geography was healthy. The problem within the discipline is that only one story is told and frequently from the perspective of a privileged subject position. To make us aware of the assumptions that sustain that narrative continuity, it is necessary to dislocate. This is the methodological importance of work by feminists and postcolonialist economic geographers; they are dislocating, disrupting, and displacing the discipline's traditional narratives, and in doing so they point to the kind of exclusive (essentialist) assumptions used to sustain those former accounts.

Compared to these recent feminists and postcolonialists, my three exemplars of dislocation may seem anemic case studies. After all, the three are white males living in the world's metropoles. That said, one reason that I used the work of Sraffa, Innis, and Lukermann (other than that I knew it well) was that methodologically all three attempted to disrupt, to make discontinuous, the prevailing Enlightenment habit of constructing complete systems of thought from supposed universals. Specifically, what marked their work out for me was their willingness to reflect upon their own local conditions and to see those conditions as important in the kind of knowledge that they presented. This is also a central epistemological contribution of feminist and postcolonial critics, although their work clearly takes on a sharper political edge than found in the trio of writers I examined.

More generally, my three exemplars were precisely that; each showed in different ways that it was possible to do a different kind of economic geography, one that shunned closure, universals, and dogmatism and embraced openness, context, and reflexivity. I wanted to show that the ideas I had discussed in the previous chapters were not just ideas but that they could be put to work; by using the writings of Sraffa, Innis, and Lukermann, I hoped to demonstrate this possibility.

In earlier drafts of this conclusion I finished by providing a self-critique and by anticipating potential criticisms of the book. My exposition of both types of criticisms became so large and unwieldy, however, that eventually I gave up on the attempt. All of this is just another way of saying that I am only too aware of the failings of this present volume. If experience is the name we give to our mistakes, then this book was perfected by experience. But as I tell my students at the end of my economic geography course, the main mistake of the discipline has been its attempt at perfection. To be human is to err, and if economic geographers concentrate on what it is to be human rather than what it is to be divine, then maybe things will come together after all.

REFERENCES

Abler, R., Adams, J. A., and Gould, P. (1972). *Spatial organization: The geographer's view of the world.* London: Prentice-Hall.

Adams, J. G. U. (1981). *Transportation planning.* London: Routledge & Kegan Paul.

Adorno, T. (1967). *Prisms.* London: Neville Spearman.

Aksoy, A., and Robbins, K. (1992). Hollywood for the 21st century: Global competition for critical mass in image markets. *Cambridge Journal of Economics, 16,* 1–22.

Alexander, P. (1964). The philosophy of science 1850–1910. In D. J. O'Conner (Ed.), *A critical history of western philosophy* (pp. 402–425). London: Macmillan–Collier.

Alonso, W. (1964). *Location and land use.* Cambridge, MA: Harvard University Press.

Amariglio, J. (1988). The body, economic discourse, and power: An economist's introduction to Foucault. *History of Political Economy, 20,* 583–613.

Amariglio, J. (1990). Economics as a postmodern discourse. In W. J. Samuels (Ed.), *Economics as discourse: An analysis of the language of economists* (pp. 15–46). Dordrecht, The Netherlands: Kluwer.

Amin, A. (1989). Flexible specialization and small firms in Italy: Myths and realities. *Antipode, 21,* 13–34.

Amin, A., and Robbins, K. (1990). The reemergence of regional economies? The mythical geography of flexible accumulation. *Environment and Planning D: Society and Space, 8,* 7–34.

Anas, A. (1982). *Residential location markets and urban transportation.* New York: Academic Press.

Anuchin, V. A. (1973). Theory of geography. In R. J. Chorley (Ed.), *Directions in geography* (pp. 43–63). London: Methuen.

Archer, K. (1987). Mythology and the problem of reading in urban and regional research. *Environment and Planning D: Society and Space, 5,* 384–393.

Arib, M., and Hesse, M. B. (1986). *The construction of reality.* Cambridge, UK: Cambridge University Press.

Aris, R., and Penn, M. (1980). The mere notion of a model. *Mathematical Modelling, 1*, 1–12.

Bagguley, P., Mark-Lawson, J., Shapiro, D., Urry, J., Walby, S., and Warde, A. (1990). *Restructuring place, class and gender.* London: Sage.

Baker, R. (1982). Place utility fields. *Geographical Analysis, 14*, 10–28.

Baldone, S. (1980). Fixed capital in Sraffa's theoretical scheme. In L. L. Pasinetti (Ed.), *Essays in the theory of joint production* (pp. 88–137). London: Macmillan.

Baldwin, R. E. (1956). Patterns of development in newly settled regions. *Manchester School of Economics and Social Studies, 24*, 161–179.

Barnbrock, J. (1976). Prolegomenon to a methodological debate on location theory: The case of von Thunen. *Antipode, 6*(1), 59–66.

Barnes, B. (1974). *Scientific knowledge and sociological theory.* London: Routledge & Kegan Paul.

Barnes, B. (1977). *Interests and the growth of knowledge.* London: Routledge & Kegan Paul.

Barnes, B., and Bloor, D. (1982). Relativism, rationalism and sociology of knowledge. In M. Hollis and S. Lukes (Eds.), *Rationality and relativism* (pp. 21–47). Cambridge, MA: MIT Press.

Barnes, T. J. (1983). *The geography of value, production and distribution: Theoretical economic geography after Sraffa.* Ph.D. dissertation, Department of Geography, University of Minnesota, Minneapolis.

Barnes, T. J. (1987a). Homo economicus, physical metaphors, and universal models in economic geography. *Canadian Geographer, 31*, 299–308.

Barnes, T. J. (1987b). A new industrial geography. *Canadian Journal of Regional Science, 10*, 97–105.

Barnes, T. J. (1989a). Rhetoric, metaphor and mathematical modelling. *Environment and Planning A, 21*, 1281–1284.

Barnes, T. J. (1989b). Structure and agency in economic geography and theories of economic value. In A. Kobayashi and S. McKenzie (Eds.), *Remaking human geography* (pp. 134–148). London: Unwin Hyman.

Barnes, T. J. (1991). Shall I compare thee to a continuous and strictly quasi-concave utility function? Or, homo economicus, part two. *Canadian Geographer, 35*, 400–404.

Barnes, T. J. (1992). Reading the texts of theoretical economic geography: The role of physical and biological metaphors. In T. J. Barnes and J. S. Duncan (Eds.), *Writing worlds: Discourse, text and metaphor in the representation of landscape* (pp. 118–135). London: Routledge.

Barnes, T. J. (1993). Whatever happened to the philosophy of science? *Environment and Planning A, 25*, 301–304.

Barnes, T. J. (1994). Five ways to leave your critic: A sociological scientific experiment in replying. *Environment and Planning A, 26*, 1653–1658.

Barnes, T. J., and Curry, M. R. (1983). Toward a contextualist approach to geographical knowledge. *Transactions, Institute of British Geographers, 8*, 467–482.

Barnes, T. J., and Curry, M. R. (1992). Postmodernism in economic geography: Metaphor and the construction of alterity. *Environment and Planning D: Society and Space, 10*, 57–68.

Barnes, T. J., and Duncan, J. S. (Eds.). (1992). *Writing worlds: Discourse, text and metaphor in the representation of landscape.* London: Routledge.

Bassett, K. (1994). "Whatever happened to the philosophy of science?": Some comments on Barnes. *Environment and Planning A, 26,* 337–342.

Becker, G. (1976). *The economic approach to human behavior.* Chicago: University of Chicago Press.

Benn, S., and Mortimore, G. (Eds.). (1976). *Rationality and the social sciences.* London: Routledge & Kegan Paul.

Bennett, R. J. (1981). Quantitative and theoretical geography in Western Europe. In R. J. Bennett (Ed.), *European progress in spatial analysis* (pp. 1–32). London: Pion.

Bennett, R. J. (1985). A reappraisal of the role of spatial science and statistical inference in geography in Britain. *L'Espace géographique, 14,* 23–28.

Bennett, R. J. (1986). Quantification and relevance. In R. J. Johnston (Ed.), *The future of geography* (pp. 211–224). London: Methuen.

Berger, C. (1976). *The writing of Canadian history. Aspects of English-Canadian historical writing: 1900–1970.* Toronto: Oxford University Press.

Berman, M. (1982). *All that is solid melts into air: The experience of modernity.* New York: Penguin.

Bernstein, R. J. (1983). *Beyond objectivism and relativism: Science, hermeneutics and praxis.* Philadelphia: University of Pennsylvania Press.

Bernstein, R. J. (1986). *Philosophical profiles.* Philadelphia: University of Pennsylvania Press.

Bernstein, R. J. (1991). *The new constellation: The ethical–political horizons of modernity/postmodernity.* Cambridge, UK: Polity Press.

Berry, B. J. L. (1959). Further comments concerning "geographic" and "economic" in economic geography. *Professional Geographer, 9,* 11–12.

Berry, B. J. L. (1993). Geography's quantitative revolution: Initial conditions. A personal memoir. *Urban Geography, 14,* 434–441.

Bharadwaj, K. (1988). Sraffa's Ricardo. *Cambridge Journal of Economics, 12,* 67–84.

Billinge, M. (1986). Economic man. In R. J. Johnston, D. Gregory, and D. M. Smith (Eds.), *The dictionary of human geography* (2nd ed., p. 122). Oxford: Blackwell.

Bird, J. (1989). *The changing worlds of geography: A critical guide to concepts and methods.* Oxford: Clarendon Press.

Black, M. (1962). *Models and metaphors: Studies in language and philosophy.* Ithaca, NY: Cornell University Press.

Blaug, M. (1980). *The methodology of economics. Or how economists explain.* Cambridge, UK: Cambridge University Press.

Bloor, D. (1973). Wittgenstein and Mannheim on the sociology of mathematics. *Studies in the History and Philosophy of Science, 4,* 173–191.

Bloor, D. (1976). *Knowledge and social imagery.* London: Routledge & Kegan Paul.

Bloor, D. (1982a). Durkheim and Mauss revisited: Classification and the sociology of knowledge. *Studies in the History and Philosophy of Science, 13,* 267–297.

Bloor, D. (1982b). Formal and informal thought. In B. Barnes and D. Edge (Eds.),

Science in context: Readings in the sociology of science (pp. 117–124). Cambridge, MA: MIT Press.

Bloor, D. (1983). *Wittgenstein: A social theory of knowledge.* London: Macmillan.

Bloor, D. (1984). The sociology of reasons: Or why "epistemic factors" are really social factors. In J. R. Brown (Ed.), *Scientific rationality: The sociological turn* (pp. 295–324). Dordrecht, The Netherlands: D. Reidel.

Bloor, D. (1988). Rationalism, supernaturalism, and the sociology of knowledge. In I. Hronsky, M. Feher, and B. Dajka (Eds.), *Scientific knowledge socialized* (pp. 55–74). Budapest: Akedemiai Kiado.

Bloor, D. (1991). *Knowledge and social imagery* (2nd ed.). Chicago: University of Chicago Press.

Boland, L. (1979). A critique of Friedman's critics. *Journal of Economic Literature, 17,* 503–522.

Boland, L. (1981). On the futility of criticizing the neo-classical maximization hypothesis. *American Economic Review, 71,* 1031–1036.

Boland, L. (1982). *The foundations of economic method.* London: George Allen & Unwin.

Boland, L. (1983). The neo-classical maximization hypothesis: Reply. *American Economic Review, 73,* 828–829.

Bondi, L. (1993). Locating identity politics. In M. Keith and S. Pile (Eds.), *Place and the politics of identity* (pp. 84–101). London: Routledge.

Booth, D. (1985). Marxism and development sociology: Interpreting the impasse. *World Development, 13,* 761–787.

Borges, J. L. (1964). *Labyrinths: Selected stories and other writings.* New York: New Directions Books.

Boventor, von, E. S. (1970). Towards a unified theory of spatial economic structure. In R. D. Dean, W. H. Leahy, and D. L. McKee (Eds.), *Spatial economic theory* (pp. 325–355). New York: Free Press. (Reprinted from the 1962 *Papers and Proceedings of the Regional Science Association, 10,* 163–180.)

Bowlby, S., Foord, J., and McDowell, L. (1986). The place of gender in locality studies. *Area, 18,* 327–331.

Bowlby, S., Lewis, J., McDowell, L., and Foord, J. (1989). The geography of gender. In R. Peet and N. J. Thrift (Eds.), *New models in geography* (Vol. 2, pp. 157–175). London: Unwin Hyman.

Braithwaite, R. B. (1960). *Scientific explanation.* New York: Harper Torchbooks.

Brebner, J. B. (1953). Harold Adams Innis as historian. *Canadian Historical Association.* Report of the annual meeting held in London, June 4–6, 1953, pp. 14–24

Breheny, M. J., and Hooper, A. (Eds.). (1985). *Rationality in planning.* London: Pion.

Britton, J. N. H., and Gilmour, J. M. (1978). *The weakest link: A technological perspective on Canadian industrial underdevelopment.* Background Study 43. Ottawa: Science Council of Canada.

Brodie, J. (1989). The political economy of regionalism. In W. Clement and G. Williams (Eds.), *The new Canadian political economy* (pp. 138–159). Montreal and Kingston: McGill–Queen's University Press.

Browett, J. (1984). On the necessity and inevitability of uneven spatial development under capitalism. *International Journal of Urban and Regional Research, 8,* 155–176.

Brown, B. (1986). Modal choice, location demand, and income. *Journal of Urban Economics, 20,* 128–139.

Browning, C. (Ed.). (1982). *Conversations with geographers: Career pathways and research styles.* University of North Carolina at Chapel Hill, Department of Geography, Occasional Paper 16.

Brueckner, J. (1978). Urban general equilibrium models with non-central production. *Journal of Regional Science, 18,* 203–215.

Buckley, K. (1958). The role of staples industries in Canadian economic development. *Journal of Economic History, 18,* 439–450.

Bunge, W. (1962). *Theoretical geography.* Lund, Sweden: C. W. K. Gleerup.

Bunge, W. (1966). *Theoretical geography* (2nd ed.). Lund, Sweden: C. W. K. Gleerup.

Bunge, W. (1971). *Fitzgerald: Geography of a revolution.* Cambridge, MA: Schenkman.

Bunge, W. (1973a). Ethics and logic in geography. In R. J. Chorley (Ed.), *Directions in geography* (pp. 317–331). London: Methuen.

Bunge, W. (1973b). The geography. *Professional Geographer, 25,* 331–337.

Bunge, W. (1977). The first years of the Detroit geographical expedition: A personal report. In R. Peet (Ed.), *Radical geography* (pp. 31–39). London: Methuen.

Bunge, W. (1979a). Fred K. Schaefer and the science of geography. *Annals, Association of American Geographers, 69,* 128–132.

Bunge, W. (1979b). Perspective on theoretical geography. *Annals, Association of American Geographers, 69,* 169–174.

Bunge, W. (1988). *The nuclear war atlas.* Oxford: Blackwell.

Burling, R. (1962). Maximization theories and the study of economic anthropology. *American Anthropologist, 64,* 802–821.

Burton, I. (1963). The quantitative revolution and theoretical geography. *Canadian Geographer, 7,* 151–162.

Buttimer, A. (1982). Musing on Helicon: Root metaphors and geography. *Geografiska Annaler, 64 B,* 89–96.

Caldwell, B. J. (1982). *Beyond positivism: Economic methodology in the twentieth century.* London: George Allen & Unwin.

Cameron, I. (1983). Metaphor in science and society. *Bulletin of Science Technology and Society, 3,* 251–292.

Carey, J. W. (1967). Harold Adams Innis and Marshall McLuhan. *Antioch Review, 27,* 5–39.

Carey, J. W. (1978). *Communication as culture: Essays on media and society.* Boston: Unwin Hyman.

Carling, A. (1986). Rational choice Marxism. *New Left Review, 160,* 24–62.

Carney, J. (1980). Regions in crisis: Accumulation, regional problems and crisis formation. In J. Carney, R. Hudson, and J. Lewis, (Eds.), *Regions in crisis* (pp. 28–59). London: Croom Helm.

Carrothers, G. P. (1956). A historical review of the gravity and potential concepts of human interaction. *Journal, American Institute of Planners, 22,* 94–102.

Casetti, E. (1993). Spatial analysis: Perspectives and prospects. *Urban Geography,* *14,* 526–537.

Castree, N. (1995). On theory's subject and subject's theory: Harvey, capital, and the limits to classical Marxism. *Environment and Planning A, 27,* 299–320.

Caves, R. E. (1960). *Trade and economic structure: Models and methods.* Cambridge, MA: Harvard University Press.

Chang, W.-C. (1976). Statistical theories and sampling practices. In D. B. Owen (Ed.), *On the history of statistics and probability* (pp. 299–315). New York: Marcel Dekker.

Chatterji, M. (1990). Postscript: The future of regional science. In M. Chatterji and R. Kuenne (Eds.), *New frontiers in regional science: Essays in honour of Walter Isard* (Vol. 1, pp. 342–351). London: Macmillan.

Chilcote, E. B., and Chilcote, R. H. (1992). The crisis of Marxism: An appraisal of new directions. *Rethinking Marxism, 5,* 84–106.

Chisholm, M. (1975). *Human geography: Evolution or revolution?* Harmondsworth: Penguin.

Chorley, R. J. (1964). Geography and analogue theory. *Annals, Association of American Geographers, 54,* 127–137.

Chorley, R. J. (1995). Haggett's Cambridge: 1957–66. In A. D. Cliff, P. R. Gould, A. G. Hoare, and N. J. Thrift (Eds.), *Diffusing geography: Essays for Peter Haggett* (pp. 355–374). Oxford: Blackwell.

Chorley, R. J., and Haggett, P. (Eds.). (1965). *Frontiers in geographical teaching.* London: Methuen.

Chorley, R. J., and Haggett, P. (Eds.). (1967). *Models in geography.* London: Methuen.

Christopherson, S. (1989a). Flexibility in the US service economy and the emerging spatial division of labour. *Transactions, Institute of British Geographers, 14,* 131–143.

Christopherson, S. (1989b). On being outside "the project." *Antipode, 21,* 83–89.

Christopherson, S., and Storper, M. (1989). The effects of flexible specialization on industrial politics and the labor market: The motion picture industry. *Industrial Labor Relations Review, 42,* 331–347.

Clark, G. L. (1983). Fluctuations and rigidities in local labour markets. Part 2: Reinterpreting contracts. *Environment and Planning A, 15,* 365–378.

Clark, G. L., Gertler, M. S., and Whiteman, J. (1986). *Regional dynamics: Studies in adjustment theory.* Boston: Allen & Unwin.

Clarke, S. (1982). *Marx, marginalism and modern sociology.* London: Macmillan.

Clement, W., and Williams, G. (1989). Introduction. In W. Clement and G. Williams (Eds.), *The new Canadian political economy* (pp. 1–15). Montreal and Kingston: McGill–Queen's University.

Cloke, P., Philo, C., and Sadler, D. (1991). *Approaching human geography: An introduction to contemporary theoretical debates.* London: Paul Chapman.

Cochrane, A. (1987). What a difference that place makes: The new structuralism of locality. *Antipode, 19,* 354–363.

Coffey, W. J. (1988). The origins of systems theory in geography. In W. J. Coffey (Ed.), *Geographical systems and systems of geography: Essays in honour of William Warntz* (pp. 9–26). London, Ontario: Department of Geography, University of Western Ontario.

Cohen, T. (1979). Metaphor and the cultivation of intimacy. In S. Sacks (Ed.), *On metaphor* (pp. 1–10). Chicago: University of Chicago Press.

Cole, J. P. (1969). Mathematics and geography. *Geography, 54,* 152–164.

Cole, J. P., and King, C. A. M. (1968). *Quantitative geography.* London: Wiley.

Cooke, P. (1987). Clinical inference and geographical theory. *Antipode, 19,* 69–78.

Cooke, P. (1988). Flexible integration, scope economies, and strategic alliances: social and spatial mediations. *Environment and Planning D: Society and Space, 6,* 281–300.

Cooke, P. (1989a). The contested terrain of locality studies. *Tijdschrift voor Economische en Sociale Geografie, 80,* 15–29.

Cooke, P. (Ed.). (1989b). *Localities: The changing face of urban Britain.* London: Unwin Hyman.

Cooke, P. (1989c). Locality, theory and the poverty of spatial variation. *Antipode, 21,* 261–273.

Cooke, P. (1990). *Back to the future: Modernity, postmodernity and locality.* London: Unwin Hyman.

Corbridge, S. (1986). *Capitalist world development: A critique of radical development geography.* London: Macmillan.

Corbridge, S. (1988). Deconstructing determinism: A reply to Michael Watts. *Antipode, 20,* 239–259.

Corbridge, S. (1989). Marxism, post-Marxism and the geography of development. In R. Peet and N. J. Thrift (Eds.), *New models in geography* (Vol. 1, pp. 224–256). London: Unwin Hyman.

Corbridge, S. (1993). Marxisms, modernities and moralities: Development praxis and the claims of distant strangers. *Environment and Planning D: Society and Space, 11,* 449–472.

Corbridge, S., Thrift, N. J., and Martin, R. L. (Eds.) (1994). *Money, space and power.* Oxford: Blackwell.

Couclelis, H. (1986). A theoretical framework for alternative models of spatial decision and behavior. *Annals, Association of American Geographers, 76,* 95–116.

Cox, K., and Mair, A. (1988). Locality and community in the politics of local economic development. *Annals, Association of American Geographers, 78,* 307–325.

Cox, K., and Mair, A. (1989). Levels of abstraction in locality studies. *Antipode, 21,* 121–132.

Cox, K., and Mair, A. (1991). From localised social structures to localities as agents. *Environment and Planning A, 23,* 197–213.

Cox, N. J. (1989). Modelling, data analysis and Pygmalion's problem. In B. Macmillan (Ed.), *Remodelling geography* (pp. 204–208). Oxford: Blackwell.

Creighton, D. B. (1957). *Harold Adams Innis: Portrait of a scholar.* Toronto: University of Toronto Press.

Crouch, R. (1979). *Human behavior: An economic approach.* North Scituate, MA: Duxbury.

Culler, J. (1983). *On deconstruction: Theory and criticism after structuralism.* London: Routledge & Kegan Paul.

Curry, M. R. (1980). *Forms of life: A Wittgensteinian view.* M.A. thesis, Department of Geography, University of Minnesota, Minneapolis.

Curry, M. R. (1985a). On rationality: Contemporary geography and the search for the foolproof method. *Geoforum, 16,* 109–118.

Curry, M. R. (1985b, April). *Universal and local models in urban geography.* Paper presented at the 81st annual meeting of the Association of American Geographers, Detroit, Michigan.

Curry, M. R. (1992a). The architectonic impulse and the reconceptualisation of the concrete in geography. In T. J. Barnes and J. S. Duncan (Eds.), *Writing worlds: Discourse, text and metaphor in the representation of landscape* (pp. 97–117). London: Routledge.

Curry, M. R. (1992b, May). *Constructing margin and frontier: Strategies of exclusion and approaches in contemporary geography.* Paper presented in honor of the retirement of Fred Lukermann, Department of Geography, University of Minnesota, Minneapolis.

Curry, M. R., and Barnes, T. J. (1988). Time and narrative in economic geography. *Environment and Planning A, 20,* 141–149.

Cutler, A., Hindess, B., Hirst, P. Q., and Hussain, A. (1977). *Marx's Capital and capitalism today* (Vol. 1). London: Routledge & Kegan Paul.

Davidson, D. (1979). What metaphors mean. In S. Sacks (Ed.), *On metaphor* (pp. 29–45). Chicago: University of Chicago Press.

Davis, J. (1988). Sraffa, Wittgenstein and neoclassical economics. *Cambridge Journal of Economics, 12,* 29–36.

Davis, P. J., and Hersh, R. (1980). *The mathematical experience.* Boston: Birkhauser.

Debreau, G. (1959). *The theory of value.* New Haven: Yale University Press.

Dennis, K. (1982). Economic theory and the problem of translation. *Economic Issues, 16,* 691–712 and 1039–1062.

Derrida, J. (1976). *Of grammatology* (translated by G. C. Spivak). Baltimore: Johns Hopkins University Press.

Derrida, J. (1983). The time of a thesis: Punctuations. In A. Montefiore (Ed.), *Philosophy in France today* (pp. 24–50). Cambridge, UK: Cambridge University Press.

Derrida, J. (1991). *The Derrida reader: Between the blinds.* Hemel Hempstead: Harvester Wheatsheaf.

Desai, M. (1979). *Marxian economics.* Towota, NJ: Littlefield & Adams.

Deutsche, R. (1991). Boy's town. *Environment and Planning D: Society and Space, 9,* 5–30.

Dewey, J. (1939). *Intelligence in the modern world.* J. Ratner (Ed.). New York: Random House.

Dickens, P. (1988). *One nation? Social change and the politics of locality.* London: Pluto Press.

Diggins, J. P. (1978). *The bard of savagery.* New York: Seabury Press.

Diskin, J., and Sandler, B. (1993). Essentialism and the economy in the post-Marxist imaginary: Reopening the sutures. *Rethinking Marxism, 6,* 28–48.

Dobb, M. H. (1940). *Political economy and capitalism.* New York: International Publishers.

Dobb, M. H. (1973). *Theories of value and distribution since Adam Smith.* Cambridge, UK: Cambridge University Press.

Doel, M. (1993). Proverbs for paranoids: Writing geography on hollowed ground. *Transactions, Institute of British Geographers, 18,* 377–394.

Drache, D. (1976). Rediscovering Canadian political economy. *Journal of Canadian Studies, 11,* 3–18.

Drache, D. (1982). Harold Innis and Canadian capitalist development. *Canadian Journal of Political and Social Theory, 6,* 35–56.

Drache, D. (1983). The crisis of Canadian political economy: Dependency theory versus the new orthodoxy. *Canadian Journal of Political and Social Theory, 7,* 25–49.

Drache, D. (1992). *The global vision of Harold Innis: Competitiveness at the cost of development.* Unpublished manuscript, Department of Political Science, York University, North York, Ontario.

Driver, F. (1992). Geography's empire: Histories of geographical knowledge. *Environment and Planning D: Society and Space, 10,* 23–40.

Dugger, W. M. (1979). The methodological differences between institutional and neoclassical economics. *Journal of Economic Issues, 13,* 899–909.

Dugger, W. M. (1992). *Underground economics: A decade of institutional dissent.* Armonk, NY: M. E. Sharpe.

Dunbar, G. S. (1985). Harold Innis and Canadian geography. *Canadian Geographer, 29,* 159–163.

Duncan, J. S., and Ley, D. F. (1982). Structural Marxism in human geography: A critical assessment. *Annals, Association of American Geographers, 72,* 30–59.

Duncan, J. S., and Ley, D. F. (Eds.). (1993). *Place/ culture/ representation.* London: Routledge.

Duncan, S. (1989). What is locality? In R. Peet and N. J. Thrift (Eds.), *New models in geography* (Vol. 2, pp. 221–252). London: Unwin Hyman.

Duncan, S., and Savage, M. (1989). Space, scale and locality. *Antipode, 21,* 179–206.

Duncan, S., and Savage, M. (1991). Commentary. *Environment and Planning A, 23,* 155–164.

Dunford, M. (1990). Theories of regulation. *Environment and Planning D: Society and Space, 9,* 297–321.

Dyck, I. (1989). Integrating home and wage work-place: Women's daily lives in a Canadian suburb. *Canadian Geographer, 33,* 329–341.

Eagleton, T. (1986). *Against the grain.* London: Verso.

Easterbrook, W. T. (1953). Innis and economics. *Canadian Journal of Economics and Political Science, 19,* 291–330.

Eatwell, J., and Panico, C. (1987). Sraffa, Piero. In J. Eatwell, M. Milgate, and P. Newman (Eds.), *The new Palgave dictionary of economics* (Vol. 4, pp. 445–452). London: Macmillan.

Elson, D. (1979). Introduction. In D. Elson (Ed.), *Value: The representation of labour in capitalism* (pp. i–v). London: CSE Books.

Elster, J. (1985). *Making sense of Marx.* Cambridge, UK: Cambridge University Press.

Elster, J. (1986). *An introduction to Karl Marx.* Cambridge, UK: Cambridge University Press.

England, K. V. L. (1993). Suburban pink collar ghettos: The spatial entrapment of women? *Annals, Association of American Geographers, 83,* 225–242.

Entrikin, J. N. (1991). *The betweenness of place: Towards a geography of modernity.* London: Macmillan.

Farjoun, E., and Machover, M. (1983). *Laws of chaos.* London: Verso and New Left Books.

Feyerabend, P. (1978). *Against method.* London: Verso.

Fischer, M., and Nijkamp, P. (1985). Developments in explanatory discrete spatial data and choice analysis. *Progress in Human Geography, 9,* 515–551.

Foord, J., and Gregson, N. (1986). Patriarchy: Towards a reconceptualization. *Antipode, 18(2),* 186–211.

Foot, S., and Webber, M. (1983). Unequal exchange and unequal development. *Environment and Planning D: Society and Space, 1,* 281–304.

Forbes, D., and Rimmer, P. (Eds.). (1984). *Uneven development and the geographical transfer of value.* Human geography monograph 16. Canberra: Research School of Pacific Studies, Australian National University.

Forman, P. (1971). Weimar culture, causality, and quantum theory, 1918–27: Adaptation by German physicists and mathematicians to a hostile intellectual environment. In R. McCormmach (Ed.), *Historical studies in physical sciences* (Vol. 3, pp. 1–115). Philadelphia: University of Pennsylvania Press.

Fotheringham, A. S. (1981). Spatial structure and distance decay parameters. *Annals, Association of American Geographers, 71,* 425–436.

Fotheringham, A. S., and O'Kelly, M. E. (1989). *Spatial interaction models: Formulations and applications.* Dordrecht: Kluwer.

Foucault, M. (1984). What is Enlightenment? In P. Rabinow (Ed.), *The Foucault reader* (pp. 32–50). New York: Pantheon.

Frege, G. (1959). *The foundations of arithmetic* (translated by J. Austin). Oxford: Blackwell.

French, H. M. (1971). The historical perspective. In H. M. French and J.-B. Racine (Eds.), *Quantitative and qualitative geography: La nécessité d'un dialogue* (pp. 1–11). Occasional papers, Department of Geography, University of Ottawa. Ottawa: University of Ottawa Press.

Friedman, M. (1953). Methodology of positive economics. In *Essays in positive economics* (pp. 3–43). Chicago: University of Chicago Press.

Gale, S. (1972). On the heterodoxy of explanation: A review of David Harvey's *Explanation in geography. Geographical Analysis, 4,* 285–332.

Garrison, W. L. (1956). Applicability of statistical inference to geographical research. *Geographical Review, 46,* 427–429.

Garrison, W. L. (1964). Presidential address: Values of regional science. *Papers of the Regional Science Association, 13,* 7–14.

Geertz, C. (1973). *The interpretation of cultures: Selected essays.* New York: Basic Books.

Geertz, C. (1983). *Local knowledge: Further essays in interpretive anthropology.* New York: Basic Books.

Geertz, C. (1984). Anti anti-relativism. *American Anthropologist, 86,* 263–278.

Georgescu-Roegen, N. (1954). Choice, expectations, and measurability. *Quarterly Journal of Economics, 68,* 502–534.

Georgescu-Roegen, N. (1968a). *Analytical economics.* Cambridge, MA: Harvard University Press.

Georgescu-Roegen, N. (1968b). Utility. In the *International encyclopedia of the social sciences* (Vol. 16, pp. 236–267). New York: Macmillan and the Free Press.

Georgescu-Roegen, N. (1971). *The entropy law and the economic process.* Cambridge, MA: Harvard University Press.

Georgescu-Roegen, N. (1973). Utility and value in economic thought. In P. Wiener (Ed.), *Dictionary of the history of ideas* (pp. 450–458). New York: Charles Scribners and Sons.

Geraets, T. (Ed.). (1979). *Rationality today.* Ottawa: University of Ottawa Press.

Geras, N. (1987). Post-Marxism? *New Left Review, 163,* 40–82.

Gertler, M. S. (1988). The limits to flexibility: Comments on the post-Fordist vision of production and its geography. *Transactions, Institute of British Geographers, 13,* 419–432.

Gertler, M. S. (1989). Resurrecting flexibility? A reply to Schoenberger. *Transactions, Institute of British Geographers, 14,* 109–112.

Gertler, M. S. (1992). Flexibility revisited: Districts, nations, states and the forces of production. *Transactions, Institute of British Geographers, 17,* 259–278.

Getis, A. (1993). Scholarship, leadership and quantitative methods. *Urban Geography, 14,* 517–525.

Gibson, K., and Graham, J. (1992). Rethinking class in industrial geography: Creating a space for an alternative politics of class. *Economic Geography, 68,* 109–127.

Giddens, A. (1976). *New rules of sociological method.* London: Hutchinson.

Giddens, A. (1977). *Studies in social and political theory.* London: Hutchinson.

Glennie, P. D., and Thrift, N. J. (1992). Modernity, urbanism, and modern consumption. *Environment and Planning D: Society and Space, 10,* 423–443.

Godelier, M. (1972). *Rationality and irrationality in economics.* New York: Monthly Review Press.

Golledge, R. G., and Amadeo, D. (1968). On laws in geography. *Annals, Association of American Geographers, 53,* 760–774.

Gould, P. (1970). Is statistix inferens the geographical name for a wild goose chase? *Economic Geography, 46,* 439–448.

Gould, P. (1979). Geography 1957–1977: The Augean period. *Annals, Association of American Geographers, 69,* 139–151.

Gould, P., and White, R. (1974). *Mental maps.* Harmondsworth, UK: Penguin.

Graham, J. (1988). Postmodernism and Marxism. *Antipode, 20,* 60–65.

Graham, J. (1990). Theory and essentialism in Marxist geography. *Antipode, 22,* 53–66.

Graham, J. (1991). Fordism/Post-Fordism, Marxism/Post-Marxism: The second cultural divide. *Rethinking Marxism, 4,* 39–58.

Graham, J. (1992a). Anti-essentialism and overdetermination—a response to Dick Peet. *Antipode, 24,* 141–156.

Graham, J. (1992b). Post-Fordism as politics: The political consequences of narratives on the left. *Environment and Planning D: Society and Space, 10,* 393–410.

Graham, J., Gibson, K., Horvath, R., and Shakow, D. (1988). Restructuring in US manufacturing: The decline of monopoly capitalism. *Annals, Association of American Geographers, 78,* 473–490.

Gregory, D. (1978). *Ideology, science and human geography.* London: Hutchinson.

Gregory, D. (1981). Alfred Weber and location theory. In D. Stoddart (Ed.), *Geography, ideology and social concern* (pp. 165–185). Oxford: Blackwell.

Gregory, D. (1982). Solid geometry: Notes on the recovery of spatial structure. In P. Gould and G. Olsson (Eds.), *A search for common ground* (pp. 187–219). London: Pion.

Gregory, D. (1989a). Areal differentiation and post-modern human geography. In D. Gregory and R. Walford (Eds.), *Horizons in human geography* (pp. 67–96). London: Macmillan.

Gregory, D. (1989b). The crisis of modernity? Human geography and critical social theory. In R. Peet and N. Thrift (Eds.), *New models in geography* (pp. 348–385). London: Unwin Hyman.

Gregory, D. (1993). Realism. In R. Johnston, D. Gregory, and D. M. Smith (Eds.), *The dictionary of human geography* (3rd ed., pp. 499–503). Oxford: Blackwell.

Gregory, D. (1994). *Geographical imaginations.* Oxford: Blackwell.

Gregory, S. (1963). *Statistical methods and the geographer.* London: Longman.

Gregory, S. (1971). The quantitative approach in geography. In H. M. French and J.-B. Racine (Eds.), *Quantitative and qualitative geography: La nécessité d'un dialogue* (pp. 25–33). Ottawa: University of Ottawa Press.

Gregson, N. (1987a). The CURS initiative: Some further comments. *Antipode, 19,* 364–370.

Gregson, N. (1987b). *Locality research: A case of conceptual duplication.* Centre for Urban and Regional Studies, University of Newcastle.

Gudeman, S. (1986). *Economics as culture.* London: Routledge & Kegan Paul.

Gudeman, S., and Penn, M. (1982). Models, meaning and reflexivity. In D. Parkin (Ed.), *Semantic anthropology* (pp. 89–106). London: Academic Press.

Gunn, G. (1987). *The culture of criticism and the criticism of culture.* Oxford: Oxford University Press.

Hadjimichalis, C. (1987). *Uneven development and regionalism.* Beckenham, Kent: Croom Helm.

Haggett, P. (1965a). Changing concepts in economic geography. In R. J. Chorley and P. Haggett (Eds.), *Frontiers in geographical teaching* (pp. 101–117). London: Methuen.

Haggett, P. (1965b). *Locational analysis in human geography.* London: Edward Arnold.

Haggett, P. (1990). *The geographer's art.* Oxford: Blackwell.

Haggett, P., and Chorley, R. J. (1965). Frontier movements and the geographical tradition. In R. J. Chorley and P. Haggett (Eds.), *Frontiers in geographical teaching* (pp. 358–378). London: Methuen.

Haggett, P., and Chorley, R. J. (1967). Models, paradigms and the new geography.

In R. J. Chorley and P. Haggett (Eds.), *Models in geography* (pp. 19–41). London: Methuen.

Haggett, P., and Chorley, R. J. (1989). Foreword. In B. Macmillan (Ed.), *Remodelling geography.* Oxford: Blackwell.

Hahn, F., and Hollis, M. (Eds.). (1979). Introduction. *Philosophy and economic theory* (pp. 1–17). Oxford: Oxford University Press.

Hanson, S. (1993). "Never question the assumptions" and other scenes from the revolution. *Urban Geography, 14, 552–556.*

Hanson, S., and Pratt, G. (1992). Dynamic dependencies: A geographical investigation of local labor markets. *Economic Geography, 68, 373–405.*

Hanson, S., and Pratt, G. (1995). Introduction. *Gender, work, and space.* London: Routledge.

Haraway, D. (1991). Situated knowledges: The science question in feminism and the privilege of partial perspective. In *Simians, cyborgs, and women: The reinvention of nature* (pp. 183–201). New York: Routledge.

Harcourt, G. C. (1972). *Some Cambridge controversies in the theory of capital.* Cambridge, UK: Cambridge University Press.

Harding, S. G. (Ed.). (1976). *Can theories be refuted?* Dordrecht, The Netherlands: D. Reidel.

Hardy, G. H. (1967). *A mathematician's apology.* Cambridge, UK: Cambridge University Press.

Harland, R. (1987). *Superstructuralism: The philosophy of structuralism and post-structuralism.* London: Methuen.

Harris, B. (1985). Urban simulation models in regional science. *Journal of Regional Science, 25, 545–567.*

Harris, C., and Nadji, M. (1985). The spatial context of the Arrow–Debreau general equilibrium system. *Journal of Regional Science, 25, 1–10.*

Hartshorne, R. (1955). "Exceptionalism in Geography" re-examined. *Annals, Association of American Geographers, 45, 205–244.*

Harvey, D. (1967). Models of the evolution of spatial patterns in human geography. In R. J. Chorley and P. Haggett (Eds.), *Models in geography* (pp. 549–608). London: Methuen.

Harvey, D. (1969). *Explanation in geography.* London: Edward Arnold.

Harvey, D. (1973). *Social justice and the city.* London: Edward Arnold.

Harvey, D. (1974). Class monopoly rent: Finance capital, and the urban revolution. *Regional Studies, 8, 239–255.*

Harvey, D. (1982). *Limits to capital.* Chicago: University of Chicago Press.

Harvey, D. (1984). On the history and present condition of geography: An historical materialist manifesto. *Professional Geographer, 36, 1–10.*

Harvey, D. (1985a). *Consciousness and the urban experience.* Baltimore: Johns Hopkins University Press.

Harvey, D. (1985b). *The urbanization of capital.* Baltimore: Johns Hopkins University Press.

Harvey, D. (1986). The geopolitics of capitalism. In D. Gregory and J. Urry (Eds.), *Social relations and spatial structures* (pp. 128–163). London: Macmillan.

Harvey, D. (1987). Three myths in search of a reality in urban studies. *Environment and Planning D: Society and Space, 5, 367–376.*

Harvey, D. (1989). *The condition of postmodernity: An enquiry into the origins of cultural change.* Oxford: Blackwell.

Harvey, D. (1992). Postmodern morality plays. *Antipode, 24,* 300–326.

Harvey, D., and Scott, A. J. (1989). The practice of human geography: Theory and empirical specificity in the transition from Fordism to flexible accumulation. In B. Macmillan (Ed.), *Remodelling geography* (pp. 217–229). Oxford: Blackwell.

Hausman, D. M. (1981). *Capital, profits, and prices: An essay in the philosophy of economics.* New York: Columbia University Press.

Hay, A. M. (1985). Scientific method in geography. In R. J. Johnston (Ed.), *The future of geography* (pp. 129–142). London: Methuen.

Haynes, K., and Stubbings, R. (1985). Geography, science and concept change: The ecology of Toulmin—a commentary. *Scientific Geography Newsletter, 2,* 10–15.

Hempel, C. G. (1958). The theoretician's dilemma. In H. Feigl, G. Maxwell, and M. Scriven (Eds.), *Minnesota studies in the philosophy of science* (Vol. 2, p. 50). Minneapolis: University of Minnesota Press.

Hempel, C. G., and Oppenheim, P. (1948). Studies in the logic of explanation. *Philosophy of Science, 15,* 135–175.

Henderson, W., Dudley-Evans, T., and Backhouse, R. (Eds). (1993). *Economics and language.* London: Routledge.

Hesse, M. B. (1963). *Models and analogies in science.* London: Steed and Ward.

Hesse, M. B. (1980). *Revolutions and reconstructions in the philosophy of science.* Brighton: Harvester Wheatsheaf.

Hesse, M. B. (1987). Tropical talk: The myth of the literal. *Proceedings of the Aristotelian Society, 61,* 297–311.

Hicks, J. (1976). Some questions of time in economics. In A. Tang, F. Westfield, and J. Worky (Eds.), *Evolution, welfare and time in economics* (pp. 135–141). Lexington, MA: Lexington Books.

Hilts, V. (1973). Statistics and social science. In R. N. Giere and R. S. Westfall (Eds.), *Foundations of the scientific method in the nineteenth century* (pp. 206–233). Bloomington: University of Indiana Press.

Hindess, B. (1988). *Choice, rationality and social theory.* London: Unwin Hyman.

Hirst, P. Q., and Zeitlin, J. (1991). Flexible specialization versus post-Fordism: Theory, evidence and policy implications. *Economy and Society, 20,* 1–56.

Hobbes, T. (1914). *Leviathan.* London: J. M. Dent & Sons. (Original published 1651)

Hodgson, G. M. (1981). Critique of Wright: 1. Labour and profits. In I. Steedman and P. M. Sweezy (Eds.), *The value controversy* (pp. 75–99). London: Verso and New Left Books.

Hodgson, G. M. (1988). *Economics and institutions: A manifesto for a modern institutional economics.* Cambridge, UK: Polity Press.

Hollis, M. (1983). Rational preferences. *Philosophical Forum, 14,* 246–262.

Hollis, M., and Lukes, S. (1982). *Rationality and relativism.* Cambridge, MA: MIT Press.

Hollis, M., and Nell, E. J. (1975). *Rational economic man: A philosophical critique of neo-classical economics.* Cambridge, UK: Cambridge University Press.

Hoover, E. M. (1963). Presidential address: Whence regional scientists. *Papers of the Regional Science Association, 11,* 7–16.

Howard, M. (1987). Economics on a Sraffian foundation. *Economy and Society, 16,* 317–340.

Hudson, B. (1977). The new geography and the new imperialism: 1870–1918. *Antipode, 9,* 12–19.

Hudson, R. (1989). Labour market changes and new forms of work in old industrial regions: Maybe flexibility for some but not flexible accumulation. *Environment and Planning D: Society and Space, 7,* 5–30.

Hutchinson, T. (1938). *The significance and basic postulates of economic theory.* London: Macmillan.

Innis, H. A. (1930). *The fur trade in Canada: An introduction to Canadian economic history.* Toronto: University of Toronto Press.

Innis, H. A. (1935). The role of intelligence: Some further notes. *Canadian Journal of Economics and Political Science, 1,* 280–287.

Innis, H. A. (1946). *Political economy and the modern state.* Toronto: Ryerson.

Innis, H. A. (1950). *Empire and communications.* Toronto: University of Toronto Press.

Innis, H. A. (1951). *The bias of communication.* Toronto: University of Toronto Press.

Innis, H. A. (1956a). The teaching of economic history in Canada. In M. Q. Innis (Ed.), *Essays in Canadian economic history* (pp. 3–16). Toronto: University of Toronto Press.

Innis, H. A. (1956b). Transportation as a factor in Canadian economic history. In M. Q. Innis (Ed.), *Essays in Canadian economic history* (pp. 62–77). Toronto: University of Toronto Press.

Innis, H. A. (1956c). The work of Thorstein Veblen. In M. Q. Innis (Ed.), *Essays in Canadian economic history* (pp. 17–26). Toronto: University of Toronto Press.

Irvine, J., and Miles, I. (1979). Statistics teaching in social science: A problem with history. In J. Irvine, I. Miles, and J Evans (Eds.), *Demystifying social statistics* (pp. 11–26). London: Pluto Press.

Isard, W. (1956). *Location and space economy.* New York: Wiley.

Isard, W. (1990). Regional science: Some retrospect, remarks on its scope and nature, and some prospects. In C. Smith (Ed.), *Location analysis and general theory: Economic, political, regional, and dynamic. Selected papers of Walter Isard* (Vol. 1, pp. 293–229). London: Macmillan.

Isard, W., in association with Bramhall, D., Carrothers, G., Cumberland, J., Moses, L., Price, D., and Schooler, E. (1960). *Methods of regional analysis: An introduction to regional science.* New York: Wiley.

Isard, W., in association with Smith, T., Isard, P., Tung, T., and Dacey, M. (1969). *General theory: Social, political, economic and regional.* Cambridge, MA: MIT Press.

Isard, W., and Dacey, M. (1962). On the projection of individual behavior in regional analysis I and II. *Journal of Regional Science, 4,* 1–34 and 51–83.

Isard, W., and Ostroff, D. (1960). General interregional equilibrium. *Journal of Regional Science, 2,* 67–74.

268 – References

Isard, W., and Reiner, T. A. (1966). Regional science: Retrospect and prospect. *Papers of the Regional Science Association, 16,* 1–16.

Jackson, P. (1991). Mapping meanings: A cultural critique of locality studies. *Environment and Planning A, 23,* 215–228.

Janelle, D. G., and Janelle, B. (1988). Patterns of contact and influence in the life of a spatial scientist: William Warntz. In W. J. Coffey, (Ed.), *Geographical systems and systems of geography: Essays in honour of William Warntz* (pp. 189–202). London, Ontario: Department of Geography, University of Western Ontario.

Jevons, W. (1970). *The theory of political economy.* Harmondsworth, UK: Penguin.

Johnson, H. G. (1974). The current and prospective state of economics. *Australian Economic Papers, 13,* 1–27.

Johnson, M. (Ed.). (1981). Introduction. In *Philosophical perspectives on metaphor* (pp. 3–47). Minneapolis: University of Minnesota Press.

Johnston, R. J. (1991). *Geography and geographers: Anglo-American geography since 1945* (4th ed.). London: Edward Arnold.

Katz, C. (1992). All the world is staged: Intellectuals and the project of ethnography. *Environment and Planning D: Society and Space, 10,* 495–510.

Keeble, D. E. (1980). Industrial decline, regional policy and the urban–rural manufacturing shift in the United Kingdom. *Environment and Planning A, 12,* 945–962.

Keeble, D. E. (1982). A response to Sayer's reply by Keeble. *Environment and Planning A, 14,* 124–125.

Keith, M., and Pile, S. (Eds.). (1993). *Place and the politics of identity.* London: Routledge.

King, L. J. (1993). Spatial analysis and the institutionalization of geography as a social science. *Urban Geography, 14,* 538–551.

Klamer, A. (1984). *The new classical economics: Conversations with the new classical macroeconomists and their opponents.* Brighton: Harvester Wheatsheaf.

Klamer, A. (1988). Economics as discourse. In N. deMarchi (Ed.), *The Popperian legacy in economics* (pp. 259–278). Cambridge, UK: Cambridge University Press.

Kline, M. H. (1980). *Mathematics: The loss of certainty.* New York: Oxford University Press.

Knight, F. (1956). *On the history and method of economics.* Chicago: University of Chicago Press.

Knorr-Cetina, K. D. (1981). *The manufacture of knowledge: An essay on the constructionist and contextual nature of science.* New York: Pergamon.

Knorr-Cetina, K. D. (1983). The ethnographic study of scientific work: Towards a constructivist interpretation of science. In K. D. Knorr-Cetina and M. Mulkay (Eds.), *Science observed: Perspectives on the sociology of science* (pp. 115–140). London: Sage.

Knorr-Cetina, K. D., and Mulkay, M. (1983). Introduction. In K. D. Knorr-Cetina and M. Mulkay (Eds.), *Science observed: Perspectives on the sociology of science* (pp. 1–17). London: Sage.

Koestler, A. (1964). *The sleepwalkers*. Harmondsworth, UK: Penguin.

Kroker, A. (1984). *Technology and the Canadian mind: Innis/McLuhan/Grant*. Montreal: New World Perspectives.

Kuenne, R. (1990). Walter Isard: Scholar, teacher and founder. In M. Chatterji and R. Kuenne (Eds.), *New frontiers in regional science: Essays in honour of Walter Isard* (Vol. 1, pp. 1–9). London: Macmillan.

Kuhn, T. (1970). *The structure of scientific revolutions* (2nd ed.). Chicago: University of Chicago Press.

Laclau, E., and Mouffe, C. (1985). *Hegemony and socialist strategy: Towards a radical democratic politics*. London: Verso.

Laclau, E., and Mouffe, C. (1987). Post-Marxism without apologies. *New Left Review, 166*, 79–106.

Lakatos, I. (1971). History of science and its rational reconstruction. In R. Buck and R. Cohen (Eds.), *PSA 1970: In memory of Rudolph Carnap. Boston studies in the philosophy of science* (Vol. 8, pp. 91–139). Dordrecht, The Netherlands: D. Reidel.

Lancaster, K. (1966). A new approach to consumer theory. *Journal of Political Economy, 74*, 132–157.

Landry, D., and MacLean, G. (1991). Rereading Laclau and Mouffe. *Rethinking Marxism, 4*, 41–60.

Latour, B. (1987). *Science in action: How to follow scientists and engineers through society*. Milton Keynes: Open University.

Latour, B. (1993). *We have never been modern*. Brighton, UK: Wheatsheaf.

Latour, B., and Woolgar, S. (1979). *Laboratory life: The construction of scientific facts*. Beverly Hills, CA: Sage.

Lawson, H. (1985). *On reflexivity: The post-modern predicament*. London: Hutchinson.

Laxer, G. (1991). Introduction. In *Perspectives on Canadian economic development: Class, staples, gender and elites* (pp. ix–xvii). Toronto: Oxford University Press.

Lefeber, L. (1958). *Allocation in space: Production, transport and industrial location*. Amsterdam: North Holland.

Lentricchia, F. (1983). *Criticism and social change*. Chicago: University of Chicago Press.

Leslie, D. A. (1993). Femininity, post-Fordism, and the "new traditionalism." *Environment and Planning D: Society and Space, 11*, 689–708.

Lever, W. (1985). Theory and methodology in industrial geography. In M. Pacione (Ed.), *Progress in industrial geography* (pp. 10–39). Beckenham, Kent: Croom Helm.

Levine, A. L. (1974). This age of Leontieff . . . and who? *Journal of Economic Literature, 12*, 872–881.

Levine, A. L., Sober, E., and Wright, E. O. (1987). Marxism and methodological individualism. *New Left Review, 162*, 67–84.

Lewis, P. W. (1972). Three related problems in the formulation of laws in geography. In W. K. D. Davies (Ed.), *The conceptual revolution in geography* (pp. 157–162). London: University of London Press. (First published in 1965 in *Professional Geographer, 17*, 24–27)

Ley, D. F. (1978). Social geography and social action. In D. F. Ley and M. S. Samuels (Eds.), *Humanistic geography: Prospects and problems* (pp. 41–57). Chicago: Maaroufa Press.

Liebenstein, H. (1966). Allocative efficiency vs. X-efficiency. *American Economic Review, 56,* 392–415.

Liossatos, P. (1980). Unequal exchange and regional disparities. *Papers of the Regional Science Association, 45,* 87–103.

Lipietz, A. (1986). New tendencies in the international division of labour: Regimes of accumulation and modes of regulation. In A. J. Scott and M. Storper (Eds.), *Production, work, territory* (pp. 16–39). London: Unwin Hyman.

Lippi, M. (1979). *Value and naturalism in Marx.* London: New Left Books.

Livingstone, D. N. (1992). *The geographical tradition: Episodes in the history of a contested enterprise.* Oxford: Blackwell.

Livingstone, D. N., and Harrison, R. T. (1981). Meaning through metaphor: Analogy as epistemology. *Annals, Association of American Geographers, 71,* 95–107.

Lovering, J. (1990). Fordism's unknown successor: A comment on Scott's theory of flexible accumulation and the re-emergence of regional economies. *International Journal of Urban and Regional Research, 14,* 158–171.

Lovering, J. (1991). Theorizing postfordism: Why contingency matters (a further response to Scott). *International Journal of Urban and Regional Research, 15,* 298–301.

Lowe, A. (1951). On the mechanistic approach to economics. *Social Research, 18,* 403–434.

Lucas, R. A. (1971). *Minetown, milltown, railtown: Life in Canadian communities of single industry.* Toronto: Toronto University Press.

Lukermann, F. E. (1958). Towards a more geographic economic geography. *Professional Geographer, 10,* 2–10.

Lukermann, F. E. (1959a, January 20). The changing pattern of flour mill location. *Northwestern Miller,* pp. 33–36.

Lukermann, F. E. (1959b, January 27). The changing pattern of flour mill location. *Northwestern Miller,* pp. 12–14.

Lukermann, F. E. (1959c, February 10). The changing pattern of flour mill location. *Nortwestern Miller,* pp. 12–14.

Lukermann, F. E. (1959d, February 24). The changing pattern of flour mill location. *Northwestern Miller,* pp. 12–15.

Lukermann, F. E. (1959e, March 24). The changing pattern of flour mill location. *Northwestern Miller,* pp. 12, 14, and 16–17.

Lukermann, F. E. (1959f, March 31). The changing pattern of flour mill location. *Northwestern Miller,* pp. 12–16.

Lukermann, F. E. (1959g, April 28). The changing pattern of flour mill location. *Northwestern Miller,* pp. 12–16.

Lukermann, F. E. (1960a). The changing pattern of cement mill location in N. America. *Przeglad Geograficzny, 32,* 537–559.

Lukermann, F. E. (1960b). The geography of cement? *Professional Geographer, 12*(4), 1–6.

Lukermann, F. E. (1961). The role of theory in geographical inquiry. *Professional Geographer, 13,* 1–6.

Lukermann, F. E. (1964a). *Geography among the sciences.* Manuscript, Department of Geography, University of Minnesota, Minneapolis.

Lukermann, F. E. (1964b). Geography as a formal intellectual discipline and the way in which it contributes to human knowledge. *Canadian Geographer, 8,* 167–172.

Lukermann, F. E. (1965a). The "calcul des probabilités" and the École française de géographie. *Canadian Geographer, 9,* 128–137.

Lukermann, F. E. (1965b). Geography: De facto or de jure. *Journal of the Minnesota Academy of Science, 32,* 189–196.

Lukermann, F. E. (1966). Empirical expressions of nodality and hierarchy in a circulation manifold. *East Lakes Geographer, 2,* 17–44.

Lukermann, F. E., and Porter, P. W. (1960). Gravity and potential models in economic geography. *Annals, Association of American Geographers, 50,* 493–504.

Machlup, F. (1978a). Homo-economicus and his class mates. In *Methodology of economics and other social sciences* (pp. 267–281). London: Academic Press.

Machlup, F. (1978b). The universal bogey: Economic man. In *Methodology of economics and other social sciences* (pp. 283–301). London: Academic Press.

MacKenzie, D. A. (1979). Eugenics and the rise of mathematical statistics in Britain. In J. Irvine, I. Mills, and J. Evans (Eds.), *Demystifying social statistics* (pp. 39–50). London: Pluto Press.

MacKenzie, D. A. (1981). *Statistics in Britain 1865–1930: The social construction of scientific knowledge.* Edinburgh: Edinburgh University Press.

MacKenzie, S., and Rose, D. (1983). Industrial change, the domestic economy and home life. In J. Anderson, S. Duncan, and R. Hudson (Eds.), *Redundant space in cities and regions* (pp. 155–200). New York: Academic Press.

Mainwaring, L. (1984). *Value and distribution in capitalist economies.* Cambridge, UK: Cambridge University Press.

Mair, A. (1986). Thomas Kuhn and understanding geography. *Progress in Human Geography, 10,* 345–370.

Mann, M. (1986). *The sources of social power* (Vol. 1). Cambridge, UK: Cambridge University Press.

Mannheim, K. (1936). *Ideology and utopia.* New York: Harcourt, Brace & World.

Marcus, G., and Fisher, M. (1986). *Anthropology as cultural critique: An experimental moment in the human sciences.* Chicago: University of Chicago Press.

Marsden, P. (1992). Real regulation reconsidered. *Environment and Planning A, 24,* 751–767.

Marshall, J. S. (1985). Geography as a scientific enterprise. In R. J. Johnston (Ed.), *The future of geography* (pp. 113–128). London: Methuen.

Marx, K. (1976). *Capital* (Vol. 1). Harmondsworth: Penguin.

Massey, D. (1973). A critique of industrial location theory. *Antipode, 5(3),* 33–39.

Massey, D. (1978). Survey: Regionalism: Some current issues. *Capital and Class, 6,* 106–123.

Massey, D. (1979). A critical evaluation of industrial location theory. In F. Hamilton and G. Linge (Eds.), *Spatial analysis: Industry and the industrial environment* (pp. 57–72). Chichester: Wiley.

Massey, D. (1984a). Industrial location: Some thoughts and observations. *ESRC Newsletter, 51*, xv.

Massey, D. (1984b). *Spatial divisions of labour: Social structures and the geography of production*. London: Macmillan

Massey, D. (1986). New directions in space. In D. Gregory and J. Urry (Eds.), *Social relations and spatial structures* (pp. 9–19). London: Macmillan.

Massey, D. (1991a). Flexible sexism. *Environment and Planning D: Society and Space, 9*, 31–57.

Massey, D. (1991b). The political place of locality studies. *Environment and Planning A, 23*, 267–281.

Massey, D. (1992). Space, place and gender. *LSE Magazine, 4(1)*, 132–134.

Massey, D. (1993). Power, geometry and a progressive sense of place. In J. Bird et al. (Eds.), *Mapping the futures: Local culture, global change* (pp. 59–69). London: Routledge.

Massey, D., and Meegan, R. (1982). *Anatomy of job loss: The how, why and where of employment decline*. London: Methuen.

Mayhew, A. (1988). The beginnings of institutionalism. In M. R. Tool (Ed.), *Evolutionary economics: Vol. 1. The foundations of institutional thought* (pp. 21–48). Armonk, NY: M. E. Sharpe.

McCloskey, D. N. (1985). *The rhetoric of economics*. Madison: University of Wisconsin Press.

McDowell, L. (1986). Beyond patriarchy: A classed-based explanation of women's subordination. *Antipode, 18(3)*, 311–321.

McDowell, L., and Court, G. (1994a). Missing subjects: Gender, power and sexuality in merchant banking. *Economic Geography, 70*, 229–251.

McDowell, L., and Court, G. (1994b). Performing work: Bodily representations in merchant banks. *Environment and Planning D: Society and Space, 12*, 727–750.

McDowell, L., and Massey, D. (1984). A woman's place? In D. Massey and J. Allen (Eds.), *Geography matters! A reader* (pp. 128–147). Cambridge, UK: Cambridge University Press.

McKenzie, R. (1978). On the methodological boundaries of economics. *Journal of Economic Issues, 12*, 627–645.

McLuhan, M. (1953). The later Innis. *Queen's Quarterly, 60*, 386–394.

Meek, R. (1976). *Studies in the labour theory of value* (2nd ed.). London: Lawrence and Wishart.

Melody, W. H. (1981). Introduction. In W. H. Melody, L. Salter, and P. Heyer (Eds.). *Culture, communication and dependency: The tradition of H. A. Innis* (pp. 3–12). Norwood, NJ: Ablex.

Merton, R. K. (1973). *The sociology of science*. Chicago: University of Chicago Press.

Milberg, W. (1991). Marxism, post-structuralism, and the discourse of economists. *Rethinking Marxism, 4*, 93–104.

Miller, R. (1991). Selling Mrs. Consumer: Advertising in the age of suburban socio-spatial relations, 1910–30. *Antipode, 23*, 263–301.

Mirowski, P. (1981). Is there a mathematical neoinstitutional economics? *Journal of Economic Issues, 15*, 593–613.

Mirowski, P. (1984a). Physics and the "marginalist revolution." *Cambridge Journal of Economics, 8,* 361–379.

Mirowski, P. (1984b). The role of conservation principles in twentieth-century economic theory. *Philosophy of the Social Sciences, 14,* 461–473.

Mirowski, P. (1986a). Introduction. Paradigms, hard cores, and fuglemen in modern economic theory. In P. Mirowski (Ed.), *The reconstruction of economic theory* (pp. 1–11). Boston: Kluwer–Nijhoff.

Mirowski, P. (1986b). Mathematical formalism and economic explanation. In P. Mirowski (Ed.), *The reconstruction of economic theory* (pp. 179–240). Boston: Kluwer–Nijhoff.

Mirowski, P. (1988). The philosophical foundations of institutional economics. In *Against mechanism: Protecting economics from science* (pp. 106–133). Towota, NJ: Rowman & Littlefield. (Reprinted from the 1987 *Journal of Economic Issues, 21,* 1001–1038.)

Mirowski, P. (1989). *More heat than light. Economics as social physics, physics as nature's economics.* Cambridge, UK: Cambridge University Press.

Mirowski, P. (1990). Learning the meaning of a dollar: Conservation principles and the social theory of value in economic theory. *Social Research, 57,* 689–717.

Mirowski, P. (1991). Postmodernism and the social theory of value. *Journal of Post-Keynesian Economics, 13,* 565–582.

Morgan, K., and Sayer, A. (1985). A "modern" industry in a mature region: The remaking of management-labour relations. *International Journal of Urban and Regional Research, 9,* 383–404.

Morishima, M., and Cataphores, G. (1978). *Value, exploitation and growth.* New York: McGraw-Hill.

Morrill, R. (1993). Geography, spatial analysis and social science. *Urban Geography, 14,* 442–446.

Morris, M. (1992). The man in the mirror: David Harvey's "Condition" of postmodernity. *Theory, Culture and Society, 9,* 253–279.

Moses, L. N. (1958). Location theory and production. *Quarterly Journal of Economics, 72,* 259–272.

Mouzelis, N. (1988). Marxism or post-Marxism? *New Left Review, 167,* 107–123.

Mulligan, G. (1983). Central place populations: A micro-economic consideration. *Journal of Regional Science, 23,* 83–92.

Murgatroyd, L., and Urry, J. (1983). The restructuring of a local economy: The case of Lancaster. In J. Anderson, S. Duncan, and R. Hudson (Eds.), *Redundant spaces in cities and regions* (pp. 67–98). London: Academic Press.

Muth, R. (1985). Models of land-use, housing and rent: An evaluation. *Journal of Regional Science, 25,* 293–306.

Myers, G., and Papageorgiou, Y. Y. (1991). Homo economicus in perspective. *Canadian Geographer, 35,* 380–399.

Myrdal, G. (1969). *The political element in the development of economic theory.* New York: Simon and Schuster.

Nagel, E. (1961). *The structure of science: Problems in the logic of scientific explanation.* New York: Harcourt, Brace & World.

Napoleoni, C. (1978). Sraffa's "tabula rasa." *New Left Review, 112,* 75–77.

Napolitano, G. (1984–1985). The "secret life" of a great intellectual. *Science and Society, 48,* 216–219.

Neill, R. (1991). *A history of Canadian economic thought.* London and New York: Routledge.

Nelson, K. (1986). Female labour supply characteristics and the suburbanization of low-wage office work. In A. J. Scott and M. Storper (Eds.), *Production, work, territory: The geographical anatomy of industrial capitalism* (pp. 149–171). Boston: Allen & Unwin.

Niedercorn, J., and Ammari, N. (1987). New evidence on the specification and performance of neoclassical gravity models in the study of urban transportation. *Annals of Regional Science, 21,* 56–64.

Norris, C. (1987). *Derrida.* Cambridge, MA: Harvard University Press.

Oakes, G. (1986). Introduction: Rickert's theory of historical knowledge. In H. Rickert (Ed.), *The limits of concept formation in the natural sciences: A logical introduction to the historical sciences* (pp. vii–xxx). Cambridge, UK: Cambridge University Press.

Olsson, G. (1965). *Distance and human interaction: A review and bibliography.* Philadelphia: Regional Science Research Institute.

Olsson, G. (1970). Explanation, prediction, and meaning variance: An assessment of distance interaction models. *Economic Geography, 46,* 223–233.

Olsson, G. (1980). *Birds in egg/Eggs in bird.* London: Pion.

Olsson, G. (1991). *Lines of power/Limits to language.* Minneapolis: University of Minnesota Press.

Olsson, G. (1992). Lines of power. In T. J. Barnes and J. S. Duncan (Eds.), *Writing worlds: Discourse, text and metaphor in the representation of landscape* (pp. 85–96). London: Routledge.

Olsson, G., and Gale, S. (1968). Spatial theory and human behavior. *Papers of the Regional Science Association, 21,* 229–242.

Oppenshaw, S. (1989). Computer modelling in human geography. In B. Macmillan (Ed.), *Remodelling geography* (pp. 70–88). Oxford: Blackwell.

Parker, I. (1977). Harold Innis, Karl Marx and Canadian political economy. *Queen's Quarterly, 84,* 545–563.

Parker, I. (1985). Harold Innis: Staples, communications, and the economics of capacity, overhead costs, rigidity, and bias. In D. Cameron (Ed.), *Explorations in Canadian economic history: Essays in honour of Irene M. Spry* (pp. 73–93). Ottawa: University of Ottawa Press.

Parker, I. (1988). Harold Innis as a Canadian geographer. *Canadian Geographer, 32,* 63–69.

Parr, J. (1990). *The gender of breadwinners: Women, men and change in two industrial towns, 1880–1950.* Toronto: University of Toronto Press.

Pasinetti, L. L. (1977). *Lectures in the theory of production.* New York: Columbia University Press.

Patterson, G. (1990). *History and communications: Harold Innis, Marshall McLuhan, and the interpretation of history.* Toronto: University of Toronto Press.

Pearson, K. (1970). Notes on the history of correlation. In E. S. Pearson and M.

G. Kendall (Eds.), *Studies in the history of statistics and probability* (pp. 185–206). London: Griffin.

Peck, J. A., and Tickell, A. (1992). Local modes of social regulation? Regulation theory, Thatcherism and uneven development. *Geoforum, 23,* 347–383.

Peet, R. (1992). Some questions for anti-essentialism. *Antipode, 24,* 113–130.

Perroux, F. (1950). Economic space and its applications. *Quarterly Journal of Economics, 64,* 89–104.

Pfouts, R. W. (1958). Discussion: Population projection by means of income potential models. *Papers of the Regional Science Association, 4,* 155–158.

Pickering, A. (Ed.). (1992). *Science as practice and culture.* Chicago: University of Chicago Press.

Pickering, A. (1993). The mangle of practice: Agency and emergence in the sociology of science. *American Journal of Sociology, 99,* 559–589.

Piore, M. J., and Sabel, C. F.(1984). *The second industrial divide: Possibilities for prosperity.* New York: Basic Books.

Pitfield, D. (Ed.). (1984). *Discrete choice models in regional science.* London papers in regional science, 14. London: Pion.

Polanyi, K. (1968). *Primitive, archaic and modern economies* (edited by G. Dalton). Boston: Beacon.

Pollitt, B. H. (1988). The collaboration of Maurice Dobb in Sraffa's edition of Ricardo. *Cambridge Journal of Economics, 12,* 55–66.

Popper, K. (1945). *The open society and its enemies* (2 vols.). London: Routledge & Kegan Paul.

Porter, T. M. (1986). *The rise of statistical thinking 1820–1900.* Princeton, NJ: Princeton University Press.

Pratt, A. C. (1991). Discourses of locality. *Environment and Planning A, 23,* 257–266.

Pratt, G. (1993). Feminist geographies. In R. J. Johnston, D. Gregory, and D. M. Smith (Eds.), *The dictionary of human geography* (3rd ed., pp. 192–196). Oxford: Blackwell.

Pratt, G., and Hanson, S. (1993). Women and work across the life course: Moving beyond essentialism. In C. Katz and J. Monk (Eds.), *Full circles: Geographies of women over the life course* (pp. 27–54). London: Routledge.

Pratt, G., and Hanson, S. (1994). Geography and the construction of difference. *Gender, Place and Culture, 1,* 5–29.

Pred, A. (1967). *Behavior and location* (Part 1). Lund, Sweden: C. W. K. Gleerup.

Pringle, R. (1989). *Secretaries talk.* London: Verso.

Przeworski, A. (1985). Marxism and rational choice. *Politics and Society, 15,* 379–409.

Pyke, F., Becattini, G., and Sengenberger, W. (1990). *Industrial districts and inter-firm co-operation in Italy.* Geneva: International Institute for Labour Studies.

Quigley, J. (1983). Consumer's choice of dwelling, neighborhood and public service. *Regional Science and Urban Economics, 15,* 41–63.

Quine, W. V. (1979). A postscript on metaphor. In S. Sacks (Ed.), *On metaphor* (pp. 159–160). Chicago: University of Chicago Press.

Rabinow, P. (1986). Representations are social facts: Modernity and post-modernity in anthropology. In J. Clifford and G. Marcus (Eds.), *Writing culture: The poetics and politics of ethnography* (pp. 234–261). Berkeley: University of California Press.

Resnick, S. A., and Wolff, R. D. (1987). *Knowledge and class: A Marxian critique of political economy.* Chicago: University of Chicago Press.

Resnick, S. A., and Wolff, R. D. (1992). Reply to Richard Peet. *Antipode, 24,* 131–140.

Richards, I. A. (1936). *The philosophy of rhetoric.* Oxford: Oxford University Press.

Richards, M. (1982). Disaggregate demand models—promises and prospects. *Transportation Research, 16,* 339–344.

Richards, S. (1987). *Philosophy and sociology of science* (2nd ed.). Oxford: Blackwell.

Richardson, H. (1977). *The new urban economics.* London: Pion.

Robbins, L. (1935). *An essay on the nature and significance of economic science* (2nd ed.). London: Macmillan.

Robinson, J. V. (1964). *Economic philosophy.* Harmondsworth, UK: Penguin.

Robinson, J. V. (1965). *Collected economic papers* (Vol. 3). Oxford: Blackwell.

Robinson, J. V. (1979). History versus equilibrium. In *Collected economic papers* (Vol. 5, pp. 48–58). Oxford: Blackwell.

Roemer, J. (1982). *A general theory of exploitation and class.* Cambridge, MA: Harvard University Press.

Roemer, J. (Ed). (1986). *Analytical Marxism.* Cambridge, UK: Cambridge University Press.

Roncaglia, A. (1978). *Sraffa and the theory of prices.* London: Wiley.

Roosevelt, F. (1974). Cambridge economics as commodity fetishism. *Review of Radical Political Economy, 7,* 1–32.

Rorty, R. (1979). *Philosophy and the mirror of nature.* Princeton, NJ: Princeton University Press.

Rorty, R. (1982). *The consequences of pragmatism (essays 1972–80).* Minneapolis: University of Minnesota Press.

Rorty, R. (1987). Hesse and Davidson on metaphor. *Proceedings of the Aristotelian Society, supplementary volume, 61,* 283–296.

Rorty, R. (1989). *Contingency, irony and solidarity.* Cambridge, UK: Cambridge University Press.

Rorty, R. (1991a). *Essays on Heidegger and others. Philosophical papers* (Vol. 2). Cambridge, UK: Cambridge University Press.

Rorty, R. (1991b). *Objectivity, relativism, and truth. Philosophical papers* (Vol. 1). Cambridge, UK: Cambridge University Press.

Rose, G. (1989). Locality studies and waged labour: An historical critique. *Transactions, Institute of British Geographers, 14,* 317–328.

Rose, G. (1993). *Feminism and geography: The limits of geographical knowledge.* Minneapolis: University of Minnesota Press.

Rosenberg, A. (1976). *Microeconomic laws: A philosophical analysis.* Pittsburgh: University of Pittsburgh Press.

Rosenberg, A. (1979). Can economic theory explain everything? *Philosophy of the Social Sciences, 9,* 509–529.

Rosenberg, A. (1983). If economics isn't a science, what is it? *Philosophical Forum*, *14*, 296–314.

Rosenberg, A. (1985). *The structure of biological science.* Cambridge, UK: Cambridge University Press.

Rotstein, A. (1977). Innis: the alchemy of fur and wheat. *Journal of Canadian Studies, 12*, 6–31.

Rouse, J. (1987). *Knowledge and power: Towards a political philosophy of science.* Ithaca, NY: Cornell University Press.

Rouse, J. (1992). What are cultural studies of scientific knowledge? *Configurations, 1*, 1–22.

Rozen, M. (1985). Maximizing behavior: Reconciling neo-classical and xfficiency approaches. *Journal of Economic Issues, 19*, 661–685.

Rubin, I. (1972). *Essays on Marx's theory of value.* Detroit: Black and Red Press.

Ruccio, D. (1991). Postmodernism in economics. *Journal of Post-Keynesian Economics, 13*, 495–510.

Sabel, C. F. (1989). Flexible specialization and the re-emergence of regional economies. In P. Q. Hirst and J. Zeitlin (Eds.), *Reversing industrial decline? Industrial structure and policy in Britain and her competitors* (pp. 17–70). Oxford: Berg.

Sack, R. D. (1972). Geography, geometry and explanation. *Annals, Association of American Geographers, 62*, 61–78.

Sahlins, M. (1972). *Stone age economics.* New York: Aldine.

Said, E. (1978). *Orientalism.* New York: Harper.

Salais, R., and Storper, M. (1992). The four "worlds" of contemporary industry. *Cambridge Journal of Economics, 16*, 169–193.

Samuels, W. J. (1990). The self-referentiality of Thorstein Veblen's theory of the preconceptions of economic science. *Journal of Economic Issues, 24*, 695–718

Samuelson, P. A. (1963). Discussion. *American Economic Review Papers and Proceedings, 53*, 231–236.

Samuelson, P. A. (1964). Theory and realism: A reply. *American Economic Review, 54*, 736–739.

Samuelson, P. A. (1972). Maximum principles in analytical economics. *American Economic Review, 62*, 249–262.

Samuelson, P. A. (1987). Sraffian economics. In J. Eatwell, M. Milgate, and P. Newman (Eds.), *The new Palgave dictionary of economics* (Vol. 4, pp. 452–461). London: Macmillan.

Sarre, P. (1987). Realism in practice. *Area, 19*, 3–10.

Savage, M., Barlow, J., Duncan, S., and Saunders, P. (1987). "Localities research": The Sussex Programme on economic restructuring, social change and the locality. *Quarterly Journal of Social Affairs, 3*, 27–51.

Sayer, A. (1976). A critique of urban modelling: From regional science to urban and regional political economy. *Progress in Planning, 6*, 187–254.

Sayer, A. (1979a). Epistemology and conceptions of people and nature in geography. *Geoforum, 10*, 19–44.

Sayer, A. (1979b). Understanding urban models versus understanding cities. *Environment and Planning A, 11*, 853–862.

Sayer, A. (1982a). Explaining manufacturing shift: A reply to Keeble. *Environment and Planning A, 14,* 119–125.

Sayer, A. (1982b). Explanation in economic geography: Abstraction versus generalization. *Progress in Human Geography, 6,* 65–85.

Sayer, A. (1984). *Method in social science: A realist approach.* London: Hutchinson.

Sayer, A. (1985a). The difference that space makes. In D. Gregory and J. Urry (Eds.), *Social Relations and Spatial Structures* (pp. 49–66). Oxford: Blackwell.

Sayer, A. (1985b). Realism in geography. In R. J. Johnston (Ed.), *The future of geography* (pp. 159–173). New York: Methuen.

Sayer, A. (1987). Hardwork and its alternatives. *Environment and Planning D: Society and Space, 5,* 395–399.

Sayer, A. (1989a). The "new" regional geography and problems of narrative. *Environment and Planning D: Society and Space, 7,* 253–276.

Sayer, A. (1989b). On the dialogue between humanism and historical materialism in geography. In A. Kobayashi and S. MacKenzie (Eds.), *Remaking human geography* (pp. 206–226). London: Unwin Hyman.

Sayer, A. (1989c). Postfordism in question. *International Journal of Urban and Regional Research, 13,* 666–695.

Sayer, A. (1991). Behind the locality debate: Deconstructing geography's dualisms. *Environment and Planning A, 23,* 283–308.

Sayer, A. (1993). Postmodernist thoughts in geography: A realist view. *Antipode, 25,* 320–344.

Sayer, A., and Walker, R. (1992). *The new social economy: Reworking the division of labour.* Oxford: Blackwell.

Schaefer, F. K. (1953). Exceptionalism in geography: A methodological introduction. *Annals, Association of American Geographers, 43,* 226–249.

Schefold, B. (1980). Fixed capital as a joint product and the analysis of accumulation with different forms of technical progress. In L. L. Pasinetti (Ed.), *Essays on the theory of joint production* (pp. 138–217). London: Macmillan.

Schell, M. (1991). Interview. *Massachusetts, 2,* 9.

Schneider, M. (1959). Gravity models and trip distribution theory. *Papers of the Regional Science Association, 5,* 51–56.

Schoenberger, E. (1989). Thinking about flexibility: A response to Gertler. *Transactions, Institute of British Geographers, 14,* 98–108.

Scott, A. J. (1976). Land use and commodity production. *Regional Science and Urban Economics, 6,* 147–160.

Scott, A. J. (1979). Commodity production and the dynamics of land use differentiation. *Urban Studies, 16,* 95–104.

Scott, A. J. (1982). Industrial patterns and the dynamics of industrial activity in the modern metropolis. *Urban Studies, 19,* 111–142.

Scott, A. J. (1983). Industrial organization and the logic of intra-metropolitan location I: Theoretical considerations. *Economic Geography, 59,* 233–250.

Scott, A. J. (1985). Location processes, urbanization and territorial development: An exploratory essay. *Environment and Planning A, 17,* 479–501.

Scott, A. J. (1986a). High technology industry and territorial development: The rise of the Orange County complex, 1955–84. *Urban Geography, 7,* 3–45.

Scott, A. J. (1986b). Industrialization and urbanization: An agenda. *Annals, Association of American Geographers, 76,* 25–37.

Scott, A. J. (1988a). Flexible production systems in regional development: The rise of new industrial spaces in North America and Western Europe. *International Journal of Urban and Regional Research, 12,* 171–186.

Scott, A. J. (1988b). *Metropolis: From the division of labor to urban form.* Berkeley: University of California Press.

Scott, A. J. (1988c). *New industrial spaces.* London: Pion.

Scott, A. J. (1991a). Flexible production systems: Analytical tasks and theoretical horizons—a reply to Lovering. *International Journal of Urban and Regional Research, 15,* 130–134.

Scott, A. J. (1991b). A further rejoinder to Lovering. *International Journal of Urban and Regional Research, 15,* 231.

Scott, A. J., and Storper, M. (1986). *Production, work, territory: The geographical anatomy of industrial capitalism.* London: Allen & Unwin.

Scott, A. J., and Storper, M. (1987). High technology industry and regional development: A theoretical critique and reconstruction. *International Journal of Social Science, 122,* 215–232.

Scott, A. J., and Storper, M. (1992). Regional development reconsidered. In H. Ernste and V. Meier (Eds.), *Regional development and contemporary industrial responses: Extending flexible specialization* (pp. 3–24). London: Belhaven.

Seal, H. L. (1970). The historical development of the Gauss linear model. In E. S. Pearson and M. G. Kendall (Eds.), *Studies in the history of statistics and probability* (pp. 207–230). London: Griffin.

Searle, G. (1976). *Eugenics and politics in Britain 1900–1914.* Leyden, The Netherlands: Noordhoff.

Seckler, D. (1975). *Thorstein Veblen and the institutionalists.* London: Macmillan.

Sen, A. (1979). Rational fools: A critique of the behavioural foundations of economic theory. In F. Hahn and M. Hollis (Eds.), *Philosophy and economic theory* (pp. 87–109). Oxford: Oxford University Press.

Senstat, J., and Constantine, G. (1975). A critique of the foundations of utility theory. *Science and Society, 39,* 157–179.

Shackle, G. (1972). *Epistemics and economics.* Cambridge, UK: Cambridge University Press.

Shaikh, A. (1981). The poverty of algebra. In I. Steedman and P. M. Sweezy (Eds.), *The value controversy* (pp. 266–300). London: Verso and New Left Books.

Shapin, S. (1975). Phrenological knowledge and the social structure of early nineteenth-century Edinburgh. *Annals of Science, 32,* 219–243.

Shapin, S., and Schaffer, S. (1985). *Leviathan and the air-pump.* Princeton, NJ: Princeton University Press.

Shaw, M., and Miles, I. (1979). The social roots of statistical knowledge. In J. Irvine, I. Miles, and J. Evans (Eds.), *Demystifying social statistics* (pp. 27–38). London: Pluto Press.

Sheppard, E. S. (1978). Theoretical underpinnings of the gravity hypothesis. *Geographical Analysis, 10,* 386–402.

Sheppard, E. S. (1979). Notes on spatial interaction. *Professional Geographer, 31,* 386–402.

Sheppard, E. S. (1980). The ideology of spatial choice. *Papers of the Regional Science Association, 45,* 197–213.

Sheppard, E. S. (1984). The distance decay gravity model debate. In G. L. Gaile and C. J. Wilmott (Eds.), *Spatial statistics and models* (pp. 367–388). Dordrecht: D. Reidel.

Sheppard, E. S. (1990). Transportation in a capitalist space economy: Transportation, circulation time and transportation innovations. *Environment and Planning A, 22,* 1007–1024.

Sheppard, E. S., and Barnes, T. J. (1986). Instabilities in the geography of capitalist production: Collective versus individual profit maximization. *Annals, Association of American Geographers, 76,* 493–507.

Sheppard, E. S., and Barnes, T. J. (1990). *The capitalist space economy: Geographical analysis after Ricardo, Marx and Sraffa.* London: Unwin Hyman.

Shields, R. (Ed.) (1992). *Lifestyle shopping. The subject of consumption.* Andover, UK: Routledge and Chapman Hall.

Sibley, D. (no date). *Spatial applications of exploratory data analysis.* CATMOG number 49. Norwich, CT: Geo Abstracts.

Sibley, D. (1981). The notion of order in spatial analysis. *Professional Geographer, 33,* 1–5.

Simon, H. (1957). *Models of man.* New York: Wiley.

Simon, H. (1976). From substantive to procedural rationality. In S. Latsis (Ed.), *Method and appraisal in economics* (pp. 129–148). Cambridge, UK: Cambridge University Press.

Slater, D. (1992a). On the borders of social theory: Learning from other regions. *Environment and Planning D: Society and Space, 10,* 307–328.

Slater, D. (1992b). Theories of development and politics of the postmodern: Exploring a border zone. *Development and Change, 23,* 283–319.

Slater, D. (1993). The geographical imagination and the enframing of development theory. *Transactions, Institute of British Geographers, 18,* 419–437.

Smith, C. (Ed.). (1990). Introduction. In *Locational analysis and general theory: Economic, political, regional and dynamic. Selected papers of Walter Isard* (Vol. 1, pp. 1–11). London: Macmillan.

Smith, N. (1982). Gentrification and uneven development. *Economic Geography, 58,* 139–155.

Smith, N. (1984). *Uneven development: Nature, capital and the reproduction of space.* Oxford: Blackwell.

Smith, N. (1986). On the necessity of uneven development. *International Journal of Urban and Regional Research, 10,* 87–104.

Smith, N. (1987). Dangers of the empirical turn: Some comments on the CURS initiative. *Antipode, 19,* 59–68.

Smith, N., and Katz, C. (1993). Grounding metaphor: Towards a spatialized politics. In M. Keith and S. Pile (Eds.), *Place and the politics of identity* (pp. 67–83). London: Routledge.

Smith, T. (1975). An axiomatic theory of spatial discounting behavior. *Papers of the Regional Science Association, 34,* 31–44.

Soja, E. W. (1980). The socio-spatial dialectic. *Annals, Association of American Geographers, 70,* 207–225.

Soja, E. W. (1986). Taking Los Angeles apart: Some fragments of a critical human geography. *Environment and Planning D: Society and Space, 4,* 255–272.

Soja, E. W., Morales, R., and Wolff, G. (1983). Urban restructuring: An analysis of social and spatial changes in Los Angeles. *Economic Geography, 59,* 195–230.

Soper, K. (1986). *Humanism and anti-humanism: Problems in European thought.* London: Hutchinson.

Sorokin, P. (1937–1941). *Social and cultural dynamics* (4 vols.). New York: American Book Company.

Spivak, G. C. (1988). Can the subaltern speak? In C. Nelson and L. Grossberg (Eds.), *Marxism and the interpretation of culture* (pp. 271–313). Urbana: University of Illinois Press.

Spry, I. M. (1981). Overhead costs, rigidities of productive capacity and the price system. In W. H. Melody, L. Salter, and P. Heyer (Eds.), *Culture, communication and dependency: The tradition of H. A. Innis* (pp. 155–166). Norwood, NJ: Ablex.

Sraffa, P. (1925). Sulle relazioni fra costo e quantita prodotta. *Annali di Economia, 2,* 277–328.

Sraffa, P. (1926). The laws of return under competitive conditions. *Economic Journal, 36,* 535–550.

Sraffa, P. (1960). *Production of commodities by means of commodities: Prelude to a critique of political economy.* Cambridge, UK: Cambridge University Press.

Stamp, L. D., and Beaver, S. H. (1947). *The British Isles.* London: Longman.

Steedman, I. (1977). *Marx after Sraffa.* London: New Left Books.

Steedman, I., and Sweezy, P. M. (Eds.). (1981). *The value controversy.* London: Verso and New Left Books.

Stewart, J. Q. (1958). Discussion: Population projection by means of income potential models. *Papers of the Regional Science Association, 4,* 153–154.

Stewart, J. Q., and Warntz, W. (1958). Macrogeography and social science. *Geographical Review, 48,* 167–184.

Stigler, G. J. (1953). Sraffa's Ricardo. *American Economic Review, 43,* 586–599.

Stigler, G. J. (1973). The adoption of marginal utility theory. In R. Collison Black, A. Coats, and C. Goodwin (Eds.), *The marginal revolution in economics* (pp. 305–320). Durham, NC: Duke University Press.

Stigler, S. M. (1986). *The history of statistics: The measurement of uncertainty before 1900.* Cambridge, MA: Harvard University Press.

Stoddart, D. (1986). *On geography and its history.* Oxford: Blackwell.

Storper, M. (1985a). Oligopoly and the product cycle: Essentialism in economic geography. *Economic Geography, 61,* 260–282.

Storper, M. (1985b). Technology and spatial productive relations: Disequilibrium interindustry relationships and industrial development. In M. Castells (Ed.), *High technology, space and society* (pp. 265–283). Beverly Hills, CA: Sage.

Storper, M. (1987). The post-Enlightenment challenge to Marxist urban studies. *Environment and Planning D: Society and Space, 5,* 418–426.

Storper, M. (1990). Responses to Amin and Robbins: Michael Storper replies. In
F. Pyke, G. Beccantini, and W. Sengenberger (Eds.), *Industrial districts and
interfirm cooperation in Italy* (pp. 228–237). Geneva: International Labour
Office.

Storper, M. (1993). Flexible specialization in Hollywood: A response to Aksoy
and Robbins. *Cambridge Journal of Economics, 17,* 479–484.

Storper, M., and Scott, A. J. (1988). The geographical foundations and social
relations of flexible production complexes. In J. Wolch and M. Dear (Eds.),
The power of geography: How territory shapes social life (pp. 21–40).
Boston: Unwin Hyman.

Storper, M., and Walker, R. (1989). *The capitalist imperative: Territory, technology
and industrial growth.* Oxford: Blackwell.

Sullivan, A. (1986). A general equilibrium model with agglomeration economies
and decentralized employment. *Journal of Urban Economics, 20,* 55–74.

Suppe, F. (1977). *The structure of scientific theories* (2nd ed.). Urbana: University
of Illinois Press.

Taffe, E. J. (1993). Spatial analysis: Development and outlook. *Urban Geography,
14,* 422–433.

Taylor, C. (1986). Spatial utility equilibrium and city size distribution in a central
place system. *Journal of Urban Economics, 19,* 1–22.

Taylor, P. J. (1976). An interpretation of the quantification debate in British
geography. *Transactions, Institute of British Geographers, 1,* 129–142.

Thoben, H. (1982). Mechanistic and organistic analogies in economics reconsidered. *Kyklos, 35,* 292–306.

Thompson, D. W. (1917). *On growth and form.* Cambridge, UK: Cambridge
University Press.

Thrift, N. J. (1983). On determination of social action in space and time.
Environment and Planning D: Society and Space, 1, 23–57.

Thrift, N. J. (1995). Peter Haggett's life in geography. In A. D. Cliff, P. R. Gould,
A. G. Hoare, and N. J. Thrift (Eds.), *Diffusing geography. Essays for Peter
Haggett* (pp. 375–395). Oxford: Blackwell.

Tickell, A., and Peck, J. A. (1992). Accumulation, regulation and the geographies
of post-Fordism: Missing links in regulationist research. *Progress in Human
Geography, 16,* 190–218.

Tuan, Y.-F. (1978). Sign and metaphor. *Annals, Association of American Geographers, 68,* 363–372.

Unwin, D. J. (1978). Quantitative and theoretical geography in the United
Kingdom. *Area, 10,* 337–344.

Urry, J. (1987). Survey 12: Society, space and locality. *Environment and Planning
D: Society and Space, 5,* 435–444.

Veblen, T. (1919). *The place of science in modern civilization and other essays.*
New York: B. W. Huebsch.

von Mises, L. (1963). *Human action* (3rd ed.). Chicago: Contemporary Books.

Wachterhauser, B. (Ed.). (1986). *Hermeneutics and modern philosophy.* Albany:
State University of New York Press.

Walker, R. (1978). Two sources of uneven development under advanced capitalism: Spatial differentiation and capital mobility. *Review of Radical Political Economy, 10,* 28–37.

Walker, R. (1988). The geographical organization of production systems. *Environment and Planning D: Society and Space, 7,* 377–408.

Wallace, I. (1978). Towards a humanized conception of economic geography. In D. F. Ley and M. S. Samuels (Eds.), *Humanistic geography: Problems and prospects* (pp. 91–108). Chicago: Maaroufa.

Warde, A. (1985). Spatial change, politics and the division of labour. In D. Gregory and J. Urry (Eds.), *Social relations and spatial structures* (pp. 190–212). London: Macmillan.

Warf, B. (1988). Regional transformation, everyday life, and Pacific Northwest lumber production. *Annals, Association of American Geographers, 78,* 326–346.

Warf, B. (1993). Postmodernism and the localities debate: Ontological questions and epistemological implications. *Tijdschrift voor Economische en Sociale Geografie, 84,* 162–168.

Warntz, W. (1957). Transportation, social physics, and the law of refraction. *Professional Geographer, 9,* 2–7.

Warntz, W. (1959). *Toward a geography of price: A study in geo-econometrics.* Philadelphia: University of Pennsylvania Press.

Warntz, W. (1965). *Macrogeography and income fronts.* Monograph series number 3. Philadelphia: Regional Science Research Institute.

Warntz, L. (1984). Trajectories and co-ordinates. In M. Billinge, D. Gregory, and R. L. Martin (Eds.), *Recollections of a revolution: Geography as spatial science* (pp. 134–150). London: Macmillan.

Watkins, M. H. (1963). A staple theory of economic growth. *Canadian Journal of Economics and Political Science, 29,* 141–158.

Watkins, M. H. (1982). The Innis tradition in Canadian political economy. *Canadian Journal of Political and Social Theory, 6,* 12–34.

Watson, A. J. (1977). Harold Innis and classical scholarship. *Journal of Canadian Studies, 12,* 45–61.

Watts, M. J. (1988). Deconstructing determinism: Marxisms, development theory and a comradely critique of *Capitalist world development. Antipode, 20,* 142–168.

Watts, M. J. (1993). Development I: Power, knowledge, discursive practice. *Progress in Human Geography, 17,* 252–272.

Webber, M. J. (1972). *Impact of uncertainty on location.* Cambridge, MA: MIT Press.

Webber, M. J. (1982). Agglomeration and the regional question. *Antipode, 14,* 1–11.

Webber, M. J. (1984). *Explanation, prediction and planning: The Lowry model.* London: Pion.

Webber, M. J. (1987). Quantitative measurement of some Marxist categories. *Environment and Planning A, 19,* 1303–1321.

Weber, S., and Wiesmeth, H. (1987). Contract equilibrium in a regulated rental housing market. *Journal of Urban Economics, 21,* 59–68.

Weinstein, M. (1986). Liberalism goes post-modern: Rorty's pragmatism. *Canadian Journal of Political and Social Theory, 10,* 10–19.

Wernick, A. (1986). The post-Innisian significance of Innis. *Canadian Journal of Political and Social Theory, 10,* 128–150.

Wilber, C. K., and Harrison, R. S. (1978). The methodological basis of institutional economics: Pattern, model, storytelling, and holism. *Journal of Economic Issues, 12,* 61–89.

Williams, G. (1983). *Not for export: Towards a political economy of Canada's arrested industrialization.* Toronto: McClelland and Stewart.

Williams, S. (1981). Realism, Marxism and human geography. *Antipode, 13*(2), 1–8.

Williamson, O. (1975). *Markets and hierarchies.* New York: Free Press.

Willis, P. (1978). *Learning to labour: How working class kids get working class jobs.* Farnborough: Saxon House.

Wilson, A. G. (1969). Notes on some concepts in social physics. *Papers of the Regional Science Association, 22,* 159–193.

Wilson, A. G. (1972). Theoretical geography: Some speculations. *Transactions, Institute of British Geographers, 57,* 31–44.

Wilson, B. (Ed.). (1970). *Rationality.* Oxford: Blackwell.

Wittgenstein, L. (1922). *Tractatus logico-philosophicus.* London: Kegan Paul.

Wittgenstein, L. (1964). *Remarks on the foundations of mathematics* (edited by G. von Wright, R. Rhees, and E. G. Anscombe). Oxford: Blackwell.

Wittgenstein, L. (1976). *Wittgenstein's lectures on the foundations of mathematics, Cambridge, 1939.* Ed. C. Diamond. Brighton: Harvester Press.

Wolch, J., and Dear, M. (Eds.). (1988). *The power of geography: How territory shapes social life.* Boston: Unwin Hyman.

Wolff, R. D., and Resnick, S. A. (1987). *Economics: Marxian versus neoclassical.* Baltimore: Johns Hopkins University Press.

Wolff, R. P. (1982). Piero Sraffa and the rehabilitation of classical political economy. *Social Research, 49,* 209–238.

Wolpert, J. (1964). The decision process in a spatial context. *Annals, Association of American Geographers, 54,* 537–558.

Wong, S. (1973). The F-twist and the methodology of Paul Samuelson. *American Economic Review, 63,* 312–325.

Wong, S. (1978). *The foundations of Paul Samuelson's revealed preference theory.* London: Routledge & Kegan Paul.

Woolgar, S. (1988). *Science: The very idea.* London: Tavistock.

Wright, E. O. (1981). Reconsiderations. In I. Steedman and P. M. Sweezy (Eds.), *The value controversy* (pp. 130–162). London: Verso and New Left Review Books.

Wrigley, N., and Bennett, R. J. (Eds.). (1981). *Quantitative geography: A British view.* London: Routledge & Kegan Paul.

Young, R. (1990). *White mythologies: Writing history and the West.* London: Routledge.

INDEX

Engels, Frederick, 136
Enlightenment, 3–16, 19, 21, 23, 26, 28–31, 36,
    40, 41, 49, 246–247
    defined, 6–10
Entrikin, Nicholas, 240–241, 244
Entropy maximization model, 17, 116, 119, 250
Environment and Planning A, 155
Epistemology, 8, 47, 56, 81, 92–95, 125
    architectonic, 10
    foolproof methods and, 6, 7, 55, 81–83, 89,
        95, 97, 99, 108, 124
    foundationalism, 7–10, 55, 171
    inductivism and, 89, 90
Equilibrium
    history and, 222–223, 235, 241–242
    social physics and, 234
*Essay on the Nature and Significance of
    Economic Science* (Robbins), 224
Essentialism, 7–10, 23, 30, 39, 41, 53, 54, 60,
    98–99, 151, 202, 209–210, 230–231, 250
    class and, 74–75
    definitions of "woman," 47
    economic geography and, ch. 2
    economics and, 69, 72
    local knowledge as a critique of, 95
    Marxism and, 77
    neoclassical economics and, 77
    Rorty's critique of, 55–56
Ethnography, 44–45, 81, 114, 214, 244
    economic geography and, 97, 99
Expanded reproduction, 34
Eugenics, 163, 182
Experimental science, 6
Explanation in Geography (Harvey), 18–19,
    103, 105–106, 121–122
Extremal theory, 85, 86. *See also* Constrained
    maximization

Fallibilism, 22
Falsification, difficulties of, 93, 114–115
Farjoun, Emmanuel, 57, 62
Feminist theory, 5, 8, 14, 45, 146, 251
    liberal, 45
    Marxist, 45–46, 48
    postcolonial, 45–47
Feyerabend, Paul, 82, 111, 121, 150
Finitism, 119
Fish, Stanley, 69
Fitzgerald (Bunge), 136
Flexible production, 5, 4, 11, 31–40, 49
    compared to locality research, 31–32, 39–40
    industrial districts and, 33, 36
    progressive tendencies within, 36–37
Flexible specialization, 32, 33, 35–38, 155
Flour milling, 230–231, 234–237, 246
Foolproof methods, 6, 7, 81–83, 89, 95, 97, 99,
    124
Foord, Jo, 29
Fordism, 33–36
Fotheringham, Stewart, 157
Foucault, Michel, 8, 9, 14, 43, 153, 204
Foundationalism, 7–10, 98, 108–109, 115, 151,
    171
Fraser, Nancy, 8
Frege, Gottlob, 175, 176
Freud, Sigmund, 151
Friedman, Milton, 93
Frontiers in Geographical Teaching (Chorley and
    Haggett, eds.), 141, 145
Frye, Northrop, 206

Functionalism, 25, 34–35
    a posteriori, 32, 34
    structural, 129, 233–234, 237, 242–244

Gadamer, Hans-Georg, 55
Galton, Francis, 179, 180–181, 183
Galileo, 156
Garin–Lowry model, 200–201
Garrison, William, 135, 169
Geertz, Clifford, 69, 82, 247
Gender, 45, 46
Generalization, 16
*General Theory of Money, Employment and
    Interest* (Keynes), 187
Geographer's Art, The (Haggett), 140
Geometry, 169–170
    William Bunge and, 137–139
    Peter Haggett and, 140–141
Georgescu-Roegen, Nicholas, 60, 61, 64–66, 68
German locational school, 130–132, 136, 139
Gertler, Meric, 36, 37, 121
Gibson, Katherine, 41
Giddens, Anthony, 24–25
Gödel's incompleteness theorem, 173
Golledge, Reginald, 147
Graham, Julie, 37, 38, 41–42, 70, 79
Gramsci, Antonio, 187, 189
Grand theory, 98–99
Gravity model, 4, 97, 116, 118, 148–149, 156–
    159, 233, 250
    empirical justification, 156–157
    rationalist justification, 156–157
Gregory, Derek, 6, 7, 12, 25, 123, 147, 171, 235
Gregory, Stanley, 170–171
Gregson, Nicky, 27
Growth poles, 20, 33, 116
Gudeman, Steven, 193, 194, 209

Hagerstrand, Torsten, 145
Haggett, Peter, 105, 121–122, 125, 140–145, 170
    compared to William Bunge, 141
    use of models, 141–142
Hanson, Susan, 47, 48, 125
Hardy, Godfrey, 172
Harland, Richard, 166
Haraway, Donna, 8, 251
Harré, Rom, 15
Harris, Britton, 87
Harrison, Richard, 149
Harrison, Robert, 213
Hartshorne, Richard, 137
Harvey, David, 11–15, 18, 22–25, 32, 39, 45,
    89, 103–107, 119, 121–122, 147, 149, 155,
    158, 169, 200, 220
    batlike terms, 12
    tension between Enlightenment and
        anti-Enlightenment views, 12
    theory of accumulation, 12, 40, 58–60
Hausman, Daniel, 196, 202
Hegemony and Socialist Strategy (Laclau and
    Mouffe), 74
Heidegger, Martin, 8, 55, 146
Hempel, Carl, 106
Hersh, Reuben, 173
Hesse, Mary, 111, 114–115, 117–118, 149, 153
    network model, 115–116, 118
Hicks, John, 222
Hilbert, David, 173
Hinterland, 216. *See also* Periphery